I0458790

BABY BUMP & BEYOND
Devotional for New Moms

DAILY ENCOURAGEMENT FOR THE JOURNEY OF MOTHERHOOD

ANCHORED GRACE PUBLISHING

© Copyright 2025
All rights reserved.
Anchored Grace Publishing
Binnovate Publishers

The content contained within this book may not be reproduced, duplicated or transmitted without direct written permission from the author or the publisher. Under no circumstances will any blame or legal responsibility be held against the publisher, or author, for any damages, reparation, or monetary loss due to the information contained within this book. Either directly or indirectly. You are responsible for your own choices, actions, and results.

A Gift for You

Thank you for choosing this devotional.

To support your journey of faith, we created a special gift bundle for our readers.

Inside the Anchored Grace Reader Gift Bundle, you will receive:

A free digital devotional

Printable prayer journal pages

Scripture reflection cards

Bonus devotionals for different seasons of life

Daily encouragement from Anchored Grace

Simply scan the QR code below or visit the link to receive your free bundle.

devo.anchoredgraces.com/newmomsgift

Scan the QR code with your phone camera or type the link into your browser.

We pray these resources continue to encourage your heart each day.

Embrace the sacred journey of motherhood as a divine partnership, where every heartbeat echoes God's promise of love and hope.

Psalm 139:13-14 (NIV) - "For you created my inmost being; you knit me together in my mother's womb. I praise you because I am fearfully and wonderfully made; your works are wonderful, I know that full well."

DEVOTIONAL

In the quiet stillness of anticipation or the joyful chaos of newborn cries, know that every moment of this sacred journey is steeped in divine purpose. Just as God intricately knitted you together, crafting your unique essence, He is now weaving a new life within you or cradled in your arms. Each tiny heartbeat is a profound echo of God's loving promise, reminding you that you are part of something far greater than yourself—a beautiful partnership in creation.

As you embrace the tender vulnerability of motherhood, take comfort in Psalm 139:13-14, where you are reminded of your own sacred creation. Reflect on how wonderfully made you are, a living testament to the artistry of God. In those moments of doubt or exhaustion, let His strength fill you, assuring you that this journey is both a gift and a ministry. Hold tight to the hope that rises with each day, for you are fearfully made, entrusted with an eternal love that shapes not just your heart, but the heart of your child. Embrace this divine partnership; it is a pathway where love and hope flourish in every heartbeat.

DAILY REFLECTION

In this sacred journey of motherhood, how can you lean into the divine promise of love and hope that resonates within every heartbeat of your child, and what does that reveal about your own identity as a beloved creation of God?

PRAYER

Dear Lord, in this sacred moment of anticipation or in the tender chaos of my newborn's cries, I breathe in Your promise of love and hope. Help me to embrace the beautiful vulnerability of motherhood as I navigate this divine partnership, knowing that every heartbeat echoes Your artistry. Grant me strength in moments of doubt, reminding me that I am wonderfully made and entrusted with this precious life, an eternal reflection of Your boundless grace. Amen.

January 2

On this day of new beginnings, reflect on the miracle of creation in your womb and the divine love that surrounds your journey into motherhood. Trust that God's strength is with you as you nurture this precious gift, turning each moment into a testament of hope and faith.

Psalm 127:3 - "Children are a heritage from the Lord, offspring a reward from him."

DEVOTIONAL

In this beautiful season of transition, as you cradle your precious newborn or anticipate their arrival, embrace the deep truth found in Psalm 127:3 — "Children are a heritage from the Lord, offspring a reward from him." Each gentle breath and tiny heartbeat is a testament to the extraordinary gift of life that God has entrusted to you. As you nurture this new life, remember that it is not only your child who will be shaped by your love but you, too, will be transformed by the deepening of your faith and the breadth of your love.

In the quiet moments of late-night feedings or the dizzying days of adjustment, take comfort in the knowledge that God journeys alongside you. When doubt and exhaustion seep into your heart, let His strength cradle you, assuring you that you are not alone. Trust in His promise that every tear, every smile, every struggle, and every joy is woven into the beautiful tapestry of motherhood. Hold fast to the hope that you are lovingly nurturing a future filled with potential, poured out by the very hands of your Creator.

DAILY REFLECTION

In the quiet moments of your journey into motherhood, how can you open your heart to see God's unwavering presence as both a source of strength and a gentle reminder of the sacred gift that your child truly is?

PRAYER

Dear Lord, in this tender season of nurturing new life, I come before You with a heart full of gratitude and anticipation. As I hold this precious gift in my arms or await their arrival, fill me with the strength to embrace the challenges and joys of motherhood, knowing that every moment is steeped in Your divine purpose. May Your unwavering love sustain me in the quiet hours, reassuring me that I am never alone on this journey, and may my faith blossom as I witness the miracle of life unfold before my eyes. Amen.

As you nurture new life, remember that God's love envelops you and your baby. Trust in His guidance and grace as you embark on this sacred journey of motherhood, filled with hope and joy. Let every moment be a reminder of His promises, bringing peace to your heart.

Isaiah 66:13 - "As a mother comforts her child, so will I comfort you; and you will be comforted over Jerusalem."

DEVOTIONAL

As you embark on this sacred journey of motherhood, know that God's love surrounds you in ways both gentle and profound. Just as a mother wraps her arms around her child, offering warmth and solace, so too does God embrace you in this transition, inviting you to find comfort in His presence. The moments of uncertainty you may face—the sleepless nights, the worries, the joys—are all held tenderly within His caring hands. Isaiah reminds us, "As a mother comforts her child, so will I comfort you." Imagine that divine comfort washing over you like a soft blanket, easing your fears and filling you with the assurance that you are not alone. In those quiet moments with your newborn, when you feel the weight of responsibility, remember that your journey is not just about guiding a tiny life; it is a path where God's love illuminates every step. May you find strength in His embrace, knowing that His love will guide you as you nurture, teach, and grow alongside your child. Trust in this sacred relationship, and allow His comfort to be the foundation of the beautiful bond you are beginning to cultivate.

DAILY REFLECTION

How can you pause in the midst of sleepless nights and motherhood's challenges to embrace the comforting presence of God, allowing His love to guide you through each precious moment with your little one?

PRAYER

Dear Lord, in this wondrous season of motherhood, I come before You with a heart full of gratitude and awe. As I cradle my little one, may I feel the warmth of Your love wrapping around us, offering strength in the sleepless nights and reassurance in moments of doubt. Help me to trust in Your embrace, as I nurture and guide this precious life, knowing that I am not alone on this sacred journey. Amen.

January 4

In this sacred season of new beginnings, may the miracle of new life remind you of God's endless love and faithfulness. Trust in His guidance as you nurture your little one, and find strength in His promises during these tender moments of motherhood.

Jeremiah 29:11 -"For I know the plans I have for you," declares the Lord, "plans to prosper you and not to harm you, plans to give you hope and a future."

DEVOTIONAL

As you cradle this tiny miracle in your arms, remember God whispers to your heart through the tender words of Jeremiah 29:11, "For I know the plans I have for you." These plans, dear new mother, are woven into the very fabric of this precious life you are nurturing. The journey ahead may feel overwhelming at times, filled with both joy and uncertainty; yet in every moment, rest assured that God's design is unfolding even when you cannot see it.

On sleepless nights and in quiet, sacred moments, allow yourself to breathe deep, trusting that every tear and every smile contributes to a greater story— one that God has intricately crafted for both you and your child. Your love, however small it may feel day-to-day, reflects the boundless love our Creator has for both of you. So, as you navigate this beautiful chaos, cling to the hope that God's plans are good, filled with promise and purpose. Trust in His guidance, and let His peace cradle both you and your little one in the days to come.

DAILY REFLECTION

In the midst of sleepless nights and newfound responsibilities, how can you consciously embrace the assurance that God's plans for you and your baby are unfolding with grace, even when the path ahead feels uncertain?

PRAYER

Dear Lord, as I hold this precious gift in my arms, help me to trust in Your divine plan for our lives. In moments of uncertainty and overwhelm, remind me that each day is guided by Your loving hand, weaving together the joys and struggles into a beautiful tapestry of purpose. Grant me the peace to nurture this new life with unwavering faith, knowing that Your love surrounds us both with every heartbeat. Amen.

Step into the vibrant joy of the Resurrection this Easter season. Celebrate the new life and hope found in Christ, reminding first-time mothers that just as new beginnings blossom, their journey is a beautiful testament to faith and love.

Proverbs 3:5-6: "*Trust in the Lord with all your heart and lean not on your own understanding; in all your ways submit to him, and he will make your paths straight.*"

DEVOTIONAL

As you embark on this beautiful journey of motherhood, let the words of Proverbs 3:5-6 resonate deeply within your spirit: "Trust in the Lord with all your heart and lean not on your own understanding." Each day may present its own set of challenges, filled with moments of self-doubt and uncertainty. Remember, it's perfectly okay to feel overwhelmed; every mother experiences this at some point. When you're unsure, lean into Him and allow His gentle guidance to cradle your heart.

In fostering your child's growth, you are not just nurturing their body but also their soul. This sacred trust invites you to submit your fears and questions to God's loving embrace, knowing that He is crafting a path that leads to grace and wisdom. Embrace this season of dependence, for in this surrender, you will discover the strength to meet each day with courage and love. As you seek Him in every decision, He will illuminate the way, reassuring you that you are never alone in this beautiful calling of motherhood.

DAILY REFLECTION

In moments of uncertainty on this nurturing journey, how can you intentionally surrender your fears to God, trusting that His guidance will illuminate the path forward for both you and your child?

PRAYER

Dear Lord, as I embark on this sacred journey of motherhood, help me to trust in Your guidance with every beat of my heart. When self-doubt whispers in the quiet moments and challenges seem overwhelming, may I lean into Your embrace, finding strength in surrender and peace in Your presence. Lord, illuminate my path as I nurture my child's body and soul, reminding me that in reliance upon. You, I am never alone in this beautiful calling. Amen.

As you embark on the transformative journey of motherhood, remember that just as God breathed life into creation, He lovingly guides you through each moment of nurturing and growth. Trust in His promise that every new beginning is imbued with hope, grace, and unwavering love.

2 Corinthians 5:17 - "Therefore, if anyone is in Christ, he is a new creation. The old has passed away; behold, the new has come."

DEVOTIONAL

As you cradle that tiny life in your arms, let the truth of 2 Corinthians 5:17 wash over you: "Therefore, if anyone is in Christ, he is a new creation. The old has passed away; behold, the new has come." In these delicate moments of motherhood, you are not only nurturing a new life but also embracing your own renewal through Christ. Each giggle, every coo, and even the sleepless nights are reminders of the fresh beginning God has gifted you. Like spring flowers blossoming after a long winter, you are being transformed in ways you may not yet fully understand. Trust that just as He breathed life into creation, He breathes His grace and love into your journey, equipping you to navigate the beautiful chaos of motherhood. Hold onto the promise that in this new season, you are deeply cherished and continuously remade into His image. Embrace this profound adventure, knowing God walks alongside you every step of the way.

DAILY REFLECTION

In this sacred season of nurturing new life, how might you invite God into your journey as a mother, allowing His love and grace to transform not only your little one but also your own heart and spirit?

PRAYER

Dear Lord, as I hold this precious life in my arms, help me to embrace the beauty of new beginnings that You so graciously provide. Fill my heart with Your peace and strength, reminding me that just as You have made me new in Christ, You are nurturing this little one in profound ways. May each moment of motherhood draw me closer to Your love, and may I always see the glimpses of Your promise in the laughter, the cries, and the quiet stillness of our days together. Amen.

January 7

Embrace the miracle of new life as you nurture your child in faith. Trust that God's love will guide you, providing the strength and wisdom you need in every moment of motherhood.

Isaiah 40:11 - "He tends his flock like a shepherd. He gathers the lambs in his arms and carries them close to his heart; he gently leads those that have young."

DEVOTIONAL

As you cradle your newborn in your arms, take a moment to pause and reflect on the profound truth of Isaiah 40:11. In this sacred season of your life as a first-time mother, you are not just nurturing a child; you are immersed in a divine embrace, a living testament to God's love. Just as a shepherd gathers his flock and carries the lambs close to his heart, so too does God wrap you and your baby in His tender care. Each sleepless night and whispered prayer carries echoes of that love, reminding you that you are never alone. Trust that in the exhilarating highs and daunting lows of motherhood, His guiding hand is there, offering strength when you feel weak and wisdom in the moments of uncertainty. Allow yourself to lean into that love and let it shape the beautiful bond you nurture with your child. Embrace this miracle of new life, for within it lies a divine calling— one that will draw you closer to God's heart and allow you to reflect His grace in your little one's life. Your journey of motherhood is not just about raising a child, but about nurturing faith in the very essence of your family.

DAILY REFLECTION

How can you intentionally create moments of prayer and connection with God as you nurture your newborn, inviting both His strength and wisdom into your evolving journey of motherhood?

PRAYER

Dear Lord, in this sacred moment of cradling new life, I thank You for the miracle of motherhood. As I nurture my baby, may Your love surround us, filling our hearts with strength and wisdom through every joy and challenge we face together. Guide me with Your gentle hand, that I may reflect Your grace and embrace this divine calling, trusting completely in Your faithful presence. Amen.

One Week Together

You've just completed your first week of devotionals.

If these reflections have brought peace or encouragement into your day, would you consider sharing a short Amazon review?

devo.anchoredgraces.com/newmoms

Your words help other women discover devotionals that may support them on their own faith journey.

Thank you for spending these moments in reflection.

The journey of motherhood begins with God's profound gift of new life. Trust in His guidance as you nurture your child, knowing each moment is a sacred opportunity to reflect His love and grace. Embrace the joy and challenges with prayer, leaning on Him for strength and wisdom.

Psalm 115:14-15 - "May the Lord cause you to flourish, both you and your children. May you be blessed by the Lord, the Maker of heaven and earth."

DEVOTIONAL

As you embark on this beautiful journey of motherhood, remember that within every heartbeat and tiny kick lies the profound gift of new life, a testament to God's unwavering love. Psalm 115:14-15 whispers a promise of blessing not just for you, but for your child as well—how precious it is to know that you and your baby are wrapped in God's grace. In the quiet moments when joy is overwhelming or the challenges feel insurmountable, pause and seek His presence in prayer. Each sleepless night and soft coo is an opportunity to reflect the love that God pours into your heart, allowing it to overflow to your little one. You are not alone in this; His guiding hand will cradle and strengthen you, leading you through both the laughter and the tears. Embrace your unique journey, knowing that every moment is sacred and infused with purpose. Let this divine adventure of nurturing and growing together be filled with trust, prayer, and an unshakeable faith in the goodness of His plans for you and your child.

DAILY REFLECTION

In the delicate balance of joy and challenge that motherhood brings, how can you actively seek God's presence in your moments of doubt, allowing His grace to guide you as you nurture the precious new life in your care?

PRAYER

Dear Lord, as I stand on the threshold of motherhood, I am filled with awe and gratitude for the precious gift of new life within me. Guide my heart with Your steadfast love, that I may nurture my child with wisdom and grace, reflecting Your goodness in every moment. Strengthen me through the challenges and illuminate my path with the joy that flows from trusting in You, knowing that both my little one and I are cradled in Your eternal embrace. Amen.

Today, reflect on the miraculous journey of motherhood, where each moment is a divine invitation to trust in God's promise. In the quiet of uncertainty, find strength in His unwavering love as you nurture new life.

Isaiah 50:4 - "The Sovereign Lord has given me a well-instructed tongue, to know the word that sustains the weary. He wakens me morning by morning, wakens my ear to listen like one being instructed."

DEVOTIONAL

As you embark on this beautiful yet challenging journey of motherhood, take a moment to breathe in the wonder of new life. Each tiny kick, each coo, is a reminder of the miraculous gift entrusted to you. In the quiet moments of uncertainty, when the weight of responsibility feels heavy, remember that God has equipped you with a "well-instructed tongue." Just like Isaiah, He directs your heart to speak words of life and comfort, both to your little one and to yourself. Embrace the mornings as sacred; they are invitations to listen for His guiding voice amidst the din of sleepless nights. A low His unwavering love to envelop you, providing strength when your spirit feels weary. Today, surrender your fears and anxieties, trusting that the One who knows you intimately will sustain you through every challenge. Celebrate each moment, for in nurturing this new life, you reflect the heart of the Creator who wonders over you with delight.

DAILY REFLECTION

In the sacred and often overwhelming moments of your motherhood journey, how can you actively seek God's presence to transform your fears into trust and your doubts into declarations of love for your new life?

PRAYER

Dear Lord, in this sacred journey of motherhood, I come to You with a heart full of wonder and a spirit sometimes trembling with uncertainty. As I nurture this precious life, remind me that every kick, every sigh, is Your gentle way of inviting me to trust in Your promises. Fill my weary soul with Your unwavering love, and let me find strength in my vulnerability, knowing that I am never alone. Guide my words and my heart as I embrace this calling, and help me to celebrate each moment with gratitude for the beautiful gift You've entrusted to me. Amen.

On this blessed journey of motherhood, remember that every moment—whether waiting for your little one or cradling them close—reflects God's perfect timing. Trust in His plan, for your heart is already nurturing the sacred bond of love and grace.

Isaiah 40:31 - "But those who hope in the Lord will renew their strength. They will soar on wings like eagles; they will run and not grow weary, they will walk and not be faint."

DEVOTIONAL

On this blessed journey of motherhood, each moment is woven with divine purpose. Whether you find yourself cradling your newborn or eagerly anticipating their arrival, remember that every heartbeat echoes God's perfect timing. In the stillness of the night or the gentle flutter of tiny kicks, let your heart be attuned to His whispers of love and assurance. You are not alone; God is crafting your unique story, a tapestry of grace that will unfold as your bond deepens. With each day, your strength will renew, as Isaiah 40:31 promises. Trust that even in the most overwhelming moments, He is your anchor, and you will soar on wings of hope. Embrace this sacred journey, for you are nurturing not only a child but also a legacy of faith and love.

DAILY REFLECTION

As you cradle your new blessing in your arms or feel those joyful flutters within, how can you open your heart to embrace the unique timing of God's plan for your journey into motherhood, trusting that each moment is a cherished step in nurturing both your child and your faith?

PRAYER

Dear God, in this sacred journey of motherhood, I lift my heart to You, grateful for the gift of new life and the joy it brings. Whether I am waiting with anticipation or holding my little one close, help me to feel Your presence in every heartbeat and every tiny kick. Grant me strength and peace as I trust in Your perfect timing, knowing that You are weaving a beautiful story through this journey of love and grace. Amen.

As you nurture new life, remember that God entrusted you with a precious gift. Lean into His endless love and wisdom as you experience the joy and challenges of motherhood, knowing His presence surrounds you every step of the way.

Matthew 19:14 - "But Jesus said, 'Let the little children come to me and do not hinder them, for to such belongs the kingdom of heaven.'"

DEVOTIONAL

As you cradle your little one in your arms, take a moment to absorb the profound truth that you hold a precious gift—a miracle entrusted to you by the Creator of life. In Matthew 19:14, Jesus welcomes children with open arms, reminding us that in their innocence, they embody the essence of the Kingdom of Heaven. Each smile, every gentle coo, and even the sleepless nights are sacred moments, woven together by God's love and purpose for both you and your child.

Embrace the challenges of motherhood as opportunities to lean deeper into His endless wisdom and grace. When uncertainty creeps in or your heart feels heavy, remember that you are not alone; His presence surrounds you, offering comfort and strength. Your journey may be filled with ups and downs, but trust that every step is a path lit by the divine. Through each day, you are nurturing not only a new life but also your own spirit—crafted beautifully in the image of God's love.

DAILY REFLECTION

How can you cultivate a deeper sense of gratitude for the tiny moments of joy and challenge in motherhood as you embrace the sacred responsibility of nurturing the life God has entrusted to you?

PRAYER

Dear Lord, as I cradle this precious life in my arms, may I always remember the sacred trust You have bestowed upon me. In moments of joy and in times of doubt, grant me the strength to lean into Your unwavering love and wisdom, knowing that You are ever-present. Help me to embrace each day, cherishing the miracles of motherhood and nurturing not only my child but also the spirit You have created within me. Amen.

As you cradle new life in your arms, let this season of Advent remind you that God's greatest gift came as a child. Trust in His promises as you nurture your little one, knowing that each moment is filled with divine purpose and love.

Luke 1:30-31: - "But the angel said to her, 'Do not be afraid, Mary, for you have found favor with God. And behold, you will conceive in your womb and bear a son, and you shall call his name Jesus.'"

DEVOTIONAL

As you cradle new life in your arms, this season of Advent envelops you in a profound truth: God's greatest gift came as a child, just as your little one has entered the world. Remember the angel's words to Mary, a young mother herself, who was greeted with both the wonder and weight of divine favor. "Do not be afraid," he said, acknowledging the swirling emotions of anticipation and anxiety that come with new life. In your journey of motherhood, trust that each moment, both joyful and challenging, holds a divine purpose woven by God's loving hands.

As you nurture your baby, reflect on the miracle that unfolded in Mary's womb—God with us, a promise fulfilled, and a reminder that His presence is as constant and comforting as your embrace. Let each coo and sigh from your child echo the assurance that you are not alone; the very essence of love and grace has been entrusted to you. With every heartbeat you hold close, may you find peace in the journey ahead, illuminated by the gift of Jesus and the hope of His everlasting love.

DAILY REFLECTION

In this sacred season of Advent, how can you let the love and promise of Christ's birth guide your heart as you navigate the beautiful yet daunting moments of nurturing your little one?

PRAYER

Dear Lord, as I cradle this fragile gift of life in my arms, remind me that just as You sent Your Son as the greatest treasure, my child is a reflection of Your love and promise. Help me to embrace the joy and uncertainty of motherhood, finding strength in Your guiding presence, and may each moment be a sacred reminder of the divine purpose held within these tender days. Grant me the grace to nurture with both wisdom and patience, knowing that in every coo and sigh, Your love surrounds us—comforting, encouraging, and eternally near. Amen.

On this sacred journey of motherhood, trust that God's love envelops you and your child. As you nurture new life, remember that His strength is your foundation, guiding each moment with grace and hope. Embrace the beauty of this gift, knowing you are never alone.

1 Peter 5:7 - "Cast all your anxiety on him because he cares for you."

DEVOTIONAL

As you stand on the threshold of motherhood, either cradling your little one or awaiting their arrival, feel the tender embrace of God's love surrounding you. Each kick and gentle sigh remind us that life begins anew, a divine gift woven with purpose and grace. In moments of uncertainty, when doubts creep in or exhaustion settles around you, remember the truth of 1 Peter 5:7: "Cast all your anxiety on him because he cares for you." It's in these quiet, vulnerable moments that His strength becomes your foundation— steady, unwavering, and ever-present. Allow His love to soothe your worries, replacing them with a profound sense of peace, knowing that you're never alone on this sacred journey. Embrace the beauty of nurturing new life, and trust that as you care for your child, you are also cradled gently in His arms. Together, navigate this remarkable season with faith, knowing that every challenge is met with grace and every day is filled with hope.

DAILY REFLECTION

In the midst of sleepless nights and endless joys, how can you intentionally invite God's presence into your daily moments of motherhood, trusting His love to guide and uplift you as you nurture this precious new life?

PRAYER

Dear Lord, as I step into this sacred journey of motherhood, I ask for Your gentle presence to surround me and my child. Help me to embrace each moment with faith, surrendering my anxieties into Your loving hands, knowing that Your strength will guide me through both the joys and challenges. May Your love fill our days with peace and remind me that I am never alone, cradled in Your grace as I nurture this precious new life.

As you welcome the miracle of new life, remember that God intricately weaves His love and purpose into each moment of motherhood. Trust in His guidance as you nurture your child, knowing that His grace will sustain you through both joys and challenges.

1 Thessalonians 5:16-18 -"Rejoice always, pray continually, give thanks in all circumstances; for this is God's will for you in Christ Jesus."

DEVOTIONAL

As you cradle this precious new life in your arms, take a moment to pause and breathe in the beauty of the miracle before you. The journey of motherhood is unlike any other—filled with moments that stretch your heart, your patience, and your understanding. In those late-night feedings and quiet, sleepless hours, remember 1 Thessalonians 5:16-18: "Rejoice always, pray continually, give thanks in all circumstances." These words are not just a call to action; they are a loving reminder from God that every tiny smile, every coo, and yes, even every tear is woven into His perfect tapestry of purpose for both you and your child. Trust that in the whirlwind of emotions—joy, fear, love, and exhaustion—God's grace is your constant companion. As you nurture your little one, let your heart be a mirror of His love, reflecting hope and joy even in the smaller, challenging moments. Embrace the richness of this experience, knowing that with each prayer and every whisper of gratitude, you are inviting His guidance into your journey. You are not alone; He is with you in every moment, encouraging you to rejoice and to thrive as you embark on this incredible adventure of motherhood.

DAILY REFLECTION

In the midst of sleepless nights and tender first moments, how can you open your heart to recognize and cherish the divine guidance that infuses every aspect of your journey as a new mother?

PRAYER

Dear Lord, as I hold this miraculous gift in my arms, I pause to marvel at the love and purpose You have woven into each moment of our journey. Grant me the strength to embrace both the joys and challenges of motherhood, and fill my heart with gratitude for the whispered blessings of each day. May Your grace guide me through the sleepless nights and joyful smiles, as I nurture this precious child and reflect Your love in all that I do. Amen.

As you nurture new life, remember that God's love guides you through each moment of joy and uncertainty. Trust in His wisdom to strengthen your heart, and lean on His promises as you cherish this sacred journey of motherhood.

2 Timothy 3:15-16 - "And how from infancy you have known the Holy Scriptures, which are able to make you wise for salvation through faith in Christ Jesus. All Scripture is God-breathed and is useful for teaching, rebuking, correcting and training in righteousness."

DEVOTIONAL

As you embrace the tender moments of nurturing your little one, remember that this sacred journey of motherhood is steeped in both joy and uncertainty. Just as the Apostle Paul reminded Timothy of the wisdom found in Scripture from infancy, you too may find solace in God's words as you guide your child. How beautiful it is that even in sleepless nights and overwhelming emotions, God's love is the gentle compass that steers you through the chaos and wonder of new life. His promises are like whispers of reassurance, inviting you to trust in His wisdom as you navigate this transformative role.

In your moments of doubt or fear, cling to the truth that the Scriptures are alive and powerful, meant for teaching and instilling strength. Allow Jesus, the embodiment of that wisdom, to cradle your heart and nurture your spirit. Cherish each day, for every instance you nurture your child, you are also nurturing your own faith—a beautiful cycle woven by the grace of God.

DAILY REFLECTION

In the quiet moments when your heart swells with love or aches with uncertainty, how can you intentionally invite God's gentle guidance into your journey of motherhood, trusting in His promises to illuminate the path before you?

PRAYER

Dear Lord, as I embrace the miracle of new life, I seek Your guiding light in the moments of joy and uncertainty. May Your love surround me, filling my heart with strength and reassurance as I nurture my child and foster my faith. Help me to trust in Your wisdom, remembering that every sleepless night and emotional wave is a part of this sacred journey, woven by Your grace. Amen.

Creating new life is a reflection of God's love and creativity. As you navigate the joys and challenges of motherhood, lean into His strength and grace, trusting that He has a purpose for every moment. Your journey is a sacred blessing, intricately woven into His divine plan.

Psalm 113:9 - "He gives the barren woman a home, making her the joyous mother of children. Praise the Lord!"

DEVOTIONAL

As you embark on this beautiful journey of motherhood, remember that each flutter of your baby's movements and every late-night feeding is a testament to God's intricate design. In Psalm 113:9, we are reminded that He transforms lives, turning emptiness into abundance and longing into joy. Embrace the moments of stillness as sacred, where you can feel His presence wrapping around you like a warm embrace, whispering that you are never alone in this beautiful chaos. The challenges you face may sometimes seem daunting, but take heart; they are a part of a greater tapestry woven by His loving hands. Trust that your unique path is filled with purpose, and lean into His strength when you feel weary. With each smile and coo of your little one, acknowledge the reflection of God's creativity at work in your life and your child's. As you nurture this new life, let your heart overflow with praise, knowing that you are a joyful testament to His love.

DAILY REFLECTION

In the quiet moments of motherhood, how can you seek to embrace God's presence as a source of strength and comfort, recognizing that each challenge you encounter is part of His beautiful design for your journey?

PRAYER

Dear Lord, as I embark on this miraculous journey of motherhood, I thank You for the precious life growing within me or nestled in my arms. Help me to embrace each moment, from the joy-filled giggles to the weary nights, as sacred reflections of Your unfathomable love and creativity. Grant me Your strength when the days feel overwhelming and remind me to see Your purpose woven through every challenge and triumph, knowing that I am never alone in this beautiful chaos. Amen.

Each new life is a precious gift, reminding us of God's unwavering love and faithfulness. As you welcome your little one, lean into the hope and joy that comes from trusting in His perfect plan. Remember, your journey as a mother reflects His boundless grace and the beauty of creation.

Isaiah 66:9 - "Shall I bring to the moment of birth and not give delivery?" says the LORD. "Shall I, who cause delivery, shut up the womb?" says your God.

DEVOTIONAL

As you cradle your newborn in your arms, let the profound truth of Isaiah 66:9 wash over you: the God who brings life into the world is also the One who delights in your journey of motherhood. Each tiny sigh and gentle movement is a sacred reminder of His unwavering love, woven meticulously into the fabric of your child's being. Reflect on the miracle of this moment—your body, a vessel of divine purpose, nurtured and sustained by His grace. Every challenge faced during your pregnancy, every painful moment of labor, now blossoms into the sweet reality of life, just as He promised. In the quiet hours of night, when doubts may creep in, remember that your little one is not just a gift but a testament to His faithfulness. Trust in His perfect plan for both you and your child, knowing that you are accompanied by His boundless mercy each step of the way. Embrace this new chapter with hope and joy, allowing it to illuminate the remarkable beauty of creation as you embark on this incredible journey of motherhood.

DAILY REFLECTION

As you hold your precious child close, how can you actively embrace the hope and joy in trusting God's perfect plan for your journey of motherhood amidst the challenges you may face?

PRAYER

Dear Lord, as I hold this precious gift in my arms, may I always remember that Your love and faithfulness surround us both. Help me to embrace the challenges and joys of motherhood, trusting in Your perfect plan for our lives, and allowing Your grace to guide me through each moment. In this sacred journey, fill my heart with hope and joy, and let me reflect Your boundless love in all I do. Amen.

January 18

Embrace the miracle of new life, where God's grace cradles your heart. In each moment of uncertainty and joy, trust that He guides your journey as a mother, nurturing both you and your little one with boundless love.

Isaiah 49:15-16 - "Can a mother forget the baby at her breast and have no compassion on the child she has borne? Though she may forget, I will not forget you. See, I have engraved you on the palms of my hands; your walls are ever before me."

DEVOTIONAL

As you cradle your newborn, a profound miracle unfolds in your arms—a testament to God's infinite grace and love. In moments of uncertainty, whether it's a late-night cry or a tiny hiccup, remember the promise in Isaiah: just as a mother instinctively nurtures, God's heart is ever-present, cradling you both. Picture your child's name engraved on the palms of His hands, a beautiful assurance that you are never alone in this journey. Embrace the joy that breathes through each giggle and the worries that weigh in quiet moments; both are beautifully intertwined in the tapestry of motherhood. Let His love fill the spaces where anxiety tries to creep in, reminding you of His unwavering presence. With every smile, every sigh, trust that He is guiding you—and your little one—through the ebb and flow of this sacred time. You are wrapped in His boundless love, tenderly nurtured as you learn the dance of grace and strength.

DAILY REFLECTION

In the quiet moments as you cradle your little one, how can you open your heart to fully embrace the grace and guidance God offers, transforming each challenge into a cherished part of this miraculous journey of motherhood?

PRAYER

Dear Lord, in this sacred season of new life, fill the hearts of first-time mothers with Your overwhelming grace and peace. As they cradle their little ones, may they feel Your nurturing embrace surrounding them both, reminding them that in every moment of joy and uncertainty, You are there, whispering love and comfort. Help them to trust in Your perfect guidance as they embark on this journey, cherishing each precious giggle and navigating the worries with confidence, knowing that their child is forever held in Your hands. Amen.

January 19

The miracle of new life reflects God's boundless love and grace. As you nurture your precious child, remember that each tiny heartbeat is a reminder of His faithfulness. Trust in His guidance and strength for this beautiful journey of motherhood.

Isaiah 44:24 - "This is what the Lord says—your Redeemer, who formed you in the womb: I am the Lord, the Maker of all things, who stretches out the heavens, who spreads out the earth by myself."

DEVOTIONAL

As you cradle your little one, take a moment to soak in the miracle of new life. Each tiny heartbeat is not just a rhythm; it is the sweet echo of God's unwavering love and grace. In Isaiah 44:24, we are reminded that the Lord, our Redeemer, formed you and your child in the womb. His creative power stretched across the heavens and the earth, and now, that same divine artistry is manifested right in your arms. This sacred journey of motherhood may sometimes feel daunting, filled with sleepless nights and endless uncertainties. Yet, in those moments of doubt, remember that you are not alone; the Creator of all things is guiding you, empowering you to nurture this precious gift. Lean on Him for strength, and trust that His faithfulness will carry you through each day, revealing the beauty of His plan in your life and in your child's. You are a vessel of His love, and your journey is a testament to both His artistry and His grace.

DAILY REFLECTION

How can embracing the miracle of your child's life deepen your understanding of God's unwavering love and strengthen your trust in His guidance during this transformative journey of motherhood?

PRAYER

Dear Lord, as I cradle my precious child, help me to be ever mindful of the miracle You've woven into my arms. Let each tiny heartbeat remind me of Your limitless love and the grace that surrounds this beautiful journey of motherhood. Grant me the strength to nurture this little life and the wisdom to trust in Your guiding hand, knowing that in every challenge, Your faithfulness shines brightly. Amen.

During this tender season of new life, find peace in God's promise to always care for you and your child. Trust that His strength sustains you through sleepless nights and joyful discoveries, reminding you that you are never alone on the journey of motherhood.

Matthew 11:28-30 - "Come to me, all you who are weary and burdened, and I will give you rest. Take my yoke upon you and learn from me, for I am gentle and humble in heart, and you will find rest for your souls. For my yoke is easy and my burden is light."

DEVOTIONAL

In the beautiful chaos of motherhood, where sleepless nights blend into tender mornings, God extends an invitation to you: "Come to me." Like the gentle embrace of a warm blanket, His promise to care for you and your child envelops the uncertainties that often cloud your heart. Each coo and cry from your little one is a reminder of the sacred trust placed in your hands, and in those moments of weariness, remember that His strength sustains you. As you navigate the rollercoaster of emotions—joy, anxiety, sweetness, and fatigue—rest in His assurance that you are not alone on this journey. When you feel overwhelmed, allow yourself to lean into His yoke; in your humility, you'll find His gentleness lifting your burdens. Embrace the discoveries that each day brings, knowing that every challenge is a stepping stone in your growth as a mother. In the tender season of new life, let God's unwavering love be the anchor that steadies your soul, guiding you through both the struggles and the joys.

DAILY REFLECTION

In the midst of the beautiful chaos of your new motherhood journey, how can you intentionally lean into God's promise of strength and comfort during those moments when exhaustion threatens to overshadow your joy?

PRAYER

Dear Lord, in this sacred journey of motherhood, I seek Your gentle embrace, feeling the weight of sleepless nights and the joy of tiny moments. Hold me close as I navigate both the chaos and the beauty, reminding me that your strength is my guiding light. Help me to trust in Your promise of care, that I may find peace in the heart of this tender season, knowing I am never alone. Amen.

January 21

On this journey of new life, trust in God's promise of strength and provision. He holds every moment of your motherhood with love, guiding you through the joys and challenges ahead. Embrace His presence as you nurture this precious gift.

Philippians 4:19 - "And my God will meet all your needs according to the riches of his glory in Christ Jesus."

DEVOTIONAL

As you embark on this wondrous journey of motherhood, remember that you are not alone in your hopes and uncertainties. The days ahead may be filled with moments of sheer joy intertwined with moments of doubt, but Philippians 4:19 reassures us that God will supply all your needs according to His limitless riches. In the quiet of the night when you cradle your little one, feel His presence wrapping around both of you, guiding your every step. Trust that the strength to face the challenges will rise within you, sourced from a love that knows no bounds. Each whisper of worry or pang of fear can be transformed into a prayer, reminding you that God's heart is ever-present in your journey. Embrace your role as nurturer, confident that in every heartbeat and every tear, His grace sustains you. Let His promises ignite the joy of your new beginning, and rest in the assurance that you are cradled in divine love, nurturing this precious gift with a faith that flourishes daily.

DAILY REFLECTION

In this sacred season of new beginnings, how can you lean into God's promise of provision and strength, allowing His love to transform your fears into faith as you embrace each moment of this beautiful journey into motherhood?

PRAYER

Dear Lord, In this tender season of new life, I seek Your strength and guidance as I embrace the joys and uncertainties of motherhood. Wrap Your loving arms around me and my little one, filling my heart with peace and assurance that Your presence is with us every step of the way. Help me to trust in Your promise, knowing that through every challenge, Your grace will nourish my spirit and ignite the love that surrounds this precious gift. Amen.

Three Weeks of Reflection

You've now spent several weeks walking through these devotionals.

If this book has encouraged your heart, a brief Amazon review helps other women find the same encouragement.

devo.anchoredgraces.com/newmoms

Your experience may guide someone else toward the hope they are searching for.

Thank you for being here.

January 22

On this journey of motherhood, trust in God's perfect timing and grace as you nurture new life. Each moment, whether joyful or challenging, is a sacred reminder of His presence and love in your growing family. Celebrate the gift of this new chapter, knowing you are never alone.

Isaiah 30:18 - "Yet the Lord longs to be gracious to you; therefore he will rise up to show you compassion. For the Lord is a God of justice. Blessed are all who wait for him!"

DEVOTIONAL

In the tender journey of motherhood, each heartbeat you feel and every kick you experience is a sacred reminder of God's precious gift. Isaiah 30:18 reminds us that the Lord longs to be gracious to you, and as you embrace this new chapter, trust that His timing is perfect, even in the most challenging moments. It's easy to feel overwhelmed amid sleepless nights and endless questions, but know that each struggle is laced with grace, a divine whisper assuring you that you are never alone in this nurturing role. As you cradle your little one, remember that your love mirrors the compassion God has for you—infinitely patient and profoundly deep. Celebrate the joy of your child's first smile, but also embrace the days filled with uncertainty, for all these moments are woven into the tapestry of your growing family. In the stillness of those quiet nights, feel the Lord rising up around you, bringing tenderness, strength, and an unshakeable peace. Blessed are those who wait upon Him, for it is in the waiting that His love transforms your heart, preparing you to be the incredible mother you are destined to be.

DAILY REFLECTION

In the midst of sleepless nights and tender moments with your newborn, how can you lean into God's gentle embrace and trust that each challenge is an opportunity to deepen your faith in His perfect timing and grace?

PRAYER

Dear Lord, in the quiet moments of this beautiful journey, I come to You, heart full of wonder and trepidation. Help me to trust in Your perfect timing as I nurture this new life, embracing the joy and challenges alike. May Your grace envelop me, reminding me that I am never alone, and may my love for my child reflect the boundless compassion You have shown me. Amen.

January 23

In this sacred season of new beginnings, cherish the miracle of life blooming within you or cradled in your arms. Trust in God's perfect plan as He weaves your journey of motherhood, bringing grace and strength to each precious moment. Lean on faith as you nurture the heart He has entrusted to you.

Psalm 68:6 - "God sets the lonely in families, He leads out the prisoners with singing; but the rebellious live in a sun-scorched land."

DEVOTIONAL

In this sacred season of new beginnings, as you cradle the miracle of life in your arms or feel the gentle rhythm of your child's movements within, take a moment to pause and breathe in the beauty of this journey. Psalm 68:6 reminds us that God places the lonely in families—a promise that extends to you, dear mother, as you experience the profound transformation of life and love. Each tiny heartbeat, each tender cry, is a testament to God's perfect plan for you and your little one, woven together in a tapestry of grace. As days unfold, trust in the strength that rises in nurturing this fragile heart, knowing you are never alone in this journey. Lean on faith, inviting God's wisdom to flow through the moments of joy and uncertainty alike. Embrace the laughter, the late nights, and even the tears, for they are chapters in a beautiful story authored by the Creator Himself. Remember, you are held in the embrace of a family formed by His love—a family that grows with each heartbeat you cherish.

DAILY REFLECTION

In this sacred season of new beginnings, how can you open your heart to fully embrace the extraordinary journey of motherhood, trusting that each challenge and joy is woven into God's divine plan for you and the precious life you hold?

PRAYER

Dear Lord, in this sacred season of new beginnings, I thank You for the miracle of life that fills my heart with awe and wonder. As I cradle this precious child or carry the gift within, grant me the grace to embrace each moment, trusting in Your perfect plan. May Your strength guide me through sleepless nights and joyful days, reminding me that I am never alone on this journey of motherhood. Amen.

January 24

As you cradle your newborn, remember that each tiny heartbeat is a testament to God's faithfulness. In the quiet moments of joy and uncertainty, lean on His promises, knowing that His strength will support you in this beautiful and transformative season of motherhood.

Isaiah 41:10 - "So do not fear, for I am with you; do not be dismayed, for I am your God. I will strengthen you and help you; I will uphold you with my righteous right hand."

DEVOTIONAL

As you cradle your newborn, feel the soft rise and fall of their tiny chest, a precious reminder of God's unwavering faithfulness. Each heartbeat echoes a promise, whispered into the fabric of your new life as a mother. In those quiet moments, when uncertainty lingers and joy floods your heart, hold tightly to His words: "Do not fear, for I am with you." God knows this journey can feel overwhelming; He intertwines His strength with your every doubt. When you feel the weight of responsibility resting heavy on your shoulders, remember that you are not alone—He holds you up with His righteous right hand. Embrace the beautiful mess of motherhood, knowing that every sleepless night and every tender gaze is part of a sacred transformation. Your heart is now intertwined with His, and in each moment, He invites you to lean into His grace.

DAILY REFLECTION

In this sacred season of new beginnings, how can you pause to acknowledge God's presence in your heartache and joy, allowing His strength to cradle both you and your precious child?

PRAYER

Dear Lord, as I cradle this precious life in my arms, may I forever remember that each tiny heartbeat is a testament to Your unwavering love. In moments of uncertainty and joy, I surrender my worries to You, trusting that Your strength will carry me through the beautiful chaos of motherhood. Help me to embrace each day with grace, knowing that I am never alone on this journey, for You are my constant companion and support. Amen.

January 25

As you welcome new life into your world, may you find strength and joy in God's promises. Trust that He is with you every step of the way, nurturing both you and your child as you navigate this beautiful journey of motherhood.

Isaiah 40:29-31 - He gives power to the weak, and to those who have no might He increases strength. Even the youths shall faint and be weary, and the young men shall utterly fall, but those who wait on the Lord shall renew their strength; they shall mount up with wings like eagles, they shall run and not be weary, they shall walk and not faint.

DEVOTIONAL

As you cradle your newborn in your arms, each tiny breath a reminder of the miraculous gift of life, remember that God sees the beauty and challenge of this sacred journey. In moments of exhaustion, when the weight of sleepless nights and the rhythm of endless feeding seem overwhelming, take heart in His promise: "He gives power to the weak." You are not alone in this experience; your every longing and struggle is known to Him. As you nurture this new life, the same God who formed your child intricately within you is there to renew your strength, just as a mother's heart gives life to hope and dreams. Trust in His timing, for those who wait on the Lord will find the wings to rise above fatigue and uncertainty. Lean into His presence when you feel weary. Embrace each moment—both challenging and joyous— knowing that in the tapestry of motherhood, He weaves love, resilience, and grace into every thread of your journey.

DAILY REFLECTION

In this sacred season of new life, how can you invite God's presence to transform your weary moments into opportunities for grace and deeper connection with your child?

PRAYER

Dear Lord, as I hold this precious new life in my arms, I ask for Your strength to wash over me, filling my heart with Your unwavering joy. In the quiet moments of exhaustion, remind me of Your promises and that I am never alone in this journey. Help me to embrace each day with grace, trusting that You nurture both my child and me, crafting a beautiful tapestry of love that reflects Your divine plan. Amen.

Nurturing a new life brings both joy and challenges. As you care for your little one, let God's love guide your heart and strengthen your spirit. Trust in His promise that you are never alone on this beautiful journey of motherhood.

1 Thessalonians 5:11 - "Therefore encourage one another and build each other up, just as in fact you are doing."

DEVOTIONAL

In this sacred season of nurturing new life, embrace the beautiful yet challenging adventure of motherhood. As you cradle your little one, may you feel the warmth of God's love surrounding you, whispering strength and encouragement into your weary spirit. Motherhood is a tapestry woven with joy and fatigue, laughter and tears, and through it all, remember you are never alone. In those quiet moments, when the world feels overwhelming, look to 1 Thessalonians 5:11, which reminds us to encourage one another and lift each other up. Share your hopes, your fears, and your triumphs with trusted friends or family; they are your allies in this journey. As you pour into the life of your child, let God pour His love back into you, filling every corner of your heart. Trust that each challenge you face is laced with His promise of support, transforming your journey into a beautiful, faith-filled story of love and resilience.

DAILY REFLECTION

In the midst of sleepless nights and tender moments, how can you consciously invite God's love into your daily struggles as a new mother, allowing it to transform your challenges into opportunities for growth and deeper connection?

PRAYER

Dear Lord, in this sacred journey of motherhood, I come before You with a heart both joyous and weary. As I nurture this new life, grant me the strength to embrace each challenge and the grace to recognize the beauty in every moment. Fill my spirit with Your unwavering love, allowing it to flow through me and into my child, reminding me that I am never alone on this incredible path. Amen.

January 27

Embrace the gift of new life as you navigate the tender moments of motherhood. In this season of growth and transformation, trust in God's perfect timing and provision. Remember, you are never alone—His presence surrounds you in every joy and challenge.

Isaiah 43:19 - "See, I am doing a new thing! Now it springs up; do you not perceive it? I am making a way in the wilderness and streams in the wasteland."

DEVOTIONAL

As you step into the beautiful, sometimes overwhelming journey of motherhood, remember the promise that God is doing a new thing in your life. Isaiah 43:19 reminds us that, even in moments of uncertainty, His presence is our guiding light amid the wilderness of sleepless nights and the joyful chaos of baby smiles. Each day brings its own challenges and triumphs, and in those tender moments, take a breath and embrace the growth that is unfolding within you and around you.

You are nurturing not just a child but a remarkable journey, and God's provision is woven into every moment, whether it's a midnight lullaby or a shared giggle. Trust that in this season of transformation, you are equipped with the love and strength that come from above. Keep your heart open to the new joys and lessons, even when they come shrouded in surprise or struggle. Remember, sweet momma, you are never alone; He is with you, preparing paths of peace where there once was uncertainty, and streams of grace in every challenge you face.

DAILY REFLECTION

In the quiet moments of your day, how can you intentionally seek God's presence to find comfort and strength as you nurture the miracle of new life within and around you?

PRAYER

Dear Lord, as I embrace this precious gift of new life, I ask for Your guiding light to illuminate my path through the tender moments of motherhood. In the sleepless nights and joyous first smiles, help me to trust in Your perfect timing and provision. Wrap me in Your comforting presence, reminding me that I am never alone as I navigate the beautiful chaos of this journey. Amen.

January 28

Amid the beauty and challenges of new motherhood, find strength in God's promise that He is with you always, nurturing both you and your little one. Trust that His grace fills every moment, bringing peace and joy as you step into this sacred journey.

Deuteronomy 31:6 – "Be strong and courageous. Do not be afraid or terrified because of them, for the Lord your God goes with you; he will never leave you nor forsake you."

DEVOTIONAL

As you embark on this beautiful journey of motherhood, remember that each moment—both the blissful and the challenging—is cradled in the loving arms of God. Like a comforting whisper in the night, His promise in Deuteronomy 31:6 reminds you that you are never alone. The feelings of uncertainty and fear may wash over you like waves crashing on the shore, but take heart; God walks alongside you. You may find strength in those quiet moments, holding your little one close, as His grace fills the room, inviting peace into your heart. Every sleepless night and every weary day is an opportunity to witness His nurturing spirit, not only within you but also as you care for your precious child. Trust in His promise—He will never leave you nor forsake you—as you cultivate this sacred bond with your baby. Embrace the joy amid the chaos, knowing that God's love envelops you both, drawing you deeper into the beauty of this new life.

DAILY REFLECTION

In this tender season of nurturing your little one, how can you open your heart to recognize and embrace God's unwavering presence, transforming moments of fear into opportunities for grace and connection?

PRAYER

Dear Lord, in this tender journey of motherhood, I lift my heart to You, feeling the weight of both joy and uncertainty. As I hold my little one close, remind me of Your unwavering presence, wrapping us in Your love and grace. Help me to embrace each moment—be it peaceful or challenging—with the assurance that I am never alone, for You walk beside me, nurturing both my spirit and the precious life I've been blessed with. Amen.

January 29

As you nurture new life, reflect on God's perfect love that envelops both you and your baby. Trust in His strength for each moment, knowing that in every heartbeat and tiny breath, His grace fills your journey of motherhood.

Romans 15:13 – "May the God of hope fill you with all joy and peace as you trust in him, so that you may overflow with hope by the power of the Holy Spirit."

DEVOTIONAL

As you cradle your precious new life, take a moment to bask in the profound love of a God who understands the depths of your heart. Each gentle heartbeat you feel is not just a reminder of your baby's presence but a testament to the God of hope who breathes life into every moment. In the quiet hours of the night, when the weight of uncertainty or fatigue may attempt to cloud your spirit, remember that His grace surrounds you like a warm embrace, empowering you with strength you didn't know you had. Just as you nurture your little one with tender care, trust that God nurtures you, filling you with joy and peace that can only come from Him. Allow His love to overflow in your life, infusing your moments with hope, even as you navigate the challenges of motherhood. As you lean into Him, watch as the Holy Spirit transforms your fears into faith, and your worries into worship. Embrace this journey, knowing that in every tiny breath and every soft coo, you are enveloped in perfect love—a love that never fails.

DAILY REFLECTION

In the quiet, tender moments with your newborn, how can you consciously invite God's perfect love into your heart, allowing it to transform your doubts into hope and your worries into a profound sense of peace?

PRAYER

Dear Lord, as I cradle this precious life in my arms, help me to feel Your love enveloping us both. In the moments of tiredness and uncertainty, remind me that Your grace is my strength, filling my heart with peace and joy. May every heartbeat and gentle coo deepen my trust in You, turning my fears into faith as I navigate this beautiful journey of motherhood. Amen.

January 30

In this sacred season, may the miracle of new life draw you closer to God's perfect love. Trust in His plan as you nurture your little one, and find strength in His promises each day of this beautiful journey.

Isaiah 54:13-14 - "All your children shall be taught by the Lord, and great shall be the peace of your children. In righteousness you shall be established; you shall be far from oppression, for you shall not fear; and from terror, for it shall not come near you."

DEVOTIONAL

In this sacred season of nurturing new life, take a moment to pause and reflect on the miracle unfolding within you. As you cradle your little one in your arms or feel their tiny kicks within, remember the promise of Isaiah 54:13-14—a promise woven into the very fabric of motherhood. Your child is touched by the hand of the Lord, destined to be taught His ways, enveloped in a peace that only He can provide. Though there may be sleepless nights and moments of uncertainty, trust that God has a perfect plan for both you and your baby. With each coo and cry, embrace the beautiful reality that you are not alone; His love surrounds you and empowers you to face the challenges ahead. It is in your gentle nurturing that you will instill the values of faith, hope, and love, allowing God's righteousness to flourish in your home. Lean into His promises, and find strength in knowing that fear and oppression have no place in your journey as a mother.

DAILY REFLECTION

In the tender moments of your baby's first cries or gentle sighs, how can you invite God's perfect love to guide you through the unknowns of motherhood, nurturing not just your child, but your own heart in trust and faith?

PRAYER

Dear Lord, in this sacred season of new beginnings, I come before You with a heart full of wonder and gratitude. As I nurture this precious life within me or in my arms, remind me that Your love is ever-present, guiding each step of this beautiful journey. Help me to trust in Your perfect plan, embracing the joy amidst the uncertainties, and filling our home with faith, hope, and love that reflects Your divine grace. Amen.

January 31

As you nurture this precious new life, remember the words of Psalm 139:13-14: "For you created my inmost being; you knit me together in my mother's womb." Trust in God's perfect design for both you and your baby, for each moment of this journey is a sacred gift. Rejoice in the miraculous love that binds you together.

Psalm 128:3-4: "Your wife will be like a fruitful vine within your house; your children will be like olive shoots around your table. Yes, this will be the blessing for the man who fears the Lord."

DEVOTIONAL

As you cradle this precious new life in your arms, let the profound truth of Psalm 139:13-14 wash over you: "For you created my inmost being; you knit me together in my mother's womb." Each soft breath, every delicate movement, is a testament to the loving handiwork of God, who designed both you and your child with purpose and care. In the quiet moments, when you gaze into your baby's eyes, remember that this journey you're on is not just a path of sleepless nights and endless feedings, but a sacred voyage woven with divine intention. Hold fast to the promise found in Psalm 128:3-4, as your little ones encircle your table, a living symbol of God's blessings. Your home and heart are now witnesses to the miraculous love that binds you together, a love that strengthens with every diaper change and midnight cuddle. Embrace the joy and challenges alike, for they are threads in the beautiful tapestry of motherhood. In these fleeting moments, rejoice in the gift of being a mother, and trust that every step along the way is held securely in God's embrace.

DAILY REFLECTION

As you hold your newborn close, how can you find peace and gratitude in the delicate balance between the challenges of motherhood and the profound love that God knit into your unique journey together?

PRAYER

Dear Lord, in this sacred season of new beginnings, I lift up every first-time mother who cradles her little one in her arms. May she feel the depth of Your love knitted into every moment, understanding that both she and her baby are woven into Your perfect plan. Grant her the grace to embrace the joys and challenges of motherhood, reminding her that each soft breath and gentle coo is a precious whisper of Your divine handiwork. Amen.

In this sacred journey of motherhood, remember that God's love is your anchor. As you nurture new life, trust in His guidance and wisdom, knowing He equips you for every challenge and joy that lies ahead. Surrender your worries, for you are not alone; His presence walks beside you each day.

Psalm 73:26 - "My flesh and my heart may fail, but God is the strength of my heart and my portion forever."

DEVOTIONAL

As you embark on this sacred journey of motherhood, each moment filled with awe and tenderness, remember that God's love is your steadfast anchor. The days may blend into late-night feedings and tender cries, but amidst the whirlwind, His gentle presence embraces you, whispering of strength when you feel weak. Psalm 73:26 assures us, "My flesh and my heart may fail, but God is the strength of my heart and my portion forever." In those moments of doubt or fear, let that verse be a comforting balm to your soul, reminding you that you are never alone. Every challenge you meet and every joy you cherish is part of a divine tapestry that He weaves with love. Surrender your worries at His feet, for He has equipped you with everything you need for this beautiful calling. Trust in His guiding hand, and allow your heart to be filled with peace, knowing you are cradled in His unending grace.

DAILY REFLECTION

In the quiet moments of this sacred journey, how can you actively remind yourself that God's unwavering love is your anchor amidst the joys and challenges of motherhood?

PRAYER

Dear Lord, as I step into this sacred journey of motherhood, I ask for your tender guidance and strength. In the quiet moments of love and the chaos of sleepless nights, remind me that your unwavering presence is my anchor, and your boundless grace holds me close. Help me to trust in your plans, surrender my worries, and find solace in the knowledge that I am never alone on this beautiful path you have laid before me. Amen.

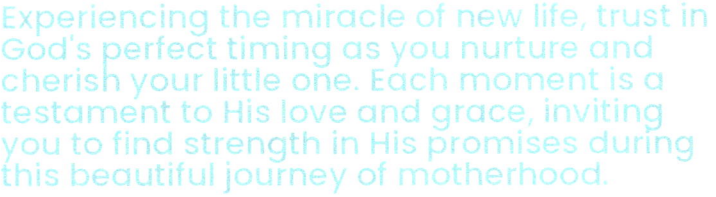

Experiencing the miracle of new life, trust in God's perfect timing as you nurture and cherish your little one. Each moment is a testament to His love and grace, inviting you to find strength in His promises during this beautiful journey of motherhood.

Isaiah 43:4 - "Since you are precious and honored in my sight, and because I love you, I will give people in exchange for you, nations in exchange for your life."

DEVOTIONAL

As you cradle your newborn in your arms, take a moment to absorb the overwhelming love swirling around you. Isaiah 43:4 reminds us of the deep value God places on each life, including the precious little one you have brought into the world. In this sacred time, the miracle of new life reveals His wondrous design and the incredible journey ahead. Trust in His perfect timing as you nurture and cherish every tiny milestone; each coo and smile is a testimony to His grace and everlasting love.

Though there may be days filled with uncertainty or exhaustion, remember that you are fearfully and wonderfully made for this role. Just as He cherishes you, you now have the privilege of cherishing another soul, teaching them about this divine love that intertwines your lives. Lean into His promises during this beautiful journey of motherhood, for with each heartbeat, you're reminded of the hope and joy He imparts not only to you but through you to the world.

DAILY REFLECTION

In the quiet moments with your little one, how can you embrace the truth that each tiny laugh and flutter is not just a reminder of their precious life, but also a beautiful invitation to trust in God's perfect timing and love as you navigate the wonders and challenges of motherhood?

PRAYER

Dear Lord, as I hold my little one close, let the magnitude of this love sink deep into my heart. Help me to embrace each precious moment as a reflection of Your grace, trusting in Your perfect timing through the exhaustion and uncertainty. May I nurture this tiny life with the same depth of love You pour into me, guiding them to know the beauty of Your promises and the hope that flows from our bond. Amen.

Today's journey is a beautiful reminder of God's promise in new life. Trust in His grace as you welcome this precious child, knowing that He walks alongside you through every moment of joy and challenge.

John 10:10 - "I have come that they may have life, and have it to the full."

DEVOTIONAL

As you embrace the beautiful chaos of motherhood, take a moment to breathe in the miracle that is your child. In John 10:10, Jesus promises abundance — a life filled with joy, love, and purpose. This new journey, with its mix of sleepless nights and tender whispers, is a sacred tapestry woven by God's hand. Each coo, each tiny finger wrapped around yours, is a reminder that you are not alone; He walks beside you in every joyful giggle and every moment of uncertainty.

Trust in His grace, for it flows endlessly like the love you feel for your little one. Motherhood will challenge you like never before, yet it will also unveil depths of strength and tenderness you never knew you possessed. Today, let your heart overflow with gratitude for the life you hold, and rest in the assurance that God's promise surrounds you, filling your days with His boundless love.

DAILY REFLECTION

In the tender moments of sleepless nights and soft whispers, how can you intentionally recognize and embrace God's grace as a source of strength and comfort on this remarkable journey of motherhood?

PRAYER

Dear Lord, as I cradle this precious gift in my arms, I am reminded of the miracle of new life that reflects Your boundless love. Help me to lean into Your grace during the sleepless nights and unparalleled joys, trusting that in every messy moment of motherhood, Your presence is my comfort and strength. May my heart overflow with gratitude, as I embrace this beautiful journey, grounded in the promise that You are always by my side. Amen.

As you cradle new life in your arms, remember that God's love surrounds you and your child. In this sacred season, find strength and grace in His promises, trusting that He will guide you in nurturing your little one with faith. Let each gentle moment be a reminder of His unending support in your journey of motherhood.

Psalm 31:24 - "Be strong and take heart, all you who hope in the Lord."

DEVOTIONAL

As you cradle the precious new life in your arms, let each soft breath remind you of the love that weaves through your journey, a love that flows from your Creator. In these tender moments, feel God's embrace wrapping around you, filling the quiet spaces with His unwavering support. The days may be long and the nights filled with uncertainty, yet trust that He holds you and your child, guiding every step of motherhood with grace. Remember the words of Psalm 31:24 — "Be strong and take heart, all you who hope in the Lord." This hope, like a gentle whisper, invites you to lean into the promises He has made; promises that will sustain you through sleepless nights and joyful milestones alike. Embrace the challenges with a heart full of faith, for each struggle is woven into the beautiful tapestry of your family's story. In every gentle moment, find reassurance in knowing that you are never alone on this sacred journey; God's love nurtures you both, today and always.

DAILY REFLECTION

In the quiet moments when you hold your child close, how can you intentionally invite God's loving presence into your journey, allowing His promises to illuminate the path of motherhood ahead?

PRAYER

Dear Lord, as I cradle this precious life, help me to sense Your love surrounding us in every gentle breath and heartbeat. Grant me the strength and grace to nurture my child with faith, trusting in Your promises to guide us through this beautiful yet daunting journey of motherhood. May each moment of doubt transform into a testament of Your unwavering support, reminding me that I am never alone. Amen.

As you cradle new life, remember that God's love is the foundation of this journey. Each moment of nurturing your child reflects His grace, inviting you to trust in His plan and find strength in His presence.

1 Corinthians 13:4-7 - "Love is patient, love is kind. It does not envy, it does not boast, it is not proud. It does not dishonor others, it is not self-seeking, it is not easily angered, it keeps no record of wrongs. Love does not delight in evil but rejoices with the truth. It always protects, always trusts, always hopes, always perseveres."

DEVOTIONAL

As you cradle your precious new life, take a moment to breathe in the sweetness of this gift. Each coo and gentle sigh is a reminder of God's unwavering love that envelops both you and your little one. In these early days, the profound truth found in 1 Corinthians 13:4-7 becomes your guiding light: love is patient, love is kind. Embrace the challenges of sleepless nights and the joys of tiny milestones; know that these moments are woven with grace. Remember that God's love invites you into a beautiful dance of nurturing, where His strength supports your every step. As you cultivate this new life, trust in His perfect plan, allowing His love to shape your heart and your home. Here, in this sacred journey of motherhood, you are never alone; His presence is your constant companion, and His love is the foundation upon which you will build their life.

DAILY REFLECTION

In this tender season of motherhood, how can you intentionally invite God's love into the daily rhythms of nurturing your child, allowing His grace to illuminate the challenges and joys you encounter?

PRAYER

Dear Lord, as I cradle this precious gift in my arms, I am reminded of the deep well of Your love that surrounds us. Help me to embrace each sleepless night and fleeting moment with grace and patience, trusting in Your perfect plan for our lives. May Your presence be my strength and my guide, weaving love into the fabric of our home and nurturing my heart to embrace this beautiful journey of motherhood. Amen.

On this day, as new life enters the world, remember God's promise in Psalm 127:3: "Children are a heritage from the Lord." Trust in His faithfulness as you nurture this precious gift, knowing that His love surrounds you both in every moment.

1 John 3:1 - "See what great love the Father has lavished on us, that we should be called children of God!"

DEVOTIONAL

As you cradle your little one today, take a moment to reflect on the profound truth encompassed in Psalm 127:3: "Children are a heritage from the Lord." Each coo, every tiny hand grasping yours, is a reminder of the sacred gift you hold—one that is woven together by God's own hands. In this season of new beginnings, let the weight of this blessing fill your heart with both awe and gratitude.

1 John 3:1 beautifully proclaims, "See what great love the Father has lavished on us." His love doesn't just touch you; it envelops your child, showering both of you with sweetness and care. As you nurture this precious life, trust in His unwavering faithfulness; He is with you in the quiet hours and the chaotic ones, whispering reassurances into the depths of your soul. Each day, allow His love to ripple through your parenting journey, illuminating the path ahead with hope and joy. Embrace this incredible adventure, for you are not alone; you are held in the arms of a loving Father who rejoices in the beautiful story He is writing through you both.

DAILY REFLECTION

In the tender moments of your day as a new mother, how can you consciously invite God's love to shape not only your heart but also the precious life cradled in your arms, reminding you that both of you are cherished treasures in His divine plan?

PRAYER

Dear Lord, as I hold my little one close, I am overwhelmed by the marvel of Your creation and the love that surrounds us. Help me to embrace each moment of this journey, trusting in Your promise that this child is a precious gift and a heritage from You. Grant me the wisdom and grace to nurture their spirit as I lean on Your unfailing love, knowing that You guide us both with gentle hands through every joy and challenge. Amen.

As you welcome new life into the world, remember that God's grace surrounds you daily. His strength will guide you through the joys and challenges of motherhood, reminding you that you are never alone in this sacred journey. Trust in His plan as you nurture your little one with love and faith.

2 Corinthians 12:9 - But he said to me, "My grace is sufficient for you, for my power is made perfect in weakness." Therefore I will boast all the more gladly about my weaknesses, so that Christ's power may rest on me.

DEVOTIONAL

As you cradle the new life in your arms, embrace the profound truth that God's grace envelops you daily. Each moment, from the sweet coos to the sleepless nights, is drenched in His love and strength. Remember, He says, "My grace is sufficient for you," a promise that whispers assurance in your toughest moments. As you navigate the joys and challenges of motherhood, allow your vulnerabilities to transform into sources of strength. When fatigue weighs heavily on your shoulders, lean into His promise; it is in your moments of weakness that His power shines brightest. Trust that you are never alone in this sacred journey, for God walks beside you, guiding your steps. With each tender caress, nurture your little one not just with love, but with the faith that blooms when you surrender to His will.

DAILY REFLECTION

In this tender season of your life, how can you open your heart to recognize and receive God's grace in both the joyful milestones and the quiet struggles of motherhood?

PRAYER

Dear Lord, as I hold this precious new life in my arms, I am filled with awe and gratitude for Your boundless grace. In moments of joy and in times of challenge, remind me that Your strength is my foundation. Help me to trust in Your divine plan as I nurture this little one, filling our days with love, faith, and the comforting assurance that I am never alone on this sacred journey. Amen.

As you welcome new life, find strength in God's promises. Each tiny heartbeat is a reminder of His grace, guiding you through the joys and challenges of motherhood. Trust in His unfailing love as you nurture this precious gift.

James 1:17 - "Every good and perfect gift is from above, coming down from the Father of the heavenly lights, who does not change like shifting shadows."

DEVOTIONAL

As you cradle the tiny life nestled in your arms, remember that each heartbeat is a miraculous melody, echoing the perfect gift given to you by God. In the gentle rhythm of your child's breathing, you can hear the whispers of His promises, reminding you that His grace wraps around you like a warm blanket on a cold night. Motherhood is a journey woven with joy and challenges; there will be sleepless nights and moments of doubt, but through it all, trust in the unfailing love that surrounds you.

Just as the sun rises each day, bringing warmth and light, God's blessings shine upon you, steadfast and unchanging. You are not embarking on this path alone; the Father of the heavenly lights walks beside you, illuminating your way with His love. Embrace the beauty of each small moment, for they are precious threads in the tapestry of your little one's life. Allow the love of Christ to sustain you and fill your heart with hope as you nurture this wonderful gift from above.

DAILY REFLECTION

In this sacred season of new beginnings, how can you intentionally carve out moments of stillness to reflect on God's promises, allowing His love to fill your heart and guide your steps as you embark on this incredible journey of motherhood?

PRAYER

Dear Lord, as I cradle this precious life in my arms, I thank You for the miracle of each tiny heartbeat. Remind me, in the quiet moments and the chaos, that Your promises are my strength and Your grace wraps around us like a gentle embrace. Help me to trust in Your unfailing love, nurturing this gift with a heart full of hope and faith, knowing that I am never alone in this beautiful journey of motherhood. Amen.

Embrace the miracle of new life, knowing that each moment is a gift from God. As you nurture your little one, trust in His guidance and strength, for you are never alone on this sacred journey of motherhood.

Psalm 34:18 - "The Lord is close to the brokenhearted and saves those who are crushed in spirit."

DEVOTIONAL

As you cradle your precious little one, remember that in each soft sigh and gentle smile, God is whispering His love into your heart. The journey of motherhood is unlike any other, filled with moments of pure joy and, at times, overwhelming challenges. Psalm 34:18 reminds us that the Lord is near, especially when our spirits feel crushed under the weight of worry or fatigue. It's in these tender moments of vulnerability that His strength covers us. Embrace the miracle of new life—each day holds the potential for joy, discovery, and growth. Allow yourself to lean into God's guidance; He walks beside you, illuminating your path with unwavering support. Take a deep breath, trust in His presence, and remember—you are never alone in this sacred journey of nurturing and loving.

DAILY REFLECTION

How can you intentionally savor the fleeting moments of joy and challenge in your new role as a mother, allowing God's presence to remind you that you are beautifully supported in this sacred journey?

PRAYER

Dear Lord, as I hold this miracle of new life in my arms, I thank You for the gift of motherhood. Help me to embrace every moment, both joyful and challenging, knowing that You are with me in the quiet whispers of the day. Grant me strength and wisdom as I nurture my little one, and remind me that Your love surrounds us both, guiding our hearts on this sacred journey. Amen.

May the miracle of new life remind you of God's unconditional love and faithfulness. Each moment, from the first kick to the gentle coos, reflects His divine plan for your family. Trust that He walks alongside you, guiding every step of this beautiful journey.

Genesis 1:27-28 - "So God created mankind in his own image, in the image of God he created them; male and female he created them. God blessed them and said to them, 'Be fruitful and increase in number; fill the earth and subdue it.'"

DEVOTIONAL

As you cradle your newborn, can you feel the weight of a miracle resting in your arms? Each tiny breath, each flutter of their heart, echoes the profound truth that you are participating in a divine narrative crafted by God Himself. Just as He created humanity in His very image, so too has He entrusted you with the sacred task of nurturing this precious life. Remember, dear mother, that every kick you felt was a testament to His faithfulness and every coo is a reminder of your child's unique place in His creation. God's call to "be fruitful and multiply" isn't merely a command; it's an invitation to experience His abundant love in the most intimate way. Embrace the delightful chaos and the quiet moments, for in them lie the whispers of His guidance. Trust that as you navigate this beautiful journey of motherhood, you are never alone—He walks beside you, illuminating every step with His unwavering presence.

DAILY REFLECTION

In the stillness of these precious moments with your baby, how can you open your heart to recognize the unique ways God's unwavering love is reflected in your journey of motherhood?

PRAYER

Dear Lord, as I hold this precious gift in my arms, I am in awe of the miracle of new life that reflects Your unfathomable love. Thank You for entrusting me with this sacred journey; may each tender moment remind me of Your faithfulness and guide me to nurture this little one in the light of Your grace. Help me to embrace both the chaos and the quiet, knowing that You are with me every step of the way, illuminating my path with Your unending presence.

In this sacred season of new beginnings, may the love you feel for your child mirror the boundless grace God provides. Trust that in each moment of uncertainty, His presence guides you, nurturing both you and your little one with strength and joy. Your journey as a mother is a beautiful reflection of God's unending faithfulness.

Galatians 5:22-23: "But the fruit of the Spirit is love, joy, peace, forbearance, kindness, goodness, faithfulness, gentleness and self-control. Against such things, there is no law."

DEVOTIONAL

As you embark on this sacred journey of motherhood, remember that each moment with your child is a tapestry woven with love, joy, and grace. The new life you hold n your arms reflects the boundless love that God has for each of us, a love that empowers and sustains. In times of sleepless nights and uncertain days, lean into the promise of Galatians 5:22-23; know that His Spirit fills you with the gifts of gentleness, patience, and unwavering joy. Even in the chaos that sometimes feels overwhelming, trust that God is present, comforting you and nurturing both your soul and your baby's spirit. Your heart is a vessel of His faithfulness, teaching you resilience in ways you never imagined. Embrace the highs and lows, for they are all part of the beautiful calling to be a mother. In this hallowed season of new beginnings, let your love for your child mirror the grace that God showers upon you.

DAILY REFLECTION

In this sacred season of new beginnings, how can you consciously embody the grace and love God showers upon you as you navigate the beautiful complexities of motherhood and deepen your bond with your child?

PRAYER

Dear Lord, in this sacred season of new beginnings, I thank You for the precious gift of my child. As I navigate the whirlwinds of motherhood, fill my heart with Your boundless grace, allowing my love to reflect the nurturing presence that surrounds us. May Your strength be my anchor in moments of doubt, and Your joy be my guiding light, reminding me that in every challenge and joy, I am enveloped in Your unending faithfulness. Amen.

The joy of new life brings both wonder and responsibility. Trust in God's guidance as you nurture this precious gift, knowing He equips you with strength and wisdom for each step on this beautiful journey of motherhood.

Proverbs 31:25-27 - "She is clothed with strength and dignity; she can laugh at the days to come. She speaks with wisdom, and faithful instruction is on her tongue. She watches over the affairs of her household and does not eat the bread of idleness."

DEVOTIONAL

As you embrace the miracle of new life, take a moment to breathe in the joy and wonder that surrounds you. Each tiny heartbeat brings forth dreams and hopes, along with a gentle reminder of the responsibility that lies ahead. Proverbs 31:25-27 assures us that despite the challenges, you are clothed with strength and dignity—these are gifts bestowed upon you by God. In your moments of doubt or exhaustion, remember that your anxieties can be replaced with laughter, for you have been entrusted with a precious life that will enrich your soul. Let wisdom be your guiding light; speak words of encouragement to both your little one and yourself. As you nurture this gift, lean into God's embrace, knowing He has equipped you with the strength and insight needed for every step of this journey. Celebrate the small victories and cling to His promises, for you are not alone in this beautiful adventure of motherhood. Your heart is a garden, blooming with love, resilience, and the reassurance that God walks beside you always.

DAILY REFLECTION

In the gentle chaos of these early days, how can you embrace the divine strength and wisdom God has gifted you, transforming moments of uncertainty into opportunities for growth and connection with your little one?

PRAYER

Dear Lord, in the quiet moments of motherhood, as I cradle this new life, I am awash in wonder and joy, feeling both the weight and beauty of the responsibility You've placed in my hands. Grant me the strength and wisdom to nurture this precious gift, reminding me that even amid doubt and exhaustion, I can lean into Your embrace and find solace in Your promises. May my heart overflow with love, resilience, and laughter, as I walk this sacred journey with You by my side. Amen.

On this journey of motherhood, find peace in the quiet moments of prayer, knowing that God's love envelops you and your child. Trust in His guidance as you nurture this precious life, and remember that with each heartbeat, His faithfulness grows stronger.

Philippians 4:6-7: "Do not be anxious about anything, but in every situation, by prayer and petition, with thanksgiving, present your requests to God. And the peace of God, which transcends all understanding, will guard your hearts and your minds in Christ Jesus."

DEVOTIONAL

As you embark on this beautiful journey of motherhood, take a moment to breathe deeply and embrace the stillness that surrounds you. In those quiet moments, remember Philippians 4:6-7, which gently reminds us to lean into prayer, casting aside your worries and fears. Each heartbeat of your child is a sacred reminder of God's faithfulness and love, enveloping both you and your little one in a warm embrace.

With every prayer you whisper, whether in joy or uncertainty, know that God is listening, ready to guide you through the stormy waters and the serene shores of parenting. Trust in His unfailing presence as you nurture this precious life; your love, rooted in faith, will blossom in ways you cannot yet imagine. Let go of anxiety and allow His peace—one that transcends all understanding —to guard your heart and mind, fortifying you in the beautiful, albeit challenging, moments ahead. Embrace the journey, dear mother, for you are never alone; God walks with you every step of the way.

DAILY REFLECTION

In the quiet moments of motherhood, how can you intentionally invite God's peace into your heart and trust in His unending love as you nurture your child?

PRAYER

Dear Lord, in these tender moments of motherhood, I come to You seeking peace amidst the joys and uncertainties. Surround me and my child with Your love, and let each heartbeat remind us of Your unwavering faithfulness. Grant me the strength to trust Your guidance as I nurture this precious life, knowing that even in stillness, Your presence envelops us both. Amen.

February 14

In this tender season of new life, remember that God's love envelops you and your baby. As you navigate the challenges of motherhood, trust in His guidance and find strength in His promises, knowing you are never alone on this beautiful journey.

John 14:27 - "Peace I leave with you; my peace I give to you. Not as the world gives do I give to you. Let not your hearts be troubled, neither let them be afraid."

DEVOTIONAL

In the gentle unfolding of these precious days, as you cradle your newborn close, remember that you are enveloped in a love far deeper than the challenges you may face. The journey of motherhood may feel overwhelming, filled with moments of uncertainty and sleepless nights, yet it is in these spaces that God's grace shines brightest. Lean into His promise of peace, for He assures you in John 14:27, "Peace I leave with you; my peace I give to you." This is not a fleeting peace that the world offers, but a steadfast, nurturing grace that flows from the heart of your Creator.

When your heart pulses with anxiety, remind yourself that you are not alone; His presence is a constant embrace, wrapping around you both. Allow His peace to quiet your fears and illuminate the path ahead, guiding your steps as you learn to nurture not just your baby, but yourself. Embrace each moment—each coo, each cry—as a sacred opportunity to grow in love, grace, and faith. In knowing you are nurtured by His grace, you will find the strength to nurture your little one, walking confidently in this beautiful, transformative journey of motherhood.

DAILY REFLECTION

In this sacred journey of motherhood, how can you open your heart to receive the unwavering grace of God, allowing it to fill your moments of uncertainty with peace and reassurance as you nurture both your baby and your own soul?

PRAYER

Dear Lord, in this beautiful yet daunting season of motherhood, I seek Your presence to cradle both me and my newborn in Your nurturing embrace. Grant me the grace to embrace each moment—each joy and each challenge—while filling my heart with Your peace that surpasses understanding. Help me to trust in Your promises, knowing that as I care for my little one, I am also being lovingly cared for in Your infinite love. Amen.

As a first-time mother, your journey unfolds with the miracle of new life, reminding you of God's unwavering love and grace. Trust in His guidance as you nurture this precious gift, knowing that every moment is imbued with divine purpose. Embrace the beauty of this season, for you are part of His tapestry of creation.

1 Samuel 1:27-28 - "I prayed for this child, and the Lord has granted me what I asked of him. So now I give him to the Lord. For his whole life he will be given over to the Lord."

DEVOTIONAL

As you hold this tiny miracle in your arms, remember the profound truth found in 1 Samuel 1:27-28: "I prayed for this child, and the Lord has granted me what I asked of him." Each coo and every gentle sigh is a reminder of the unwavering love that God has for you and your little one. This journey into motherhood is not just a physical evolution; it is an embrace of the divine, a sacred partnership where you nurture not only the body but the spirit of a child entrusted to you. In moments of uncertainty, lean into His grace, knowing that He walks alongside you, guiding your heart and hands. Every little moment, from sleepless nights to joyful giggles, is etched with purpose, as you are woven into the beautiful tapestry of God's creation. Cherish this season, for it is a chapter that reflects His love so vividly, reminding you that you are beautifully designed for this role. Trust in His perfect timing, for you are exactly where you need to be, enveloped in His promises.

DAILY REFLECTION

How can you see the hand of God weaving His love and purpose into the small, everyday moments of your new journey as a mother?

PRAYER

Dear Lord, as I cradle this precious new life in my arms, I marvel at the gift You have entrusted to me. Grant me the wisdom to nurture both body and spirit, reminding me that every moment—be it a soft coo or a sleepless night—holds a piece of Your divine purpose. Help me to embrace this journey with a heart full of gratitude, trusting in Your unwavering love and guidance as I navigate the beautiful tapestry of motherhood. Amen.

As you cradle the miracle of new life, remember that God's love surrounds you and your little one. Trust in His strength during these transformative days, and let His grace guide you in every moment of joy and challenge.

Philippians 4:13 - "I can do all things through Christ who strengthens me."

DEVOTIONAL

As you cradle the miracle of your new life, take a moment to breathe in the sacredness of this gift. Each tiny breath, each soft coo, is a reminder of God's love wrapping around you both like a warm embrace. In these transformative days, when exhaustion and joy intertwine, remember Philippians 4:13: "I can do all things through Christ who strengthens me." Let this promise anchor you, whispering that you are not alone. When challenges feel overwhelming, pause and lean into His strength, knowing that the struggles are part of a beautiful journey. Trust in His grace to guide your heart as you navigate this new path—moments of pure joy will rise alongside the difficult days. Each smile and every sleepless night are threads woven into the tapestry of motherhood, showcasing the incredible bond formed through love and faith.

DAILY REFLECTION

In the quiet moments when the weight of motherhood feels heavy, how can you intentionally invite God's love into your heart and home, transforming exhaustion into gratitude as you embrace the journey with your little one?

PRAYER

Dear Lord, as I hold this precious new life in my arms, I am overwhelmed by the miracle You have blessed me with. Please fill my heart with Your love and strength, guiding me through both the tender joys and the exhausting nights, reminding me that I am never alone in this journey. Grant me the grace to embrace each moment, trusting that every challenge is woven into the beautiful story of motherhood, a testament to Your faithful presence in our lives. Amen.

God's love shines brightly in the miracle of new life, reminding us that each tiny heartbeat echoes His divine purpose. As you nurture this precious gift, trust in His steadfast presence to guide and strengthen you through every sleepless night and overwhelming joy. Rejoice, for you are not alone in this sacred journey of motherhood.

Luke 1:45 - "Blessed is she who has believed that the Lord would fulfill his promises to her."

DEVOTIONAL

As you cradle your little one, each gentle breath a reminder of God's unfathomable love, let the miracle of new life draw you deeper into His embrace. In the quiet moments, when the world feels overwhelmingly filled with both joy and uncertainty, remember that His promises resonate through every tiny heartbeat. Luke 1:45 encourages us to embrace faith amidst the chaos: "Blessed is she who has believed that the Lord would fulfill his promises to her." These words whisper assurance to your weary heart, inviting you to trust that He is ever-present, guiding you through sleepless nights and the whirlwind of emotions that motherhood brings. Each smile, each coo, is a reflection of His divine purpose at work within your family. You are not alone; His steadfast presence surrounds you, nurturing your spirit as you navigate this sacred journey. Rejoice in this beautiful season, for God's love shines brightly, lighting your path as you nurture this precious gift.

DAILY REFLECTION

How can you more deeply embrace God's unwavering presence in your heart as you navigate the beautiful chaos of motherhood, trusting that each moment of uncertainty is woven into His divine plan for you and your baby?

PRAYER

Dear Lord, in this tender season of nurturing new life, help me to feel Your presence wrapped around us like a warm embrace. As I witness each tiny heartbeat, may Your love remind me that we are not alone, and may my heart be filled with faith in Your steadfast promises. Grant me strength for the sleepless nights and grace amidst the overwhelming joy, guiding me to cherish every fleeting moment as a reflection of Your divine purpose. Amen.

As new life unfolds, find peace in the promise of God's presence during this transformative journey. Trust that His strength will guide you through each moment, bringing comfort and joy as you nurture your little one. Embrace this sacred season with the assurance that you are never alone; His love surrounds every step of motherhood.

Matthew 28:20: "And surely I am with you always, to the very end of the age."

DEVOTIONAL

As you stand on the threshold of motherhood, cradling new life in your arms or feeling those tender kicks within, allow yourself a moment to breathe deep and embrace this sacred journey. Matthew 28:20 reminds us, "And surely I am with you always, to the very end of the age." In the early hours when the world seems still and your heart races with awe and uncertainty, remember that God walks beside you, cradling both your fears and joys. Every sleepless night and quiet moment spent nurturing your little one is filled with His divine presence, offering strength when you feel weary and joy amidst the challenges. Trust in the promise that His love envelops you, illuminating the path as you discover the beauty of this new chapter. Let His gentle whispers guide your heart, reassuring you that you are never alone in this transformative experience. Embrace the grace of each day, for in the chaotic and tender moments of motherhood, His faithfulness shines brightest, transforming your challenges into cherished memories. God's love is a constant, holding you securely as you nurture this precious gift of life.

DAILY REFLECTION

In the quiet moments of your journey into motherhood, how can you consciously invite God's presence into your heart, allowing His love to transform your fears into cherished memories as you nurture this precious life?

PRAYER

Dear Lord, as I embark on this tender journey of motherhood, I seek Your presence to envelop me with peace and strength. In moments of uncertainty and joy, guide my heart to trust in Your unwavering love, reminding me that I am never alone. May each day be a reflection of Your grace and a celebration of the precious life I hold, as I nurture with the assurance that You walk beside me always. Amen.

February 19

As you cradle new life in your arms, remember that every moment is a blessing filled with God's grace. Trust His plan for you and your child, nurturing not just body, but spirit, through prayer and love. Embrace this sacred journey with faith that He guides each step.

Proverbs 22:6 - "Train up a child in the way he should go; even when he is old he will not depart from it."

DEVOTIONAL

As you cradle new life in your arms, cherish each gentle breath and tiny movement, for these moments are exquisite gifts from God, washed in His grace. The journey of motherhood unfolds in the quiet whispers of the heart, where the weight of responsibility mingles with boundless joy. In Proverbs 22:6, we are reminded that nurturing your child is not merely a duty but a divine calling—an invitation to guide their spirit as tenderly as you hold their tiny frame. Trust in God's plan for both of you; the path may twist and turn, but He walks beside you, lighting the way with unwavering love. Each prayer you lift is a thread woven into the fabric of your child's faith—a powerful legacy you are beginning to build together. Embrace the sacred rhythm of this new chapter, where your love becomes a beacon of hope and resilience. Remember, as you guide your child toward the light, you, too, are held firmly in the embrace of His unending grace.

DAILY REFLECTION

As you hold this precious gift, how can you intentionally weave moments of prayer and love into your daily routine, nurturing not only their body but also their spirit in the light of God's grace?

PRAYER

Dear Lord, as I cradle this precious life in my arms, fill my heart with gratitude for each fleeting moment and every blessing that comes with motherhood. Strengthen my spirit with Your wisdom, guiding me through the challenges and joys of this sacred journey—help me nurture not just their body, but their soul, as I lean on Your unwavering love. May the prayers I whisper bring comfort and light to both our lives, as I trust in Your divine plan for our family. Amen.

As you nurture new life, remember that God entrusts you with this precious gift. Seek His strength and wisdom in every moment, trusting that His love surrounds you and your baby, fostering a bond that reflects His divine care.

Exodus 23:25 - "Worship the Lord your God, and his blessing will be on your food and water. I will take away sickness from among you."

DEVOTIONAL

As you embark on this beautiful journey of motherhood, the weight of responsibility mingles with the joy of nurturing new life. In the quiet moments—those late-night feedings, the gentle lullabies, and the sweet hand grasps—God's love envelops you. Exodus 23:25 reminds us that as we worship and focus our hearts on the Lord, His blessings flow into the very fabric of our daily lives, ensuring that our nourishment is not just physical, but spiritual as well. Trust that He goes before you, safeguarding your baby from sickness and surrounding you both with His divine care. Each little cry, every coo, is a beautiful reminder of God's grace and presence in your life. As you cradle this precious gift, seek His strength in the uncertainties, and let the bond you share be a reflection of His unending love. You are not alone; He is with you every step of the way, weaving His purpose through your beautiful journey of motherhood.

DAILY REFLECTION

In the tender moments of motherhood, how can you invite God's presence into your heart, allowing His strength to transform your worries into trust as you cherish each new day with your little one?

PRAYER

Dear Lord, as I cradle this precious life in my arms, I am overwhelmed with gratitude for the gift of motherhood. Infuse my heart with your strength and wisdom in each moment of joy and uncertainty, reminding me that your love surrounds us both. May every tiny cry and gentle coo draw me closer to you, fostering a bond that reflects your infinite grace and comfort.

February 21

As you cradle the new life in your arms, remember that just as God knit you together in your mother's womb, He is weaving a beautiful tapestry in your child's life. Trust His guidance with each moment, knowing your love is a reflection of His grace.

Ephesians 2:10 - "For we are God's handiwork, created in Christ Jesus to do good works, which God prepared in advance for us to do."

DEVOTIONAL

As you cradle the precious life in your arms, remember that this moment is a divine intersection between artistry and purpose. Just as God intricately knit you together in your mother's womb, He is weaving an extraordinary tapestry in your child's life, with each thread representing His love and intention. Ephesians 2:10 reminds us that we are His handiwork, crafted with purpose to fulfill the good works He has prepared for us. In the quiet, sleepless nights and joyful mornings, trust that your love—raw, tender, and unconditional—is a mirror reflecting His grace. With every coo and sigh, you are not just nurturing a child but nurturing the masterpiece that God envisions. Allow yourself to lean into the journey, knowing that each moment, both challenging and beautiful, is part of a divine story being written together. So breathe deep, cherish every fleeting second, and walk in faith, for He has great plans for both you and your little one.

DAILY REFLECTION

In the quiet beauty of your child's every sigh and coo, how can you consciously recognize and embrace the divine purpose that God is weaving through both of your lives in this sacred season of motherhood?

PRAYER

Dear Lord, as I cradle this precious life in my arms, I am reminded of the beautiful work You are crafting in both of us. Guide me in these fragile moments; help me to trust that Your love weaves through our journey, illuminating our path with grace and hope. Thank you for this sacred gift—may my heart reflect Your endless love as we embrace the tapestry of our lives together. Amen.

As you navigate the beautiful journey of motherhood, remember that God's love cradles you and your baby in every moment. Trust in His provision, as you discover the depths of His grace in sleepless nights and joyful milestones. Your little one is a precious gift, cherished and held in divine purpose.

Hebrews 13:5-6 - "Keep your lives free from the love of money and be Content with what you have, because God has said, 'Never will I leave you; never will I forsake you.' So we say with confidence, 'The Lord is my helper; I will not be afraid. What can mere mortals do to me?'"

DEVOTIONAL

As you journey through the transformative season of motherhood, may you find solace in the gentle embrace of God's unwavering love. Each moment, from the quiet nights cradling your newborn to the exhilarating first milestones, is seasoned with His grace, reminding you that you are not alone. In the complexities of this new role, remember that your little one is a cherished gift, intricately woven into God's divine plan, just as you are. When weariness settles in and uncertainty looms, hold fast to His promise: "Never will I leave you; never will I forsake you." Your heart may swell with joy, or ache with doubt, yet know that both emotions are a part of this grand tapestry of motherhood. With confidence, proclaim, "The Lord is my helper." In this sacred space, where love and vulnerability intertwine, let your spirit be nourished by the boundless provisions of our Creator. Trust that His embrace surrounds both you and your baby, infusing each day with purpose and peace.

DAILY REFLECTION

In the tender moments of motherhood, how can you intentionally recognize and embrace the whispers of God's love and provision amid the challenges and joys you experience with your little one?

PRAYER

Dear Lord, in this sacred journey of motherhood, I seek Your guidance and embrace amid both the quiet and chaotic moments. Wrap my weary heart in Your love, and remind me daily that each cry and coo is a precious note in the symphony of Your divine plan. Grant me the strength to cherish these fleeting days and to trust fully in Your provision, knowing that I am never alone on this beautiful path. Amen.

As you cradle your newborn, remember that God entrusts you with this precious gift, just as He entrusted Mary with Jesus. May your journey of motherhood be filled with His peace and guidance, reminding you that His strength is made perfect in your weakness.

Luke 1:38 - "I am the Lord's servant," Mary answered. "May your word to me be fulfilled." Then the angel left her.

DEVOTIONAL

As you cradle your newborn, feel the weight of that precious gift in your arms, akin to Mary holding the infant Jesus. In the quiet moments of the night, when all is still except for the soft breaths of your little one, remember Mary's profound acceptance: "I am the Lord's servant." Just as she embraced her divine calling with courage and grace, so too are you called to embrace the journey of motherhood with faith and trust. This path may sometimes feel overwhelming, with whispers of doubt flooding your mind, but take heart—His strength is made perfect in your weakness. Each moment with your child is an echo of God's love and trust as He watches you nurture, teach, and guide. Lean into His peace, which surpasses all understanding, as He walks alongside you. In these tender moments, may you continually hear His gentle reminder: you are never alone.

DAILY REFLECTION

In the sacred stillness as you cradle your newborn, what whispers of God's strength and guidance are calling you to embrace the beautiful yet daunting journey of motherhood, echoing Mary's unwavering faith?

PRAYER

Dear Lord, as I cradle this precious gift in my arms, I am filled with gratitude for the trust You have placed in me. In the quiet moments, when uncertainty whispers in the night, remind me of Mary's courage and faith. May Your strength embrace me, turning my worries into peace, as I embark on this beautiful journey of motherhood. Let me feel Your presence in every gentle breath and tiny sigh, knowing that I am never alone in this sacred calling. Amen.

As you cradle your newborn, remember that each moment is a sacred gift, echoing God's promise of new life. Trust in His unfailing love as you navigate this precious journey of motherhood, shaping not just your child's life, but your own heart and faith.

John 16:21 - "A woman giving birth to a child has pain because her time has come; but when her baby is born she forgets the anguish because of her joy that a child is born into the world."

DEVOTIONAL

As you cradle your newborn, take a moment to breathe in the miracle unfolding in your arms. John 16:21 speaks to the heart of your journey— the labor pains that echo the trials of motherhood, now overshadowed by the sheer joy of new life. Each tiny heartbeat reminds us that even in hardship, God's promise of renewal stands firm. Trust in His unfailing love as you navigate sleepless nights and pastel-colored dreams, for these moments shape not only your child's path but carve deeper into your own heart and faith. With every coo and giggle, let go of past worries and embrace the sacred gift of now. This journey, filled with both challenges and delights, is a divine tapestry being woven by the hands of your Creator. Remember that you are not alone; His presence wraps around you like a soft blanket, comforting and guiding you as you embrace this beautiful adventure of motherhood.

DAILY REFLECTION

As you hold your little one close, how can you surrender your worries to God and embrace this season of motherhood as a profound opportunity for your own spiritual growth and intimacy with Him?

PRAYER

Dear Lord, as I hold my precious newborn, I am in awe of the miracle of life wrapped in my arms. Help me to cherish these fleeting moments and remind me of Your unwavering love through every trial and joy of motherhood. Grant me the strength to embrace this journey with an open heart, trusting in Your divine plan as I shape not only my child's future but also my faith and love for You. Amen.

God's love flows through the miracle of new life, reminding first-time mothers that each moment— whether waiting in anticipation or holding their little one—is a sacred journey. Trust in His guidance as you nurture this precious gift, knowing that He is with you every step of the way.

Psalm 145:9 The LORD is good to all; he has compassion on all he has made.

DEVOTIONAL

As you stand on the threshold of motherhood, whether cradling your newborn or feeling those first fluttering kicks, remember that each moment is a divine tapestry woven from love and hope. Psalm 145:9 reminds us that "The LORD is good to all; he has compassion on all he has made." In this sacred journey, God's love flows through every heartbeat and every gentle breath, reminding you that you are never alone. When doubts or fears begin to stir, take a moment to pause and let His compassion wrap around you like a warm embrace. Trust in His guidance, knowing that He has entrusted you with a precious gift—an extension of His grace and kindness. Each late-night feeding, every coo, and every smile is a reminder that you are participating in the miracle of creation. Allow yourself to lean into His presence during this transformative time, for He walks with you every step of the way, cherishing both you and your little one.

DAILY REFLECTION

In the quiet moments of waiting or the sweet chaos of nurturing your newborn, how can you more deeply embrace the truth that God's love is interwoven into every experience, guiding you through this sacred journey of motherhood?

PRAYER

Dear Lord, in the tender moments of anticipation and the joy of holding my little one, I thank You for the profound gift of new life that flows from Your endless love. As I navigate the waves of motherhood, may I feel Your compassion surrounding me, reminding me that I am never alone. Grant me the strength to embrace each moment as a sacred part of this journey, and may Your guidance illuminate my path, nurturing the precious bond You have blessed me with. Amen.

As you nurture new life, remember that God's love surrounds you in this sacred journey of motherhood. Lean on His strength and wisdom, for every moment of uncertainty is an opportunity to deepen your faith. Trust that, just as He knit your child together in the womb, He is intricately involved in every step of your parenting path.

Romans 8:28 - "And we know that in all things God works for the good of those who love him, who have been called according to his purpose."

DEVOTIONAL

As you embark on this beautiful and transformative journey of motherhood, take a moment to embrace the sacredness of the life you now nurture. Each flutter and every kick remind you that God's love wraps around you like a comforting embrace, whispering reassurance in the quiet stillness of night. In the midst of sleepless nights and moments of uncertainty, remember that He who knit your precious child together in your womb is also guiding your every step.

Hold onto Romans 8:28, for it reassures you that God is working through every challenge for your good, weaving together a tapestry of grace and love in your family's life. Trust that He has equipped you with strength and wisdom, even in your most vulnerable moments. With each decision, each doubt, lean into Him, knowing that our Lord rejoices in your heart's desire to nurture and protect this new life. You are not alone; His presence surrounds you, filling the gaps with hope and courage, ensuring that every tear and smile is under His gentle watch.

DAILY REFLECTION

In this sacred journey of motherhood, how can you intentionally seek God's presence in both your joyful moments and your moments of doubt, allowing His unwavering love to guide and strengthen you as you nurture this precious new life?

PRAYER

Dear Lord, as I cradle this new life in my arms, I feel both the joy and weight of the journey ahead. Surround me with Your unconditional love, guiding me through moments of doubt and uncertainty. Help me to trust in Your divine plan, knowing that each challenge I face is an opportunity to grow in faith and grace, all under Your watchful care. Amen.

Trust in God's perfect timing and provision as you welcome new life. Each moment is a reminder of His faithfulness, guiding you through the joys and challenges of motherhood.

Psalm 37:5-6 - "Commit your way to the Lord; trust in him and he will do this: He will make your righteous reward shine like the dawn, your vindication like the noonday sun."

DEVOTIONAL

As you cradle the tiny life in your arms, each moment becomes a beautiful tapestry woven with joy and uncertainty. In this sacred journey of motherhood, remember to commit your way to the Lord, for He guides your footsteps through both the light and shadows. Psalm 37:5-6 whispers His promise: trust in Him, and like the dawn breaking over the horizon, He will illuminate your path. The sleepless nights and overwhelming emotions might sometimes cloud your spirit, but rest assured, His perfect timing and provision are at work. Every giggle, every tiny coo is a testament to His faithfulness, a reminder that you are not alone in this tender season. Embrace the challenges, knowing that He transforms your struggles into the vibrant glow of joy and fulfillment. As you nurture this new life, allow your heart to trust deeply in the One who has knitted your little one in His love, guiding you both into the bright future He has prepared.

DAILY REFLECTION

How can you embrace the delicate balance of joy and uncertainty in motherhood while trusting that God's perfect timing is shaping both you and your child in profound ways?

PRAYER

Dear Lord, as I embrace this new life before me, fill my heart with trust in Your perfect timing and provision. In moments of joy and uncertainty, remind me that Your faithfulness is woven into each experience of motherhood. Help me to lean on You, believing that with every challenge comes the promise of Your light guiding our way. Amen.

In this sacred season of new beginnings, may you find strength in God's promises as you cradle the miracle of life in your arms. Trust that His unwavering love surrounds you, guiding you through the joys and challenges of motherhood. Each tender moment is a reflection of His grace, reminding you that you are never alone in this journey.

Matthew 6:26 - "Look at the birds of the air; they do not sow or reap or store away in barns, and yet your heavenly Father feeds them. Are you not much more valuable than they?"

DEVOTIONAL

In this sacred season of new beginnings, as you cradle the precious life entrusted to you, pause and breathe deeply in the stillness of these moments. The journey of motherhood is a profound tapestry woven with both joy and uncertainty; allow yourself to feel the full spectrum of emotions that come with it. Remember the promise found in Matthew 6:26, where Jesus reminds us of the caring hand of our Heavenly Father. Just as He provides for the birds, nurturing them without their toil, know that you too are cherished, valued, and held in His loving embrace.

Each soft coo and gentle sigh from your little one is a sacred reminder of His grace surrounding you—a grace that is truly sufficient for every challenge and delight you will face. In times of fatigue or doubt, let your heart be anchored in the unwavering love of God, for He walks with you, whispering reassurance amid the chaos. As you embrace the tender moments, trust that you are never alone; His strength is made perfect in your fragility, guiding you, loving you, and filling you with the courage to be the mother He has called you to be.

DAILY REFLECTION

In this holy season of new beginnings, how might embracing the tender, fragile moments of motherhood open your heart to trust in God's unwavering love and the unique grace He offers you and your child?

PRAYER

Dear Lord, as this new life rests in my arms, I thank You for the incredible gift of motherhood. In moments of doubt and weariness, remind me of Your unwavering presence, cradling me in Your love and grace. Help me to embrace each joyful sigh and challenging tear, trusting that Your strength is at work in me, guiding my every step on this sacred journey. Amen.

It seems like you've entered a reference error, which commonly occurs in spreadsheet applications like Excel when a formula refers to an invalid cell or range. If you can provide more context or clarify what you're trying to achieve, I'd be happy to assist you further!

Luke 1:46-47 -"And Mary said: 'My soul glorifies the Lord and my spirit rejoices in God my Savior.'"

DEVOTIONAL

As you embark on this beautiful journey of motherhood, take a moment to reflect on Mary's words in Luke 1:46-47: "My soul glorifies the Lord and my spirit rejoices in God my Savior." Just as Mary carried the miraculous gift of life within her, you too carry the promise and potential of a new life. In the early days of motherhood, amidst the exhaustion and worries, allow yourself the grace to rejoice.

Consider how Mary, despite her circumstances, celebrated the profound truth of God's goodness. In those quiet, late-night moments, when your heart swells with love or fear, remember to pause and glorify God for the blessing you hold in your arms. Every cry is a reminder of His faithfulness, every sleepless night an opportunity for prayer. Embrace the joy and the challenges; they are woven into the rich tapestry of your new role. Like Mary, rejoice in your spirit, knowing that God walks with you through every step of this extraordinary journey.

DAILY REFLECTION

In the tender moments of your motherhood journey, how can you find the strength to rejoice in God's goodness, even when the burdens feel heavy and the nights are long?

PRAYER

Dear Lord, as I stand at the beginning of this sacred journey into motherhood, I ask for Your grace to fill my heart with joy amidst the uncertainties. Help me to embrace each moment with gratitude, even when the nights are long and the challenges seem overwhelming. Remind me to rejoice in the miracle I hold, finding Your presence in every heartbeat and every cry, just as Mary did. Amen.

In this sacred season of anticipation and new beginnings, trust in God's perfect plan as you nurture the precious gift of life. Remember, each moment of your journey is wrapped in His love, guiding you as you embrace the miraculous role of motherhood.

Psalm 40:5 - Many, O Lord my God, are the wonders you have done. The things you planned for us no one can recount to you; were I to speak and tell of them, they would be too many to declare.

DEVOTIONAL

In this sacred season of anticipation and new beginnings, dear mother, allow yourself to be enveloped by the wonders God has in store for you and your little one. Psalm 40:5 whispers of the countless blessings intertwined with your journey, each moment a testament to His divine craftsmanship. As your heart swells with joy and perhaps a touch of anxiety, remember that your feelings are both valid and precious — just like the life you are nurturing.

Embrace the quiet moments of reflection, for in them, you'll find His love anchoring your spirit, reminding you that you are not alone on this journey. The days ahead may be filled with sleepless nights and deep questions, but every challenge is accompanied by His grace, guiding you as you grow into the miraculous role of motherhood. Trust in His perfect plan, even when the path seems uncertain, and rejoice in the beauty of this remarkable bond. Count the wonders He is weaving into your story, for in those wonders lies the essence of pure love.

DAILY REFLECTION

In this precious season of nurturing new life, how can you embrace the divine threads of joy and uncertainty that God intricately weaves into your journey of motherhood?

PRAYER

Dear Lord, in this sacred season of anticipation, I surrender my heart to You as I embrace the miracle of motherhood. May Your love guide me through every joy and uncertainty, reminding me that I am never alone in this journey. Help me to find peace in the quiet moments and trust in Your perfect plan, as I nurture this precious gift of life with grace and gratitude. Amen.

As you cherish the new life within your arms, remember that just as God knitted each of us together in our mother's womb, He is intimately involved in your journey of motherhood. Trust in His grace to guide you through the joys and challenges of nurturing this precious gift.

Colossians 3:23-24 - "Whatever you do, work heartily, as for the Lord and not for men, knowing that from the Lord you will receive the inheritance as your reward. You are serving the Lord Christ."

DEVOTIONAL

As you cradle this new life in your arms, take a moment to pause and cherish the miracle of motherhood. In these tender moments, remember that just as the Lord intricately wove you together in your mother's womb, He is endlessly weaving His love and grace into your journey of nurturing your child. Each sleepless night and every joyful giggle is an act of worship, a chance to serve the Lord with all your heart.

Colossians 3:23-24 reminds us that every diaper changed and every quiet lullaby sung is more than a task; it's a holy calling. Trust that even in the weary days, God's strength is made perfect in your weakness. You are not alone—His presence walks with you through the challenges, and His joy fills the moments of bliss. Embrace this journey and let each day be an offering of love, for you are part of a divine tapestry, lovingly crafted by His hands.

DAILY REFLECTION

In the quiet moments as you cradle your little one, how can you choose to see each challenge of motherhood as a sacred thread woven into the beautiful tapestry of God's love and grace?

PRAYER

Dear Lord, as I cradle this precious gift in my arms, I am overwhelmed by the miracle of motherhood. Help me to cherish each moment, both the joys and the challenges, as I lean into Your grace and guidance. May every sleepless night and joyful laugh draw me closer to You, reminding me that I am never alone in this journey. Embrace us with Your love as I nurture this beautiful life, and fill my heart with strength and peace for each day ahead. Amen.

On this journey of motherhood, trust in God's perfect timing and provision. As you nurture the new life entrusted to you, remember His grace is sufficient in every moment of uncertainty. Embrace each day with hope, knowing you are wonderfully supported.

2 Corinthians 9:8 - "And God is able to bless you abundantly, so that in all things at all times, having all that you need, you will abound in every good work."

DEVOTIONAL

As you stand on the threshold of motherhood, cradling the gift of new life in your arms or feeling the flutter of anticipation within, remember that each moment is woven with divine purpose. The journey ahead may be filled with joy, fear, and countless uncertainties, but trust that God's timing is perfect, sculpting your path uniquely and beautifully. In those quiet nights when doubt whispers in the dark, cling to His promise from 2 Corinthians 9:8—His grace is more than enough for every trial you face. You are not alone; God, in His abundance, has provided the strength and wisdom you need to nurture the precious life entrusted to you. Allow yourself to embrace the imperfection of this journey, resting in the knowledge that you are wonderfully supported by a loving Father. Each day is an opportunity to witness His provision and goodness, to spread hope through your love. Trust wholeheartedly, knowing that with each small step of faith, you are growing into the mother He has created you to be.

DAILY REFLECTION

In the quiet moments between heartbeats and fervent prayers, how can you intentionally recognize and embrace God's grace in the unpredictable rhythm of your new motherhood journey?

PRAYER

Dear Lord, as I embark on this beautiful yet uncertain journey of motherhood, I lay my fears and joys before You. Help me to trust in Your perfect timing and to embrace each moment with hope, knowing Your grace is sufficient for every trial. Surround me with Your love and strength, reminding me that I am never alone as I nurture this precious life, crafted by Your hand. Amen.

In this sacred season of new beginnings, find strength in God's promise: "Before I formed you in the womb, I knew you." As you nurture your little one, trust that you are enveloped in divine love and purpose, ready to discover the beauty of motherhood together.

Jeremiah 1:5 - "Before I formed you in the womb, I knew you, and before you were born I consecrated you; I appointed you a prophet to the nations."

DEVOTIONAL

In this sacred season of new beginnings, you find yourself at the threshold of motherhood, a journey woven with love, joy, and divine purpose. Remember the words of Jeremiah 1:5: "Before I formed you in the womb, I knew you." Just as God has known your child since the beginning, rest assured that He has intricately crafted you for this beautiful role, bringing strength and wisdom to nourish your little one. Each small kick, each gentle coo, is a reminder that you are part of a greater plan, designed by the hands of a loving Creator.

As you nurture your baby, allow His promise to wrap around you like a warm embrace, affirming that you are never alone in this journey. Trust that in the quiet moments—those late-night feedings or peaceful snuggles—you are unfolding new layers of love and purpose. Together with your child, you will discover the beauty of motherhood, revealing the wonders of faith, hope, and resilience. Embrace this sacred calling, for you are profoundly cherished, equipped with everything you need to illuminate this new chapter in both your lives.

DAILY REFLECTION

In the midst of sleepless nights and tender moments, how can you embrace the truth that both you and your precious child are cherished creations of a loving God, uniquely designed for this journey of motherhood together?

PRAYER

Dear Lord, as I embark on this sacred journey of motherhood, I seek Your strength and guidance. Wrap me in Your divine love as I nurture this precious life, reminding me that I am woven into Your beautiful plan. Grant me the grace to embrace each moment, knowing that I am cherished and supported in the miracle of new beginnings. Amen.

In the tender moments of motherhood, trust in God's perfect timing and provision for your growing family. As you nurture new life, remember that every heartbeat is a gift wrapped in His love and grace. Find joy and strength in His promises as you step into this beautiful journey.

Psalm 127:1-2: "Unless the Lord builds the house, the builders labor in vain. Unless the Lord watches over the city, the guards stand watch in vain. In vain you rise early and stay up late, toiling for food to eat—for he grants sleep to those he loves."

DEVOTIONAL

In the tender moments of motherhood, when the world feels both overwhelmingly beautiful and daunting, remember that you are not alone—God is intricately involved in your journey. Psalm 127:1-2 gently reminds us that no matter how hard we strive, without His guiding hand, our efforts may fall short. Each little heartbeat you feel is a divine reminder of His perfect timing and provision, a grace gift that fills your home with profound love and purpose.

As you nurture this new life, let your worries and fears fade as you entrust your family to the One who understands every tear and every joy. It's in the late-night feedings and the early morning cuddles that His presence washes over you, gifting you with strength to embrace both the challenges and beauty of motherhood. Find joy in His promises, for He is the true architect of your family, and in Him, you can rest assured that everything you need will be provided. Cherish this journey, knowing that every moment is wrapped in His love, crafted specifically for you.

DAILY REFLECTION

In the quiet moments of gentle rocking and soft whispers, how can you open your heart to trust in God's perfect timing, allowing His love and grace to wash over you as you embrace the beautiful uncertainty of motherhood?

PRAYER

Dear Lord, in these tender moments of motherhood, I come before You with a heart filled with wonder and anxiety. As I nurture this precious new life, remind me that Your timing is perfect and Your love never fails. Help me to entrust my fears and joys into Your hands, knowing that every heartbeat is a gift of grace. Fill me with the strength to embrace this beautiful journey, and let me find solace in Your promises as I seek to be the mother You've called me to be. Amen.

As you nurture the precious life within or cradle your newborn, remember that God's love envelops both you and your child. Trust in His guidance, allowing faith to strengthen the bond you share and illuminate the path ahead. Each moment is a sacred blessing, woven with divine purpose.

1 John 4:19 - "We love because he first loved us."

DEVOTIONAL

As you tenderly nurture the precious life growing within you or cradle your newborn in your arms, remember that God's love envelops you both like a warm embrace. In this sacred space of motherhood, each heartbeat punctuates His faithfulness, a gentle whisper of assurance: you are not alone. Trust in His guidance; He has carefully woven your journey together with grace and purpose. Each moment spent in quiet reflection or the sweetness of a lullaby is a reminder of the divine bond you are creating, one filled with joy, uncertainty, and unwavering love.

In those late night feedings or amidst the tender coos, let 1 John 4:19 resonate in your heart: "We love because He first loved us." As you pour love into this tiny being, know that you are embodying the very essence of God's affection. Allow His love to strengthen the bond you share, illuminating the path ahead with hope and tranquility. In every beautiful and challenging moment, you are living out a promise— one that challenges you to trust, to nurture, and to thrive, together in His everlasting love.

DAILY REFLECTION

As you cradle your newborn and reflect on the journey of motherhood, how can you open your heart to receive the depth of God's love and allow it to guide you through both the sweet and challenging moments of nurturing this precious life?

PRAYER

Dear Lord, in this sacred season of my life, I thank You for the precious gift of motherhood, for each heartbeat that echoes Your love. As I cradle this tiny life, remind me daily that I am enveloped in Your grace, and guide my heart to trust in Your divine purpose. May every moment, be it filled with joy or uncertainty, draw me closer to You, as I nurture this child with the same boundless love You have given me. Amen.

Through the sacred journey of motherhood, God's love envelops you, bringing comfort and strength. As you nurture new life, trust that His grace will guide your heart and hands in each precious moment.

Psalm 46:1-2 - "God is our refuge and strength, an ever-present help in trouble. Therefore we will not fear, though the earth give way and the mountains fall into the heart of the sea."

DEVOTIONAL

As you embark on this sacred journey of motherhood, remember that you are never alone. In the stillness of night, when your heart races with both joy and trepidation, Psalm 46:1-2 reminds us that God is our refuge and strength. Each gentle coo and every little kick is a testament to His love enveloping you, whispering assurance amidst the uncertainties. The overwhelming moments, when doubt creeps in like a shadow, are transformed by His ever-present help, guiding your heart and hands as you nurture this precious new life. Trust in His grace, for it is more sufficient than any worry that may burden your spirit. Take a deep breath, feel the rhythm of your heartbeat synchronize with your baby's, and know that you are cradled in divine support. In this season of both chaos and wonder, let His comforting presence be your anchor, filling you with strength and peace.

DAILY REFLECTION

In this tender season of motherhood, how might you open your heart to embrace the stillness and seek God's guiding presence, even in moments of uncertainty and chaos?

PRAYER

Dear Lord, as I step into the beautiful chaos of motherhood, I seek Your comfort and strength to guide me through every heartbeat and every tender moment. Embrace my heart with Your grace, soothing the fears that linger in the quiet, and remind me that Your love is the anchor I need. May each coo and gentle sigh be a reminder of Your presence, filling me with peace as I nurture this precious new life. Amen.

Trust in God's perfect timing as you welcome new life, for each day brings His grace into your journey. As you nurture your child, remember that you are cradled in His love, equipped with strength and wisdom for this sacred role. Rejoice in the gift of motherhood, knowing that His faithfulness will guide you every step of the way.

Psalm 145:18-19 - "The LORD is near to all who call on him, to all who call on him in truth. He fulfills the desires of those who fear him; he hears their cry and saves them."

DEVOTIONAL

As you embrace the beauty of new life, remember that each moment is woven together by God's perfect timing. The journey of motherhood, with all its joys and challenges, is a divine tapestry—a reflection of His grace and love that envelops you as you nurture your little one. In the quiet hours, when doubt or fear creeps in, hold close the promise of Psalm 145:18-19. Know that the Lord is near, always listening to your heart, ready to fulfill the deepest longings of your soul. Even in the midst of sleepless nights and overwhelming choices, trust that He has equipped you with the strength and wisdom you need for this sacred role. Let His faithfulness be a balm to your spirit, reminding you that you are never alone in this journey. Rejoice, dear mother, in the precious gift of your child, for each day is a new testament to His unwavering love and guidance along the way.

DAILY REFLECTION

In this tender season of new life, how can you consciously lean into God's perfect timing and embrace the moments of joy and uncertainty, trusting that He is guiding you with love as you nurture your precious child?

PRAYER

Dear Lord, as I embark on this beautiful journey of motherhood, I surrender my worries and embrace Your perfect timing with an open heart. In the quiet moments of doubt, help me to feel Your love cradling me like the precious life I hold, reminding me that I am never alone in this sacred calling. May Your faithfulness shine bright in each day, guiding me with strength and wisdom, as I celebrate the incredible gift of my child. Amen.

Embrace the miracle of new life with faith and gratitude. In this sacred season, remember that every challenge and joy in motherhood is a reflection of God's love— a love that nurtures you and your little one every step of the way.

Colossians 3:17 - "And whatever you do, whether in word or deed, do it all in the name of the Lord Jesus, giving thanks to God the Father through him."

DEVOTIONAL

In this beautiful season of new beginnings, as you cradle that precious life in your arms, take a moment to pause and reflect on the immense gift you've been given. Every tiny breath, every gentle coo, is a sacred pause orchestrated by the hands of our Creator. Motherhood can feel overwhelming, but remember, it is in both the challenges and delights that God's love intricately weaves itself into the fabric of your journey.

Colossians 3:17 reminds us to ground every action, every whisper of love, in gratitude for the Lord. As you navigate sleepless nights and the sweet chaos of new motherhood, let each moment be a prayer—offered in joy and perseverance. Embrace the miracle of new life with faith, knowing that God walks beside you, nurturing your heart as you nurture your child. In gratitude, may you find strength; in faith, may you discover an unbreakable bond that mirrors the divine love bestowed upon both you and your little one.

DAILY REFLECTION

In the midst of sleepless nights and joyful milestones, how can you intentionally recognize and cherish the moments where God's love reveals itself in the depths of your new journey as a mother?

PRAYER

Dear Lord, in this joyful whirlwind of new life, I pause to thank You for the incredible gift You have bestowed upon me. As I cradle my little one, may each breath and every gentle coo remind me of Your immeasurable love, nurturing both me and my child through the challenges and delights of motherhood. Grant me the strength to embrace this sacred journey with open arms, walking in faith and gratitude as You guide us every step of the way.
Amen.

Trust in God's perfect timing as you welcome new life. In moments of uncertainty, remember that His strength will guide you and His love will fill your heart, crafting a beautiful beginning for you and your little one.

Hebrews 11:1 - "Now faith is the assurance of things hoped for, the conviction of things not seen."

DEVOTIONAL

As you stand on the threshold of motherhood, the anticipation can feel both exhilarating and overwhelming. Remember, dear one, that you are not alone in this journey; each moment of uncertainty invites you deeper into the heart of God. Hebrews 11:1 reassures us that faith is the assurance of things hoped for, the conviction of things not seen. In this sacred time of waiting and nurturing, let your heart rest in the knowledge that God's timing is perfect.

When sleepless nights and restless thoughts arise, close your eyes and breathe in His strength, which flows like a gentle river, calming the storms within. Embrace those moments when you feel vulnerable, for His love fills every crack in your heart, crafting a beautiful beginning for both you and your little one. Trust that as each day unfolds, you are being lovingly guided, and the love that surrounds you will be the foundation on which your family grows. Cherish this miraculous journey, for it is a testimony of hope and faith blooming in your life.

DAILY REFLECTION

In the quiet moments as you cradle your new life, how can you lean into God's promise of strength and love to transform your uncertainties into a profound trust in His perfect timing?

PRAYER

Dear Lord, as I embark on this sacred journey into motherhood, I place my heart into Your hands, trusting in the beautiful timing You have set before me. In moments when doubt seeps in, wrap me in Your strength and love, reminding me that even in uncertainty, I am held by a greater purpose. May Your presence fill my days with peace and joy as I welcome this new life, crafting a story woven with hope and faith. Amen.

As a new life begins, take a moment to reflect on the miracle of creation and the love that surrounds you. In the quiet moments of motherhood, remember that God walks this journey with you, offering strength and grace for each challenge. Trust in His perfect plan for you and your child.

Colossians 1:16-17 - "For by him all things were created, in heaven and on earth, visible and invisible, whether thrones or dominions or rulers or authorities—all things were created through him and for him. And he is before all things, and in him all things hold together."

DEVOTIONAL

As you cradle this new life in your arms, take a deep breath and let the miracle of creation wash over you. In these precious moments, relish the warmth of love that envelops you both – a love that mirrors the heart of our Creator. Colossians 1:16-17 reminds us that all things, including your baby, are intricately woven together by God's hands, each detail echoing His wondrous design. When exhaustion grips you and doubt creeps in, know that even in the chaos of motherhood, He is present, holding both you and your child in a tender embrace. Trust that His perfect plan unfolds in your journey, guiding you through each challenge with strength and grace. Remember, you are not alone; the same Divine Spirit that brought forth your child walks with you, illuminating every step of this awe-inspiring path. Cherish each moment, for you are part of a sacred story, beautifully crafted by the One who holds all things together.

DAILY REFLECTION

In the tender hours of motherhood, how can you intentionally invite God's presence into your daily moments, allowing His strength and grace to transform your challenges into sacred memories of love and connection with your child?

PRAYER

Dear Lord, as I cradle this precious life in my arms, I am in awe of the miracle of creation that blooms before me. In the quiet moments and amidst the chaos, fill me with your strength and grace, reminding me that I am never alone on this journey. Help me trust in Your perfect plan, embracing each challenge and delight, and may I always recognize the warmth of Your love surrounding us as we grow together in Your sacred story. Amen.

As you nurture the precious life within you or hold your newborn in your arms, remember that just as God lovingly formed each of us, He is intricately weaving His plans for your family. Trust in His perfect timing and seek His strength in this beautiful season of motherhood.

Psalm 20:4 - "May He grant you according to your heart's desire, and fulfill all your purpose."

DEVOTIONAL

As you cradle your precious child, your heart swells with a reflection of God's love and creativity. In this intimate moment, you're reminded that just as He meticulously crafted every detail of your life, He is also weaving the tapestry of your new family's journey. Embrace the quiet whispers of the Holy Spirit guiding you, nurturing both your little one's needs and your own. You may feel a myriad of emotions—sudden joy mingled with solemn responsibility, a true testament to the depth of love that God places within a mother's heart. Remember Psalm 20:4, which assures you that He grants you the desires of your heart; trust that He is shaping your family's purpose even amidst sleepless nights and uncertain days. Lean into His strength, finding comfort in the knowledge that you are not alone in this journey. Allow this season of motherhood to deepen your faith, unfolding the boundless plans He has for you and your child, each day a new chapter in His divine story.

DAILY REFLECTION

In this sacred moment of nurturing your child, how might you recognize God's whispers of love and purpose in the vibrant chaos of motherhood, and what steps will you take to embrace His plans for your family during this extraordinary journey?

PRAYER

Dear Lord, as I cradle this precious life I've been entrusted with, envelop me in Your divine peace and wisdom. Help me to recognize the beauty in each moment, even when shadows of uncertainty loom, and let my heart be open to the whispers of Your love and guidance. May my journey through motherhood be a sacred chapter woven with Your grace, where I find strength in my vulnerability and joy in the everyday miracles of nurturing my child. Amen.

This season of new beginnings mirrors the miraculous journey of motherhood. Trust in God's perfect timing as you nurture the precious life within or cradle your newborn, drawing strength from His unwavering love and guidance. Remember, you are never alone on this sacred path.

Romans 5:3-4 - "Not only so, but we also glory in our sufferings, because we know that suffering produces perseverance; perseverance, character; and character, hope."

DEVOTIONAL

As you stand on the threshold of motherhood, whether awaiting the arrival of your little one or cradling them for the first time, remember that this season is not just about new beginnings; it's also about the profound transformation of your heart and spirit. Romans 5:3-4 reminds us that through our struggles—fatigue, uncertainty, and the overwhelming responsibility—God is weaving a tapestry of perseverance, character, and ultimately, hope. Each sleepless night may feel heavy, and each moment of doubt may seem insurmountable, but know that these trials are shaping you into the mother you were destined to be, one filled with strength and love that reflects God's unwavering care.

In these sacred moments, take a breath, close your eyes, and feel the divine presence surrounding you, reminding you that you are never alone on this journey. Your cries and joys are heard; your heart, stretched wide, is understood. As you nurture this precious life, trust in the perfect timing of God's plan—each tiny giggle, each new milestone is a beautiful testament that you are cradling a miracle. Embrace this sacred path with hope, for in every challenge lies the seeds of growth and the promise of a flourishing future.

DAILY REFLECTION

In this tender season of your life, how can you recognize and celebrate the moments of grace amidst the challenges, allowing God's love to guide you through the beautiful, chaotic journey of motherhood?

PRAYER

Dear Lord, as I embark on this sacred journey of motherhood, I ask for your gentle guidance and unwavering strength. Help me to embrace each moment—both the joys and the challenges—trusting in your perfect timing as I nurture this precious life. May your love surround me, reminding me that I am never alone, and may my heart be filled with hope and resilience, growing into the mother you have called me to be. Amen.

On this journey of motherhood, trust in God's perfect timing as you nurture new life. Every moment is a sacred gift, and God walks alongside you through the joys and challenges of this beautiful calling. Hold fast to His promises, for He has equipped you for this divine role.

Hebrews 10:23 - "Let us hold unswervingly to the hope we profess, for he who promised is faithful."

DEVOTIONAL

As you embark on this beautiful journey of motherhood, remember that every moment is not just a milestone but a sacred gift from above. In these early days, whether you're feeling the quickening of new life or cradling your precious newborn, trust in God's perfect timing—He knows every beat of your heart and every flutter of your baby's. While the nights may be long and the days full of uncertainty, cling to the promise found in Hebrews 10:23: "Let us hold unswervingly to the hope we profess, for he who promised is faithful."

In the challenging moments when doubts creep in, remind yourself that God has equipped you with everything you need for this divine role of nurturing a new life. Each small triumph, each tear, and every joyful laugh are woven into your unique tapestry of motherhood, and God walks alongside you through it all. He is there in the quiet breaths and in the chaos, faithfully guiding you. Embrace this season wholeheartedly, knowing that you are not alone; His love will fill the spaces of uncertainty with grace and assurance.

DAILY REFLECTION

In this sacred journey of motherhood, how can you lean into God's unwavering faithfulness during both the tender moments and the trials, trusting that He is shaping you into the mother your child needs?

PRAYER

Dear Lord, as I step into this sacred journey of motherhood, I ask for Your gentle guidance. Help me to trust in Your perfect timing and to see each fleeting moment as a cherished gift, knowing that You walk beside me through every joy and challenge. Fill my heart with Your unwavering hope, reminding me that I am equipped for this divine calling, and may Your love envelop my family, bringing peace to our hearts and strength to our days. Amen.

The journey of motherhood begins with a beautiful blend of hope and responsibility. Trust in God's guidance as you nurture the precious life entrusted to you; each day is a testament to His love. Remember, His strength is your refuge in this sacred adventure.

2 Timothy 1:7 - "For God has not given us a spirit of fear, but of power and of love and of a sound mind."

DEVOTIONAL

As you stand on the threshold of motherhood, the path ahead may feel both exhilarating and daunting, a beautiful blend of hope and responsibility. Each kick, each flutter reminds you of the precious life entrusted to your care—an exquisite gift woven by God's own hands. As you nurture this new creation, lean into the promise of 2 Timothy 1:7: "For God has not given us a spirit of fear, but of power and of love and of a sound mind." In moments of uncertainty, when sleepless nights loom or the weight of responsibility presses down, remember that His strength is your refuge. Allow His love to envelop you, giving you the courage to face the unknown. This sacred adventure is more than just a journey; it's a daily testament to His unwavering love as you grow alongside your little one. Trust in His guidance, for with every heartbeat, you are embracing the extraordinary work He has begun in you and your child.

DAILY REFLECTION

In this miraculous journey of motherhood, how can you intentionally seek God's guidance in moments of uncertainty, allowing His love and strength to transform your fears into a deeper bond with your precious child?

PRAYER

Dear God, as I embark on this sacred journey of motherhood, I marvel at the gift you have entrusted to my care. In moments of uncertainty and wonder, I seek Your strength to guide me, enveloping me in Your love as I nurture this precious life. May I embrace each day with courage, trusting in Your wisdom, and remembering that this beautiful blend of hope and responsibility is wrapped in Your unfailing grace. Amen.

As a first-time mother, your journey into motherhood is a beautiful reflection of God's nurturing love. Trust that He equips you with strength and wisdom for every challenge. In your moments of uncertainty, lean into His presence, for He cherishes your heart and your child.

1 Thessalonians 5:24 - "The one who calls you is faithful, and he will do it."

DEVOTIONAL

As you cradle the fragile new life in your arms, remember that this journey of motherhood mirrors the tender love God has for you. Each miraculous moment—from the gentle kicks within to the first soft coos—echoes the divine promise that you are not alone. In the midst of sleepless nights and the whirlwind of emotions, hold onto the truth of 1 Thessalonians 5:24: "The one who calls you is faithful, and he will do it." This is not just a calling into motherhood; it's a sacred promise that God will equip you with strength and wisdom for every challenge you encounter. When doubt creeps in and insecurity whispers loudly, lean deeper into His presence, for He delights in your heart and cherishes your child. Trust that your moments of uncertainty are pathways for you to discover His infinite grace. Know that in leaning on Him, you're not only nurturing your baby but also nurturing your own spirit, enveloped in His faithful love.

DAILY REFLECTION

In this sacred season of your new journey, how can you cultivate a deeper trust in God's promises as you navigate the beautiful, yet challenging moments of motherhood?

PRAYER

Father in heaven, as I embrace this precious gift of life, I ask for Your gentle guidance in every moment of doubt and joy. Wrap me in Your loving presence, bestowing upon me strength and wisdom, so I can nurture my child as You nurture me. In the quiet of the night and the beauty of each new day, remind me that Your faithfulness carries us both, and that I am never alone on this sacred journey. Amen.

In this season of rapid growth, just as a baby experiences bursts of development, let us reflect on our own spiritual growth. May we lean into God's nurturing presence, allowing Him to stretch and strengthen our faith in this transformative time.

Ephesians 4:15-16 - "Instead, speaking the truth in love, we will grow to become in every respect the mature body of him who is the head, that is, Christ. From him the whole body, joined and held together by every supporting ligament, grows and builds itself up in love, as each part does its work."

DEVOTIONAL

In the tender moments of a baby's growth spurt, we witness miraculous transformations—tiny limbs stretch, curious sounds emerge, and new milestones are reached. This phase, filled with excitement and uncertainty, mirrors our own spiritual journeys as we navigate the seasons of our lives. Just as a baby relies on the loving embrace of caretakers, we, too, can find comfort in God's nurturing presence during our times of rapid growth. Ephesians 4:15-16 reminds us that our maturation is a communal journey, intertwined with others as we are spiritually knit together by love. As we speak truth into our lives and the lives of those around us, we cultivate an environment where faith can flourish. This transformative time calls us to lean into God, trusting that He is shaping us into more profound reflections of Christ. Let us embrace this season of growth with open hearts, anticipating the beautiful new beginnings that await us in faith.

DAILY REFLECTION

In what ways is God inviting you to surrender your fears and embrace the beautiful stretching of your spirit during this season of growth, trusting that His loving presence will guide and support you through every transformative milestone?

PRAYER

Dear Lord, in this sacred season of growth, we thank You for the transformative work You are doing in our lives. Help us to embrace the stretching and the strengthening, just as a baby eagerly welcomes new experiences, trusting that each moment is shaped by Your loving hands. May we lean into Your presence, finding solace and strength in community as we journey together toward a deeper understanding of Your grace. Amen.

God has entrusted you with the beautiful gift of new life. As you nurture this precious child, remember that His love surrounds both you and your little one, offering strength and peace in each tender moment.

1 John 4:9-10 - "This is how God showed his love among us: He sent his one and only Son into the world that we might live through him. This is love: not that we loved God, but that he loved us and sent his Son as an atoning sacrifice for our sins."

DEVOTIONAL

In the tender stillness of the night, as you cradle your newborn close, remember that this fragile life is a remarkable reflection of God's profound love. Just as He sent His Son, Jesus, into the world, He has entrusted you with a precious gift—a tiny heart that beats in rhythm with yours. The journey of motherhood can often feel daunting, filled with sleepless nights and countless uncertainties, yet in these moments, God whispers His promise of strength and peace. With each little coo and soft sigh, allow yourself to be enveloped in His love, knowing that you are not alone. Embrace the vulnerability that comes with nurturing this new life; it is here that you will discover the depths of your own capacity to love. Each stumble and triumph in this beautiful chaos is a reminder of His grace, poured out over you and your little one. Take heart, dear mother, for in your hands lies the opportunity to raise a child who will know the vastness of God's love, just as you do.

DAILY REFLECTION

As you hold your little one close in the quiet moments of the night, how can you intentionally invite God's love into your nurturing, allowing it to transform your fears into a profound sense of peace and purpose?

PRAYER

Dear Lord, as I hold this precious gift in my arms, help me to feel the depth of Your love surrounding us both. Grant me the strength to embrace the uncertainties of motherhood and the peace that comes from knowing I am never alone. May each moment of joy and challenge draw me closer to You, revealing the beauty of Your grace in our lives. Amen.

As you cradle the precious life entrusted to you, remember that God's love flows through every moment of motherhood. Trust in His guidance as you nurture this new gift, knowing that in your vulnerability, His strength is made perfect. Rejoice in the journey, for you are beautifully fashioned for this sacred role.

1 Thessalonians 2:7-8 - "But we were gentle among you, just as a nursing mother cherishes her own children. So, affectionately longing for you, we were well pleased to impart to you not only the gospel of God, but also our own lives, because you had become dear to us."

DEVOTIONAL

As you cradle the precious life entrusted to you, take a moment to breathe in the incredible gift of motherhood. In those hushed moments of night, when the world outside seems still, remember that just as a nursing mother cherishes her child, so too does God cradle you in His unwavering love. 1 Thessalonians 2:7-8 reminds us that love is not merely a feeling, but a gentle action—one that nurtures and sustains. Your vulnerability in these early days is not a weakness; it is a sacred space where His strength can shine through your journey. Each coo and cry is a reflection of your devotion, whispering the truth that you were beautifully fashioned for this role. Embrace the messiness and joy, knowing that in every moment you are imparting not only care but a glimpse of the Gospel itself. Trust in His guidance, and rejoice, for through you, His love flows into this new life, shaping hearts for generations to come.

DAILY REFLECTION

As you navigate the tender moments of motherhood, how can you intentionally embrace your own vulnerability, allowing it to transform into a source of strength that reflects God's unwavering love to your child?

PRAYER

Dear Lord, - in this sacred season of motherhood, I come before You with a heart full of gratitude and awe. As I cradle this precious life, may Your unwavering love envelop me, bringing comfort in my moments of doubt and strength in my vulnerability. Help me to embrace each fleeting moment, knowing that in nurturing this child, I am reflecting Your tender care and shaping a legacy of love that will echo through generations. Amen.

March 21

"Experience the miracle of new life this season. As you nurture your little one, remember that God entrusted you with this precious gift, filling your journey with hope, strength, and divine love."

Luke 18:16-17: "But Jesus called the children to him and said, 'Let the little children come to me, and do not hinder them, for to such belongs the kingdom of God. Truly, I say to you, whoever does not receive the kingdom of God like a child shall not enter it.'"

DEVOTIONAL

As you cradle your little one in your arms, take a moment to breathe in the miracle of new life. Each coo and giggle reflects the gentle whispers of God's love, reminding you that He has entrusted you with this incredible blessing. In this season, as you nurture your child, may you also embrace the joy and wonder of God's creation. Jesus welcomed children with open arms, illustrating the purity of faith that you, too, are invited to emulate. Just as they trust you completely, allow yourself to trust in God's unwavering strength and guidance during this transformative journey. Remember that with each tiny hand that wraps around your finger, you are not alone; His love surrounds you, infusing your heart with hope. Let your days be filled with the beauty of His promise, as you witness the unfolding of a divine masterpiece in the life of your little one.

DAILY REFLECTION

How can you find moments of joy and gratitude in the everyday chaos of motherhood, allowing God's love to weave strength and hope through your nurturing journey?

PRAYER

Dear Lord, in this sacred season of new life, I thank You for the precious gift of my child. As I hold them close, may I feel Your love wrapping around us, filling our hearts with strength and hope. Help me to cherish each moment, guiding me to nurture their spirit as I learn to trust in Your divine presence, knowing that I am never alone on this beautiful journey. Amen.

As you nurture new life, remember that God's love envelops both you and your child. Trust in His guidance with each tiny heartbeat, knowing that His grace equips you for this sacred journey of motherhood.

Psalm 46:5 - "God is within her, she will not fall; God will help her at break of day."

DEVOTIONAL

As you tread the beautiful yet overwhelming journey of motherhood, take a moment to dwell in the comforting truth of Psalm 46:5: "God is within her, she will not fall; God will help her at break of day." In the quiet stillness of midnight feedings or the gentle rhythm of your baby's breath, remember that God's love surrounds both you and your little one. Each tiny heartbeat resonates with the promise that you are not alone; His grace weaves through the fabric of your days, infusing them with strength and purpose. Nurturing new life is both a privilege and a challenge, and in moments of uncertainty, you may feel like the weight of the world rests on your shoulders. Yet, trust that the One who formed your child is also guiding you as a mother. When doubts creep in, remind yourself that even in your weakest moments, His power sustains you. Embrace this sacred journey, knowing that with every step, His love envelops you; His presence is your anchor. Surrender your worries to Him, for He is right there, nurturing your heart as you nurture your child.

DAILY REFLECTION

In this tender season of your life, how can you intentionally embrace God's presence in your heart as you nurture your little one, allowing His love to transform your moments of uncertainty into opportunities for trust?

PRAYER

Dear Lord, as I embrace the beauty and challenges of motherhood, I thank You for the gift of this little life. Fill my heart with Your peace in the quiet moments and strengthen me when I feel overwhelmed. Help me to trust in Your unwavering love and guidance, knowing that with each heartbeat, I am enveloped in Your grace. Amen.

As you navigate the miraculous journey of motherhood, remember that God's love surrounds you and your newborn. Trust in His guidance as you cherish each precious moment, knowing He equips you with strength and wisdom for this new adventure.

Romans 8:31-32 - "What, then, shall we say in response to these things? If God is for us, who can be against us? He who did not spare his own Son, but gave him up for us all—how will he not also, along with him, graciously give us all things?"

DEVOTIONAL

As you stand on the threshold of motherhood, with a tiny heartbeat nestled close to yours, embrace the overwhelming love that surrounds you. Romans 8:31-32 reminds us that if God is for us, no obstacle can stand in the way of His grace. Picture this moment: the gentle rise and fall of your baby's breath as you marvel at the miracle of life. With each sleepless night and every uncharted territory of parenting, remember that God didn't spare His own Son in His love for us—so rest assured, He is abundantly generous in providing you the wisdom and strength you need for this journey. Trust in His guidance as you navigate the joys and challenges, knowing that each smile, cry, and coo are sacred moments infused with His presence. Cherish these early days; they are fleeting yet foundational. In your heart, let this promise bloom: you are never alone; God's love and provision will sustain you through every precious moment.

DAILY REFLECTION

In this tender season of new life, how can you open your heart to fully embrace the depths of God's love and wisdom guiding you through each fleeting moment with your newborn?

PRAYER

Dear Lord, as I embark on this beautiful journey of motherhood, I thank You for the precious life nestled in my arms. Grant me the strength and wisdom to embrace each moment, whether it brings joy or challenge, trusting that Your love surrounds us both. Help me to see Your grace in every cry, every laugh, and every sleepless night, reminding me that I am never alone on this miraculous path. Amen.

Embrace the beautiful journey of motherhood as a sacred calling. Trust that God equips you with strength and wisdom, guiding you through each moment of joy and challenge. In this season, lean into prayer and community, knowing you are never alone on this path.

Joshua 1:9 - "Have I not commanded you? Be strong and courageous. Do not be afraid; do not be discouraged, for the Lord your God will be with you wherever you go."

DEVOTIONAL

As you stand on the threshold of motherhood, whether cradling your newborn or reveling in the anticipation of their arrival, remember that this journey is a sacred calling. In moments of joy and in the midst of uncertainty, lean on the promise found in Joshua 1:9: "Have I not commanded you? Be strong and courageous." The weight of responsibility may feel heavy at times, but know that God equips you with all the strength and wisdom you need. You are not alone; your heart might swell with love, but moments of fear and doubt can creep in too. In those times, let prayer be your refuge and community your support. Embrace the beautiful chaos of motherhood, for each challenge is a chance to witness God's faithfulness. Trust that you are upheld by His unwavering presence as you navigate this remarkable path.

DAILY REFLECTION

How can you intentionally seek God's strength and the support of your community as you embrace both the joys and challenges of this sacred journey into motherhood?

PRAYER

Dear Lord, as I embark on this sacred journey of motherhood, I surrender my fears and uncertainties into Your hands. Fill my heart with the strength and wisdom I need to embrace each moment—both the joyous and the challenging—knowing that Your love surrounds and supports me. Grant me the courage to trust in Your guidance, and may I find comfort in prayer and the embrace of my community, reminding me that I am never alone on this beautiful path. Amen.

As a first-time mother, the journey of nurturing new life reflects God's entrusting us with His creation. In these tender moments of expectancy or holding your newborn, find strength and comfort in His promise: "I will not leave you or forsake you" (Hebrews 13:5). Trust His guidance as you step into this beautiful calling of motherhood.

Hebrews 13:5 - "I will never leave you nor forsake you."

DEVOTIONAL

As you embark on this profound journey of motherhood, each flutter, each kick, and each coo is a reminder of the sacred trust God has placed in you. In these quiet moments of expectancy, when you dream about the life that is growing within, hold fast to His promise: "I will never leave you nor forsake you" (Hebrews 13:5). Embrace the mix of excitement and anxiety, for in your heart lies a divine calling—a love that mirrors God's own nurture for creation. As you cradle your newborn, every gaze, every heartbeat echoes His unwavering presence beside you. Remember, dear mother, that He walks alongside you in sleepless nights and joyful mornings alike, filling your heart with unexplainable strength. Lean into His guidance; your moments of uncertainty are met with His everlasting grace. Let this journey deepen your faith and remind you that you are never alone in this beautiful calling.

DAILY REFLECTION

As you cradle your little one close to your heart, what fears or joys can you lay before God, trusting that in every moment of motherhood, He walks with you and nurtures you just as you nurture your child?

PRAYER

Dear Lord, in this sacred season of waiting and wonder, fill the hearts of first-time mothers with Your peace and assurance. As they nurture new life, remind them of Your constant presence in every flutter and every gentle coo, embracing them with strength in the moments of joy and uncertainty. Empower them to trust in Your promise that they are never alone on this beautiful journey of motherhood. Amen.

In this sacred season of new beginnings, reflect on God's promise to nurture and guide you through the joys and challenges of motherhood. Trust in His unwavering love as you cradle your little one, knowing you are never alone on this beautiful journey.

Matthew 6:30-31 - "But if God so clothes the grass of the field, which is alive today and tomorrow is thrown into the furnace, will he not much more clothe you, O you of little faith? Therefore do not be anxious, saying, 'What shall we eat?' or 'What shall we drink?' or 'What shall we wear?'"

DEVOTIONAL

In this sacred season of new beginnings, dear mother, your heart is filled with a tender blend of joy and anxiety as you cradle your little one. Remember, as the grass of the field is clothed in beauty and care, so too will God clothe you with grace and strength for this new chapter of your life. Matthew 6:30-31 reassures us that if God provides for the needs of nature, how much more will He tend to you and your precious child? Your journey into motherhood may sometimes feel overwhelming, but take comfort in knowing that you are not alone; His unwavering love surrounds you like a gentle embrace. Each moment, whether filled with laughter or tears, is held in the palms of His hands. Trust in this divine promise, and as you nurture your little one, let Him guide you with wisdom and reassurance. Embrace these fleeting days, knowing that every day brings new miracles woven into the fabric of your heart.

DAILY REFLECTION

How can you intentionally seek and recognize God's presence in the everyday moments of nurturing your little one, transforming challenges into cherished memories of His unwavering love?

PRAYER

Dear God, in this sacred season of new beginnings, I come before You with a heart brimming with both joy and uncertainty. As I hold my little one close, remind me of Your unfailing love and the strength You grant me daily. Help me to trust in Your guidance through the challenges and triumphs of motherhood, knowing that I am never alone on this beautiful journey. Amen.

March 27

In the joyous journey of motherhood, find strength in the promise of new life. Trust that God, who knit your little one together in the womb, will guide you through every moment of uncertainty and joy. Rejoice in this sacred calling, knowing His love surrounds both you and your child.

Matthew 1:23 - "Behold, the virgin shall conceive and bear a son, and they shall call his name Immanuel, which means, God with us."

DEVOTIONAL

In this beautiful season of new beginnings, as you embark on the joyous journey of motherhood, take a moment to reflect on the profound truth found in Matthew 1:23: "Behold, the virgin shall conceive and bear a son, and they shall call his name Immanuel, which means, God with us." Just as Mary was entrusted with the sacred gift of life, so too has God chosen you to nurture and cherish the little one growing within you or in your arms. In times when uncertainty clouds your path or exhaustion weighs upon your heart, remember that you are not alone. God, who intricately knit your child together in your womb, is ever-present, guiding you with His gentle love and wisdom. Every coo, every sleepless night, and every moment of sweet joy is wrapped in His grace. Embrace this sacred calling; it is a testament to His unfailing love that surrounds both you and your child. Rejoice in each milestone, for within them lies the promise of new life—His presence, Immanuel, shining brightly in your motherhood journey.

DAILY REFLECTION

In the tender moments of your journey as a mother, how can you consciously seek and celebrate the presence of Immanuel, feeling His embrace in both the challenges and joys that shape your daily life?

PRAYER

Dear Lord, in this sacred season of new beginnings, I thank You for the precious gift of life that has filled my heart with joy and wonder. As I navigate the beautiful journey of motherhood, help me to lean into Your presence, trusting that in moments of uncertainty, Your love will cradle both me and my child. Let each day be a celebration of Your grace, as I rejoice in the small milestones and feel Your guiding hand in every precious moment. Amen.

March 28

Trust in the Lord's perfect timing; each moment of motherhood is a divine gift. As you nurture this precious life, remember that God's love surrounds you, guiding every step of your journey. Lean on His strength and find peace in the beautiful chaos of new beginnings.

Galatians 4:4-5: "But when the set time had fully come, God sent his Son, born of a woman, born under the law, to redeem those under the law, that we might receive adoption to sonship."

DEVOTIONAL

In this sacred season of motherhood, whether you're eagerly awaiting the arrival of your little one or cradling them gently in your arms, remember that each moment unfolds according to God's perfect timing. As we read in Galatians 4:4-5, "But when the set time had fully come, God sent his Son," we are reminded that creation itself is a masterpiece of divine precision, intertwining moments to fulfill His glorious purpose. Just as Christ came into the world at just the right time, so too has your child arrived in your life, a cherished gift woven into the fabric of your story. In each sleepless night and joyful smile, feel His love enveloping you, guiding your heart and hands through the delightful chaos of new beginnings. There will be days when doubts and fears cast a shadow, and that's okay—lean on His strength, for His grace is sufficient and His peace will anchor your soul. Embrace the beautiful mess of new motherhood; it is here, in these precious moments, that God whispers His love, reminding you that you are not alone. Trust in His timing, for every day is a testament to His faithfulness and love, a whisper of the new life He is nurturing within and around you.

DAILY REFLECTION

In this season of profound change and new beginnings, how can you truly embrace the unique timing of your motherhood journey, trusting that each moment—be it joyous or challenging—is a tender expression of God's unwavering love for you and your child?

PRAYER

Dear Lord, in this tender moment of motherhood, I come to You with a heart full of gratitude and wonder. Thank You for the precious gift of my child, a blessing woven into my story with such perfect timing. Help me to embrace the beautiful chaos of these early days, trusting in Your unfailing love and guidance. When doubts arise, remind me that I am not alone, and let Your peace wash over me, assuring me that each moment is filled with divine purpose. Amen.

March 29

As you nurture new life, remember God's unwavering love strengthens your journey. Trust in His plans for you and your child, finding peace in every moment as you embrace the joy and challenges of motherhood.

Psalm 42:1-2: "As the deer pants for the water brooks, so pants my soul for You, O God. My soul thirsts for God, for the living God. When shall I come and appear before God?"

DEVOTIONAL

As a first-time mother, each moment of nurturing new life is tinged with wonder and trepidation. You may feel like that deer, longing for the cool waters of reassurance in a world that can often feel overwhelming. In times of quiet reflection, remember that God's unwavering love flows like a gentle stream, ready to nourish your soul as you care for your little one. Just as a mother's heart beats in rhythm with her child's needs, God's heart beats with love and support for you. Trust in His perfect plans for you and your child, embracing the joy and challenges that each day brings. In the midst of sleepless nights and uncharted territories, lean into His presence, for it is there that peace awaits. As you seek Him, you'll find the strength to rise and the grace to embrace your incredible journey of motherhood.

DAILY REFLECTION

In this sacred season of nurturing new life, how can you lean into God's unwavering love to transform moments of uncertainty into opportunities for deeper trust and joy in your journey as a mother?

PRAYER

Dear Lord, as I embark on this sacred journey of motherhood, grant me the strength to embrace both the joys and challenges that come my way. Fill my heart with peace amidst the uncertainty, reminding me of Your unwavering love that flows through every moment. Help me to trust in Your perfect plan for my child and me, and let my soul be nourished by Your presence as I nurture this new life.

God's promise of new beginnings shines brightly in the journey of motherhood. As you nurture this precious life, remember that His strength fuels your love, guiding each step of your beautiful adventure.

1 Corinthians 10:13 – "No temptation has overtaken you except what is common to mankind. And God is faithful; he will not let you be tempted beyond what you can bear."

DEVOTIONAL

As you embark on this wondrous journey of motherhood, remember that each day brings the promise of new beginnings. Your heart swells with love, yet the path you tread may sometimes feel daunting. In those moments of doubt or overwhelm, rest assured that God's faithfulness accompanies you, just as He has before. 1 Corinthians 10:13 reminds us that you are never alone in your struggles; every challenge reflects the shared experiences of humanity. God promises to sustain you, providing you with the strength to embrace both the joys and trials of nurturing your little one. Cling to that promise, knowing it is His grace that fuels your love and guides your footsteps on this beautiful adventure. As you nurture this precious life, trust that God's light shines even in the darkest valleys, illuminating the love that will shape generations to come.

DAILY REFLECTION

In the tender moments of motherhood, how can you open your heart to truly see God's hand guiding you through the highs and lows, transforming each challenge into an opportunity for deeper love and faith?

PRAYER

Dear Lord, as I stand on the threshold of this new chapter, I thank You for the gift of motherhood and the precious life I am entrusted to nurture. When the weight of uncertainty bears down on my heart, remind me of Your unwavering presence and the strength that flows from Your love. May Your light guide my every step, illuminating my path with hope and grace as I embrace both the joys and challenges of this beautiful adventure. Amen.

As you cradle your newborn, remember that God has entrusted you with a precious gift. This season of motherhood is a beautiful reminder of His endless love, guiding you to nurture and protect your child with faith and grace. Trust in His presence as you navigate this transformative journey.

Proverbs 31:25-26 – "She is clothed with strength and dignity; she can laugh at the days to come. She speaks with wisdom, and faithful instruction is on her tongue."

DEVOTIONAL

As you cradle your newborn, feel the weight of the precious gift that lies in your arms—a reminder of God's boundless love. In this tender moment, reflect on Proverbs 31:25-26: "She is clothed with strength and dignity; she can laugh at the days to come." Each day will bring new challenges and joys, but within you lies the strength to embrace them with grace. Your journey into motherhood is not just about nurturing another life, but it's also a call to grow in wisdom and faith. Trust that God is guiding your every step, planting faithful instruction on your heart. As you nurture your child, remember that you are also being nurtured by His presence. Allow His love to fill you, giving you the courage to face unknown tomorrows, and laugh at the adventures that lie ahead.

DAILY REFLECTION

In this sacred moment of cradling your newborn, how can you invite God's love into your heart to empower your journey of motherhood, transforming both your fears and joys into laughter and grace?

PRAYER

Dear Lord, as I cradle this tiny miracle in my arms, help me to feel the depth of Your love and the sacred joy of motherhood. Grant me strength and wisdom to nurture this child with grace, trusting in Your guidance through the uncertainties ahead. May each challenge become a stepping stone to deeper faith, and may I always remember that Your loving presence surrounds us both, filling our days with laughter and hope. Amen.

April 1

"With the joy of new life cradled in your arms, remember that God's love nurtures you as you nurture your child. Trust in His grace to guide you through each sleepless night and give you strength for every tender moment."

Colossians 3:12-13 - "Therefore, as God's chosen people, holy and dearly loved, clothe yourselves with compassion, kindness, humility, gentleness and patience. Bear with each other and forgive one another if any of you has a grievance against someone. Forgive as the Lord forgave you."

DEVOTIONAL

As you cradle the joy of new life in your arms, take a moment to breathe in the profound beauty and responsibility of motherhood. Each tiny sigh and gentle coo is a reminder of how deeply you are loved by your Creator, who delights in the tender love you pour into your child. In the stillness of the night, when exhaustion weighs heavy on your heart, remember that God's grace wraps around you like a soft blanket, offering comfort and strength. Colossians 3:12-13 reminds us to clothe ourselves with compassion and kindness—not just towards your little one but also towards yourself. It's okay to feel overwhelmed; it's part of this incredible journey. As you encounter challenges and sleepless nights, forgive yourself as God forgives you, and remember that each moment is a chance to grow —not just as a mother, but as His beloved child. Trust that in your vulnerability, His love will cradle you just as you cradle your baby, guiding you through this sacred adventure.

DAILY REFLECTION

In the quiet moments when your heart is both overflowing with love and weighed down by fatigue, how can you intentionally seek God's grace to nurture not just your child, but also your own weary spirit?

PRAYER

Dear Lord, in this beautiful yet overwhelming season of new motherhood, I seek Your gentle embrace. Wrap me in Your love, Lord, as I nurture this precious life, and remind me to shower myself with the same grace I extend to my child. When the nights grow long and weariness settles in, fill my heart with Your strength and fill my soul with Your peace, guiding me through each tender moment as we grow together in Your boundless love. Amen.

April 2

On this day, celebrate the miracle of new life with gratitude and joy. As a first-time mother, lean into the promises of God, who knit your baby together in the womb. Trust that His grace will guide you through the challenges and joys of motherhood, surrounding you with His love every step of the way.

1 Chronicles 28:20 - "Be strong and courageous, and do the work. Do not be afraid or discouraged, for the Lord God, my God, is with you."

DEVOTIONAL

On this special day, as you cradle the miracle of new life in your arms, let gratitude overflow in your heart. Each tiny finger and delicate feature is a testament to God's incredible handiwork, reminding you that He personally knit your baby together with purpose and love. In this season of joy and wonder, it's normal to feel a mix of excitement and uncertainty. Remember the promise found in 1 Chronicles 28:20: "Be strong and courageous, and do the work." Every cry, every sleepless night, and every burst of laughter is a moment filled with His grace, guiding you through the beautiful chaos of motherhood. Trust that you are not alone—His presence envelops you, lifting you when you feel weary and celebrating alongside you in each triumph. Embrace this sacred journey, knowing that your heart has expanded in ways you never imagined, filled with a love that is as deep as God's unending faithfulness. Today, celebrate the miracle of your little one, for He has made all things new.

DAILY REFLECTION

How can you intentionally pause today to recognize and celebrate the unique miracle of your baby's life, allowing gratitude to fill your heart and trusting in God's unwavering promises as you navigate the beautiful journey of motherhood?

PRAYER

Dear Lord, as I hold this precious new life in my arms, my heart swells with gratitude for the miracle You have created. Help me to embrace each moment— every challenge, every joy—knowing that Your grace surrounds us. Instill in me the courage to trust in Your promises, guiding my steps through both the beautiful chaos and the tender moments of motherhood. Amen.

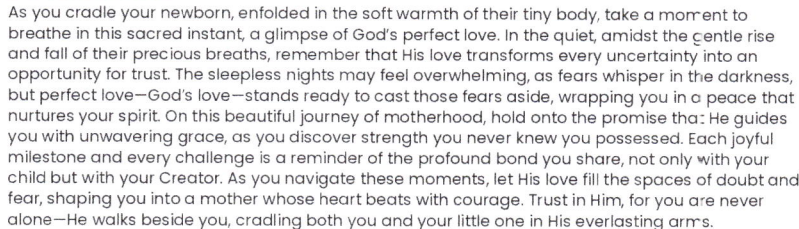

As you cradle your newborn, remember that God's love transforms every moment of motherhood. Trust in His guidance as you navigate this beautiful journey, knowing that His strength sustains you in both sleepless nights and joyous milestones.

1 John 4:18 - "There is no fear in love. But perfect love drives out fear, because fear has to do with punishment. The one who fears is not made perfect in love."

DEVOTIONAL

As you cradle your newborn, enfolded in the soft warmth of their tiny body, take a moment to breathe in this sacred instant, a glimpse of God's perfect love. In the quiet, amidst the gentle rise and fall of their precious breaths, remember that His love transforms every uncertainty into an opportunity for trust. The sleepless nights may feel overwhelming, as fears whisper in the darkness, but perfect love—God's love—stands ready to cast those fears aside, wrapping you in a peace that nurtures your spirit. On this beautiful journey of motherhood, hold onto the promise that He guides you with unwavering grace, as you discover strength you never knew you possessed. Each joyful milestone and every challenge is a reminder of the profound bond you share, not only with your child but with your Creator. As you navigate these moments, let His love fill the spaces of doubt and fear, shaping you into a mother whose heart beats with courage. Trust in Him, for you are never alone—He walks beside you, cradling both you and your little one in His everlasting arms.

DAILY REFLECTION

In the tender moments spent with your newborn, how can you intentionally invite God's presence into your heart, transforming your worries into a deeper trust in His unwavering support as you embrace the beautiful chaos of motherhood?

PRAYER

Dear Lord, as I hold my newborn close, I thank You for this sacred gift—a reminder of Your perfect love. In the quiet moments and sleepless nights, let Your peace wash over me, dispelling my fears and filling my heart with strength. Guide me through this beautiful journey of motherhood, Lord, and may I always feel Your presence cradling both me and my little one in Your everlasting embrace. Amen.

As you cradle new life in your arms, remember that God's love envelops both you and your child. Trust in His guidance as you navigate this beautiful journey of motherhood, knowing that every moment is filled with grace and purpose.

Song of Solomon 8:6-7 - "Set me as a seal upon your heart, as a seal upon your arm; for love is as strong as death, jealousy as cruel as the grave; its flames are flames of fire, a most vehement flame. Many waters cannot quench love, nor can the floods drown it. If a man would give for love all the substance of his house, it would be utterly despised."

DEVOTIONAL

As you cradle that precious new life in your arms, let the profound love that God has for both you and your child wrap around you like a warm embrace. In this sacred moment, remember the words from the Song of Solomon: love is a force unmatched, a flame that cannot be extinguished by any storm. Your journey into motherhood is lined with moments of joy and trials, each one a testament to the strength of the love you carry. Trust in God's guidance as you navigate late-night feedings, tender first smiles, and everything in between. Feel His presence with you, offering grace when you are weary and joy when you least expect it. Just as you seal your love upon your child's heart, know that God's love is sealing your bond, infusing every interaction with purpose. Embrace this beautiful adventure, for you are not alone; His love is steadfast, a foundation upon which your family will flourish.

DAILY REFLECTION

In this tender season of motherhood, how can you intentionally seek and reflect God's unwavering love in the small yet profound moments shared with your newborn?

PRAYER

Dear God, in this precious moment, as I hold my child close, I feel Your love envelop us both. Grant me the strength to embrace the joys and challenges of motherhood, and may Your guidance light my path. Help me to nurture this little life with the same unwavering love that You have for us, reminding me that in every tear and smile, Your grace is with us, shaping our journey together. Amen.

"Embrace the miracle of new life with unwavering faith, trusting in God's perfect timing. In each moment of motherhood, remember His promises are a source of strength and comfort, guiding you through the tender journey ahead."

Luke 1:37 - "For with God nothing will be impossible."

DEVOTIONAL

As you cradle your tiny miracle, remember that each heartbeat is a testament to the extraordinary work of our Creator. In the sacred dance of motherhood, challenges may rise, yet your faith can rise even higher. Luke 1:37 whispers a gentle reminder: "For with God, nothing will be impossible." Hold onto this promise during sleepless nights and uncertain days; God's timing is immaculate, and His plans are woven into every moment you spend nurturing new life. Embrace the joy of first kicks, the sweetness of giggles, and the quiet moments of connection—these are threads in the tapestry of your journey, intricately designed by His loving hands. When doubt creeps in, let His promises wrap around you like a warm blanket, providing strength and reassurance that you are never alone. With unwavering faith, trust that you are equipped and guided through this tender adventure, for you are leaning into the greatest miracle of all.

DAILY REFLECTION

How can you hold onto God's promises during the quiet moments of motherhood, allowing His faithfulness to transform your doubts into a deeper trust as you embrace the miracle of your new life?

PRAYER

Dear God, as I cradle this precious miracle in my arms, fill my heart with unwavering faith in Your perfect timing. Help me to find strength in Your promises during the sleepless nights and quiet moments, reminding me that each kick and giggle is a sacred blessing woven into my journey. May Your love wrap around me like a warm blanket, reminding me that I am never alone, and equip me to embrace the beauty and challenges of motherhood with grace, trusting in the miracle of new life that You have so lovingly given. Amen.

As you cradle your newborn, remember that God has woven hope and purpose into this new life. Trust in His promises as you nurture and guide your child, knowing each moment is a divine blessing. In the joy and challenges of motherhood, find strength in prayer and grace in His presence.

Psalm 78:4-7: "We will not hide them from their children, but tell to the coming generation the glorious deeds of the Lord, and his might, and the wonders that he has done. He established a testimony in Jacob and appointed a law in Israel, which he commanded our fathers to teach to their children, that the next generation might know them, the children yet unborn, and arise and tell them to their children, so that they should set their hope in God and not forget the works of God, but keep his commandments."

DEVOTIONAL

As you cradle your newborn, let your heart swell with the beauty of God's intricate design, woven into every tiny finger and fluttering heartbeat. In these sacred moments, remember the promise that each child carries with them—a life imbued with hope and purpose, destined to reflect the glorious deeds of the Lord. Amid the sleepless nights and joyful firsts, you embark on a remarkable journey of nurturing, one that calls you to be their spiritual guide and storyteller. With each gentle word you whisper, each lullaby you sing, you weave the story of His might into the very fabric of their being. Psalm 78:4-7 reminds us of the importance of passing down the truths of our faith; how beautiful it is that you are their first teacher, shaping their understanding of God's love. In moments of doubt or weariness, lean into prayer, where you find strength and grace in His unwavering presence. Trust in His promises as you nurture and guide your child, knowing that every fleeting moment is a divine blessing meant to be cherished and celebrated. As you embrace the joys and challenges of motherhood, may your heart be filled with peace, knowing that you are part of His extraordinary plan.

DAILY REFLECTION

In the quiet moments as you cradle your newborn, how can you actively embrace the hope and purpose that God has placed within them, allowing His promises to guide your journey of motherhood amidst both the joys and the challenges?

PRAYER

Dear Lord, as I cradle my precious newborn in my arms, I am in awe of the beautiful design You have woven into this tiny life. Grant me the wisdom and strength to nurture them with love and faith, instilling in their heart the truths of Your promise and purpose. In the quiet moments and the chaotic ones, may I always find solace in Your presence, leaning on You for grace as I embark on this sacred journey of motherhood. Amen.

Trust in God's plan for you and your newborn, for each moment in this new journey is a gift. Lean into His strength as you nurture this precious life, knowing that His love surrounds you both.

Exodus 14:14 – "The Lord will fight for you; you need only to be still."

DEVOTIONAL

As you cradle your newborn in your arms, remember that this sacred moment is part of God's intricate plan for your life. The journey of motherhood is filled with uncertainty and joy, a tapestry woven with each cry, each giggle, and each quiet moment of wonder. Just as the Israelites stood at the edge of the Red Sea, unsure of what lay ahead, you may feel overwhelmed by the vastness of your new role. In these moments, take heart in Exodus 14:14: "The Lord will fight for you; you need only to be still." Allow His strength to fill the spaces of doubt within you. When sleepless nights feel heavy and the weight of responsibility is daunting, remember that His love wraps around both you and your child like a gentle embrace, guiding you through this miraculous adventure. Trust in the process, for each day is a gift—a time to nurture not only your baby but your heart in His unwavering grace. Lean into this trust, knowing that as you surrender to His plan, you are held and cherished in ways beyond all understanding.

DAILY REFLECTION

In the beautiful chaos of these early days with your newborn, how can you intentionally pause to recognize the sacred gift of each moment, trusting that God's love and strength are guiding both you and your child through this transformative journey?

PRAYER

Dear God, in this tender season of motherhood, I place my trust in Your perfect plan for me and my little one. Help me to find strength in Your presence during the sleepless nights and unpredictable days, knowing that Your love envelops us both. Teach me to cherish each moment as a beautiful gift, guiding me to nurture my child with the grace and patience that mirrors Your own. Amen.

As you welcome new life, remember that God's love surrounds you in this sacred journey of motherhood. Trust in the strength He provides as you nurture your child, reflecting His grace and tenderness in your new role.

Psalm 136:1-3 – "Give thanks to the Lord, for He is good. His love endures forever. Give thanks to the God of gods. His love endures forever. Give thanks to the Lord of lords: His love endures forever."

DEVOTIONAL

As you step into the beautiful chaos of motherhood, whether welcoming a tiny newborn or adjusting to the sweet rhythms of a growing infant, let the truth of Psalm 136:1-3 wash over you like a gentle embrace. "Give thanks to the Lord, for He is good. His love endures forever." In these precious moments, as you cradle your little one close, remember that you are enveloped in God's unwavering love—a love that saw you through the sleepless nights and joyful mornings. Reflect on the countless ways His goodness manifests in your journey, reminding you that each small milestone is a reflection of His grace. Trust in the strength God provides, for just as He tenderly nurtures you, He empowers you to nurture your child. This sacred bond mirrors His love in profound and beautiful ways; each lullaby, every gentle touch, is an echo of His tenderness. As you navigate the challenges and triumphs of motherhood, let gratitude fill your heart, transforming moments of doubt into opportunities for deeper connection with Him. Breathe deeply, knowing you are not alone—His love endures forever, guiding you on this precious path.

DAILY REFLECTION

In what ways can you consciously embrace and reflect God's enduring love in the everyday moments of nurturing your little one, transforming the challenges of motherhood into cherished connections with Him?

PRAYER

Dear Lord, as I cradle this precious new life, I am reminded of Your ever-present love that surrounds us. Grant me the strength to nurture my child with Your grace and tenderness, turning moments of uncertainty into opportunities to grow closer to You. In the beautiful chaos of motherhood, help me to always give thanks for Your enduring goodness, resting in the truth that we are blessed beyond measure by Your unfailing love.

With each tiny heartbeat, God whispers His promise of love and new beginnings. Trust in His guidance as you nurture this child, knowing that you are never alone in this journey of motherhood.

1 Chronicles 29:11-12 - "Yours, Lord, is the greatness and the power and the glory and the majesty and the splendor, for everything in heaven and earth is yours. Yours, Lord, is the kingdom; you are exalted as head over all. Wealth and honor come from you; you are the ruler of all things."

DEVOTIONAL

As you cradle your new baby, each tiny heartbeat is a gentle reminder of the incredible journey you've embarked upon. In this sacred moment, consider the words from 1 Chronicles 29:11-12: "Yours, Lord, is the greatness and the power and the glory." The heartbeat you hear is not just a biological miracle; it is a testament to God's faithfulness and His promise of love. He has entrusted you with this precious life, and in your nurturing arms, His majesty rests. Motherhood can feel overwhelming, but remember, you are never alone. Just as the fabric of the universe is woven by His hands, your path is guided by His love. Trust in that divine guidance, and let His strength fortify you as you create a world for your child—a world filled with faith, warmth, and unending love. Each day, take a moment to pause, listen, and revel in the whispers of God, knowing that every heartbeat is an invitation to grow alongside your little one.

DAILY REFLECTION

As you listen to your baby's gentle heartbeat, what fears or hopes surface within you, and how can you invite God's love to guide you through each moment of this beautiful yet uncertain journey of motherhood?

PRAYER

Dear Lord, as I hold this precious life in my arms, I am in awe of Your promise woven into each tiny heartbeat. Help me to trust in Your guidance as I navigate the beautiful and overwhelming journey of motherhood. Fill my heart with Your love, reminding me that in days of uncertainty, I am never alone, for Your whispers of assurance are always near. Amen.

On this day, as you cradle new life, remember that God lovingly knits together each precious child in your womb. Trust in His divine plan and find strength in the quiet moments, for your journey of motherhood is a sacred gift filled with His unfailing love and grace.

Genesis 4:1 - "Now Adam knew Eve his wife, and she conceived and bore Cain, saying, 'I have gotten a man with the help of the Lord.'"

DEVOTIONAL

As you cradle new life in your arms or gently feel its flutter within, pause for a moment to reflect on the sacredness of this journey. Just as Adam recognized the precious gift of Cain with gratitude, you too are invited to acknowledge the miracle unfolding within you. Each movement, each heartbeat is a testament to God's faithfulness—a reminder that He lovingly knits together every precious child, instilling them with purpose and love. In the stillness of the night or during soft, quiet moments, let His presence surround you, bringing comfort and strength to your heart. Motherhood is a beautiful tapestry woven with threads of joy, worry, and unwavering grace. Embrace this sacred gift, trusting in His divine plan for your family, knowing that you are not alone. Allow His love to fill your moments, guiding you as you nurture this life and grow together in faith.

DAILY REFLECTION

In the tender moments when you hold your child close, how can you recognize and embrace the unique purpose that God has woven into their very being, and how might that awareness transform your journey of motherhood?

PRAYER

Dear Lord, in this sacred moment, I thank You for the precious life I cradle, for each heartbeat and flutter is a reminder of Your unfailing love and grace. Help me to trust in Your divine plan as I navigate the joys and challenges of motherhood, and may I find strength in Your presence, embracing the journey ahead with a heart full of gratitude and hope. Amen.

April 11

God's love is reflected in the miracle of new life. As you navigate the joys and challenges of motherhood, lean on His strength and wisdom, trusting that each moment is a divine gift. Let His peace cradle you in the tender journey of nurturing your little one.

Psalm 126:3 - "The LORD has done great things for us, and we are filled with joy."

DEVOTIONAL

As you embark on this sacred journey of motherhood, take a moment to soak in the beautiful reality that God has chosen you to nurture a miracle. Psalm 126:3 beautifully reminds us, "The LORD has done great things for us, and we are filled with joy." In the quiet moments, when your heart swells with love for your little one, remember that this joy is a reflection of His divine handiwork. Each coo, each tiny grasp of your finger, unfolds a story of love that God weaves into your lives. Yet, as you navigate the sleepless nights and the uncertainties of motherhood, lean into His strength, for you are not alone. His wisdom can guide you when doubts arise and His peace can cradle your heart amid the chaos. Trust that every moment with your child is a precious gift, revealing His love in ways you are yet to fully understand. Embrace this tender journey, allowing God's love to shine through you as you nurture the precious life entrusted to your care.

DAILY REFLECTION

In the quiet embrace of your little one's gaze, how can you invite God's love to fill the spaces of uncertainty and joy, transforming each fleeting moment into a cherished reflection of His grace?

PRAYER

Dear Lord, in this sacred chapter of motherhood, I thank You for the precious gift of new life before me. As I embrace the joys and challenges that come each day, may Your love fill my heart, guiding me with strength and wisdom in every moment. Cradle me in Your peace, and let Your divine presence shine through me as I nurture this little miracle, trusting that in each fleeting moment lies the essence of Your boundless love. Amen.

April 12

God's blessings overflow as you nurture this new life. Trust in His guidance, knowing each moment is a sacred opportunity to reflect His love. Your journey of motherhood is woven into His divine plan.

Matthew 5:16 - "In the same way, let your light shine before others, that they may see your good deeds and glorify your Father in heaven."

DEVOTIONAL

As you embark on this sacred journey of motherhood, remember that each moment spent nurturing your little one is a reflection of God's endless love. Your hands, cradling this precious life, are filled with the opportunity to shine His light brightly in the world. In the quiet of the night or the early morning light, as you coo softly to your baby, you are not just comforting them; you are painting a portrait of God's grace and compassion. In those challenging moments, when the weight of responsibility feels heavy, trust in His guidance—He has equipped you with everything you need to flourish. Let your heart be open to the lessons of patience, joy, and vulnerability, for they will mold you into a powerful beacon of hope. Remember, your journey is penned in His divine plan, and by embracing each day with faith, you create a legacy that glorifies your Father in heaven. Shine brightly, dear mother; your good deeds in this sacred role will illuminate the path for others and inspire them to seek His face.

DAILY REFLECTION

In the tender moments of motherhood, how can you intentionally seek God's presence to find strength and grace, allowing His love to flow through you as you nurture this new life?

PRAYER

Dear Lord, as I embrace this sacred journey of motherhood, fill my heart with Your peace and my hands with Your strength. Help me to trust in Your guidance during the sleepless nights and joyful moments alike, knowing that each day is a chance to reflect Your profound love. May I nurture this little life with grace, allowing Your blessings to overflow through my every action, so that together we may shine as a testament to Your divine plan. Amen.

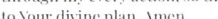

As you nurture a new life, remember that God's love envelops you both. Trust His guidance in the quiet moments, and find strength in His promises, knowing He walks alongside you through each challenge and joy of motherhood.

Matthew 6:28-30 - "And why do you worry about clothes? See how the flowers of the field grow. They do not labor or spin. Yet I tell you that not even Solomon in all his splendor was dressed like one of these. If that is how God clothes the grass of the field, which is here today and tomorrow is thrown into the fire, will He not much more clothe you—you of little faith?"

DEVOTIONAL

As you cradle your precious little one, take a moment to breathe in the wonder of new life and the profound love that surrounds you both. In the rush of late-night feedings and the overwhelming joy of first smiles, remember that just as God beautifully adorns the flowers of the field, His love envelops you in each gentle moment. Every worry you carry is a reminder that you're not alone; trust in His comforting presence. He sees you, dear mother, in your vulnerability and your joys, ready to guide you through the labyrinth of motherhood. When uncertainty looms, reflect on His promises: He cares for the smallest details of your life and will sustain you. Let your faith bloom like those flowers, radiant and unburdened, knowing that He is by your side. Embrace the journey with a heart open to His love, for you are beautifully crafted for this sacred role of nurturing and guiding the life entrusted to you.

DAILY REFLECTION

In the quiet moments of motherhood, how can you intentionally recognize and embrace God's love as a source of strength and reassurance amidst the challenges and joys you face with your little one?

PRAYER

Dear Lord, as I cradle this precious life in my arms, envelop me and my little one with Your unwavering love. In moments of exhaustion and joy, remind me that I am not alone, and guide me gently with Your promises. Help me to embrace each challenge and delight as a part of Your beautiful plan, nurturing not just my child, but my faith as well. Amen.

As you welcome new life, remember that God's grace surrounds you in this sacred journey of motherhood. Trust in His plan, finding strength in each moment, whether in joy or in challenge. You are not alone—He walks with you through this beautiful transformation.

Psalm 139:15-16 - "My frame was not hidden from you when I was made in the secret place, when I was woven together in the depths of the earth. Your eyes saw my unformed body; all the days ordained for me were written in your book before one of them came to be."

DEVOTIONAL

As you cradle this precious life, take a moment to breathe deeply and savor the miracle held in your arms. Psalm 139 reminds us that God intricately weaves each of us into existence, uniquely crafted with purpose and love. In the quiet moments of awe and wonder, acknowledge that this journey of motherhood is not just a series of tasks, but a sacred dance with the Creator who knows every detail of your new child's life. When days feel heavy and doubts creep in, remember that God's grace envelops you like a warm embrace, guiding you through challenges with unwavering strength. Trust that His plan unfolds not just in serene, joyful moments, but also in the messy, chaotic ones that test your heart. You are not alone; His presence is a constant companion, reminding you that it's okay to seek help and lean on others. As you navigate this profound transformation, cherish each moment—both radiant and trying—knowing that your journey is beautifully ordained. With every heartbeat, you're writing a story of love, resilience, and grace that mirrors the divine love showered upon you.

DAILY REFLECTION

In the tender quiet of your new reality, how can you invite God's grace into both the joyful milestones and the challenging moments of motherhood, recognizing that each heartbeat is a reminder of His unwavering love and presence in your sacred journey?

PRAYER

Dear Lord, as I nurture this precious new life, help me to embrace both the joy and the uncertainty of motherhood. May Your grace wrap around me, offering strength in moments of doubt and comfort in times of chaos. Remind me that each day is a sacred opportunity to witness Your love woven into our journey, guiding me in both the beautiful and the challenging moments. Amen.

God's love envelops you in this beautiful journey of motherhood, whether you're awaiting your little one's arrival or cradling them in your arms. Trust that He equips you with strength and wisdom, providing comfort in the sleepless nights and joy in each tiny milestone. Remember, His grace is enough for every moment, guiding you in this divine calling.

Psalm 90:17 - "May the favor of the Lord our God rest on us; establish the work of our hands for us—yes, establish the work of our hands."

DEVOTIONAL

As you step into the sacred journey of motherhood, whether you are eagerly counting down the days until your baby arrives or cherishing the quiet moments with your newborn in your arms, remember that you are enveloped in God's unfathomable love. Each flutter, each coo, each tiny finger gripping your own, is an echo of His grace surrounding you, reminding you that you are not alone in this beautiful adventure. The sleepless nights may seem daunting, yet within those weary hours lies a tender intimacy, a sacred space where your heart blooms, trusting in His strength to sustain you. Psalm 90:17 tells us, "May the favor of the Lord our God rest on us; establish the work of our hands for us—yes, establish the work of our hands." Embrace this promise, for every fleeting smile and milestone is a testament to His faithfulness and the goodness He has woven into your path. In your moments of doubt, pause and reflect on the loving presence that guides you, reassuring you that His grace is sufficient for every challenge and joy. Allow His wisdom to fill your heart, nurturing your spirit as you navigate this divine calling, and know that each day you are doing the beautiful work of love, hand in hand with your Creator.

DAILY REFLECTION

In the tender moments of anticipation or in the quiet joy of cradling your newborn, how can you intentionally recognize and embrace God's loving presence guiding you through each challenge and triumph on this beautiful journey of motherhood?

PRAYER

Dear Lord, as I embark on this sacred journey of motherhood, let Your love envelop me in every moment, whether I am waiting in anticipation or holding my little one close. Grant me strength to embrace the sleepless nights and wisdom to cherish each small milestone, knowing that Your grace is my constant companion. May Your presence fill my heart with peace and joy, reminding me that in this beautiful calling, I am never alone. Amen.

April 16

As you nurture the precious gift of life within you or hold your newborn close, remember that God lovingly knits every child with purpose and promise. Trust in His strength daily, for He equips mothers with wisdom and grace to guide their little ones on the path of faith. Embrace this sacred journey, knowing His love is your foundation.

Psalm 112:1-2: "Praise the Lord! Blessed is the man who fears the Lord, who greatly delights in his commandments! His offspring will be mighty in the land; the generation of the upright will be blessed."

DEVOTIONAL

As you cradle the miracle growing within you or hold your newborn close, take a moment to pause and reflect on the divine artistry at work. Psalm 112:1-2 reminds us of the profound connection between our love for God and the legacy we pass on to our children. Each tiny heartbeat is a testament to God's purpose and promise, wrapped in a love that surpasses understanding. In the quiet moments of sleepless nights and whispered prayers, remember that He has equipped you with an abundance of wisdom and grace for this sacred role. Reflect on the joy of nurturing this life, knowing that your faith will shape not only your child's heart but also the generations to come. Hold tightly to His love as your foundation, for it will guide you through the storms and joys ahead. Trust that your journey as a mother is beautifully woven into His grand design.

DAILY REFLECTION

In the quiet moments when you watch your little one sleep, how can you lean into God's promise of purpose in their life, allowing your love and faith to be the guiding light on their journey?

PRAYER

Dear God, as I cradle this precious life within me, or hold my newborn in my arms, I stand in awe of the miracle You have created. Grant me the strength and wisdom to nurture this child with love, always trusting in Your guidance. May Your promise fill my heart with peace, and may every moment, no matter how challenging, draw me closer to You, reminding me that Your love is the very foundation upon which this beautiful journey is built. Amen.

"Trust in God's perfect timing as you welcome new life into the world. In moments of uncertainty and joy, remember that He has lovingly designed every step of your journey as a mother. Each tiny heartbeat is a reminder of His boundless grace and faithfulness."

Lamentations 3:22-23 - "The steadfast love of the LORD never ceases; His mercies never come to an end; they are new every morning; great is Your faithfulness."

DEVOTIONAL

As you stand on the threshold of motherhood, each flutter and kick reminds you of the miracle unfolding within you. In the waiting—the long nights, the uncertainty, and the moments filled with both joy and apprehension—remember the promise of Lamentations 3:22-23. Just as the dawn brings fresh mercies each morning, so too does God bring a new grace to your heart with every tiny heartbeat you feel. Embrace this season of anticipation, for it is woven with His perfect timing, a tapestry of love and faithfulness. In times of doubt, when the world feels overwhelming, allow His steadfast love to cradle your soul. This journey may not unfold as you imagined, but trust that every step is crafted by a loving Father who knows you intimately. As you welcome new life, cling to the truth that His grace is abundant, and His provisions are perfectly timed, guiding you through each day with the unwavering assurance that you are not alone.

DAILY REFLECTION

As you embrace the miracle of new life, how can you surrender your doubts and fears to God, trusting in His perfect timing to shape your journey of motherhood with grace and love?

PRAYER

Dear Lord, as I embrace this sacred journey of motherhood, help me to trust in Your perfect timing, even amid the uncertainties and overwhelming moments. Remind me that every flutter and kick is a testament to Your grace, and may Your steadfast love cradle my heart through the joys and trials ahead. Teach me to find peace in Your promises, knowing that You are intricately weaving my path and guiding me with gentle assurance. Amen.

As you cherish the miracle of new life, take comfort in knowing that God's love envelops both you and your little one. In this sacred journey of motherhood, trust in His guidance and strength, nurturing your heart with His promises and grace.

Psalm 30:5 - "For his anger lasts only a moment, but his favor lasts a lifetime; weeping may stay for the night, but rejoicing comes in the morning."

DEVOTIONAL

As you cradle your precious child, remember that each tiny heartbeat echoes the miracle of God's love surrounding you. Psalm 30:5 reminds us that while the journey of motherhood can bring moments of uncertainty and even tears, His favor is a light that lasts a lifetime. In the stillness of night, when worries may creep in, trust that God holds both you and your little one in His tender embrace. Your heart may feel overwhelmed with the weight of new responsibilities, but take solace in knowing that His strength is made perfect in your weakness. Each morning brings a fresh opportunity for joy, as His grace nurtures your spirit and guides your steps. Cherish these fleeting moments, allowing the laughter and love of your baby to wash away fears and doubts. Take comfort in knowing that God's promises are true, and that with every sunrise, He brings hope anew.

DAILY REFLECTION

How can you surrender your worries to God today, allowing His unwavering love to transform your moments of uncertainty into a celebration of the beautiful journey of motherhood?

PRAYER

Dear Lord, as I hold my child close, I am in awe of the miracle You have woven into our lives. Surround us with Your unwavering love and fill our hearts with the reassurance that in moments of uncertainty, Your strength and grace are our guiding light. Help me to savor each fleeting moment, trusting that my fears are gently cradled in Your hands and that every day is a new gift of hope and joy. Amen.

As you cradle your newborn, remember that just as God knit them together in your womb, He continues to guide each step of your journey. In moments of doubt or fatigue, lean into His grace, for He promises to be your strength and support, filling your heart with love and peace. Trust in His perfect timing and plan for your growing family.

Psalm 55:22 - Cast your burden on the Lord, and He will sustain you; He will never permit the righteous to be moved.

DEVOTIONAL

As you hold your precious newborn close, feel the gentle rhythm of their heartbeat—a reminder of how intricately God has woven their existence within you. Each moment with your little one is a sacred gift, a testament to His loving craftsmanship. In days filled with joys and challenges, you may find yourself weary or uncertain, questioning if you're enough. It's in these moments of doubt that God invites you to lean into His grace, reassuring you that His strength will uphold you. Remember, just as He carefully planned the life of your child, He also orchestrates every step of your journey as a mother. Trust in His perfect timing; He knows your heart and the unique path ahead for your growing family. As Psalm 55:22 reminds us, cast your burdens upon the Lord—He is ever-present to sustain you, enveloping you in His unwavering love and peace.

DAILY REFLECTION

In the quiet moments when you gaze at your sleeping child, how can you invite God's grace into your heart to transform your worries into peace, trusting that each precious beat of their heart is a testament to His unwavering plan for your lives?

PRAYER

Dear Lord, as I cradle this precious gift in my arms, I am awed by the miracle of Your creation. In the quiet moments of uncertainty and fatigue, remind me that Your strength is my anchor, and that Your love surrounds us both. Help me to trust in Your perfect plan for our family, knowing that each heartbeat is a testament to Your faithfulness and grace. Amen.

As you cradle your little one, find strength in the promise of new life, echoing God's love and grace. Trust that each small moment is a sacred gift, filled with divine purpose and joy. Let your heart be steadfast, for God's presence surrounds you and your child on this beautiful journey.

Titus 2:4-5: "Then they can urge the younger women to love their husbands and children, to be self-controlled and pure, to be busy at home, to be kind, and to be subject to their husbands, so that no one will malign the word of God."

DEVOTIONAL

As you cradle your little one, feel the warmth of new life enveloping you, a tangible echo of God's unwavering love and grace. Each coo, each tiny grasp of your baby's hand, is a sacred moment, imbued with purpose and joy that God so lovingly orchestrates in your life. Remember that as you nurture this precious gift, you are also wrapped in the gentle embrace of God's unwavering presence, guiding you along this beautiful journey of motherhood. In the hustle and bustle of caring for your little one, take time to breathe and reflect on the importance of loving your family with the grace that God extends to you. Titus 2 reminds us of the beauty in self-control, kindness, and nurturing a loving home. Every diaper change, every sleepless night is an opportunity to display the love that God has for you and your family, a reminder that you are not alone. Keep your heart steadfast, knowing that your commitment to love and nurture brings glory to God's word and grace in your home.

DAILY REFLECTION

In the tender moments spent with your little one, how can you consciously embrace God's unwavering presence, allowing His grace to shape your journey of motherhood and deepen the love that fills your home?

PRAYER

Dear God, as I cradle this precious gift in my arms, help me to embrace the beauty of these fleeting moments, feeling Your love wrap around us both. Strengthen my heart during the sleepless nights and the chaotic days, reminding me that every act of care is a reflection of Your grace. May I find joy in this sacred journey of motherhood, trusting that Your presence guides us, filling our home with warmth and purpose. Amen.

April 21

God lovingly equips mothers with strength and grace for the journey ahead. As you nurture new life, remember that His presence guides each step, providing comfort and wisdom. Trust in His perfect plan for you and your baby.

Psalm 22:9-10 - "Yet you brought me out of the womb; you made me trust in you, even at my mother's breast. From birth I was cast on you; from my mother's womb you have been my God."

DEVOTIONAL

As you embark on this beautiful journey of motherhood, remember that you are not alone. Psalm 22:9-10 reminds us that from the very beginning, God has been woven into the fabric of your life and your baby's. In those quiet, tender moments as you cradle your newborn, feel the essence of His strength wrapping around you, bolstering your spirit when uncertainty creeps in. Every time you soothe your baby or whisper words of love, you're echoing the gentle whispers of God who calls you His own. Trust in His perfect plan; He has equipped you with the grace and wisdom needed for each day's challenges and joys. Let His presence guide you, reminding you that you are both nurturer and nurtured, held in a sacred embrace. Embrace this sacred role, knowing that through every trial and triumph, He lovingly walks beside you.

DAILY REFLECTION

In the quiet moments of motherhood, how can you attune your heart to recognize God's gentle whispers guiding you through the beautiful yet challenging path of nurturing your little one?

PRAYER

Dear Lord, as I step into the beautiful journey of motherhood, I seek Your strength and grace to fill my heart. In the quiet moments with my little one, may I always feel Your guiding presence, nurturing both of us with love and wisdom. Help me to trust in Your perfect plan, embracing the sacred role of nurturing while being held in Your embrace. Amen.

April 22

In this sacred season of new beginnings, reflect on the miracle of life you hold in your arms. Trust in God's unwavering presence as you nurture your little one, knowing that each moment is a divine gift filled with love and purpose.

Genesis 9:7 - "And you, be fruitful and multiply; bring forth abundantly in the earth and multiply in it."

DEVOTIONAL

In this sacred season of new beginnings, you find yourself cradling a precious miracle—the tiny life that rests securely in your arms. Each soft breath, each gentle sigh, reminds you of the wonder that God has woven into this moment. As you gaze into the eyes of your little one, let the truth of Genesis 9:7 wash over you: "And you, be fruitful and multiply; bring forth abundantly in the earth and multiply in it." This command is not just a directive; it is a sacred invitation to trust in God's unwavering presence as you nurture and guide your child. Every feed, every late-night cuddle, and every coo is a divine gift, brimming with love and purpose, an eternal echo of God's promise to you. Know that you are not alone in this journey; the Creator is with you in every joyful laugh and sleepless night. Embrace the beauty of your new role, for you are a vital part of this incredible tapestry of life, designed with love and intention.

DAILY REFLECTION

In the quiet moments when you gaze upon your little one, how can you intentionally seek God's guidance to nurture not just their life, but the love that blooms within your own heart?

PRAYER

Dear Lord, as I cradle this precious life in my arms, I am filled with awe at the miracle You have entrusted to me. Help me to embrace each moment with love and gratitude, knowing that Your presence surrounds us in every joy and challenge. Grant me the wisdom to nurture this little one with tenderness, reminding me that in each coo and cuddle, Your divine purpose is beautifully unfolding. Amen.

God treasures the gift of new life. As you prepare to welcome your little one or cherish those precious early days, trust that His strength surrounds you and His love is woven through every moment of motherhood.

Isaiah 44:3-4: "For I will pour water on the thirsty land, and streams on the dry ground; I will pour my Spirit upon your descendants, and my blessing on your offspring. They shall spring up among the grass like willows by flowing streams."

DEVOTIONAL

As you stand on the brink of motherhood, whether counting down the days or cradling your newborn, remember that God cherishes this sacred journey. Isaiah 44:3-4 whispers a promise: "I will pour out my Spirit upon your descendants." In these tender moments, His Spirit surrounds you, infusing your heart with strength and love as you navigate the joys and challenges of new life. Every coo, every gentle cry, is a reminder that your little one is a blessing, blossoming like willow branches by flowing streams—a testament to God's abundance. In the quiet hours of the night or the bustling days filled with milestones, trust that His presence is woven throughout. You are not alone; His grace will sustain you, nourishing your spirit as you nurture your child. Embrace the beauty of each heartbeat and the miracle of your baby's first smile, for they are the waters that refresh your soul and remind you of His faithfulness. God treasures this precious life, and so should you.

DAILY REFLECTION

How can you intentionally pause in the midst of the joys and challenges of motherhood to recognize and celebrate the sacred gift of your little one as a reflection of God's unwavering love and presence in your journey?

PRAYER

Dear Lord, as I prepare to welcome this little miracle into the world, I thank You for the sacred gift of new life that fills my heart with awe. Surround me with Your strength and love in each tender moment, reminding me that I am never alone in this journey of motherhood. Help me to cherish every coo and gentle cry, seeing in them the beauty of Your faithfulness and the abundance of Your grace. Amen.

As you cradle this precious life, remember that each coo and sigh reveals the beauty of God's creation. In this sacred moment, acknowledge the gift of new beginnings and the divine purpose woven into your child's heart. Celebrate the joy and hope that come with every tiny heartbeat, reflecting the love of our Creator.

Luke 1:44 - For behold, when the sound of your greeting came to my ears, the baby in my womb leaped for joy.

DEVOTIONAL

As you cradle this precious life in your arms, take a moment to breathe in the sacredness of this new beginning. Each tiny coo and gentle sigh is a melody that sings of God's intricate design, a reminder that this child is a masterpiece, crafted with divine purpose and love. Just as Elizabeth felt her baby leap at the sound of Mary's greeting, know that your little one responds in a profound way to the world around them, full of joy and promise. In these quiet moments, reflect on the journey that brought you to this point—the hopes, the dreams, the prayers that have woven a tapestry of anticipation and love. Celebrate the miracle of creation unfolding before you; every heartbeat is a testament to God's faithfulness and grace. Embrace this sacred trust, and be assured that the hand of the Creator lovingly guides your child's path, infusing every moment with His light and joy. Remember, you are not just holding a baby; you are welcoming a life filled with potential, a reflection of the infinite love that brought it into being.

DAILY REFLECTION

As you gently rock your child in your arms, what hopes and dreams for their future do you hear whispering in your heart, and how might these evolve into prayers of gratitude and purpose in the days to come?

PRAYER

Dear Lord, as I cradle this precious life in my arms, I am overwhelmed by the miracle of Your creation. Thank You for this new beginning filled with joy and promise; may I nurture this child with the same love and grace that You bestow upon us. Help me to always recognize the divine purpose within their tiny heart, and lead us on a journey of faith where every coo and sigh is a reminder of Your everlasting presence.

April 25

On this day, reflect on the miracle of provision as Jesus feeds the multitude. Just as God supplied the needs of the hungry crowd, trust that He meets your needs today, nurturing your spirit with His Word and grace. Let gratitude overflow as you share His blessings with others.

John 6:11-12 - "And Jesus took the loaves, and when He had given thanks, He distributed them to those who were seated; so also the fish, as much as they wanted. And when they had eaten their fill, He told His disciples, 'Gather up the leftovers, that nothing may be lost.'"

DEVOTIONAL

On this day, as we recount the miracle of Jesus feeding the 5,000, allow your heart to be stirred by the depth of His provision. Picture the scene: a vast crowd, hungry and weary, yet in the hands of Jesus, a few loaves and fish became more than enough. In your own life, do you sometimes feel as if you are just a fragile handful, unsure if you can meet the demands around you? Remember, just as Jesus gave thanks before sharing the bread, our own gratitude is a powerful act of faith that unlocks the abundance of God's grace. He sees your needs—spiritually, emotionally, and physically—and invites you to trust that He will nurture you in the same way. Reflect on the moments of overflowing blessings and let them spark gratitude in you. As you recognize what you have received, look for ways to share those blessings, knowing that in giving, you mirror the heart of Christ, ensuring that nothing is lost but rather multiplied. May your spirit be filled today, knowing that every meal of grace He provides is both for you and for the world around you.

DAILY REFLECTION

In what areas of your life are you holding back from trusting in God's abundant provision, and how can embracing gratitude transform those moments into opportunities for sharing His blessings with others?

PRAYER

Dear Lord, as I reflect on the miracle of provision in the feeding of the multitude, I stand in awe of Your boundless grace. Remind me today that in my moments of doubt or scarcity, You hold the power to transform my vulnerabilities into blessings—both for myself and others. May my heart overflow with gratitude as I share Your goodness with the world, trusting that every act of kindness, no matter how small, echoes the love You generously bestow upon us all. Amen.

April 26

In the quiet of the night, as you cradle your newborn, remember that God is with you in every sleepless hour. This sacred moment mirrors His love—patient and unwavering—inviting you to rest in His presence amid the challenges of parenthood.

Psalm 27:14 - "Wait for the Lord; be strong, and let your heart take courage; wait for the Lord!"

DEVOTIONAL

In the stillness of the night, as you cradle your newborn in your arms, the world outside fades into silence, leaving only the soft whispers of their breath. This first sleepless night may feel overwhelming, yet it is a sacred moment—an invitation to connect deeply with God's unwavering presence. Just as your heart swells with love for your little one, remember that God's love envelops you, patient and steadfast, through every challenge of parenthood. In this quiet hour, you may feel weary, but Psalm 27:14 reminds us to "wait for the Lord; be strong, and let your heart take courage." As you rock your baby and embrace the beauty of this fleeting time, lean into the promise that God is with you, infusing your tired soul with strength. These nights of sleeplessness are not mere trials; they are holy moments where grace is found in your vulnerability. Turn your heart toward Him, finding rest not in sleep, but in the embrace of His love that carries you through the darkness.

DAILY REFLECTION

In this sacred hour of your newborn's first sleepless night, how can you surrender your weariness to the Lord, allowing His unwavering love to transform your exhaustion into a deeper connection with Him?

PRAYER

Dear Lord, in this sacred stillness of the night, as I cradle my newborn close, help me to feel Your presence wrapped around us like a warm embrace. In these moments of weariness, fill my heart with Your unwavering love and peace, reminding me that, though I may be tired, I am not alone. Grant me the strength to face the challenges of parenthood, and let each soft sigh of my child draw me deeper into Your grace, allowing me to find rest in Your faithful presence.

April 27

On this day of reflection, recognize the unexpected messiness of life, much like the first diaper blowout. In the chaos, seek God's grace and strength, trusting that He is present amid the surprises and challenges of parenthood, guiding you through every trial with love and wisdom.

2 Corinthians 4:8-9: "We are hard pressed on every side, but not crushed; perplexed, but not in despair; persecuted, but not abandoned; struck down, but not destroyed."

DEVOTIONAL

Today, as we reflect on the unexpected moments of life, let us recall the bewildering experience of a first diaper blowout—a moment that surely leaves us both frazzled and filled with laughter. Just like this little mess, parenthood often sweeps us into chaos we never anticipated, leaving us feeling hard pressed and bewildered. Yet, as we face these overwhelming challenges, let us remember the promise found in 2 Corinthians 4:8-9. Though we may be perplexed, we are not in despair; though we may feel struck down by the trials, we are not destroyed. In those frantic moments, God whispers to us reassurance amid the chaos, reminding us that His grace is abundant and His strength sustains us. As you navigate the ups and downs of parenting, be assured that you are never alone. Trust in His loving guidance, knowing that even in the messiest of moments, His presence is a testament to the joy and wisdom that come with nurturing life.

DAILY REFLECTION

In the midst of the delightful chaos of your child's first diaper blowout, how can you embrace the grace God offers, transforming this unexpected mess into a moment of gratitude for His unwavering presence in your parenting journey?

PRAYER

Dear Lord, in the midst of the chaos and unexpected surprises of parenthood, I seek Your grace to embrace the messiness of life. Help me to find joy in the bewildering moments, knowing that Your unwavering presence guides me through every trial with love and wisdom. May I always remember that even in the wildest of days, Your strength is my anchor and Your love sustains me.

April 28

On this day in the Christian calendar, reflect on the purity and renewal that comes from Christ's love, mirroring the transformation of baptism. Just as He washes away our sins, may we find strength to let go of the past and embrace the new life He offers. Celebrate the cleansing power of grace in your journey today.

Titus 3:5-6 - "He saved us, not because of righteous things we had done, but because of His mercy. He saved us through the washing of rebirth and renewal by the Holy Spirit, whom He poured out on us generously through Jesus Christ our Savior."

DEVOTIONAL

Today, as we pause to reflect on the gift of baptism, let us hinge our hearts on the transformative power of Christ's love. Like the water that flows gently but resolutely, His grace washes away our burdens, our regrets, and our old identities, inviting us into a beautiful renewal. Remember, it is not our deeds that earn this salvation; instead, it is the boundless mercy of His heart that cleanses us completely. As you prepare for the first bath at home, may it serve as a tangible reminder of the washing of rebirth, a moment to let go of all that weighs you down and step into the vibrant life He promises. The Holy Spirit stirs within us, pouring out a lavish abundance of renewal—embrace it wholeheartedly! Today is not just about cleansing the body; it is an invitation to refresh your spirit and rejoice in the new beginnings He lays before you. Trust in His promise of grace, and allow yourself to bask in the beauty of being made whole again.

DAILY REFLECTION

As you prepare for this ritual of cleansing, what burdens or past regrets will you consciously release into His transformative love, allowing Christ's grace to wash over you and renew your spirit in this sacred moment?

PRAYER

Dear Lord, as I embrace this sacred moment of cleansing, help me to fully release the burdens I carry and step into the new life You offer. May the water that washes over me remind me of Your boundless grace and the purity of Your love, renewing my spirit and heart with each drop. Teach me to trust in Your transformative power, finding strength in Your mercy as I celebrate the gift of rebirth and the vibrant journey ahead.

In the quiet moments of changing a diaper, remember that each small act of love nurtures not just the child, but your spirit as well. Just as God cherishes us in our messiness, approach this task with grace and gratitude, knowing you're building a foundation of care and faith.

Galatians 5:13-14 - "For you were called to freedom, brothers. Only do not use your freedom as an opportunity for the flesh, but through love serve one another. For the whole law is fulfilled in one word: 'You shall love your neighbor as yourself.'"

DEVOTIONAL

In the quiet moments of changing a diaper, when the world fades away to the rhythm of tender care, remember that each small act of love nurtures both the child and your spirit. This seemingly mundane task is a sacred opportunity to reflect on God's own unfailing love for us—love that enters into our messiness without hesitation. Just as your hands diligently clean and comfort, so too does God embrace us in our times of need, inviting us to serve with grace and gratitude. In Galatians 5:13-14, we are reminded that our freedom is not for ourselves alone, but a call to love and serve others. You are building a foundation of care and faith that will shape not just your child's heart, but your own as well. Embrace this moment; it may feel small, but in the eyes of Heaven, it is a demonstration of profound love. May you find joy and strength in the simplicity of each diaper change, knowing you are fulfilling a deep divine purpose.

DAILY REFLECTION

In the stillness of this moment, as you change a diaper, how can you consciously embrace the sacredness of this act as a reflection of God's unwavering love, illuminating the profound beauty found in serving even amidst life's messiest tasks?

PRAYER

Dear Lord, in this quiet moment of diaper changing, help me to recognize the sacredness in this small act of love. May your grace fill my heart, reminding me that even in the messiness of parenthood, I am embracing my child as you embrace us—with unwavering love. Grant me the strength to nurture not just my little one, but my spirit as well, knowing that each act of care reflects your divine purpose in our lives. Amen.

On this day of reflection, consider how God shapes us through our challenges, much like a newborn gaining strength in tummy time. Each difficulty is an opportunity to grow closer to Him, finding strength and resilience in faith as we develop and flourish in His love.

James 1:2-4 - "Consider it pure joy, my brothers and sisters, whenever you face trials of many kinds, because you know that the testing of your faith produces perseverance. Let perseverance finish its work so that you may be mature and complete, not lacking anything."

DEVOTIONAL

On this special day of reflection, let us lean into the wisdom found in James 1:2-4. Much like a newborn discovering the strength within during tummy time, we too are invited to embrace our challenges as sacred moments of growth. Each trial we encounter is a chance to develop endurance, a divine workout that strengthens our faith muscles. Imagine the sheer joy a baby experiences as they push through discomfort, inching closer to the remarkable gift of mobility. In our moments of struggle, God is shaping us, transforming our pain into purpose, inviting us to rise up and flourish in His love. Rather than shying away from difficulties, let's celebrate them, knowing they draw us nearer to the heart of our Creator. Today, may we find pure joy, not just in the victories, but in every moment of perseverance that leads us toward maturity in our walk with Him.

DAILY REFLECTION

In the gentle struggle of your own "tummy time" moments, how can you embrace the discomfort as a catalyst for growth, pressing closer to God's unwavering love and discovering the strength He has uniquely placed within you?

PRAYER

Dear Lord, as we embark on this day of reflection, may we embrace the challenges that stretch us, just as a newborn learns to rise during tummy time. Help us to find joy in each struggle, knowing that You are sculpting our hearts and deepening our faith through every trial. May we draw closer to You in our moments of discomfort, finding strength in Your love and purpose amidst our journeys. Amen.

May 1

As you attend your first postpartum checkup, remember that this new season of motherhood is infused with God's grace. Trust in His guidance as you prioritize your health, allowing His strength to refresh you for the journey ahead. Celebrate the life within you and the love that surrounds you.

Psalm 90:12 - "So teach us to number our days that we may get a heart of wisdom."

DEVOTIONAL

As you sit in the waiting room for your first postpartum checkup, take a deep breath and allow the gravity of this moment to settle within you. This new chapter of motherhood isn't just a shift in responsibilities; it's a divine calling filled with God's grace. Each day ahead is a gift, a chance to nurture the new life entrusted to your care while also tending to your own heart and health. Remember Psalm 90:12—"So teach us to number our days that we may get a heart of wisdom." This wise heart invites you to recognize the beauty and challenges of each moment, embracing both with gratitude. As you prioritize your well-being, trust in His guidance to refresh your spirit and strength for the journey ahead. Celebrate not just the life you brought into the world, but also the love that envelops you, for every heartfelt embrace and gentle word is a reminder of His presence in your life. In this sacred season, let God's love infuse every step you take, knowing you are not alone on this remarkable path of motherhood.

DAILY REFLECTION

In this moment of reflection during your postpartum checkup, how can you embrace the grace of God in your journey of motherhood, acknowledging both the beautiful gift of new life and the importance of caring for your own heart?

PRAYER

Dear Lord, as I sit in this waiting room, I thank You for the precious gift of motherhood and the life You have entrusted to my care. Help me to embrace this new journey with grace, nurturing both my child and my own heart. Give me strength for the challenges ahead, and may Your love surround me, reminding me that I am never alone in this sacred season of my life. Amen.

May 2

Trust in God's plan as you approach your baby's first pediatrician appointment. Just as Jesus welcomed the little children, embrace this moment with faith, knowing He guides each step of your parenting journey. Find peace in His presence and strength in His promises.

Mark 10:16 - "And He took the children in His arms, put His hands on them and blessed them."

DEVOTIONAL

As you step into the pediatrician's office with your little one, take a moment to breathe deeply and absorb the significance of this day. Just as Jesus welcomed children, embracing them with open arms, He is with you now, guiding you through the uncertainties of parenthood. In this very moment, trust in His divine plan; He knows your baby's needs even before you do. Let your heart find peace in the knowledge that you are not alone; every worry and every joy is held tenderly in His hands. Reflect on the blessing Jesus bestowed upon the children, and remember that He brings the same care and love to your family. Each step you take on this journey has been witnessed and ordained, from sweet giggles to sleepless nights. Embrace this appointment not as a source of anxiety, but as an opportunity to witness His promises unfold in your life. With faith as your anchor, allow yourself to feel the warmth of His presence wrapping around both you and your child, promising that you are never without His guidance and grace.

DAILY REFLECTION

How can you open your heart today to fully receive the peace and guidance that flows from trusting in God's plan for your baby's health and well-being?

PRAYER

Dear Lord, as I hold my little one close and step into this pediatrician's office, I ask for Your peace to fill my heart. Help me to remember that just as You welcomed the children, You embrace us on this journey of parenthood, guiding each moment with Your love and wisdom. Strengthen my faith in Your divine plan, reminding me that both the joys and concerns of this day are cradled tenderly in Your hands. Amen.

The joy of a baby's first smile reminds us of the pure grace of God's love, reflecting His delight in our existence. Just as a parent cherishes this simple yet profound moment, God treasures each expression of joy in our lives, inviting us to share that love and delight with others.

Zephaniah 3:17 - "The Lord your God is in your midst, a mighty one who will save; he will rejoice over you with gladness; he will quiet you by his love; he will exult over you with loud singing."

DEVOTIONAL

In the quiet morning light, a baby's first smile shines like a beacon of pure joy, an irreplaceable moment that stirs the heart and stirs the soul. This delicate expression, so simple yet profound, embodies an innocence that reminds us of the grace with which God loves us. Just as a parent is captivated by their child's laughter, God rejoices over us with an overwhelming gladness that echoes through the cosmos. In Zephaniah 3:17, we find assurance that He is not just a distant observer but a loving presence, delighting in who we are. Imagine the joy swirling around that first smile, resonating with the loud singing of a Divine heart, full of love and celebration just for you. In every smile and laugh we share, God invites us to reflect that joy back into the world, spreading a love that can comfort and uplift others. As we treasure these moments, let us remember that our lives are a canvas of His delight, each smile a brushstroke of grace that paints His love for all to see.

DAILY REFLECTION

How might you cultivate and share the joy of God's love in your life today, inspired by the radiant wonder of a baby's first smile?

PRAYER

Dear Lord, thank You for the radiant joy of a baby's first smile, a precious reminder of Your boundless love and grace in our lives. Help us to embrace these moments of delight and reflect that joy to those around us, so that every laugh and smile shared becomes a brushstroke of Your love painted across our world. May we always remember that You rejoice in our existence, filling our hearts with gladness to share with others. Amen.

As we celebrate the wonder of new life, let us reflect on the joy and hope that a baby brings, reminding us of God's promises. Each tiny hiccup is a reminder of His love and care, echoing the miracle of creation in each moment. Rejoice in the gift of life and the blessings that come with it!

Matthew 18:10 - "See that you do not despise one of these little ones."

DEVOTIONAL

As we gather to celebrate the wonder of new life, let us pause and reflect on the joy and hope that a precious baby brings into our world. Each tiny hiccup is more than just a physical reaction; it is a sweet echo of God's promise—a reminder that life is a delicate, miraculous gift woven together by His loving hands. In Matthew 18:10, we are gently reminded to cherish these little ones and not to overlook their significance, for they embody the purity of trust and innocence that we so often long for in our own lives. Just as every hiccup brings a brief moment of surprise, it also stirs our hearts, reminding us of the tender moments God uses to guide us closer to Him. Let us rejoice in the gift of life, understanding that these small joys hold immense weight in the tapestry of our faith. As we hold our little ones close, may we also embrace the blessings that they bring, inspiring us to live with renewed vigor and gratitude. In celebrating this gift of life, let us also share the love and care that echoes in each heartbeat, each coo, and yes, each sweet hiccup.

DAILY REFLECTION

As we marvel at the tiny hiccups of a newborn, how can we nurture the innocent wonder within ourselves, allowing each moment of joy to deepen our understanding of God's unwavering love and promises in our own lives?

PRAYER

Dear Lord, in the gentle rhythm of each baby's hiccup, we see the delicate dance of Your creation and the profound beauty of new life. Thank You for the joy and hope that children bring to our hearts; may these tiny echoes remind us of Your endless love and the promises that guide us. Help us to cherish every moment, embracing the blessings that come with this precious gift, and may we always find joy in the surprises woven into our faith. Amen.

May 5

In this season of new beginnings, may your first outing with your baby be a joyful reminder of God's promises. Trust in His guidance as you navigate this precious journey, savoring each moment of discovery.

Deuteronomy 31:8 - "It is the Lord who goes before you. He will be with you; he will not leave you or forsake you. Do not fear or be dismayed."

DEVOTIONAL

As you prepare for your first outing with your baby, take a moment to breathe in this season of new beginnings, where every small step is a precious milestone. Deuteronomy 31:8 reminds us that "It is the Lord who goes before you." Feel the reassurance in these words as you venture out, knowing that God is walking alongside you, illuminating the path ahead. Each coo, every gaze, and the light grip of tiny fingers can serve as gentle reminders of His unwavering presence. In the moments of uncertainty or overwhelming joy, let His promise soothe your heart: you are never alone in this journey. Savor the sweet discoveries, from the wonder of nature to the tender smiles of strangers. Remember, every outing is a testament to trust—trust in His guidance and the beautiful adventure that lies ahead. Embrace this outing not just as a walk, but as a sacred celebration of your growing family, held firmly in God's loving embrace.

DAILY REFLECTION

As you step out with your little one today, how can you allow each smile and every new sight to deepen your trust in God's guiding presence, transforming this ordinary outing into a sacred moment of connection and joy?

PRAYER

Dear Lord, as I embark on this first outing with my precious baby, let my heart overflow with gratitude for this season of new beginnings. May each tiny coo and curious glance remind me of Your steadfast presence, guiding us through every moment of joy and wonder. Grant me the wisdom to savor this sacred time together, trusting that Your love surrounds us, illuminating our path with hope and grace. Amen.

May 6

On this day, reflect on the quiet strength found in Jesus' teachings, reminding us that even the smallest steps taken in faith lead to profound transformation. Let each moment be a prayer, guiding your heart and mind closer to His grace.

John 15:5 - "I am the vine; you are the branches. Whoever abides in me and I in him, he it is that bears much fruit, for apart from me you can do nothing."

DEVOTIONAL

As you embark on your first stroller walk, consider the gentle rhythm of each step as a reflection of your journey in faith. Just as a branch draws strength from the vine, so too can you find your solace in Jesus' abiding presence. In this sacred moment, allow the world around you to become a living prayer—each leaf rustling in the breeze, each smile exchanged, a testament to the beauty of His creation. Remember, the quiet strength of faith often manifests in the seemingly small moments of surrender and trust. With each gentle push of the stroller, let your heart echo the sweetness of His grace, knowing that even the smallest actions can yield a harvest of love and transformation. Abide in Him throughout your day, allowing His peace to guide you through both the simple and complex steps of life. For in Him, you will discover that every little moment carries the potential for abundant fruitfulness.

DAILY REFLECTION

In the quiet rhythm of your first stroller walk, what small step can you take today that reflects your trust in Christ, allowing His grace to transform even the simplest moments into a sacred journey?

PRAYER

Dear Lord, as I embark on this first stroller walk, help me to embrace the gentle cadence of each step as a reflection of my faith in You. May the beauty of Your creation surround me, reminding me that even the smallest actions can reveal Your incredible grace. Grant me the strength to surrender my worries, trusting that in every moment, You are nurturing the seeds of love and transformation within my heart. Amen.

As you make your first car ride with your baby, remember that every journey is a step of faith, just like the Holy Family's travels. Trust in God's guidance and protection as you share this new adventure, cherishing each moment as a gift.

Matthew 2:13-15 - "Now when they had departed, behold, an angel of the Lord appeared to Joseph in a dream, saying, 'Arise, take the young Child and His mother, flee to Egypt, and stay there until I bring you word; for Herod will seek the young Child to destroy Him.' When he arose, he took the young Child and His mother by night and departed for Egypt, and was there until the death of Herod."

DEVOTIONAL

As you embark on your first car ride with your precious little one, take a moment to reflect on the journeys of the Holy Family. Just as they were guided by divine instruction through uncertain times, you too are stepping into the unknown, cradled in God's embrace. With each mile, recognize that this expedition is not just about reaching a destination, but about forging a bond filled with love and trust. The road may be winding, and the cries of a newborn can be unsettling, yet in these moments, God's gentle presence is ever near. Trust that He is watching over you, just as He protected Mary, Joseph, and Jesus during their flight to Egypt. Embrace every laugh, every tear, and every whispered prayer along the way, for these are the treasures that will fill your heart. Cherish this adventure, knowing that with each journey, you are growing in faith and love, hand in hand with the One who guides you.

DAILY REFLECTION

As you navigate this new road of parenthood, how can you let the delicate blend of joy and uncertainty in your first car ride with your baby deepen your trust in God's unwavering presence and guidance?

PRAYER

Dear Lord, as I embark on this sacred journey with my baby, I ask for Your guiding hand to be upon us. May each mile remind us of the love and protection You offered to the Holy Family, and may the cries of my little one fill my heart with wonder and grace. Help me to embrace this adventure with joy and trust, knowing that every moment spent together is a precious gift from You. Amen.

As you dress your little one today, remember that each tiny garment is a reminder of the love and care God has for us. Just like you wrap your baby in warmth and comfort, God envelops us in His grace and protection, guiding us through every season of life. Let this moment inspire you to nurture their spirit with the same devotion.

Deuteronomy 6:6-7 - "These commandments that I give you today are to be on your hearts. Impress them on your children. Talk about them when you sit at home and when you walk along the road, when you lie down and when you get up."

DEVOTIONAL

As you carefully dress your little one today, let each tiny garment serve as a gentle reminder of the boundless love and nurturing care that God showers upon us. Just as you wrap your baby in warmth and comfort, know that God envelops our hearts in His unchanging grace, guiding us through every season of life with tender protection. In this quiet moment, reflect on the verses from Deuteronomy 6:6-7, and feel the weight of your role as a parent. As you tie tiny shoes and fasten delicate buttons, think of the commandments of love that you are called to impress upon their hearts. This is more than just dressing—this is about nurturing a spirit, fostering faith, and sharing the love of God in every interaction. With every gentle touch, let your devotion to their spirit mirror His unwavering devotion to you. May this act of dressing lead to deeper conversations about faith as your little one grows, fostering a love that echoes through generations.

DAILY REFLECTION

As you dress your little one, how can you weave the warmth of God's love into each small act, nurturing not only their body but also the spirit within, to cultivate a faith that will flourish as they grow?

PRAYER

Dear Lord, as I dress my little one in these tiny garments, I thank You for the precious gift of their life and the opportunity to wrap them in warmth and love. With each button fastened and every shoe tied, may I be reminded of Your unending grace and the nurturing care You provide. Help me to nurture their spirit with devotion, teaching them to walk in Your ways, so that they may grow to know the depth of Your love throughout their journey. Amen.

May 9

Capture the joy and innocence of your little one's first milestone, echoing the love and wonder of God's creation. Today, as you witness this beautiful moment, remember that every smile and coo reflects the light of His presence in your life.

Song of Solomon 2:10-13 - "My beloved spoke and said to me, 'Arise, my darling, come away with me, my beautiful one. See! The winter is past; the rains are over and gone. Flowers appear on the earth; the season of singing has come, the cooing of doves is heard in our land.'"

DEVOTIONAL

In the gentle embrace of your home, as the camera captures the delicate beauty of your little one's first precious moments, let your heart echo with the whispers of the divine. Just as the beloved calls forth the beauty of spring in the Song of Solomon, so too does this moment invite you to arise and embrace the joy that floods your life through your child's innocent smiles. Each coo and giggle becomes a symphony, reminding you that love's presence is woven through every tiny gesture and every sparkling gaze. Here, amidst the laughter and wonder, you glimpse a reflection of God's own heart—a heart that delights in creation and celebrates each new beginning. The winter of uncertainty fades as you are surrounded by warmth, joy, and the tender light of hope. In such moments, take a deep breath and allow His spirit to fill the room, turning ordinary circumstances into extraordinary memories. Cherish these fleeting seconds of purity, where heaven kisses earth, and remember that you are witnessing not just a milestone, but a divine covenant of love unfolding before your very eyes.

DAILY REFLECTION

As you capture the fleeting beauty of your child's first milestone, how can you allow this moment of pure joy to deepen your gratitude for the divine love that surrounds your family, reminding you of the sacredness in every shared smile and innocent gaze?

PRAYER

Dear Lord, in this sacred space filled with soft laughter and tiny miracles, we thank You for the gift of our little one, a vibrant reflection of Your love and creativity. As we capture these precious moments, may each smile resonate with Your joy, and each coo remind us of Your presence in our lives. Grant us the grace to cherish these fleeting seconds, embracing the beauty of this divine tapestry woven with hope and innocence, as we witness the unfolding of Your magnificent plan in our hearts. Amen.

May 10

In this sacred moment of diaper duty, remember that each act, however humble, is infused with grace. Just as God cherishes the tiniest beginnings, so too does He smile upon the joyful, messy milestones of new life. Celebrate the laughter and love in the midst of the unexpected!

Ephesians 5:20 - "Giving thanks always and for everything to God the Father in the name of our Lord Jesus Christ."

DEVOTIONAL

In the midst of changing a diaper, a familiar yet unexpected event unfolds—a gentle reminder that life is rich with delightful surprises, even in the most mundane tasks. As the baby giggles, and perhaps even pees, you are nudged to pause and find joy in the spontaneity of this moment. Ephesians 5:20 calls us to "give thanks always and for everything," encouraging us to embrace each little milestone with a heart full of gratitude. This sacred duty of diaper changing is more than a chore; it's a beautiful dance of grace and growth. Just as God cherishes the smallest beginnings—the tiny fingers, the first words, and even the mess that comes with it—He invites you to celebrate the laughter and love woven into these fleeting moments. Each smile shared amid the chaos is a testament to the love that fills your home. So let your heart be light, for in every diaper change, God is doing a new thing, inviting you to rejoice in the joyful noise of life.

DAILY REFLECTION

In this sacred moment of care, how can you cultivate a heart of gratitude and joy, recognizing that even the most unexpected surprises are opportunities to witness God's grace in the everyday rhythms of your life?

PRAYER

Dear Lord, in this sacred moment of diaper duty, I thank You for the gift of laughter and the joy that springs forth in unexpected ways. Help me to embrace each playful surprise with a heart full of gratitude, recognizing that in these humble tasks, You are crafting wisdom and love into our lives. As I nurture this little life, may the giggles and mess remind us both of Your boundless grace that fills our home. Amen.

May 11

On this day, reflect on the theme of Divine Guidance, trusting in God's perfect path as you navigate life's challenges. Seek His wisdom in every decision, knowing that His love lights the way forward. Allow His presence to be your comfort and strength in every moment.

Proverbs 16:9 - "In their hearts humans plan their course, but the Lord establishes their steps."

DEVOTIONAL

As you embrace today, remember that your heart may be brimming with plans and desires, but it is the Lord who truly orders your steps. Reflect on the times when life felt uncertain, and yet, when you surrendered your path to Him, you found an unexpected sense of peace. Just as a gentle light illuminates a darkened room, God's guidance brightens our way, reminding us that we are never alone in our navigation of life's challenges. Each decision, large or small, is an opportunity to seek His wisdom and lean on His understanding. Trust that His love is a steady anchor, granting you comfort when the waves of worry threaten to overcome you. Let His presence be your source of strength, a soft whisper that reassures you of His perfect plan. As you walk forward today, let your heart resonate with the promise that every step taken with Him is a step taken in love.

DAILY REFLECTION

In what areas of your life can you invite God to guide you today, trusting that His love will illuminate the path ahead even in the midst of uncertainty?

PRAYER

Dear Lord, as I step into this day, I pause to acknowledge that my plans are entrusted to You. Illuminate my path with Your divine wisdom, and grant me the grace to surrender my uncertainties into Your loving hands. May Your presence envelop me like a warm embrace, grounding my heart in peace and reminding me that even in challenges, I am never alone. Guide me gently, Lord, as I seek to walk in Your light, knowing that each step with You is a step taken in love. Amen.

May 12

As you nourish your child in a moment of vulnerability, remember that Christ, who fed the hungry and welcomed the little ones, embraces you in this sacred act. Every heartbeat and gentle cry resonates with His love, affirming that you are not just a mother, but a reflection of His grace in the world.

John 6:35 - "Then Jesus declared, 'I am the bread of life. Whoever comes to me will never go hungry, and whoever believes in me will never be thirsty.'"

DEVOTIONAL

In these tender moments, as you cradle your child against you, a sacred connection unfolds between mother and child—a fragile yet profound reminder of the love that nourishes not just the body, but the soul. Just as Christ declared, "I am the bread of life," you too partake in this divine provision, serving not only milk or formula, but a steady stream of comfort and grace that transcends the physical act of feeding. With each gentle heartbeat and soft coo, you are enveloped in the warmth of His embrace, knowing that in your vulnerability, you reflect the very essence of His love. Let the world fade away, for this is your holy ground, a place where every cry is an echo of trust and every sip a song of contentment. As you nurture your child openly and without fear, embrace the truth that you are not merely meeting a need; you are mirroring the heart of Christ who welcomes the little ones with open arms. Remember that in this beautiful act of nourishment, you are never alone; the One who fed the hungry walks beside you, cheering you on. Let each moment be steeped in prayer, knowing that your journey is infused with His grace, transforming every act of love into a powerful testament of faith.

DAILY REFLECTION

In this intimate moment of nurturing your child, how can you embrace the divine echoes of Christ's love and grace, allowing His presence to fill you with courage and joy as you openly share this sacred act with the world?

PRAYER

Dear Lord, in this tender space where vulnerability meets love, I come to You, cradling my child and my heart. May each gentle sigh and soft coo remind me that I am not alone; Your grace enfolds us both. Help me to embrace this moment, to see it as a sacred act of nourishment—where I reflect Your love and welcome, trusting that in my offering, I am part of Your divine story. Amen.

On this day of reflection, ponder the miracle of Jesus nourishing the multitudes with just five loaves and two fish. Let this remind us that even in our smallest offerings, God can produce abundance, teaching us to trust Him with the little we have.

John 6:9-11 - "There is a boy here who has five barley loaves and two fish, but what are they for so many?" Jesus then took the loaves, and when He had given thanks, He distributed them to those who were seated; so also the fish, as much as they wanted.

DEVOTIONAL

As we gather today in reflection, let us turn our hearts to the boy with five barley loaves and two fish—an unassuming gift amidst a vast need. In the face of seemingly insurmountable challenges, he could have hesitated, overwhelmed by doubt. Yet, he offered all he had, trusting that it might be enough. Jesus took those humble provisions and, with a word of thanks, transformed scarcity into abundance. In our own lives, we often feel our efforts are too small, our resources too meager to make a difference. But just as the Lord multiplied that boy's lunch, He invites us to surrender our little to His boundless grace. Let this miracle stir within us the courage to offer our own small gifts, knowing they can lead to extraordinary outcomes in His hands.

DAILY REFLECTION

In what areas of your life have you hesitated to offer what little you have, and how might surrendering those small gifts to God reveal His ability to create abundance in your circumstances?

PRAYER

Dear Lord, in the quiet of our hearts, we bring our humble offerings before You, acknowledging that sometimes they feel so small in the face of our world's great needs. Help us to remember the boy with five loaves and two fish, and ignite in us the faith to surrender our little, trusting that You can transform our meager gifts into blessings beyond our imagination. May we find courage in our vulnerability, knowing that with You, even the simplest act of sharing can create miracles of love and hope. Amen.

In the midst of postpartum storms, remember that God's love is your anchor. He sees your struggle and meets you in your tears; trust that His grace is sufficient for every moment you face. Lean on Him, for even in your brokenness, His strength can bring healing.

Psalm 147:3 - "He heals the brokenhearted and binds up their wounds."

DEVOTIONAL

As you navigate the overwhelming emotions that accompany the postpartum journey, it's easy to feel adrift, caught in a storm of confusion and heartache. Yet, in your most vulnerable moments—when tears flow freely and your spirit feels heavy—remember that God sees you. Just as a loving parent rushes to comfort a child in distress, He draws near to you, offering solace for your weary heart. Psalm 147:3 reminds us, "He heals the brokenhearted and binds up their wounds." This promise resonates deeply in the chaos of new motherhood; it whispers that your brokenness does not define you, but rather serves as the canvas upon which His grace paints restoration. Trust that His warmth envelops you, and even in your darkest hours, His strength is crafting something beautiful from your pain. Lean into this truth and know that healing is not just a distant hope—it's a journey He walks with you, hand in hand.

DAILY REFLECTION

In the whirlwind of postpartum emotions, how can you invite God into your heartache today and trust that His gentle touch will bring healing amidst your tears?

PRAYER

Dear Lord, in this tumultuous season of new motherhood, I feel overwhelmed by the weight of my emotions. As I cry out in my vulnerability, remind me that Your love surrounds me like a warm embrace. May Your strength carry me through these storms, and may I find solace in the promise that You bind up every wound, crafting beauty from my brokenness. Amen.

On this sacred occasion of welcoming your newborn into the family, remember the heart of Mary, who treasured her moments with Jesus. As you gather together, may the joy and love shared reflect the light of Christ in your lives, nurturing your little one in a home filled with faith and blessing.

Luke 2:19 - "But Mary treasured up all these things and pondered them in her heart."

DEVOTIONAL

As you welcome your precious newborn into the embrace of family, take a moment to reflect on the profound journey that Mary undertook with Jesus. In her heart, she held each moment like a fragile treasure, savoring the wonder and promise of the Savior. In this sacred gathering, let the joy that fills the room echo the love Mary felt, reminding you that every giggle, every coo, is a glimpse of God's grace woven into your life. As you share stories, laughter, and dreams, may your hearts become vessels of faith, nurturing this little one with the light of Christ. Just as Mary pondered her experiences, consider taking a moment to breathe deeply, soaking in the smiles and tender glances that surround your baby. This love, this connection, is a holy blessing meant to be cherished and passed on. May your home be a sanctuary of faith, where the legacy of Christ shines brightly for generations to come.

DAILY REFLECTION

How can you, like Mary, cultivate a heart that treasures each fleeting moment with your newborn, ensuring that the joy and love you share today become lasting legacies of faith for generations to come?

PRAYER

Dear Lord, on this sacred day of welcoming our little one, let our hearts resonate with the love that filled Mary as she cherished each moment with Jesus. May our family be a haven of faith, where every laugh and tender gaze becomes a testament to Your grace, nurturing this precious child in the warmth of Your light. Help us to treasure these fleeting moments, weaving our hopes and dreams into a legacy of love that mirrors the joy of the Savior's embrace. Amen.

On this day, let us honor and cherish the gift of mothers and maternal figures in our lives, reflecting on their unwavering love and guidance. May we celebrate their nurturing spirit and the divine strength that shapes our hearts.

Proverbs 31:28-29 - Her children rise up and call her blessed; her husband also, and he praises her. "Many women have done excellently, but you surpass them all."

DEVOTIONAL

On this day, as we pause to celebrate the extraordinary women who have nurtured our hearts, we find ourselves wrapped in a warm embrace of gratitude. Proverbs 31:28-29 beautifully reminds us that a mother's impact resonates deeply within our lives—her love, a melody that plays softly in the background of our days. It beckons us to rise and call her blessed, recognizing the countless sacrifices she has made and the strength she has instilled in us. In moments of doubt, her encouraging words become a lighthouse guiding us back to shore. As we honor her today, let us not only praise her for the roles she has played but also acknowledge the divine strength that pours forth from her spirit— a reflection of God's own love and grace. May our hearts overflow with gratitude for her unwavering commitment and endless capacity to love. Indeed, many women have done excellently, but to us, she is a unique masterpiece, unparalleled and irreplaceable.

DAILY REFLECTION

In what ways can you express your gratitude and honor the unique journey of your mother or maternal figure today, recognizing the profound influence her love and guidance has had on who you are?

PRAYER

Dear Lord, on this special day, we lift our hearts in gratitude for the remarkable mothers and maternal figures who have shaped our lives with their unwavering love. May we honor their sacrifices and celebrate the divine strength that flows through them, reflecting Your grace in every tender gesture. Help us to express our love and appreciation, ensuring that they feel cherished and understood, just as they have always embraced us with open arms. Amen.

In the hustle of your first grocery run with the baby, remember that even in the ordinary, God's grace is plentiful. Just as He provides daily bread, trust that He will supply your every need, nurturing both you and your little one with love and joy. Cherish the small moments—they are holy.

Matthew 6:11 - "Give us this day our daily bread."

DEVOTIONAL

As you embark on your first grocery run with your little one in tow, the bustle of the store may feel overwhelming amid the excitement of new beginnings. In these moments of navigating aisles and selecting fresh produce, take a deep breath and remember that God's grace surrounds you, even in the ordinary. Matthew 6:11 whispers a reminder: "Give us this day our daily bread," inviting you to trust in His provision for both you and your child. Each item you pick up is a testament to the love and sustenance He pours into your life, nurturing your family in ways seen and unseen. Pause to cherish the small moments—those glimpses of wonder in your baby's eyes as they marvel at the colors and sights around them. This trip, though seemingly mundane, is laden with holy significance; it is woven into the fabric of your family's story. As you nurture your child, rejoice in the promise that God is right there, guiding you, supplying not just your physical needs but filling your heart with joy, too. Let this first grocery run be a celebration of love, grace, and the beautiful simplicity of motherhood.

DAILY REFLECTION

In this whirlwind of your first grocery run, how can you intentionally pause and recognize the sacred threads of grace interwoven between mundane tasks and precious moments with your baby?

PRAYER

Dear Lord, as I navigate this first grocery run with my precious little one, I feel the weight of both excitement and uncertainty. Remind me to breathe deeply in the midst of the hustle, trusting that Your grace weaves through each moment, nurturing us both. Help me to savor the simple joys—the wonder in my baby's eyes and the warmth of Your love surrounding us, knowing that every step we take is a testament to Your provision and grace. Amen.

Celebrate the miracle of growth as we witness the transformation of the vulnerable infant into a flourishing believer. Just as Christ nurtured His early disciples, may we recognize the hand of God in our own journeys, joyfully reflecting on how far we've come in faith.

Luke 2:52 - "And Jesus grew in wisdom and stature, and in favor with God and man."

DEVOTIONAL

As we gather in reflection today, let us pause to celebrate the miracle of growth—a journey we often overlook in the bustle of life. Just as an infant takes its first wobbly steps, so too do we embark on our own spiritual journey, nurtured by love and grace. Remember the moments when the vulnerability of faith seemed daunting, yet we, like Jesus, have grown in wisdom and stature. Can you feel the warmth of encouragement that surrounded you as you took those sacred steps toward becoming a flourishing believer? In Luke 2:52, we witness a profound truth: Christ, though divine, embraced the fullness of human growth in all aspects—mentally, physically, and spiritually. May we find joy in acknowledging how the hand of God has guided us, gently molding our hearts along the way. Reflect on your own transformation; every struggle, every victory is a testament to His unwavering presence in our lives, celebrating not just how far we've come, but how richly we are loved.

DAILY REFLECTION

As you celebrate the growth you've experienced in your faith journey, what specific moments can you recall where you felt God's unwavering presence igniting your transformation from vulnerability to strength?

PRAYER

Dear Lord, as we pause to celebrate the miracle of growth, we thank You for the incredible journey of faith that mirrors the life of a tender infant blossoming into a vibrant believer. Help us to recognize Your loving hand in our lives, guiding us through each struggle and victory, reminding us of the warmth of Your encouragement. May we continue to walk with joy and gratitude, reflecting on how far we've come in our relationship with You, and embracing the transformation that comes from Your unfailing love. Amen.

In the moments of unexpected challenges, like a baby's first spit-up, God reminds us of the beauty in humility and grace. Just as we care for our little ones with love, trust that God's love embraces us, messy and all, guiding us through the trials of parenthood with unwavering support.

Colossians 3:12-14 - "Therefore, as God's chosen people, holy and dearly loved, clothe yourselves with compassion, kindness, humility, gentleness and patience. Bear with each other and forgive one another if any of you has a grievance against someone. Forgive as the Lord forgave you. And over all these virtues put on love, which binds them all together in perfect unity."

DEVOTIONAL

In the gentle chaos of new parenthood, few moments capture the blend of joy and mess like the first spit-up of your little one. As you stand there, a mixture of surprise and love washes over you, reminding you that this journey is beautifully imperfect. In Colossians 3:12-14, we are called to clothe ourselves with compassion, kindness, and humility—qualities essential not only for our interactions with others but also for our relationship with ourselves as parents. Just as you embrace your child with unwavering love, remembering that they will make mistakes and learn to grow, God embraces you in your parenting journey, messiness and all. Each spit-up is a moment to pause, to breathe, and to reflect on the grace that covers us like a warm blanket. Allow this challenge to cultivate patience and forgiveness within you, not only for your child but also for your own evolving self. In moments of uncertainty, rest in the assurance that God's love binds all of these virtues together, supporting you with the gentle strength you need to navigate the wild and beautiful adventure of parenthood.

DAILY REFLECTION

In the midst of your baby's unexpected messes, how can you intentionally embrace the grace that God offers, allowing it to transform your moments of frustration into opportunities for deeper connection and joy?

PRAYER

Dear Lord, in this tender moment of motherhood, as I embrace the unexpected spills and messes, remind me of Your unwavering grace that envelops both my little one and myself. Help me to find beauty in these chaotic times, to nurture patience and kindness within my heart, and to remember that even in the messiness, Your love guides us through this beautiful, imperfect journey. Amen.

As the dawn breaks and a new day begins, may we stretch our hearts toward God, welcoming His light and love. In this quiet moment of awakening, let us surrender our worries and embrace the grace He offers, trusting that each breath is a gift from above.

Psalm 5:3 - "In the morning, Lord, you hear my voice; in the morning I lay my requests before you and wait expectantly."

DEVOTIONAL

As dawn breaks and a new day stretches before us, there is a sacred invitation in that first gentle yawn. In the stillness of the morning, as we slowly emerge from the comforts of sleep, we are handed a beautiful opportunity to reach out toward God. Just like a baby stretching, we too can extend our hearts, opening ourselves to the warmth of His light and the embrace of His love. In this quiet moment, let us surrender the burdens that cling to us from yesterday; our worries, our fears, and our unanswered questions, laying them at His feet. Psalm 5:3 reminds us that the Lord is eager to hear our voice each morning; He awaits our sighs and our hopes with an abundant heart. As we breathe deeply, may we trust that every inhale is not just a breath, but a gift filled with His grace. Let us embrace this day with expectant joy, knowing that in every moment, we are cradled in His loving presence.

DAILY REFLECTION

As the morning light floods your space, what worries from yesterday are you ready to lay down at God's feet, allowing His love to fill that empty space with peace and hope?

PRAYER

Dear Lord, as the dawn unfolds and a new day embraces us, help us to stretch not just our bodies but our hearts towards You. May we release our burdens into Your gentle hands, believing in the beautiful grace that each moment holds. Let our souls inhale Your love and exhale our worries, welcoming this day with open arms and trusting Your presence to guide us through every breath.

Today, celebrate the gift of nourishment as God's perfect provision. Just as the Good Shepherd cares for His flock, may you find joy in each successful feeding, recognizing it as a moment of divine connection and blessing.

Psalm 23:1-2 - "The Lord is my shepherd; I shall not want. He makes me lie down in green pastures. He leads me beside still waters."

DEVOTIONAL

Today, as you witness the beautiful connection of nourishment between you and your little one, pause to recognize this sacred moment as a reflection of God's perfect provision. Just as a shepherd gently guides his flock, nurturing and sustaining them, so too does our Lord cradle you and your child with tender care. Each successful latch, each peaceful feeding session, is a reminder of His unwavering love—a gentle whisper affirming that in Him, you lack nothing. In these quiet moments, where time seems to stand still, you may find joy in the rhythm of your breath, the warmth of your child against you, and the knowledge that you are right where you need to be. Like the still waters that calm and refresh the soul, each feeding becomes a haven of grace, where both nourishment and love flow abundantly. Let this be a day to celebrate the gift of nourishment, recognizing that these instances are not just physical sustenance but divine connections—blessings woven into the fabric of your daily lives. Trust in the Good Shepherd, who delights in your journey and cherishes every moment shared in His care.

DAILY REFLECTION

In this sacred moment of nourishing your little one, how can you embrace the reality that each gentle latch not only feeds their body but also deepens your heart's connection to God's unwavering love and provision?

PRAYER

Dear Lord, in this tender moment of feeding, I give You thanks for the gift of nourishment that flows between me and my little one. May each successful latch be a reminder of Your perfect provision and unfailing love, filling my heart with joy as I recognize Your hand guiding us. Hold us close in this sacred connection, helping us to embrace these beautiful instances as blessings woven into our lives by Your grace. Amen.

In the midst of life's messiness and unexpected blowouts, remember that renewal is always within reach. Just as we change our clothes, God's grace allows us to shed our burdens and wear a new spirit. Trust in His promise of fresh beginnings and the joy that follows.

Isaiah 43:18-19 - "Forget the former things; do not dwell on the past. See, I am doing a new thing! Now it springs up; do you not perceive it? I am making a way in the wilderness and streams in the wasteland."

DEVOTIONAL

In the midst of life's messiness, those unexpected blowouts can feel overwhelming, can't they? Just like that moment when you realize new clothes are necessary after an accident, God invites us to exchange our burdens for the grace He freely offers. Isaiah 43:18-19 beckons us to let go of our past failures and disappointments, reminding us that His mercies are new every morning. Imagine the joy of stepping into life refreshed, with a heart unencumbered by what once was. When we trust in His promise, we uncover the beauty of renewal even in our wilderness moments. Every day is an opportunity to divest ourselves of past mistakes and don the empowering spirit He provides. Embrace the newness He brings—it's a beautiful journey toward joy amidst the chaos.

DAILY REFLECTION

In the midst of life's messy blowouts, how can you intentionally allow God's grace to refresh your spirit and help you step boldly into the new beginnings He has prepared for you?

PRAYER

Dear Lord, in the chaotic moments of life when the mess seems insurmountable, remind us that You offer a fresh start with each new dawn. Help us to release our burdens and embrace Your grace, trusting that with every change, there lies the promise of renewal and joy. May we find comfort in Your presence, knowing that even in the wilderness, You are crafting something beautiful within us. Amen.

As we celebrate the gift of life, let us take a moment to reflect on the joy and promise found in every new beginning. Just as a baby's cry signifies their arrival, let us remember that God has called us into a new season of hope and growth. Embrace the journey of nurturing faith as we welcome the light of Christ into our lives.

Revelation 21:5 - "And he who was seated on the throne said, 'Behold, I am making all things new.'"

DEVOTIONAL

As we gather to celebrate the miracle of life today, let us pause and listen closely. The first cry of a newborn is more than just sound; it is the profound declaration of hope and potential. Each infant's voice whispers promises of renewal and the beauty of divine beginnings. In Revelation 21:5, we hear the comforting words from the One seated on the throne, affirming that He is making all things new. Just as our hearts swell with the joy of a baby's arrival, God calls us into new seasons of our faith journey, urging us to embrace growth amid the unknown. Today, as we welcome this new life, let us also open our hearts to the light of Christ, eager to nurture the dreams and promises He places within us. Embrace this journey, for the future is vibrant with hope, and every new breath invites us to participate in God's beautiful unfolding story.

DAILY REFLECTION

In the quiet moments between a baby's first cries and the joys they bring, how might we better attune our hearts to recognize and embrace the new beginnings God is inviting us to nurture in our own lives?

PRAYER

Dear Lord, as we celebrate the sweet gift of life today, let our hearts be open to the wonder and promise that each new beginning brings. We thank You for the precious cries of newborns, a beautiful reminder that You are continually birthing hope and renewal within us. Help us to nurture our faith with the same tenderness we offer to this new life, embracing Your light and presence as we journey forward, trusting in the bright future You have planned for each of us. Amen.

Finding rest in God's presence mirrors the lull of a sleeping child. As you cradle your little one, remember Jesus' invitation to lay down your burdens and find peace in Him. Trust that in these quiet moments, His love nurtures both you and your baby.

Psalm 4:8 - "In peace I will lie down and sleep, for you alone, Lord, make me dwell in safety."

DEVOTIONAL

As you gently sway your little one in your arms, feel the weight of the day melt away, replaced by the sacred stillness of the moment. These tranquil seconds, where the world fades into a soft background hum, echo Jesus' invitation to find rest in Him. Just as your baby instinctively trusts in your embrace, allow yourself to lean into God's unwavering love, surrendering the anxieties that keep your heart restless. Psalm 4:8 reminds us that true safety and peace come from the Lord alone; let His presence blanket you both in tranquility. In this precious time, feel the warmth of His grace wrapping around your weary spirit, nurturing you as you nurture your child. As you hear their gentle breaths, let it be a sweet reminder that in God's care, every burden can be laid down, and every fear met with His perfect love. Trust in these moments, for His peace is not just for you, but for your precious one nestled so close.

DAILY REFLECTION

In the stillness of this moment, how can you surrender your worries to God and embrace the profound peace that envelops both you and your sleeping child?

PRAYER

Dear Lord, as I cradle my little one in my arms, help me to surrender the cares of this day into Your gentle hands. May the stillness of this moment remind me of Your unwavering love, wrapping us both in peace and comfort. Let me find rest in Your presence, trusting that in these sacred hours, my heart is renewed and my spirit refreshed by Your grace.

May 25

On this day of new beginnings, celebrate the precious milestones in our lives, just as the first signs of health and growth emerge. A fallen belly button stump signifies God's promise of life and renewal, reminding us to cherish each step in our spiritual journey. Trust in His timing and nurture the new growth within you.

Philippians 1:6 - "Being confident of this, that he who began a good work in you will carry it on to completion until the day of Christ Jesus."

DEVOTIONAL

On this day of new beginnings, we celebrate the tender milestones that mark our journeys, much like the moment when a baby's first belly button stump falls away. This simple yet profound event serves as a beautiful reminder of God's promise of life and renewal. Just as a child's first signs of health and growth fill our hearts with joy and hope, so too does our spiritual journey reveal the subtle yet powerful work of the Lord within us. Philippians 1:6 reassures us that He who began a good work in us will see it to completion, much like the nurturing care given to a new life. As you witness your own growth today, take a moment to reflect on the new beginnings around you—whether in relationships, faith, or personal endeavors. Trust in His divine timing, and nurture the budding growth within your heart. Embrace this season of renewal with gratitude, knowing that each small step is a cherished part of the beautiful tapestry He is weaving in your life.

DAILY REFLECTION

In this season of new beginnings, what cherished milestones are you being called to celebrate in your own life, and how can you embrace God's promise of renewal as you nurture the growth unfolding within you?

PRAYER

Dear Lord, as we witness the beauty of new beginnings, we thank You for the tender moments that become milestones in our lives. Just as a baby's belly button stump gently falls away, may we embrace the growth and renewal You bring forth within us. Help us to trust in Your perfect timing and nurture the fragile seeds of faith blossoming in our hearts, reminding us that every small step is part of the divine journey You have laid before us. Amen.

May 26

As you gently trim your baby's nails today, let it be a reminder of God's tender care in our lives. Just as you nurture your child's well-being, trust that God watches over us, shaping us with love and precision. Each small act reflects His attentive nature.

Psalm 139:14 - "I praise you because I am fearfully and wonderfully made; your works are wonderful, I know that full well."

DEVOTIONAL

As you take those first gentle snips to trim your baby's tiny nails, pause for a moment to reflect on the divine care that mirrors this intimate act. Each delicate stroke of the nail clippers can remind you that just as you tenderly nurture your child's well-being, God is shaping and tending to your life with precision and grace. In the quiet rhythm of this routine, consider how every small act of love reflects His attentive nature toward you and your family. The Psalmist beautifully declares, "I praise you because I am fearfully and wonderfully made; your works are wonderful, I know that full well." This truth resonates deeply, not just for your little one but for you as well, as a masterpiece of God's craftsmanship. Your baby's laughter, their tiny fingers, and even those little nails are woven with purpose, just as you are. Let this moment be a reminder that in each snip, you are participating in a divine narrative of care, wonder, and the art of growing together in faith.

DAILY REFLECTION

As you tenderly clip your baby's nails today, what does this small act of care reveal to you about God's profound and loving attention to the details of your own life?

PRAYER

Dear Lord, as I delicately tend to my baby's nails today, help me to feel Your gentle presence guiding my hands. May each small act of nurturing echo Your steadfast care in my life, reminding me that I, too, am fearfully and wonderfully made. Grant me the grace to embrace this precious journey of parenthood, knowing that in each moment I shape my child, You are shaping me as well. Amen.

As you cradle your little one, let your heart overflow with gratitude for the gift of new life. In this quiet moment, sing a lullaby of love and faith, trusting that God's peace surrounds your child. May each note be a prayer, guiding your baby into sweet slumber and deep blessings.

Psalm 127:3-5 - "Children are a heritage from the Lord, offspring a reward from him. Like arrows in the hands of a warrior are children born in one's youth. Blessed is the man whose quiver is full of them."

DEVOTIONAL

As you cradle your little one in your arms, a profound sense of gratitude washes over you, reminding you of the precious gift that new life represents. In this tender moment, as you lean in to whisper a lullaby, let every note resonate as an echo of your love and faith. Understand that this small being, nestled close to your heart, is not just a child but a blessing woven into your life by God's own hands. With each gentle lyric, trust in the embrace of God's peace, enveloping your baby in comfort and warmth, guiding them softly into slumber. Psalm 127:3-5 beautifully reminds us that children are a heritage from the Lord, a reminder that parenting is a sacred calling filled with divine purpose. Each lullaby you sing is a prayer, an intention that your child may grow in strength and wisdom, like arrows destined to leave a lasting mark in this world. Hold on to this special evening, knowing that your heart, your voice, and your love are reflections of a greater love that will accompany your child throughout their journey.

DAILY REFLECTION

In this sacred moment of singing your first lullaby, how can you invite God's presence into your heart, allowing His love to flow through every note as you nurture your precious child with gratitude and purpose?

PRAYER

Dear Lord, as I cradle this precious gift in my arms, I am overwhelmed with gratitude for the life that You have woven into our world. May each note of this lullaby be a soft prayer, wrapping my little one in Your peace and love. Help me to nurture their spirit, guiding them toward a future filled with strength and purpose, where they shine brightly as a reflection of Your light.

In the gentle light of Christ's love, we gather to share stories of hope and faith with the littlest ones. Each page turned together draws us closer to the heart of God, nurturing their spirits as we instill the joy of His Word. Let this moment inspire a lifelong journey of trust and wonder in His promises.

Psalm 119:105 - "Your word is a lamp to my feet and a light to my path."

DEVOTIONAL

In the tender moments of reading with our precious little ones, we find ourselves enveloped in the gentle glow of Christ's love. Each turn of the page is not just a story shared; it is a sacred journey into the heart of hope and faith. As we whisper the words of Scripture, let us remember the promise found in Psalm 119:105: "Your word is a lamp to my feet and a light to my path." This light illuminates not only the path ahead for us but also the pathway we lay down for our children, guiding them in wonder and trust. In these early days, as they nestle close, we nurture their spirits, instilling the beauty of His Word within them. May the stories we share inspire a lifelong curiosity about God's promises, igniting joy and comfort in their young hearts. Together, let us embrace these moments, knowing that we are crafting memories that will bloom into faith for years to come.

DAILY REFLECTION

As you cradle your little one and turn the pages of their first book, how does the tender practice of sharing stories of faith and love shape the foundation of trust and wonder in their hearts today?

PRAYER

Dear Lord, as we open the pages of each story, may Your love envelop us and every word resonate in the hearts of our little ones. Instill in them a sense of wonder and trust, nurturing their spirits with the beauty of Your Word. Help us to weave faith into these cherished moments, creating a tapestry of light that guides them throughout their lives. Amen.

Amid the waves of postpartum change, remember that your worth is rooted in God's unchanging love. Just as He clothes the lilies of the field, trust that He cares for you in every season, providing solace and renewal even through hair loss. Find strength in prayer, knowing your journey is held in His hands.

Luke 12:27-28: "Consider the lilies, how they grow: they neither toil nor spin; yet I tell you, even Solomon in all his glory was not arrayed like one of these. But if God so clothes the grass, which is alive in the field today and tomorrow is thrown into the oven, how much more will he clothe you, O you of little faith!"

DEVOTIONAL

In the tender landscape of motherhood, you may find yourself navigating waves of change that touch every part of your being, including your hair. As the locks that once flowed beautifully may begin to fall, it's easy to feel a flicker of insecurity and doubt. But take heart, dear one; your worth is not intertwined with your outward appearance. Picture the lilies, flourishing in their quiet elegance, completely reliant on the care of their Creator. Just as He adorns them with beauty beyond compare, so too does He promise to envelop you in love and grace. Allow yourself to lean into prayer during these moments of uncertainty, trusting that God holds every strand of your journey in His hands. Remember, in the eyes of the One who crafted you, you are eternally cherished—far more than the fleeting beauty of this world.

DAILY REFLECTION

In this season of new motherhood, how can you embrace the beauty of your journey, trusting that even as you navigate the uncertainties of postpartum change, God's unwavering love and care weave through every thread of your being?

PRAYER

Dear Lord, in this season of change, I come to You with a heart heavy and uncertain. Remind me that my beauty and worth are woven into Your love for me, far beyond what can be seen. As I navigate the whispers of insecurity, may I find comfort in Your presence, trusting that every strand of my journey is held tenderly in Your hands. Amen.

On this day, as the warmth of normalcy returns, find joy in the simple grace of God's presence in your life. Let each moment remind you of the freedom and renewal that His love brings, inviting you to walk confidently in His light. Embrace this new chapter, knowing He walks beside you always.

Philippians 4:4-7 - "Rejoice in the Lord always; again I will say, Rejoice. Let your reasonableness be known to everyone. The Lord is at hand; do not be anxious about anything, but in everything by prayer and supplication with thanksgiving let your requests be made known to God. And the peace of God, which surpasses all understanding, will guard your hearts and your minds in Christ Jesus."

DEVOTIONAL

As you step into the beauty of normalcy today, allow the gentle warmth of God's grace to envelop you. Just like slipping into familiar clothes brings a sense of comfort, so too does He offer you the profound assurance of His presence. In this moment, take a deep breath and find joy not only in your new chapter but in the very act of being alive, fully alive in His love. Remember that every little victory—whether it's a smile, a heartbeat, or a simple act of kindness—reflects the radiant light of Christ in you. Let the words of Philippians resonate in your heart: "Rejoice in the Lord always." With each request you bring before Him, you release your anxieties into His caring hands, allowing His peace to fill the crevices of your soul. Know that this peace surpasses all understanding, guarding your heart as you navigate the path ahead. Embrace the freedom that comes from walking with Him, for He walks beside you always, inviting you into a life rich with grace and joy.

DAILY REFLECTION

In this moment of renewed normalcy, what small joys is God inviting you to celebrate today that reflect His presence and love in your life?

PRAYER

Dear Lord, as I step into this new day wrapped in the embrace of normalcy, help me to feel the warmth of Your grace surrounding me. In each moment of joy and every small victory, may I recognize Your hand guiding my path and filling my heart with peace. Grant me the courage to walk confidently in Your light, knowing that You are always by my side, encouraging me to fully embrace the beauty of life renewed.

May 31

In the stillness of the night, when weariness weighs heavy, trust that God is present in your struggles. Each moment of quiet sacrifice nurtures not just your child, but also your spirit. Find strength in His faithfulness, knowing that your efforts echo His love.

Psalm 46:10 - "Be still, and know that I am God."

DEVOTIONAL

In the stillness of the night, when the world sleeps and your eyelids grow heavy, it may feel as if your efforts go unnoticed, your sacrifices unappreciated. Yet, in this sacred quiet, God invites you to pause and reconnect. He whispers to your weary heart with the promise found in Psalm 46:10, "Be still, and know that I am God." Each moment spent cradling your child, every gentle lullaby sung, is a testament of love that goes beyond the physical—it's a nurturing of the spirit that echoes His unwavering faithfulness. Your tiredness is not in vain; it is transformed into a beautiful tapestry of devotion. In your exhaustion, find solace in the knowledge that, even when you feel alone in the dark, His presence surrounds you, holding you close. Trust that through these midnight moments, you are not just caring for your little one but also allowing God's love to flow into your own heart, renewing your strength for the journey ahead.

DAILY REFLECTION

How can you embrace the stillness of this night to uncover the deeper ways God is nurturing both your spirit and your child's heart through your acts of love?

PRAYER

Dear Lord, in these quiet hours when fatigue wraps around me like a heavy blanket, help me to recognize Your presence in the stillness. Grant me the strength to embrace this sacred time, knowing that each moment of loving sacrifice nurtures both my child and my spirit. May Your gentle whispers of reassurance fill my heart, reminding me that even in my weariness, I am cradled in Your unending love.

On this sacred day of connection, remember that every touch is an expression of God's love. As you engage in your first skin-to-skin session, cherish the miracle of new life and the divine bond it creates, reflecting the intimacy of Christ's love for us.

1 John 4:16-17 - "So we have come to know and to believe the love that God has for us. God is love, and whoever abides in love abides in God, and God abides in them. By this is love perfected with us, so that we may have confidence for the day of judgment, because as he is, so also are we in this world."

DEVOTIONAL

On this sacred day of connection, as you embrace your newborn in the warmth of skin-to-skin contact, let each heartbeat resonate with the profound truth that God's love is tangible and real. In this intimate moment, you are not just a parent; you are a vessel of divine affection, echoing the gentle embrace of Christ, who wraps us in His unwavering care. Each touch transmits a love that surpasses understanding, reminding you that you are nurturing not just a body, but a precious soul chosen by God. Just as 1 John 4:16-17 assures us, as you abide in love, you invite God's presence into your home, strengthening the bond between you and your baby. Feel the miracle of life nestled against you, and recognize this experience as a sacred reflection of the intimate relationship God desires with each of us. With every breath and sigh, remember: you are held, and you are loved. Cherish this time, for it's a glimpse into the heart of heaven, where love is perfected in the tender moments that shape us.

DAILY REFLECTION

In this sacred moment of connection, how can you allow the warmth of your baby's presence to deepen your understanding of God's unwavering love and inspire you to embrace the tender relationships in your life?

PRAYER

Dear Lord, on this sacred day of connection, I thank You for the miraculous gift of new life nestled against my heart. As I hold my baby close, may each gentle touch whisper Your love, reminding us that we are both enveloped in Your divine embrace. Help me to nurture this precious soul with the same tenderness and joy that You extend to us, reflecting Your unwavering care in every heartbeat and sigh. Amen.

Just as a child finds comfort in a pacifier, so too do we find solace in God's presence during challenging times. Embrace this opportunity to nourish your soul with His peace, trusting that He will guide you through life's uncertainties.

Isaiah 26:3-4 - "You will keep in perfect peace those whose minds are steadfast, because they trust in you. Trust in the Lord forever, for the Lord, the Lord himself, is the Rock eternal."

DEVOTIONAL

As you introduce a pacifier to your little one, you witness a beautiful moment where a simple object brings immediate comfort and calm. Just as a child instinctively reaches for that soothing pacifier, we too are invited to seek solace in the tender embrace of God's presence during the stormy moments of life. Isaiah reminds us that when our minds are steadfast—anchored in trust—we can experience perfect peace, even in uncertainty. In the same way a pacifier can quell a child's worries, our faith becomes a source of nourishment, providing strength and serenity amidst life's chaos. Embrace this season to surrender your anxieties, knowing that you are cradled in the arms of
the eternal Rock. As you nurture your child's spirit, let this be a reminder to nurture your own, enveloped in the love and guidance of our Heavenly Father. Trust wholeheartedly, for in Him you will find the peace that surpasses all understanding—a peace that reassures you amidst life's unfolding journey.

DAILY REFLECTION

In moments when life's chaos threatens to overwhelm you, how might embracing God's presence as your comfort—just like your child finds solace in a pacifier—transform your worries into peace and strengthen your faith?

PRAYER

Dear Lord, as I introduce this simple pacifier to my little one, I am reminded of the comfort found in Your presence during life's storms. Help me to embrace this season with trust, surrendering my anxieties to You, so I may nurture both my child and my own spirit. May Your peace cradle us like a gentle whisper, guiding us through uncertainties and reassuring us with Your unwavering love. Amen.

In this season of new beginnings and fresh life, let the joy of small moments remind us of God's gracious gifts. As our little ones express their wonder through every sneeze, may we celebrate the miracle of creation and the beauty of growth in faith.

Ecclesiastes 3:1-2 - "To everything there is a season, and a time for every matter under heaven: a time to be born, and a time to die; a time to plant, and a time to pluck up what is planted."

DEVOTIONAL

In this season of new beginnings, we find ourselves immersed in the delightful chaos that comes with the joy of our little ones discovering the world around them. Each tiny sneeze—a gentle reminder of life's fragility and wonder—whispers of new beginnings, encapsulating the miracle of creation that unfolds with every breath. As we watch their innocent expressions shift from surprise to giggles, we are invited to pause and reflect on the gracious gifts God bestows upon us daily. Ecclesiastes 3 reminds us that there is a time for everything; today, let's revel in the sacred moments of growth and discovery. In the simplicity of these early experiences, we glimpse the profound beauty of God's handiwork, renewing our faith as we nurture these little souls. May our hearts be open to the lessons woven into the fabric of each new day, celebrating the little sneezes and the laughter that ensues, knowing that these fleeting moments are timeless gifts. Let us embrace this season with joy and gratitude, allowing it to draw us closer to the One who breathes life into our very being.

DAILY REFLECTION

In the delicate rhythm of our little ones' first sneezes, how can we cultivate a heart of gratitude that notices the divine fingerprints in the smallest moments of their growth and our own?

PRAYER

Dear Lord, in this beautiful season of new beginnings, we thank You for the gift of our little ones and the joyful chaos they bring. With each tiny sneeze and giggle, may we be reminded of Your loving creation and the sacred moments that nourish our faith. Help us to embrace the wonder in these simple experiences, allowing them to draw us closer to You and fill our hearts with gratitude for the incredible gift of life. Amen.

On this special day, as we celebrate the miracle of new life, let your heart be filled with wonder at God's creation. Just as a baby tracks movement with wide-eyed curiosity, may we too seek to follow the light of Christ, who guides our every step. Embrace the joy and innocence that new beginnings bring, reflecting His love in all you do.

1 Peter 2:2 - "Like newborn babies, crave pure spiritual milk, so that by it you may grow up in your salvation."

DEVOTIONAL

On this special day, as we cradle the miracle of new life before us, let your heart swell with wonder at the artistry of God's creation. Just as a baby tracks movement with wide-eyed curiosity, may we, too, gaze upon the world with a thirst for His presence, longing to follow the radiant light of Christ that illuminates our path. In this sacred moment, allow the joy and innocence of new beginnings to wash over you, reminding you of the simple yet profound love that surrounds all life. Just as a newborn craves pure spiritual milk, let your spirit hunger for the nourishment that only God can provide. Embrace the gentle whispers of His guidance, knowing that each moment is a precious gift. Reflect this love in all you do, nurturing not only your own growth but also the seeds of faith in those around you. Together, let us rejoice in the beauty of new beginnings, forever tracking the movement of God's grace in our lives.

DAILY REFLECTION

In what ways can you open your heart to the wonder of new beginnings, allowing the light of Christ to guide your steps and inspire you to nurture faith in yourself and others?

PRAYER

Dear God, on this beautiful day, we stand in awe of the miracle of new life cradled in our arms. May our hearts overflow with joy and wonder as we witness the precious innocence before us, drawing our eyes toward Your radiant light. Help us to cultivate a spirit of curiosity and love, nurturing not only our own faith but also the seeds of hope in those we encounter, as we walk together in the grace you so generously bestow. Amen.

Celebrate the beauty of new beginnings this Easter season, where the miracle of resurrection brings forth hope and renewal. Just as a baby's yawn captures the innocence of new life, let us embrace the joy of Christ's promise and the fresh start it offers us all.

2 Corinthians 4:16-18 - "Therefore we do not lose heart. Though outwardly we are wasting away, yet inwardly we are being renewed day by day. For our light and momentary troubles are achieving for us an eternal glory that far outweighs them all. So we fix our eyes not on what is seen, but on what is unseen, since what is seen is temporary, but what is unseen is eternal."

DEVOTIONAL

As we bask in the beauty of this Easter season, the gentle image of a baby yawning—caught forever in time—reminds us of the joy that accompanies new beginnings. Just as that tiny yawn signifies the delight of awakening to life, so too does the resurrection of Christ invite us to embrace the fresh starts laid before us. In 2 Corinthians 4:16-18, Paul encourages us to look beyond our struggles and acknowledge that through Christ, we are being renewed each day. These outward challenges may weigh us down, but they are mere shadows compared to the eternal glory awaiting us —a promise that outweighs every trial. Let us take a moment to reflect on the hope that springs forth from the empty tomb. Just as a baby's yawn is full of potential and innocence, God's love offers us rebirth and renewal, no matter the burdens we carry. This Easter, let's allow ourselves to celebrate each step towards renewal, trusting in the unseen beauty of the life Christ has prepared for us. Embrace the joy of new life today; for in every moment of renewal, we find a glimpse of His everlasting promise.

DAILY REFLECTION

How can you embrace the promise of renewal in your own life this Easter, allowing the gentle reminder of a baby's yawn to inspire you to let go of past burdens and awaken to the hope that Christ's resurrection offers?

PRAYER

Dear Lord, in the tender silence of this Easter morning, we pause to embrace the beauty of new beginnings. Just as a baby's yawn signifies the delight of awakening to fresh life, we thank You for the resurrection that refreshes our spirits and renews our hope. Help us to see past our struggles and celebrate the promise of rebirth, trusting that each moment brings us closer to the vibrant life You have prepared for us. Amen.

In a time of uncertainty, trust that God cares for your little one. Just as He cradles the sparrows, He watches over your baby, reminding you to lean on His peace amidst worry. Seek His wisdom and comfort in prayer, knowing He is in control.

Matthew 10:29-31 - "Are not two sparrows sold for a penny? Yet not one of them will fall to the ground outside your Father's care. And even the very hairs of your head are all numbered. So don't be afraid; you are worth more than many sparrows."

DEVOTIONAL

As a new parent, the weight of worry can feel overwhelming, especially when it comes to the health and well-being of your little one. In those quiet moments when your heart races at the thought of your baby's temperature, remember the gentle assurance that comes from Matthew 10:29-31. Just as God attentively cares for the sparrows, so too does He cradle your child in His loving arms. Each tiny heartbeat, every soft sigh, does not go unnoticed; He knows and cherishes every detail, even the very hairs on your head. When uncertainty looms, lean into His peace—allow it to wash over you like a warm embrace. In prayer, release your fears and invite His comfort into your heart, trusting that you are not alone in this journey. Breathe deeply, for you and your precious baby are held in the hands of an all-knowing and loving Father.

DAILY REFLECTION

In the midst of your worries for your baby's well-being, how can you intentionally take a moment to pause, breathe, and remind yourself of God's unwavering love and presence, just as He reassures us that not even a sparrow falls without His notice?

PRAYER

Dear Lord, in this moment of worry, I lay my fears at Your feet, trusting that You cradle my baby in Your loving hands. Remind me that just as You watch over the sparrows, You are intimately aware of every heartbeat and breath. Fill my heart with Your peace, and help me to lean on Your wisdom, knowing that I am never alone in this journey of parenthood. Amen.

On this day of reflection and family, let the love of God shine brightly in your home as you welcome a cherished grandparent. Celebrate the wisdom of generations past, and let their stories remind you of God's faithfulness through time. Rejoice together in the blessings of family and the strength found in His enduring love.

Deuteronomy 4:9 - "Only take care, and keep your soul diligently, lest you forget the things that your eyes have seen, and lest they depart from your heart all the days of your life. Make them known to your children and your children's children."

DEVOTIONAL

As we gather today, hearts warm with the love of family, let us pause to honor the special presence of a grandparent. In welcoming their wisdom into our homes, we are not just inviting stories of the past, but also the deeper truths of God's faithfulness that have traversed generations. Deuteronomy 4:9 reminds us to cherish and diligently keep these memories alive, for they are treasures that shape our identity and faith. As your cherished grandparent shares tales of their journey, listen closely; each story is a thread woven into the tapestry of your family's legacy, revealing God's hand throughout time. Let it be a day to rejoice, as the light of their experiences illuminates the path you walk together, strengthening the bonds of love and faith in your home. May the spirit of gratitude fill the air, echoing with the promise of God's enduring love, and may you pass these lessons down to your own children and beyond. Today, let us celebrate the gift of family, where God's story unfolds in every generation.

DAILY REFLECTION

As you share precious moments with your grandparent today, how can you open your heart to the wisdom of their experiences and allow their stories to enrich your understanding of God's faithfulness in your own life?

PRAYER

Dear Lord, as we gather in the warmth of family, we thank You for the gift of our beloved grandparent, whose wisdom and stories illuminate our lives. May their presence remind us of Your faithfulness woven through the fabric of our history, and grant us hearts that cherish these moments together. Let gratitude fill our homes today, as we honor the legacy of love and faith that binds us across generations. Amen.

On this day in the Christian calendar, reflect on the theme of unity and reconciliation, celebrating the love of Christ that binds us together as siblings in faith. Allow this time to deepen your commitment to nurturing relationships within the body of Christ, fostering peace and understanding among one another.

Romans 12:10-12 - "Be devoted to one another in love. Honor one another above yourselves. Never be lacking in zeal, but keep your spiritual fervor, serving the Lord. Be joyful in hope, patient in affliction, faithful in prayer."

DEVOTIONAL

On this day, as we gather in the spirit of unity and reconciliation, let us pause to embrace the profound truth that we are siblings in Christ—a picturesque tapestry woven together by His love. Romans 12:10-12 invites us into a deeper relationship, urging us to be devoted to one another, not just in our words but in the very fabric of our daily interactions. Reflect on those within your faith community: Are there divisions that need mending? Perhaps a misunderstanding that calls for grace and forgiveness? As we seek to honor one another above ourselves, let us cultivate a heart that embodies the joy and hope that comes from serving the Lord together, even in the midst of our trials. This is more than mere duty; it is the joyful dance of faith that invites us to be patient in affliction and steadfast in prayer. May this sacred moment reinforce your commitment to nurturing harmony and understanding among your brothers and sisters in Christ. In doing so, we not only strengthen our bonds but also reflect the very heart of Christ's love to the world around us.

DAILY REFLECTION

In this sacred moment of reflection, how might you extend Christ's love to heal any rifts within your community, inviting His grace to transform misunderstandings into opportunities for deeper unity?

PRAYER

Dear Lord, in this sacred moment of unity, we come before You with hearts that long for reconciliation and harmony among our brothers and sisters in Christ. Help us to recognize the beauty of our shared faith and the grace that calls us to mend our divisions, fostering understanding and love in our communities. May Your Spirit ignite within us a deep commitment to serve one another, bringing hope, joy, and the healing touch of Your love into every interaction. Amen.

June 9

On this day, as you cherish the moment when your baby's tiny fingers grasp yours for the first time, remember that God's love is like that gentle hold—infinitely strong and reassuring. Just as you guide your child, trust in the Lord to guide you, enveloping both you and your little one in His faithful embrace.

Psalm 139:16 - "Your eyes saw my unformed substance; in your book were written, every one of them, the days that were formed for me, when as yet there was none of them."

DEVOTIONAL

As you experience the profound joy of your baby's tiny fingers wrapping around yours for the very first time, take a moment to pause and reflect on the depth of this connection. In that fragile grasp, you feel an overwhelming sense of love and protection; it is a moment where two worlds collide—yours and your child's. Just as your hands provide comfort and security, remember that God's love envelops you both, infinitely strong and unfailing. Psalm 139:16 reminds us that even before your child was formed, God knew their journey and the days that lay ahead. There is a beautiful reassurance in this truth: you are not alone in this sacred venture of parenthood. Allow that gentle hold to remind you to trust in His guidance, knowing that He lovingly leads you and your little one on a path filled with grace. Embrace this season with an open heart, for in every grasp and giggle, you witness the tender hands of your Creator at work in your family.

DAILY REFLECTION

In this precious moment when your baby's tiny fingers entwine with yours, how can you surrender your anxieties and fully trust in God's unwavering guidance, knowing that He holds both you and your child in a loving embrace that far exceeds any earthly bond?

PRAYER

Dear Lord, in this precious moment when my baby's tiny fingers first wrap around mine, I am reminded of the depth of Your love that surrounds us. As I guide this little one through life, help me to trust in Your strength and wisdom, knowing that You have lovingly woven our journeys together. May each gentle grasp be a reminder of Your faithful embrace, filling our home with grace and joy. Amen.

June 10

On this day of quiet reflection, seek God's grace amidst the challenges of parenthood. Trust in His strength as you navigate the tender moments that can feel overwhelming, remembering that even in our accidental missteps, His love and guidance are always present.

James 1:5 - "If any of you lacks wisdom, let him ask of God, who gives to all liberally and without reproach, and it will be given to him."

DEVOTIONAL

On this day of quiet reflection, the stillness of the world around you is disrupted by the soft cries of your little one, causing your heart to swell with both love and concern. In the whirlwind of parenthood, it's easy to feel overwhelmed, especially when an accidental noise shatters the peace of naptime. Yet, even in these tender moments of chaos, God's grace gently surrounds you, reminding you that you are not alone. James 1:5 encourages us to reach out to our Heavenly Father when we lack wisdom, and parenting often feels like a journey into the unknown. Take a deep breath and remember that your struggles do not reflect your capabilities as a parent. Instead, they reveal your vulnerability, urging you to seek His guidance. Trust in the strength He promises, for it is in these moments of misstep that His love shines through the cracks of your perfection. As you cradle your baby, whisper a prayer for wisdom, and feel the warmth of His presence, knowing that in every challenge, His grace is sufficient, and His love never fails.

DAILY REFLECTION

In the gentle chaos of parenthood, how can you open your heart to embrace the lessons hidden in your accidental moments, trusting that God's love and wisdom will guide you through the uncertainties?

PRAYER

Dear Lord, in this moment of unexpected awakening, I come to You with a heart both weary and full. Grant me the wisdom to embrace the chaos of parenthood with grace, and remind me that even in the small missteps, Your love envelops us. Help me to find peace amidst the cries, and may Your strength uplift my spirit, guiding me through each tender moment with gentle hands. Amen.

Sorting baby clothes by size is a reminder of God's perfect timing in each season of life. Just as He knitted us together in the womb, may we find joy in the little things—preparing for the precious moments ahead with faith and hope.

Genesis 33:14 - "Please let my lord go on ahead of his servant, while I move along slowly at the pace of the droves before me and that of the children, until I come to my lord in Seir."

DEVOTIONAL

As you gently sort through the delicate fabric of baby clothes, each tiny garment represents a new chapter filled with hope and promise. Just as God intricately wove each of us in our mother's womb, you are now preparing for the joyous arrival of a new life—a beautiful reminder of His perfect timing in every season. In Genesis 33:14, we see the gracious heart of Jacob as he acknowledges the importance of pace, reflecting on his slower journey with care for the little ones. This moment of organizing isn't just a chore; it's an act of love, preparing for future memories yet to be made. Embrace the stillness, for in these quiet moments, God invites you to appreciate His providence and the preciousness of life. Each size and theme you sort speaks not just of clothing, but of the promise of laughter, learning, and the boundless love that will fill your home. Trust in His timing, and let this season of preparation fill your heart with faith and anticipation for what lies ahead.

DAILY REFLECTION

As you carefully sort through each tiny garment, how might this moment of preparation deepen your trust in God's perfect timing for the beautiful journey unfolding in your life?

PRAYER

Dear Lord, as I sort through these tiny garments, I thank You for the perfect timing woven into each stitch of this new life. Help me to embrace this season of preparation with a heart full of joy and gratitude, recognizing that every piece of clothing is a promise of love and laughter yet to come. May I find comfort in Your providence, trusting that You are guiding us gently toward the beautiful moments ahead. Amen.

On this night of peaceful rest, we reflect on the gift of stillness that comes from trusting in God's promises. Just as the Christ child brought hope into the world, may we find comfort in His presence, allowing this extended sleep to nourish our hearts and spirits for the journey ahead.

Hebrews 4:9-10: "There remains, then, a Sabbath-rest for the people of God; for anyone who enters God's rest also rests from their works, just as God did from his."

DEVOTIONAL

On this night of peaceful rest, as your little one settles into a longer slumber, we are reminded of the sacred gift of stillness that envelops us when we trust in God's promises. In the quiet of the night, when the world outside fades into a gentle hush, we have the chance to reflect on the profound hope brought into our lives by the Christ child. Just as He came to illuminate the darkness, His presence in our hearts holds the power to transform our worries into peace. Tonight, let the weight of the day's labors fall away as you embrace the rest that God offers. Hebrews 4:9-10 invites us into this divine stillness, assuring us that entering God's rest means surrendering our struggles—just as He did after creation. Allow this extended sleep to nourish not only your body but your weary soul, preparing you for the glorious journey ahead. May this moment of calmness deepen your faith, fostering trust that you are held and cherished in His embrace.

DAILY REFLECTION

In the tender stillness of this night, how can you lean deeper into the promise of God's rest, allowing the peace of His presence to wash over your heart and guide you forward with renewed hope?

PRAYER

Dear Lord, as the gentle rhythm of my baby's breath fills the night air, I pause to thank You for this precious gift of rest. In these moments of stillness, may I find comfort in Your promises, allowing Your peace to wrap around my heart like a warm blanket. Help me to release the worries of the day and embrace this time of renewal, trusting fully in Your love as I prepare for the journey ahead.

June 13

On this day, as the world witnesses a baby's first roll, remember the beauty of new beginnings in faith. Just as a child discovers the joy of movement, may we embrace our spiritual growth and the transformative power of God's love in our lives.

2 Corinthians 3:18 - "And we all, who with unveiled faces contemplate the Lord's glory, are being transformed into his image with ever-increasing glory, which comes from the Lord, who is the Spirit."

DEVOTIONAL

Today, we celebrate a precious milestone—the joy of a baby's first roll. In this simple act, we are reminded of the beauty of new beginnings and the excitement that comes with each small movement forward. Just as a baby, unaware of the world beyond their little bubble, discovers the freedom of rolling over, we too are invited to explore the breadth of God's transformative love. In 2 Corinthians 3:18, we are assured that as we behold the Lord's glory, we are being changed into His image. Reflect on your own journey; the moments you've stumbled and stood back up again are all part of God's grand design for your life. Just as a child learns through each roll, we learn and grow in faith, emerging anew each day, layer by layer, in His grace. Embrace today as a sacred invitation to lean into the Spirit, celebrating not just the precious moments of infancy in faith but the lifelong journey of transformation that lies ahead. Allow His love to guide your movements, leading you into a deeper relationship with Him.

DAILY REFLECTION

In what ways can you allow the Spirit to guide your own unfolding journey of faith, celebrating both the tumbles and triumphs that lead you closer to the heart of God?

PRAYER

Dear Lord, as we witness the delightful discovery of a baby's first roll, may we be reminded of the beauty in our own moments of growth and transformation. Help us to embrace the new beginnings in our faith, releasing our fears and stepping boldly into the movement of Your love. Guide us each day, Lord, as we learn to roll over from doubt to belief, from fear to courage, and may we reflect Your glory in every step we take on this sacred journey. Amen.

June 14

On this date, rejoice in the wonder of new beginnings and the pure joy of connection reflected in a baby's smile. Just as God delights in our joyful responses, may we also reflect His love and grace to those around us, sharing smiles of hope and kindness in our daily lives.

Psalm 100:1-3 - "Make a joyful noise to the Lord, all the earth! Serve the Lord with gladness! Come into his presence with singing! Know that the Lord, he is God! It is he who made us, and we are his; we are his people, and the sheep of his pasture."

DEVOTIONAL

As we bask in the warmth of this day, let us turn our hearts to the joyful simplicity encapsulated in a baby's first big smile. This tender expression, overflowing with purity and innocence, mirrors the delight our Heavenly Father takes in us. In Psalm 100, we are beckoned to make a joyful noise, not simply in sound, but in the way we live and love—drawing from the wellspring of God's grace. Just as a baby's smile can spark joy in the hearts of those around them, may we also be conduits of God's love, spreading kindness and hope through our own expressions of joy. Each day presents a new beginning, a fresh opportunity to serve the Lord with gladness and to come into His presence with a heart full of song. Imagine the ripple effect of our smiles—small gestures significant in their power to uplift. Today, let us be the joyful reflections of our Creator, sharing the beauty of connection and love with all we meet.

DAILY REFLECTION

How can you embody the pure joy of a baby's first smile today, allowing that innocent delight to inspire your interactions and reflect God's love to those around you?

PRAYER

Dear Lord, in the sweet simplicity of a baby's first smile, we see the purity of Your love and the joy You take in our lives. Help us to embrace each day as a new beginning, spreading smiles that reflect Your grace and kindness to those around us. May our joyful hearts uplift others, creating ripples of hope and connection in a world that longs for Your light.

June 15

God's promises are unwavering, guiding us through life's uncertainties. Just as He led the Israelites to the Promised Land, He invites us to trust Him fully, knowing His faithfulness will light our path.

Numbers 23:19 - "God is not a man, that He should lie, nor a son of man, that He should change His mind. Does He speak and then not act? Does He promise and not fulfill?"

DEVOTIONAL

In the wilderness of life, our hearts often bear the weight of uncertainty, much like the Israelites who wandered under the vast, daunting skies. Yet, amidst their trials, they learned a profound truth: God's promises are not mere words but the very foundation of hope. Numbers 23:19 reminds us that unlike human frailty, God's character is steadfast; He does not lie or shift in His intentions. As we grapple with doubts that seek to overshadow our faith, we must anchor ourselves in the assurance that His Word will never fail us. Imagine standing at the brink of your own Promised Land, feeling the tremors of fear beneath your feet. In those moments, remember that trusting in His promises illuminates our path, guiding us through the shadows of despair toward the dawn of His faithfulness. Today, surrender your worries and cling tightly to the unwavering truth that God will act on what He has spoken. Let that be your source of laughter and joy, for His plans for you are rooted in love and peace, far beyond what you can imagine.

DAILY REFLECTION

In the quiet moments of doubt, what fears are you holding onto that prevent you from fully embracing the joy and freedom found in trusting God's unwavering promises?

PRAYER

Dear Lord, in the wilderness of my uncertainties, I come before You, seeking shelter in Your promises. Help me to release my fears and embrace the laughter that stems from trusting in Your unwavering love. As I stand on the brink of my own Promised Land, may Your faithfulness illuminate my path, guiding my heart to peace and joy, even in life's most daunting moments. Amen.

June 16

Rest in the promise of God's provision; even in the quiet of night, He renews your strength. As you experience deeper sleep, may you awaken refreshed, ready to embrace each day as a gift, reflecting His grace and love in all you do.

Psalm 62:1-2 - "For God alone my soul waits in silence; from Him comes my salvation. He alone is my rock and my salvation, my fortress; I shall not be greatly shaken."

DEVOTIONAL

In the gentle embrace of night, as you lay your head to rest, remember that even in the stillness, the Lord is at work. Psalm 62 speaks to the heart of our weary souls, reminding us that true strength and renewal come from God alone. When life's demands feel overwhelming, trust that each quiet moment under His watchful eye is a promise of His provision. As you drift into peaceful slumber, envision His grace washing over you, revitalizing your spirit and fortifying your resolve. Awaken each morning not just refreshed in body, but renewed in spirit, equipped to share the love and grace you receive. His faithfulness is your fortress, steady amidst the storms of life, and when you rest in Him, you become a vessel of that grace to those around you. Embrace each day as a gift, holding close the assurance that, in every moment, God is your unwavering rock, guiding you to reflect His light in a world in need of hope.

DAILY REFLECTION

How can you intentionally invite God's peace into your nightly routine, trusting that each moment of rest you take is a renewal of His grace, empowering you to face the new day with a heart full of love and hope?

PRAYER

Dear Lord, as I surrender to the quiet of the night, help me to fully trust in Your promise of provision. May Your gentle presence renew my strength and fill me with hope, so that I awaken each day ready to reflect Your grace and love. In the stillness, I find comfort in knowing You are my fortress, guiding my heart as I embrace the gift of each new morning.

June 17

On this day, as a child first recognizes your face, reflect on God's abiding presence in our lives. Just as a baby finds comfort in a familiar visage, we are reminded of the joy and security found in recognizing Christ, our ultimate source of love and assurance.

Psalm 139:1-3 "O Lord, you have searched me and known me! You know when I sit down and when I rise up; you discern my thoughts from afar. You search out my path and my lying down and are acquainted with all my ways."

DEVOTIONAL

In the soft glow of a gentle morning light, a profound moment unfolds—a baby gazes up and suddenly recognizes your face for the first time. The sweet stirrings of joy and security in that little one's heart remind us of our own relationship with God. Just as the child finds solace in the familiar and loving visage before them, we too can find immense comfort in knowing that God sees us, knows us, and cares deeply for us. Psalm 139:1-3 beautifully echoes this truth: "O Lord, you have searched me and known me!" As we go about our days, let's pause to relish in the reality that the Creator of the universe is intimately acquainted with our thoughts, our movements, and every detail of our lives. In every moment of uncertainty, we can rest assured that we are seen and cherished by Him. Today, as you reflect on this divine recognition, let His abiding presence wash over you, offering love and assurance that surpasses every challenge we may face.

DAILY REFLECTION

How does the comforting recognition of God's presence in your life inspire you to embrace the love and assurance He offers, just as a child finds joy in the familiar gaze of a cherished face?

PRAYER

Dear Lord, in this tender moment of recognition, we are reminded of Your unwavering presence in our lives. Just as a baby finds peace in seeing a familiar face, may we find joy and comfort in knowing You, our ultimate source of love. Help us to embrace the truth that You intimately know us, holding us close through every joy and challenge, and let us rest in the assurance that we are forever cherished by You. Amen.

June 18

As you introduce your little one to tummy time, may you find joy in every challenge and growth in each small effort. Trust that just as God strengthens us through trials, your baby will thrive with every moment of perseverance. Celebrate the journey of discovery together!

1 Peter 5:10 - "And the God of all grace, who called you to his eternal glory in Christ, after you have suffered a little while, will himself restore you and make you strong, firm and steadfast."

DEVOTIONAL

As you lay your little one on their tummy for another session of discovery, take a moment to pause and reflect on the beauty and purpose of this simple yet profound practice. In these early days of little struggles, as your baby learns to lift their head and stretch their tiny limbs, consider how similar moments in our own lives reveal God's hand at work. Just as 1 Peter 5:10 reminds us that our trials lead to restoration and strength, each gentle nudge you give your child is a step toward resilience—both for them and for you. Every tiny cry and every earned smile is a testament to perseverance, a reminder that growth often comes wrapped in challenges. Celebrate these milestones, no matter how small, for they are the building blocks of your child's journey. Each day of tummy time is an invitation not just to strengthen their muscles, but also to deepen your bond and faith in the journey ahead. Embrace the joy and growth that come with each moment spent together, trusting that, just like your baby, you too will emerge stronger through your shared experiences.

DAILY REFLECTION

In the tender moments of tummy time, how can you draw strength from your baby's small victories to remind yourself of the greater journey of faith and resilience that God invites you to share?

PRAYER

Dear Lord, as I lay my precious child on their tummy, help me embrace the beauty found in each moment of struggle and discovery. Grant me the patience to celebrate these small steps, knowing that with every earned smile, we are both growing stronger in faith and love. May our shared journey of perseverance reveal Your nurturing hand at work, guiding us closer to one another and to You. Amen.

June 19

On this joyful occasion, like a first-time baby delighting in the warmth and freedom of bath time, we are reminded of the new beginnings and cleansing that God offers us in Christ. In each splash and giggle, we find echoes of His love, inviting us to rejoice in the renewal of our spirits.

Ephesians 4:22-24 - "You were taught, with regard to your former way of life, to put off your old self, which is being corrupted by its deceitful desires; to be made new in the attitude of your minds; and to put on the new self, created to be like God in true righteousness and holiness."

DEVOTIONAL

On this joyful occasion, as a first-time baby revels in the warm embrace of bath time, we are invited to experience a beautiful metaphor of renewal in Christ. Each gentle splash and cheerful giggle mirrors the delight of new beginnings that God offers us, reminding us that we are meant for joy and freedom. Just as a baby feels the soothing water enveloping them, we too can emerge from our past, shedding old ways and the weight of deceitful desires. Ephesians 4:22-24 speaks to the heart of this transformation, urging us to embrace our new selves, crafted to reflect God's righteousness and holiness. In these moments of playful innocence, we catch glimpses of God's love washing over us, inviting us to revel in the cleansing power of His grace. Let us hold onto this image of freedom and renewal, allowing the joy of our spiritual rebirth to fill our hearts as deeply as a baby's laughter fills a room. May each day be a fresh opportunity to rejoice in the new life we have in Christ, and may our spirits soar with His endless love.

DAILY REFLECTION

In what ways can you embrace the joy and freedom of your spiritual renewal, allowing the playful innocence of a baby's laughter to inspire you to let go of past burdens and fully experience the love and grace that God offers?

PRAYER

Dear Lord, in this moment of joy and play, we thank You for the beautiful gift of new beginnings and the cleansing embrace of Your love. Just as a baby delights in the warmth of bath time, may we revel in the renewal You provide, washing away our past and filling us with laughter and hope. Help us to embrace our new selves, reflecting Your holiness and joy in every splash and giggle, as we celebrate the freedom found in You. Amen.

June 20

On this special day of celebration, reflect on the joy of new beginnings and the innocence of faith, much like a child exploring the world. Just as they reach for toys with eager hands, may we reach for the gifts of grace and love God offers us daily, trusting His guidance in every step we take.

Matthew 18:3 - "And said, 'Truly I tell you, unless you change and become like little children, you will never enter the kingdom of heaven.'"

DEVOTIONAL

On this special day of celebration, we are invited to embrace the joy of new beginnings, much like a child experiencing the wonder of the world for the first time. As little ones reach for colorful toys, their eyes wide with curiosity and delight, we too are called to reach out with eager hearts for the gifts of grace that God offers us each day. In Matthew 18:3, Jesus reminds us that to enter the kingdom of heaven, we must approach life with the same innocence and trust as a child. Let us reflect on the simple beauty of faith, where daily doubts and worries fade away in the light of unwavering trust in our Creator. As you navigate your own journey, may you hold onto that childlike wonder, allowing it to inspire you to explore God's love, peace, and guidance. With each step, remember that it is through grace that we grow, just as children grow through every new experience. Today, take a moment to reach out—to God, to others, and to the extraordinary life He has planned for you.

DAILY REFLECTION

In what ways can you embrace the spirit of childlike wonder today, reaching out with open hands and an eager heart to receive the grace and love that God continually offers you?

PRAYER

Dear Lord, on this day of new beginnings, I thank You for the innocent curiosity that stirs within me, much like a child reaching for colorful toys. Help me to embrace each moment with open hands and a heart full of wonder, trusting in Your loving guidance as I navigate the beautiful tapestry of life You have woven for me. May I always look to You for grace and strength, reminding myself that like a child, my greatest treasures are found in Your endless love. Amen.

In the joyful innocence of a baby's first giggle, we glimpse the pure delight of God's creation. This week, let us celebrate the happiness that springs from simple moments, reminding us of the childlike faith we are called to nurture in our walk with Christ.

Luke 1:14 - "And you will have joy and gladness, and many will rejoice at his birth."

DEVOTIONAL

In the gentle sound of a baby's first giggle, we encounter a glimpse of heaven on earth—a sweet reminder of the pure joy that can be found in life's simplest moments. Reflecting on Luke 1:14, "And you will have joy and gladness, and many will rejoice at his birth," we can see how God has woven joy into the very fabric of creation. Just as that innocent laughter fills our hearts with warmth, so too does our Father's love overflow in the little miracles that surround us daily. This week, let's embrace and celebrate those fleeting moments that spark delight within us, nurturing the childlike faith we hold dear. Imagine the joy of a tender embrace, the brilliance of a sunset, or the laughter shared during playtime—each a reminder of God's abundant grace. As we watch little ones discover joy in their world, let us not forget to seek that same wonder in our own lives, for it is in these simple joys that we can reconnect with our Creator. May our hearts be open to the laughter, joy, and gladness that come from knowing Him, as we cultivate a faith that is as innocent and genuine as a baby's first giggle.

DAILY REFLECTION

In what small yet joyful moments this week can you find a reflection of God's love, and how can embracing these instances nurture the childlike faith within you?

PRAYER

Dear Lord, in the gentle echoes of a baby's first giggle, we catch a glimpse of Your joy woven into the fabric of life. Help us to embrace the simple moments that spark delight within our hearts, nurturing a faith as innocent and genuine as that precious laughter. May our eyes always be open to the beauty of Your creation, reminding us to rejoice amidst life's fleeting joys and to share that vibrant wonder with those around us. Amen.

In the tranquility of the park, feel the gentle whisper of God's creation, inviting you to reflect on His presence in nature. Just as this space offers rest for our souls, may your heart find peace in Him today.

Psalm 23:2-3 "He makes me lie down in green pastures. He leads me beside still waters. He restores my soul."

DEVOTIONAL

In the soothing embrace of the park, take a moment to pause and embrace the serenity that surrounds you. The gentle rustle of leaves, the soft chirping of birds, and the whispering breeze all beckon you closer to the heart of creation, where God's majesty is wonderfully displayed. As you take in the vibrant greens and the calming blues, hear His loving invitation: "Come, rest in My presence." Just as He leads us to green pastures and still waters, He longs to bring peace to the restless corners of your soul. Let the stillness of this sanctuary wash over you, reminding you that quiet moments are not merely for reflection but for restoration. In this refuge, God seeks to mend your weary spirit, rejuvenating your heart like the fresh breeze that stirs the leaves above. Lean into Him, trust in His guidance, and find true solace today, for in His presence, your soul finds its rightful home. Allow Him to refresh and renew you, cultivating a deep sense of tranquility that radiates within, even as you step back into the world.

DAILY REFLECTION

In the stillness of the park, how can you open your heart to the gentle whispers of God's creation, allowing His peace to fill the restless spaces within you?

PRAYER

Dear Lord, as I stand amidst the beauty of this park, I pause to feel the tender embrace of Your creation. In the rustling leaves and the soft whispers of the breeze, may I sense Your presence inviting me to rest and restore my weary soul. Guide my heart to be still, that I might find peace in Your love, and carry the tranquility of this moment with me into the world. Amen.

June 23

Celebrate the joyful connections that flourish in community, as Jesus welcomed children with open arms. May this playdate remind us of the innocence and beauty of faith shared among young hearts, reflecting God's love in every giggle and smile.

Mark 10:14-16 - But when Jesus saw it, he was indignant and said to them, "Let the children come to me; do not hinder them, for to such belongs the kingdom of God. Truly, I say to you, whoever does not receive the kingdom of God like a child shall not enter it." And he took them in his arms and blessed them, laying his hands on them.

DEVOTIONAL

In the laughter of children at their very first playdate, we catch a glimpse of God's kingdom unfolding before our eyes. Just as the disciples, in their eagerness to shield Jesus from the noise, attempted to push the children away, we too sometimes overlook the profound lessons hidden in their joyful innocence. Mark 10:14-16 reminds us how the heart of faith mirrors that of a child—pure, open, and ever-ready to embrace community and love. As your little ones giggle and chase one another, let this delightful interaction be a sacred reminder that in every shared smile, God's love is tangible and real. Each hug, each shared toy, each delightful squeal forms the threads of connection that weave us into a vibrant tapestry of community—a reflection of the heavenly family Jesus invites us to be a part of. May you celebrate the beauty in these connections, cherishing every moment as a blessing and a display of God's love flowing through tiny hands and little hearts. Remember, in their innocent trust and joy, we find an invitation to join them in welcoming the abundant grace of God's kingdom.

DAILY REFLECTION

In the joyful chaos of your child's playdate, how can you pause to embrace the simple, profound truth that every giggle and shared moment reflects God's love and invites you into the vibrant community He desires for us all?

PRAYER

Dear Lord, as we gather for this first playdate, may our hearts be open to the simple joys and profound lessons hiding within each giggle. Help us to embrace the beautiful connections that flourish in our community, reflecting Your love through the innocent laughter of our little ones. Let this moment serve as a reminder of the purity of faith, inviting us all to share in the grace of Your kingdom. Amen.

June 24

In the joyful simplicity of baby babble, may we learn to express our faith in pure trust, embracing the wonder of God's creation. As we celebrate this season, let our hearts resonate with the unfiltered joy of His love, trusting in His perfect plan.

Psalm 8:2 - "Out of the mouths of infants and nursing babies you have established strength because of your foes, to silence the enemy and the avenger."

DEVOTIONAL

In the tender simplicity of a baby's babble, we find a profound reflection of our faith. Each "goo" and "ga" is not just a sound, but a sweet reminder that our trust in God can be pure and unguarded, just as a baby's heart is free of the world's distractions. Psalm 8:2 beautifully captures this truth, revealing that even the faintest voices—those of infants—can carry strength and wisdom that silences doubt and fear. As we celebrate this sacred season, let us embrace the wonder of creation through innocent sounds, trusting in God's perfect plan even when we cannot see it. In the rhythm of baby babble, we are invited to express our unwavering faith, shedding pretense and hesitation. May our hearts resonate with laughter and joy, echoing the love God pours over us, filling us with hope and peace. Just as the simplest words can shake the heavens, let our lives, too, be marked by a faith that is both powerful and beautiful in its simplicity.

DAILY REFLECTION

How can you embrace the pure, joyful trust of a child in your daily walk of faith, allowing your heart to express its love for God without the noise of doubt or fear?

PRAYER

Dear Lord, in the gentle echoes of baby babble, may we find the courage to express our faith with childlike wonder. Help us to embrace the simplicity of trust, celebrating the joy of Your creation and the beauty of Your perfect plan. Let our hearts be filled with laughter and unfiltered love as we learn from the innocence of these sounds, trusting that even our smallest voices can shine with Your light. Amen.

June 25

On this 29th Sunday in Ordinary Time, reflect on the call to serve rather than be served. As Christ exemplified humility and selflessness, consider how you can embody His love in your daily interactions, becoming a source of hope and encouragement for others.

Mark 10:45 – "For even the Son of Man did not come to be served, but to serve, and to give his life as a ransom for many."

DEVOTIONAL

On this 29th Sunday in Ordinary Time, we are invited to pause and reflect on the profound truth that our Savior, the Son of Man, chose the path of service over privilege. In Mark 10:45, we see the heart of Christ's mission—not to be served, but to serve, even giving His life for us. Imagine the simple act of a child grasping a new toy, their eyes wide with wonder and joy; this is how we too should reach for opportunities to serve others, embracing our roles as bearers of His love. When we approach each day with the humility and selflessness exemplified by Christ, we not only transform our own hearts but also become beacons of hope for those around us. Reflect on your daily interactions; how can you embody this spirit of generosity? Perhaps it's through a kind word, an open ear, or an unexpected act of kindness. As we strive to serve rather than be served, let us remember that in humility lies the greatest strength, and in giving, we find true fulfillment. Each small gesture resonates far beyond us, illuminating the path for others to encounter Christ's love through our actions.

DAILY REFLECTION

In what small yet meaningful ways can you embody Christ's spirit of selfless service today, allowing your heart to open like a child's grasping a new toy, eager to share joy and love with those around you?

PRAYER

Dear Lord, in the sweetness of each small act of service, may we find the joy of giving as we reflect Your love to the world. Help us to grasp each opportunity with the same wonder as a child with a cherished toy, seeing them as moments to uplift others. As we navigate our days, instill in us the humility and selflessness of Christ, so that our lives may shine brightly as beacons of hope and encouragement for those around us. Amen.

June 26

On this day of reflection, consider the transformative power of faith in our lives, much like the hope brought by healing. As we celebrate new beginnings, let us open our hearts to the promises of renewal and courage found in Christ, trusting Him to guide us through uncertainty.

Ephesians 1:18-19: "I pray that the eyes of your heart may be enlightened, in order that you may know the hope to which he has called you, the riches of his glorious inheritance in his holy people, and his incomparably great power for us who believe."

DEVOTIONAL

Today, as we pause to reflect on the transformative power of faith, let us consider how much hope can arise from moments of uncertainty. Just as a vaccination symbolizes a step toward healing and renewal, our faith in Christ offers us a profound assurance of new beginnings. In Ephesians 1:18-19, we are reminded of the hope to which we are called, a hope imbued with the richness of His glorious inheritance. This promise invites us to trust in His incomparably great power, a power that infuses our lives with courage even in the face of the unknown. As we celebrate the grace that allows us to take these vital steps toward healing, let us keep our hearts open to the light that Christ brings into our lives. The journey may still hold challenges, but our faith can illuminate the path ahead, urging us onward and upwards. Today, let us lean into that divine guidance, allowing our hearts to be filled with hope, resilience, and the assurance that we are never alone. May each new beginning remind us of God's unyielding love and the extraordinary power that lies within us as we walk with Him each day.

DAILY REFLECTION

In what ways can you embrace the hope of renewal in your life today, allowing your faith in Christ to guide you through the uncertainties that lie ahead?

PRAYER

Dear Lord, as we stand at the threshold of new beginnings, we thank You for the hope that rises from uncertainty. Just as the first vaccination brings a promise of healing, may our faith in You imbue our hearts with courage to embrace each new day. Guide us through moments of doubt, and let Your light shine upon our paths, reminding us of the unbreakable bond of love we share with You. Amen.

On this day within the Christian calendar, let us reflect on the theme of redemption. Consider how God's grace transforms our past mistakes into a beautiful testimony of hope and renewal, reminding us that every day is another chance to live in His love and purpose.

Ephesians 1:7-8: "In him we have redemption through his blood, the forgiveness of sins, in accordance with the riches of God's grace that he lavished on us."

DEVOTIONAL

Today, as we pause to reflect on the profound theme of redemption, let us cradle our hearts in the truth of Ephesians 1:7-8. In this sacred space, we are reminded that God's grace is not merely a concept, but a deep, luxurious embrace that transforms every misstep and sorrow into a tapestry of hope. Each strand of our past—woven with regret and heartache—can be recast by the refuse of His love into a beautiful testimony of renewal. Just as the dawn breaks anew each morning, so too does His forgiveness invite us to rise, beloved, from the shadows of our mistakes. Picture the lavish richness of His grace, pouring over you like a gentle rain, softening the hardened places within and breathing life into your weary spirit. Today marks a chance to surrender to His loving purpose, to reclaim the narrative of our lives as one of joy and possibility. Embrace this moment, for you are not defined by your past, but transformed by the unfathomable depth of His redeeming love.

DAILY REFLECTION

How might you invite God's grace to reshape your story today, transforming your past experiences into a testimony of hope and renewal?

PRAYER

Dear Lord, in this sacred moment of reflection, I thank You for the gift of redemption that envelops my life. With every fragile thread of my past woven into Your masterful design, help me to embrace the hope and renewal You offer, surrendering my shame and stepping into the light of Your love. May Your grace rain down upon my heart, transforming my story into a beautiful testament of Your unfailing mercy. Amen.

As your little one experiences their first growth spurt, remember that just as God nurtures our growth in faith, He is also nurturing the miraculous development of your child. Trust in His timing and provision during this precious season of transformation.

Ephesians 3:20-21: "Now to him who is able to do immeasurably more than all we ask or imagine, according to his power that is at work within us, to him be glory in the church and in Christ Jesus throughout all generations, for ever and ever! Amen."

DEVOTIONAL

As you embrace this sweet season of your baby's first growth spurt, take a moment to marvel at the miracle unfolding before your eyes. Each tiny stretch and gasp for nourishment reminds us of how God meticulously designs every journey of growth—even in faith. Just as He nurtures our souls, providing us with all we need to flourish in His grace, He is nurturing your little one's body and spirit in profound ways. Ephesians 3:20-21 gently reminds us that God's ability to shape our lives and the life of your child is beyond what we can comprehend, igniting a trust that replaces our anxieties with hope. In these moments of tenderness, when you feel the rapid changes and the late-night feedings, remember that His divine timing is at work, orchestrating every step of this beautiful transformation. Lean into His provision and reflect on how both your faith and your child are blossoming together. May this journey fill your heart with awe and gratitude, celebrating the immeasurable love and growth God pours into your lives.

DAILY REFLECTION

As you witness your baby's rapid growth in these tender days, how can you more deeply trust in God's perfect timing, knowing that just like your child, your faith is also being lovingly nurtured through every season of change?

PRAYER

Dear Lord, in this beautiful season of my baby's first growth spurt, I stand in awe of the miracle of life unfolding before my eyes. As my little one reaches for nourishment, may I be reminded of how You nurture my own soul, guiding us both in Your divine timing. Help me to trust in Your provision, embracing this transformation with a heart full of gratitude, knowing that in every stretch and gasp,
You are cultivating love and growth within us. Amen.

June 29

On this blessed day in the Christian calendar, reflect on the precious gift of new life. Just as tiny garments symbolize growth and new beginnings, let us cherish the promise of God's love that nurtures us through every season of life. Celebrate the miracle of birth with gratitude and joy.

Isaiah 44:24-25: "I am the Lord, who has made all things, who alone stretched out the heavens, who spread out the earth by myself, who foils the signs of false prophets and makes fools of diviners, who overthrows the learning of the wise and turns it into nonsense."

DEVOTIONAL

On this blessed day in the Christian calendar, we pause to celebrate the miracle of new life, a precious gift that reminds us of God's abundant love. Just as we hold tiny garments that once adorned our little ones, we are reminded of the beauty of beginnings and the promise of growth. Each delicate stitch speaks of hope and potential, echoing God's own handiwork in creating the universe—how He stretches out the heavens and shapes the earth with purpose. Within these small clothes lies a profound truth: life is both fragile and magnificent, held within the embrace of our Creator's care. As we reflect on Isaiah 44:24-25, let us find comfort in knowing that the One who made all things also nurtures our deepest hopes and dreams. May our hearts overflow with gratitude as we witness the unfolding miracle of birth, embracing each new chapter with joy and wonder. Today, let us give thanks for the little lives entrusted to us, confident in the promise that God is ever-present in their journey.

DAILY REFLECTION

How can we more fully embrace the delicate beauty of new life, just as we cherish the tiny garments that symbolize growth, and reflect on how God's love nurtures our hopes and dreams in every season?

PRAYER

Dear Lord, as we cradle the tiny clothes that once adorned our little ones, we are reminded of Your infinite love and the miracle of new beginnings. May our hearts be filled with gratitude for each precious life, and may we always recognize the profound beauty in Your creation. Help us to nurture and cherish these gifts, trusting in Your divine purpose as we walk alongside them in their journey of growth. Amen.

June 30

Celebrate the joy of new beginnings this season, where the birth of Christ fills our hearts with wonder. Just as a baby delights in the stories shared with them, we too experience the miracle of God's love through His Word. Let every page turn lead us closer to His light.

Luke 2:10-11: "But the angel said to them, 'Do not be afraid. I bring you good news that will cause great joy for all the people. Today in the town of David a Savior has been born to you; he is the Messiah, the Lord.'"

DEVOTIONAL

As we gather in this season of wonder, let us embrace the joy of new beginnings, much like the first delighted giggles of a baby during storytime. The birth of Christ, heralded by angels and attended by shepherds, invites us to experience our own hearts igniting with joy. Just as a little one gets lost in the enchantment of tales spun with love, we too find ourselves spellbound by the narrative of God's unwavering love through His Word. Each turning page in Scripture reveals the miracle of His grace, illuminating our lives with hope and warmth. Imagine the shepherds, wide-eyed and trembling yet filled with exhilaration, as they heard the good news that echoed through the fields. "Do not be afraid," the angel reassured them—a timeless invitation for us all to step into the light rather than cling to our fears. This season, let go of hesitation and allow the profound truth of Christ's birth to envelop you, leading you ever closer to His divine embrace. Together, as we celebrate this wondrous gift, may we share the story of His love with childlike wonder and joy.

DAILY REFLECTION

In this season of wonder, how can you open your heart like a child experiencing the magic of storytime, allowing the birth of Christ to fill you with joy and draw you closer to His light?

PRAYER

Dear Lord, as we bask in the joy of new beginnings this season, help us to embrace the wonder of Your love that unfolds like a cherished story. May our hearts, like those of wide-eyed children, feel the thrill of Your miraculous presence, allowing Your light to guide us through each page of our lives. Teach us to share this divine narrative with joyous hearts, igniting the same delight in others that Your birth brings to us. Amen.

Halfway Through Our Journey

You are now halfway through this devotional journey.

Many women discover this book through the thoughtful reviews shared by readers like you.

If these pages have supported your faith and daily reflection, would you consider sharing a short review on Amazon?

Your voice may help someone else find encouragement today.

devo.anchoredgraces.com/newmoms

As you pick the first raspberries of the season, reflect on the sweetness of God's blessings in your life. Just as each berry bears the marks of growth and care, so too do our lives bear the fruits of faith cultivated through trust and obedience. Let each bite remind you of the joy found in God's provision.

Psalm 107:9 - "For he satisfies the thirsty and fills the hungry with good things."

DEVOTIONAL

As you bend down to pick the first raspberries of the season, let each plump berry remind you of the sweetness of God's abundant blessings in your life. Their vibrant red hue speaks of growth and care, mirroring the tender cultivation of your own faith through trust and obedience. Each time your hands brush against the delicate leaves, pause to reflect on how God nurtures your spirit, providing sustenance for your soul—a truth echoed in Psalm 107:9, "For he satisfies the thirsty and fills the hungry with good things." With every bite of the juicy fruit, savor the joy that comes from knowing you are richly provided for, both physically and spiritually. Just as these berries emerge after a season of waiting, remember that blessings often come after seasons of perseverance and longing. Allow the taste of each raspberry to wash over you, a reminder of God's faithfulness and the delicious fulfillment that comes from walking in His ways. As your heart rejoices in this fruitful season, may you be inspired to share these sweet blessings with others, multiplying the joy that you have found in His care.

DAILY REFLECTION

In what ways can you recognize and savor the sweet blessings God has placed in your life, much like the first raspberries of the season, as reminders of His care and faithfulness in your journey of faith?

PRAYER

Dear Lord, as I pluck these first raspberries, I am reminded of Your sweet blessings in my life. Each berry, vibrant and full, reflects the growth nurtured by Your love and grace. May my heart overflow with gratitude for Your provision, and may I share this joy with others, just as You have shared Your goodness with me. Amen.

As you celebrate the joyful milestone of a baby rolling from tummy to back, remember that growth takes time and patience. Just as a child explores new movements with trust and courage, so too are we called to trust God's plan for our own journey, allowing Him to guide us through each new turn.

Psalm 37:4-5 - "Delight yourself in the Lord, and He will give you the desires of your heart. Commit your way to the Lord; trust in Him, and He will act."

DEVOTIONAL

As you celebrate the joyful milestone of your little one rolling from tummy to back, take a moment to cherish the beauty of growth and transformation. Each tiny twist and turn is a testament to their emerging strength and trust in their ability to explore the world around them. Just like that baby, we too are on a journey filled with new movements and challenges, learning to embrace the unknown with courage. Psalm 37:4-5 reminds us, "Delight yourself in the Lord, and He will give you the desires of your heart." As you witness this precious moment, reflect on the desires God has placed within you and the plans He has for your life. Commit your path to Him, trusting that He is guiding you through every new turn, just as you guide your child through each adorable tumble. With patience and faith, embrace the journey of growth, knowing that just as your child learns to roll, you are also learning to navigate the beautiful complexity of life with God's unwavering support.

DAILY REFLECTION

In this beautiful moment of watching your child master the art of rolling from tummy to back, how can you lean into your own journey of growth, trusting that each twist and turn is divinely orchestrated and filled with purpose by God?

PRAYER

Dear Lord, in this precious moment of witnessing my little one grow and thrive, I thank You for the beauty of transformation and the gentle reminders of trust woven into our journey. As my child learns to embrace each new movement, may I too find courage in the unknown, trusting Your divine plan for my life. Guide us both in our steps, reminding us that with patience and faith, we can navigate the twists and turns ahead, hand in hand with Your unwavering love. Amen.

July 3

"Celebrating the nurturing spirit of parenthood, today's focus is on the miraculous act of feeding. Just as Christ nourishes our souls, may each bottle fed be a reminder of His provision and love. In this sacred moment, embrace the joy of bonding and the gift of sustenance."

Matthew 14:19-20 - "And he ordered the crowds to sit down on the grass, and taking the five loaves and the two fish he looked up to heaven and said a blessing. Then he broke the loaves and gave them to the disciples, and the disciples gave them to the crowds. And they all ate and were satisfied."

DEVOTIONAL

As you witness the tender bond formed during your first bottle feeding, take a moment to reflect on the sacredness of this nurturing act. Just as Christ took the five loaves and two fish, looked to heaven, and gave thanks, may each drop of milk nourish not only your child's body but also the deep connection between you both. In this simple yet profound ritual, God invites you to see His provision manifest in your life—a reminder that His love multiplies in ways we often cannot fathom. Feel the weight of responsibility transform into joy as you hold that bottle, knowing that you are playing a vital role in your child's journey. As you gaze into their eyes, filled with trust and wonder, cherish the moment as a divine conversation—a time when you offer not just sustenance, but also comfort and security. Each refusal and acceptance, each satisfied coo and sigh, speaks volumes of the bond you are nurturing under God's careful watch. Let this time be a celebration of life's miraculous cycles, where every meal shared reminds us of the Bread of Life, reflective of His endless love and provision.

DAILY REFLECTION

As you gaze into your child's eyes during this sacred feeding moment, how can you allow the profound love and nourishment you offer to deepen your understanding of God's unwavering provision in your own life?

PRAYER

Dear Lord, as I nurture my child during this first bottle feeding, let each drop of milk be a testament to Your unwavering love and provision. Help me to embrace this sacred moment of connection, transforming my heart's responsibility into joy, as I reflect on the miracle of life and the beautiful bond we are creating. May the warmth in our gaze remind me of Your nurturing spirit, and may this time together serve as a cherished reminder of Your endless grace in our lives. Amen.

July 4

Trusting someone else with your little ones can feel daunting, but remember that God is always watching over them. As you enjoy a well-deserved night out, rest in the assurance that both you and your child are cradled in His loving care.

Matthew 10:31 - "So don't be afraid; you are worth more than many sparrows."

DEVOTIONAL

As you prepare for a much-anticipated night out, a swirl of emotions might wash over you—excitement mixed with the heavy weight of uncertainty. Allow yourself to pause and breathe deeply, recognizing that entrusting your little ones to another's care can stir fears and questions. But in this moment, remember the gentle assurance of Matthew 10:31: "So don't be afraid; you are worth more than many sparrows." Just as God tenderly cares for the tiniest of His creations, He is diligently watching over your child, wrapping them in His protective embrace. Consider the bravery it takes to step away, even if just for a few hours; it's a testament to your love for both your child and your own well-being. This night is not only a gift of respite but a chance to reaffirm the beautiful rhythm of trust in God's plan. As you let go of your worries, picture your little one safely cradled in the hands of the One who knows them even better than you do. Savor the joy of the moment; take this time to recharge, while knowing you are all held steadfastly in His loving care.

DAILY REFLECTION

How might your trust in God's unceasing love and watchfulness allow you to release your worries and truly savor the joy of this well-deserved night away from home?

PRAYER

Dear Lord, as I prepare to step away for a night of much-needed rest, I feel the weight of my worries tugging at my heart. Help me to release my fears and trust in Your constant care, knowing that my little one is cradled in Your loving embrace. Remind me that in this moment of letting go, I am not just nurturing myself but also deepening my faith in Your unfailing presence. Amen.

July 5

Celebrate the gift of intimacy and connection on your first postpartum date night. This moment is a beautiful reminder of God's grace in your relationship, nurturing both love and laughter as you journey through parenthood together.

Ephesians 4:2-3- "Be completely humble and gentle; be patient, bearing with one another in love. Make every effort to keep the unity of the Spirit through the bond of peace."

DEVOTIONAL

As you prepare for your first postpartum date night, take a moment to reflect on the beautiful journey you have undertaken together. Ephesians 4:2-3 gently reminds us to embrace humility and gentleness, qualities that have surely deepened in you both after welcoming your little one. In this sacred space of connection, allow love and laughter to wash over you, serving as a balm for the fatigue and challenges that parenthood can bring. Tonight is not just a break from the routine; it's an opportunity to rekindle the spark that initially drew you together. Celebrate the gift of intimacy, knowing that laughter shared over dinner or a heartfelt conversation helps weave a stronger bond amidst the chaos. As you navigate this new chapter, may you find joy in the patience you extend to one another, nurturing a unity that reflects God's grace. Cherish each moment, for it is in these tender interactions that your love will flourish anew, resonating with the peace the Lord promises when we come together in harmony.

DAILY REFLECTION

How can embracing the humility and gentleness nurtured in your hearts through parenthood allow you to deepen your connection and celebrate the joy of intimacy in this special moment together?

PRAYER

Dear Lord, as we prepare for this precious evening together, we thank You for the gift of intimacy and connection, especially in this new chapter of our lives. Help us to embrace each moment with humility and laughter, allowing Your grace to strengthen our bond as we navigate the beauty and challenges of parenthood. May our hearts be filled with joy and our spirits renewed, as we cherish this sacred time together, reflecting Your love in our relationship. Amen.

July 6

God's strength carries you in every season, including this new chapter of motherhood. Trust in His renewal as you take those first steps back into movement, knowing He's with you in each effort and every breath.

Isaiah 43:2 - "When you pass through the waters, I will be with you; and through the rivers, they shall not overflow you."

DEVOTIONAL

As you step into this new chapter of motherhood, remember that each breath you take is a testament to the strength God has woven into the very fabric of your being. In Isaiah 43:2, we are reminded that even when the waters rise, He is right there with us, ensuring we will not be overwhelmed. Your first exercise session is more than a physical act; it's a beautiful declaration of trust in His renewing power. Allow yourself to cherish those small steps, recognizing that with every movement, you are not just reclaiming your body but embracing the journey God has laid out before you. This season may feel daunting, and the path may be uncertain, but His presence is a gentle reminder that you are never alone. Feel the weight of His love surrounding you, lifting you, encouraging you to push through the doubts and embrace the strength He's promised. As you move forward, trust that His grace will carry you through every hurdle, making you stronger not just for yourself, but for your little one who will admire the courage you embody.

DAILY REFLECTION

In this sacred journey of motherhood, how can you open your heart to experience God's renewing strength in the small, tender moments of each step you take toward reclaiming your body and spirit?

PRAYER

Dear Lord, as I take these first tentative steps into motherhood and movement, I pause to acknowledge Your unwavering strength that carries me through each challenge. Wrap me in Your love, reminding me that every breath I take is a reflection of Your grace and renewal. Help me to trust in Your presence, knowing that even in moments of doubt, You equip me for this beautiful journey, guiding my heart and body as I embrace the courage to step forward. Amen.

July 7

As a child takes their first steps, trust in God's guiding hand grows stronger. Celebrate this milestone as a reflection of His unwavering presence, leading us confidently on the journey of faith. Remember, every step in faith brings us closer to His purpose.

Psalm 37:23-24 - "The steps of a man are established by the Lord, when he delights in his way; though he fall, he shall not be cast headlong, for the Lord upholds his hand."

DEVOTIONAL

In the tender moment when your baby finds their feet, a world of possibilities unfolds, mirroring the spiritual journey we each embark upon. Just as you watch with a heart overflowing with pride and joy as they take their first wobbly steps, so too does our Heavenly Father delight in our strides of faith. Psalm 37:23-24 reminds us that every step we take is lovingly ordained by the Lord, who holds our hand even when we stumble. Celebrate this precious milestone, for it symbolizes not only physical growth but also the deepening trust in God's guiding presence. Every falter becomes an opportunity for His grace, teaching us that falling is not failure; rather, it is part of the adventure. As you cheer on your little one, remember that God stands poised to uplift us at every turn, encouraging us to delight in the journey of faith. Today, as they explore the world on tiny feet, let us also embrace each step we take, knowing that with God's unwavering support, we are confidently moving closer to His divine purpose.

DAILY REFLECTION

As you marvel at your baby's first steps, how can you more fully trust in God's guiding hand to support your own journey of faith, embracing each stumble as a testament to His unwavering love and grace?

PRAYER

Dear Lord, as my little one discovers the strength in their tiny feet, I am reminded of Your guiding hand in my own journey of faith. With each wobbly step they take, may I also embrace the courage to trust in Your promises, knowing that even in moments of uncertainty, You are there to lift us up. Help us to celebrate the beauty of growth and the grace found in each stumble, for in every step we take together, we draw closer to the purpose You have lovingly set before us. Amen.

July 8

Jesus, the Light of the World, brings hope and joy even in the darkest moments. This season, let His radiant love illuminate our paths and inspire us to share that light with others. May we reflect His grace in every step we take.

John 8:12 - Again Jesus spoke to them, saying, "I am the light of the world. Whoever follows me will not walk in darkness, but will have the light of life."

DEVOTIONAL

In the stillness of the night, like the first high-pitched squeal of a baby breaking the silence, Jesus, the Light of the World, bursts forth with a promise of hope and joy. In our darkest moments, when shadows loom large and the weight of despair feels heavy, He shines brightly, illuminating our paths with His radiant love. John 8:12 reminds us that following Him means we embrace the light of life, stepping away from the shadows of fear and loneliness. How comforting it is to know that even in the deepest valleys, His light can spark joy and stir hope within us. This season, may we be vessels of His grace, allowing His brilliance to reflect in our lives as we care for others, sharing that same light that chases away darkness. As the days grow shorter and nights seem longer, let us not forget the joyful squeals of life—each one a reminder of His presence. In every giggle, every smile, may we witness the beauty of His love and carry it forth, lighting the way for those who are still searching for hope.

DAILY REFLECTION

In what ways can you embrace the radiant love of Jesus this season and allow His light to transform your darkest moments into opportunities for hope and joy?

PRAYER

Dear Lord, in this season of darkness and longing, may Your radiant love pierce through our shadows, reminding us that even the smallest voices of joy herald Your presence. Help us to be lanterns of Your grace, reflecting the light of hope to those around us, capturing the joyful squeals of life as reminders of Your unfailing love. Fill our hearts with Your warmth, that we may illuminate the paths of others, leading them toward the joy and peace found in You. Amen.

July 9

Experience the wonder of creation as your baby responds to music, echoing the joy of Psalm 150:6—"Let everything that has breath praise the Lord." This precious moment reflects the beauty of God's artistry, inviting you to celebrate the gift of life and the rhythms of His love.

Psalm 150:6 - "Let everything that has breath praise the Lord."

DEVOTIONAL

In the soft glow of the room, as gentle melodies fill the air, you observe a breathtaking moment—the joyful response of your baby to the music. Their tiny face lights up, eyes dancing with wonder, reflecting the truth of Psalm 150:6: "Let everything that has breath praise the Lord." In this simple yet profound experience, you witness a reminder of God's handiwork, how even the smallest among us can express the innate rhythm of creation. With each coo and gurgle, your baby resonates with the symphony of life, a testament to the beauty that flows from God's heart. This is not just a moment; it is a call to worship, inviting you to join in the chorus of creation, where every breath, every heartbeat, is a song of praise. Embrace this precious gift, for in it lies the essence of His love, a reminder that even the tiniest beings carry the capacity to glorify their Creator. Today, let your heart swell with gratitude for the wondrous artistry of life, inviting you to celebrate both the music and the miracle of this new life you hold in your arms.

DAILY REFLECTION

In this moment of musical wonder, how can you treasure and nurture the joyful essence of praise within your baby, recognizing that their innocent responses are a beautiful echo of God's love and creativity?

PRAYER

Dear Lord, in this sacred moment, I thank You for the sweet gift of music and the joy it brings to my baby's heart. As their eyes light up and tiny sounds dance through the air, may we both resonate with the beauty of Your creation, celebrating each breath as a hymn of praise. Help me to cherish these fleeting moments and to recognize Your artistry in every joyful response, guiding us to worship You with the innocence and wonder that only a child possesses. Amen.

July 10

Recognizing the simple joys in life, just as a baby's first toy brings delight, reminds us of the pure joy in faith. Like that cherished toy, let us treasure our relationship with Christ, discovering the wonder in His presence every day.

Psalm 104:13-14 - "He waters the mountains from His upper chambers; the earth is satisfied by the fruit of His works. He makes grass grow for the cattle, and plants for people to cultivate—bringing forth food from the earth."

DEVOTIONAL

In the simple delight of a baby discovering their first toy, we find a beautiful echo of our faith's purest joys. Just as that cherished object brings laughter and wonder, so too does our relationship with Christ fill our days with delight. Psalm 104:13-14 reminds us of His nurturing hand —He waters the mountains and provides for all creation, revealing His constant presence in the world around us. Each time we witness a blade of grass swaying gently or a flower blooming, let it remind us of His love and care. In the rush of life, may we take a moment to embrace the small wonders—the laughter of loved ones, the warmth of sunshine, the comfort of stillness. As we treasure these simple joys, let us deepen our relationship with Christ, finding solace and satisfaction in His presence. Just as that beloved toy sparks joy in a child's heart, may we seek out the everyday moments that bring us closer to Him, cultivating gratitude for His abundant grace.

DAILY REFLECTION

What simple joys have you encountered today that remind you of Christ's presence in your life, and how can you embrace them with the same wonder a child shows for their first beloved toy?

PRAYER

Dear Lord, In the tranquil moments of life, help us to recognize the simple joys that echo the pure delight of a child's first toy. May we embrace the laughter, the gentle breezes, and the warmth of your presence, reminding us of your unwavering love and care. As we seek to treasure our relationship with You, ignite in our hearts a childlike wonder, allowing us to celebrate the everyday miracles that draw us closer to You. Amen.

As you step into today, reflect on the wonder of creation around you, recognizing each moment as a gift from God. Let His presence guide your thoughts and fill your heart with gratitude during your walk. Trust in His path, knowing He is with you every step of the way.

Psalm 19:1-4 - "The heavens declare the glory of God; the skies proclaim the work of his hands. Day after day they pour forth speech; night after night they reveal knowledge. They have no speech, they use no words; no sound is heard from them. Yet their voice goes out into all the earth, their words to the ends of the world."

DEVOTIONAL

As you embark on your first long stroller walk today, take a moment to pause and breathe in the beauty that surrounds you. Each rustle of leaves, each chirp of a bird, and the gentle caress of a breeze are echoes of God's artistry in creation. In Psalm 19:1-4, we are reminded that the heavens themselves speak of His glory, whispering truth to our hearts even without words. Allow this divine orchestra to lift your spirit, guiding your thoughts to gratitude for the simple yet profound gift of life. Trust that God walks alongside you, illuminating your path with His wisdom and love. Each step can be a prayer, each breath a reminder of His presence, shaping your journey today. Embrace the wonder of creation, knowing that with every moment, you are cradled in the arms of your Creator.

DAILY REFLECTION

As you stroll through the embrace of nature's beauty today, in what ways can you attune your heart to the whispers of gratitude for the divine presence that walks with you?

PRAYER

Dear Lord, as I take this first long stroller walk, help me to pause and truly absorb the beauty of Your creation that surrounds me. May each leaf's rustle and each bird's song draw me closer to You, filling my heart with gratitude for the simple joys of life. Guide my steps and illuminate my path with Your love, reminding me that in every moment, I am held in the gentle embrace of Your presence. Amen.

On this special outing, may you find joy in the simple moments, trusting that God's presence blesses your new experiences. As you nourish your body, remember to cherish each smile and giggle, reflecting the love and grace He bestows upon your family.

Philippians 4:4-5 - "Rejoice in the Lord always. I will say it again: Rejoice! Let your gentleness be evident to all. The Lord is near."

DEVOTIONAL

As you embark on this precious outing to a restaurant with your little one, pause to soak in the beauty of the moment. Surrounded by the hustle and bustle of life, each smile from your baby is a reminder of the gentle presence of God. Philippians 4:4-5 encourages us to rejoice always, and today, as joyful laughter fills the air, let that joy radiate through you. Remember, in these early days of parenting, it is the simple moments—like watching your child experience the world for the first time—that carry profound blessings. With every bite you take, reflect on the nourishment not just for your body, but for your soul, as you create cherished memories. Trust that God's grace surrounds your family during this delightful outing, bringing with it a sense of peace and love. Embrace the giggles, for they are the music of joy, testifying to the wonderful gift of life and the ever-present love of our Lord. Rejoice in these moments, knowing that He is near, guiding you through every new experience together.

DAILY REFLECTION

As you watch your baby marvel at the world around them during this joyful outing, what simple moment today reminds you of God's unwavering love and grace in your life's journey?

PRAYER

Dear Lord, on this special outing with our little one, we thank You for the gift of family and the joy found in simple moments. May Your presence fill this space as we savor both our meals and the laughter that echoes around us, reminding us of Your endless love. Help us to cherish each smile and discovery, trusting that in every experience, Your grace is at work, nurturing our hearts and guiding our journey together. Amen.

As you celebrate this season of new beginnings, may the joy of your baby's first holiday fill your heart with gratitude. Reflect on the gift of life and love that God has bestowed upon your family, reminding you of the promise of hope and the warmth of His presence during this special time.

John 3:16 - For God so loved the world that He gave His one and only Son, that whoever believes in Him shall not perish but have eternal life.

DEVOTIONAL

As you hold your precious baby close this holiday season, take a moment to inhale the sweet scent of new beginnings and the joy of family gathered around you. This first holiday together is not just a celebration; it's a poignant reminder of the incredible gift of life bestowed upon us by our loving Creator. In John 3:16, we are assured of God's profound love—a love so deep that He gave His one and only Son for us. As you reflect upon this, consider the depth of love you feel for your little one, a mere glimpse of the unconditional love that flows from God to His children. Cherish the laughter, the tiny smiles, and even the quiet moments of wonder as you witness the world anew through your baby's eyes. Each twinkling light, each song, each gentle hug becomes a celebration of the hope and joy that Christ brings into our lives. May this first holiday be filled with gratitude, a heart overflowing with love, and the warm embrace of His presence guiding your family into the future He has lovingly prepared for you.

DAILY REFLECTION

In this season of new beginnings, how does the miracle of your baby's first holiday deepen your understanding of God's immeasurable love for you and your family?

PRAYER

Dear God, as we gather to celebrate the miracle of our baby's first holiday, may our hearts overflow with gratitude for the gift of life and the love that binds us as a family. Allow us to see the world anew through our little one's eyes and to cherish the moments—big and small—that remind us of Your unwavering presence and the promise of hope You have given us. Fill our home with laughter, warmth, and the joy that only comes from knowing You, guiding us as we step into this beautiful season of new beginnings. Amen.

On this precious day, celebrate the moment a baby recognizes their name—a reflection of God's intimate call to each of us. Just as He knows us by name, let us rejoice in the promise that we are beloved and seen by our Creator.

John 10:3-4 - "The sheep hear his voice, and he calls his own sheep by name and leads them out. When he has brought out all his own, he goes before them, and the sheep follow him, for they know his voice."

DEVOTIONAL

Today marks a milestone, a moment when your baby's eyes light up with recognition at the sound of their name. With this small but profound event, we catch a glimpse of God's unwavering attention to us. Just as your baby eagerly responds, it is a reminder that our Creator calls each of us by name, inviting us into a relationship that is deeply personal and profoundly loving. In John 10:3-4, we read, "The sheep hear his voice, and he calls his own sheep by name." Can you feel the warmth of that promise? In a world that often feels vast and impersonal, God knows your name, your story, and your heart's longing. In this moment, rejoice not just for your little one, but for the truth that you, too, are cherished and seen. Allow this recognition to deepen your faith and ignite in your heart a desire to listen for His voice, leading you gently through each day ahead.

DAILY REFLECTION

In what ways can you attune your heart to recognize and respond to the tender call of God, just as your baby joyfully responds to their name, embracing the truth that you are known and lovingly cherished by your Creator?

PRAYER

Dear Lord, on this beautiful day, we celebrate the joy of our little one's first recognition of their name—a reminder of Your intimate and personal love for each of us. May this moment inspire us to embrace the profound truth that we are known and cherished by You, longing to hear Your voice in our lives. Help us to treasure these precious milestones and nurture our relationship with You, trusting in Your gentle guidance every step of the way. Amen.

July 15

Today, reflect on the unwavering faith that guides us through uncertainty. Trust that every challenge is an opportunity for spiritual growth, reminding us that God's plan always unfolds in perfect timing. Surrender your worries and embrace His peace.

2 Corinthians 5:7 - "For we walk by faith, not by sight."

DEVOTIONAL

As we gather today, let us turn our hearts toward the lessons of faith that illuminate our uncertain paths. In moments of doubt and fear, remember that faith is not merely believing in what we can see, but trusting in the divine guidance that often remains hidden. Reflect on 2 Corinthians 5:7, "For we walk by faith, not by sight." It serves as a gentle reminder that God's plans intertwine our struggles and triumphs, creating a tapestry of grace and growth. Each challenge we face is not a stumbling block, but a stepping stone toward spiritual maturity, a chance to lean deeper into His embrace. So, take a moment to surrender those burdens you carry. Let His peace wash over you, reassuring your heart that in every uncertainty, He is steadfast, orchestrating His perfect will. Trust in the journey, for your faith will lead you closer to the heart of God.

DAILY REFLECTION

In this moment of uncertainty, what burdens can you surrender to God, trusting that His unseen hand is shaping your journey toward a greater purpose?

PRAYER

Dear Lord, in the midst of life's uncertainties, I bring my heart before You, longing to feel Your guiding hand upon my journey. Help me to surrender my worries and embrace the peace that only You can provide, knowing that each challenge is a chance to trust in Your perfect timing. Strengthen my faith, that I may boldly walk the path You have laid for me, fully aware that Your plans are unfolding with grace and purpose. Amen.

July 16

On this special day, celebrate the gift of new life and the beauty of creation through your baby's handprint or footprint art. Each tiny mark reflects God's precious design, reminding us of His love and the divine potential in every child. Cherish these moments as a testament to His blessings.

1 Peter 2:9 - "But you are a chosen race, a royal priesthood, a holy nation, a people for his own possession, that you may proclaim the excellencies of him who called you out of darkness into his marvelous light."

DEVOTIONAL

On this sacred day, as you cradle your newborn and prepare to create lasting memories with their tiny handprints or footprints, let your heart swell with gratitude for the miracle of life. Each delicate print tells a story of God's artistry—how He intricately designed this beautiful little being, a masterpiece of His love. In 1 Peter 2:9, we are reminded that we are chosen, a royal priesthood, bringing forth the light of Christ into the world. Just as your child's innocent markings reflect their unique identity, they also herald the divine potential woven into their very being. Cherish these fleeting moments as holy reminders of God's blessings, for each print is a testament to the promise of new beginnings and uncharted paths. As you look at these precious imprints, may your heart be filled with hope, knowing that this child is called into a life of purpose and grace. In this exchange of art and love, may you celebrate not just a moment, but the unfolding narrative of God's faithfulness in your family's journey.

DAILY REFLECTION

As you gaze at your baby's tiny handprints and footprints, what dreams and hopes do you envision for this precious life, knowing that each mark is a testament to God's unique design and divine purpose?

PRAYER

Dear God, in this sacred moment, as I cradle my little one close, I thank You for the precious gift of new life. May each tiny handprint and footprint serve as a reminder of Your divine love and the beautiful story You are weaving through this child's existence. Help me to cherish these moments as reflections of Your faithfulness, embracing the unique purpose You have placed within them. Amen.

July 17

For your first splash in the pool, remember that just as Jesus calls us to step out in faith, so too are we invited to dive into new experiences. Trust that with each kick and splash, you're learning and growing in His love—just like in life, every moment is a chance to embrace His grace.

Matthew 14:27 - "But Jesus immediately said to them: 'Take courage! It is I. Don't be afraid.'"

DEVOTIONAL

As you prepare for your first splash in the pool, take a moment to reflect on the journey ahead. Just like stepping into the water, embarking on new experiences can feel daunting, but remember the words of Jesus: "Take courage! It is I. Don't be afraid" (Matthew 14:27). Each ripple and splash mirrors your own steps of faith, teaching you to trust in His presence with every kick and glide. Embrace the exhilaration of the unknown, knowing that even in discomfort, you are not alone. With each little success, you are growing stronger and more confident, learning not just about swimming, but about trusting in the grace that flows from Him. Let your heart rejoice in these moments; each is a gift that deepens your faith and relationship with God. So take a deep breath, dive in, and see how His love surrounds you— even at the edge of the pool.

DAILY REFLECTION

As you take your first splash in the pool, how can you embrace the courage to dive into new experiences, trusting that each ripple of challenge you face is a sacred opportunity to deepen your relationship with God?

PRAYER

Dear Lord, as I prepare for my first splash in the pool, help me to embrace the unknown with a heart full of courage. May each ripple remind me of Your unwavering presence, teaching me to trust in Your grace as I step out in faith. Let this new adventure be a joyful reflection of our relationship, where every kick and splash deepens my understanding of Your love. Amen.

July 18

Embrace the journey of parenthood as a divine road trip, where every mile is a chance to witness God's wonders through your baby's curious eyes. Trust in His guidance, knowing that each moment— however challenging –brings you closer to the heart of His love.

Deuteronomy 1:31 - "And in the wilderness, where you saw how the Lord your God carried you, as a father carries his son, all the way that you went until you came to this place."

DEVOTIONAL

As you embark on this first road trip with your baby, take a moment to reflect on the journey ahead—one filled with the wide-eyed wonder of new experiences and the unexpected turns of parenthood. Just as Deuteronomy 1:31 reminds us of God's gentle care, know that He carries you through each mile, nurturing both you and your child in the embrace of His love. The laughter, the cries, the curious gazes of your little one—all are invitations to witness God's wonders anew. Embrace the pauses as sacred moments, where the beauty of a sunset or the joy of a passing butterfly illuminates the path you travel together. Even when the road feels daunting, trust in His guidance; every challenge you face strengthens the bond you share and draws you closer to His heart. Allow your baby's innocence to awaken your own marvel at the world, and in those shared moments, find the divine stitched into the fabric of everyday life. Remember, this journey, though filled with uncertainty, is also a divine adventure—a testimony to the love and grace that surrounds you at every turn.

DAILY REFLECTION

How can you open your heart to the unexpected joys and challenges of this road trip, allowing each moment with your baby to deepen your appreciation for the divine love guiding your journey?

PRAYER

Dear Lord, as we set out on this first road trip with our little one, open our hearts to the beauty of each moment and the wonders reflected in our baby's gaze. May we find joy in the unexpected turns, trusting that You guide us through every mile, nurturing our bond and reminding us of Your love in all things. Help us to embrace the sacred pauses along the way, so that together, we may witness new sights and feel Your grace weaving through our journey of parenthood.

July 19

As you gather in the warmth of family, remember the joy of fellowship—a reflection of God's love and grace. Embrace this moment to share stories, laughter, and faith, strengthening the bonds that tie you together in Christ.

Hebrews 10:24-25 - "And let us consider how we may spur one another on toward love and good deeds, not giving up meeting together, as some are in the habit of doing, but encouraging one another—and all the more as you see the Day approaching."

DEVOTIONAL

As you step into the embrace of your family's home, let the warmth of their love wrap around you like a familiar blanket. Each smile, each laugh shared, is a beautiful reminder of God's grace manifesting in your lives. In this sacred gathering, take a moment to reflect on the power of fellowship; for it is in these connections that our faith flourishes. As you engage in heartfelt conversations and reminiscences, consider how these bonds are reflections of Christ's love—a tapestry woven with threads of support, encouragement, and shared belief. Remember Hebrews 10:24-25, which encourages us not just to gather, but to actively spur one another toward love and good deeds. May this visit inspire you to be an agent of joy and encouragement, uplifting not just your family members but nurturing your own spirit as well. As you enjoy this time together, let it be a reaffirmation of your commitment to meet regularly, drawing strength and inspiration from one another in anticipation of the glorious Day to come.

DAILY REFLECTION

In this cherished gathering, how can you actively cultivate the love and grace of Christ within your family, turning each shared moment into a stepping stone for deeper faith and connection?

PRAYER

Father in heaven, as I step into the embrace of my family's warmth, I thank You for this sacred gathering filled with laughter and love. May our shared stories and moments of joy be a reflection of Your grace, nurturing our spirits and strengthening our bonds in Christ. Help us to inspire one another toward love and good deeds, and may this visit be a cherished reminder of the beauty found in our fellowship, drawing us closer to You and to each other. Amen.

July 20

Even in the seemingly minor struggles, like a baby's first cough, God invites us to trust in His care and healing. As we nurture our little ones, let us remember His promise to be our comfort in every season.

Matthew 11:28-29 - "Come to me, all you who are weary and burdened, and I will give you rest. Take my yoke upon you and learn from me, for I am gentle and humble in heart, and you will find rest for your souls."

DEVOTIONAL

As you hear that first little cough from your baby, a wave of concern may wash over you. It's the first sign of something that feels all too grown-up, yet it's so small in the grand tapestry of life. In these minor struggles, God whispers to us, urging us to lean into His care, much like we rock our little ones in our arms. Remember the gentle words of Matthew 11:28-29: He invites the weary to find solace in Him. Just as we cradle our babies, God cradles us, offering His tender comfort and healing. Trust that even in this moment, as simple as it may appear, His presence surrounds you, guiding you through the unknown. Embrace this season, as you nurture your child, and be reminded that God is with you—bringing rest to your spirit and peace to your heart.

DAILY REFLECTION

In the quiet worry of that first cough, how can you intentionally surrender your anxieties to God, trusting in His promise to cradle both you and your baby with divine comfort and healing?

PRAYER

Dear Lord, in this tender moment of my baby's first cough, I come before You with a heart full of both concern and hope. Help me to trust in Your unwavering care, knowing that even these small struggles are held by Your loving hands. May I find solace in Your embrace, as I nurture my little one, and remember Your promise to bring comfort and healing in every season of life. Amen.

July 21

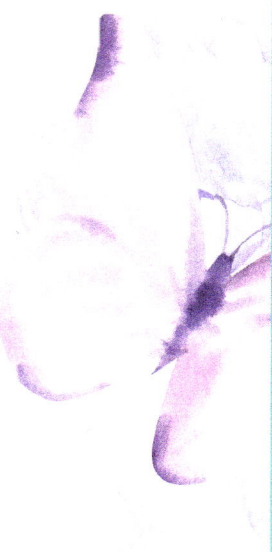

On this day, as we reflect on Christ's patience and perseverance, let parents find strength in His unwavering love while navigating the challenges of teething. May each cry be a reminder of the tender mercies that nurture growth, both in our children and in our faith.

Psalm 94:19 - "When the cares of my heart are many, your consolations cheer my soul."

DEVOTIONAL

As you cradle your little one through the discomfort of teething, reflect on the unwavering presence of Christ, who walked the path of suffering to bring us joy. In those moments when the cries seem to echo endlessly, let them become prayers that lead you closer to the heart of God. Psalm 94:19 reminds us that even when the cares of our hearts multiply, His comforting whispers can still our souls. Just as the tender mercies of God nurture our faith, may you find strength in His love amid the sleepless nights and painful bouts of fussiness. In your patience with your child, echo the patience God shows towards us as we grow and learn. Each cry, each sigh, is an opportunity to lean deeper into His grace, reminding you that you are not alone in this journey. Trust that through these challenges, both you and your child are being shaped into vessels of His glory, growing in love, resilience, and faith.

DAILY REFLECTION

In this season of teething trials, how can you transform your child's cries into a sacred reminder of Christ's enduring love, inviting you to embrace patience not only for your little one but for yourself in your own spiritual journey?

PRAYER

Dear Lord, in this tender season of teething, may Your presence be felt in every tear and every gentle cry. Grant us the grace to embrace these challenging moments, knowing that in our weariness, Your love surrounds us, nurturing both our children and our hearts. Help us cherish each sigh as a reminder of the growth You inspire, and may we find strength in Your everlasting patience as we guide our little ones through this journey. Amen.

July 22

God's abundance nourishes us in every stage of life. Just as a baby joyfully discovers the taste of solid food, we too are invited to explore the richness of His Word. May this season inspire us to savor the goodness of His love and grace.

Psalm 34:8 - "Taste and see that the Lord is good; blessed is the one who takes refuge in him."

DEVOTIONAL

As a little one takes their first delightful bites of solid food, there is a joyful wonder in discovering new tastes and textures. Each spoonful invites a reaction, a smile, perhaps even a giggle, as they begin to understand the nourishment that awaits them. In much the same way, we are called to approach the richness of God's Word with that same sense of curiosity and delight. Psalm 34:8 reminds us, "Taste and see that the Lord is good; blessed is the one who takes refuge in him." Just as every meal strengthens a baby's growth, each moment spent in His presence deepens our understanding of His abundant love and grace. This season, may we savor the sweetness of His promises, allowing them to fill us and transform us. Let us embrace the adventure of discovery, knowing that God's nourishment is ever-present, guiding us through every stage of life.

DAILY REFLECTION

In what ways can we cultivate a joyful curiosity in exploring the richness of God's Word, much like a baby excitedly discovering the delightful tastes of solid food?

PRAYER

Dear Lord, as our little ones embark on their journey of tasting solid food, may we too embrace the richness of Your Word with childlike wonder. Help us to savor each moment spent in Your presence, delighting in the sweetness of Your love and the nourishment of Your grace. Guide us to explore the depths of Your promises, filling our hearts with joy and transforming our lives through Your abundant goodness. Amen.

July 23

The joy of nurturing faith mirrors the innocence of a child's first messy meal—imperfect yet beautiful. As we celebrate the gift of grace, let's remember that it's in our messiness that God's love invites us to grow and share His abundance with others.

Matthew 18:3-4: "And said, 'Truly I tell you, unless you change and become like little children, you will never enter the kingdom of heaven. Therefore, whoever takes the lowly position of this child is the greatest in the kingdom of heaven.'"

DEVOTIONAL

In the messy joy of a child's first meal, we find a beautiful reflection of our own journey of faith. As we watch little hands smear food across their faces, we're reminded that growth comes not from perfection, but from the willingness to explore and engage with the world around us. Just as a toddler delights in the chaos of mealtime, we too are invited to embrace the messiness of our spiritual lives, understanding that it is in our vulnerability that God's grace shines brightest. Matthew reminds us that to enter the kingdom of heaven, we must adopt the humility and openness of a child. In our imperfections, we discover the depth of God's love, which cradles us like a parent nurtures a child learning to eat. Let us celebrate the beauty in our messy faith, knowing that it is in these moments of uncertainty and growth that we find ourselves fully enveloped in God's abundance. So, let us share this grace with others, inviting them to join us in the delightful mess that is life, love, and faith.

DAILY REFLECTION

In the joyful chaos of a child's first meal, how might embracing our own spiritual messiness lead us to deeper connections with God and those around us?

PRAYER

Dear Lord, as we witness the joy and chaos of a child's first meal, may it remind us of the beauty in our own imperfect journeys of faith. Help us embrace our messiness with open hearts, knowing that it is in our struggles and vulnerabilities that Your grace shines most brightly. Teach us to nurture this grace within ourselves and others, inviting all into the delightful, messy dance of love and growth that reflects Your boundless abundance. Amen.

July 24

In the midst of life's challenging firsts, remember God's unchanging love and comfort. Just as He nurtures us through our trials, we can trust Him to guide us through the discomforts of parenting, teaching us resilience and grace. Lean on His strength as you care for your little one—He is always with you.

2 Corinthians 1:3-4 - "Blessed be the God and Father of our Lord Jesus Christ, the Father of mercies and God of all comfort, who comforts us in all our affliction."

DEVOTIONAL

In the tender chaos of your first parenting experience, as your little one wrestles with discomfort, remember that you are not alone. The moment you notice that first diaper rash can feel overwhelming—your heart aches for your baby's pain, and uncertainty weighs heavily upon you. Yet, in this dissonance of joy and worry, God whispers His unwavering presence into your heart. Just as He promises to comfort us in our afflictions, He is there beside you, offering strength to navigate the trials of parenthood. This is a season not only of challenge but of profound growth; every tear shed and every sleepless night is woven into a tapestry of resilience and grace. As you tenderly care for your little one, take a moment to lean into His love, knowing that every struggle is a chance to deepen your trust in Him. His mercies are new each morning, just as your love for your child grows—may you find peace in that truth today.

DAILY REFLECTION

In the quiet moments of worry as you soothe your little one through their first discomfort, how can you open your heart to receive God's nurturing love, trusting that every challenge is a step toward deeper faith and resilience?

PRAYER

Dear Lord, in this tender moment of heartache and healing, I lift up my little one to You. As we navigate the discomforts of diaper rash and the uncertainties that come with new parenthood, remind me of Your unwavering love and presence. Grant me the strength to offer comfort and care, helping me to trust in Your grace as we grow together through these precious firsts. Amen.

July 25

On this joyful day, find laughter in God's grace, celebrating His steadfast love that brings light to our hearts. Let every giggle serve as a reminder of His unending joy, guiding us in faith and reminding us that His blessings abound. Shine brightly as you share this divine joy with others!

Psalm 126:2-3 - "Then our mouth was filled with laughter, and our tongue with shouts of joy; then they said among the nations, 'The Lord has done great things for them.' The Lord has done great things for us; we are glad."

DEVOTIONAL

On this joyful day, let us embrace the laughter that flows from our hearts as a gift of God's grace. Psalm 126:2-3 reminds us that the laughter of His people rings out like a melody, echoing the wonderful things He has done. With every cheer and giggle, we are not simply finding joy; we are proclaiming the steadfast love of our Creator who transforms our sorrows into shouts of gladness. Picture the scene: laughter spilling forth like a bright stream, touching everyone around us and inviting them into the warmth of His blessings. In a world that often feels heavy, let our joy shine as a testament to God's unwavering presence in our lives. As we share in this divine joy, we become vessels of light, illuminating the path for others to witness His greatness. So, let's fill our days with more than just smiles—let our love for Him ignite hearty belly laughs that spread His joy to all we encounter!

DAILY REFLECTION

How can you invite the laughter and joy of God's grace into your day, turning everyday moments into celebrations of His unwavering love and transforming your heart into a wellspring of light for others?

PRAYER

Dear Lord, on this joyful day, we come before You with hearts overflowing with laughter, grateful for the grace that fills our lives. May each giggle and hearty belly laugh remind us of Your steadfast love and the boundless joy You bring into our hearts. Help us to share this divine light with others, radiating Your blessings and inviting all to experience the warmth of Your goodness.

July 26

This day reminds us of the unwavering journey of faith, much like a child's first attempt to crawl—full of wobbles yet fueled by purpose. May we lean into God's grace, trusting that each earnest step brings us closer to Him. Even in our struggles, remember: movement towards the Light is a victory in our walk with Christ.

Proverbs 24:16 - "For though the righteous fall seven times, they rise again, but the wicked stumble when calamity strikes."

DEVOTIONAL

As we reflect on this day, let us think of a child's first attempts to crawl. There's a beautiful wobble, a tentative yet determined push towards discovery, much like our faith journey. We will stumble, we will falter—but Proverbs 24:16 assures us that each fall does not define us. The strength to rise again is a gift from God, a whisper of His grace encouraging us to keep moving forward. Just as a child learns to trust in their own strength, may we lean into our Father's gentle hands that guide us closer to His heart. Every small victory, each step toward the Light, is a testament to our resilience in Christ. Embrace the process, for in our striving, we are reminded that His light never dims, even amid our struggles.

DAILY REFLECTION

In what ways can you embrace the wobbles in your own faith journey, trusting that each small step toward God is not just a movement, but a profound victory in His love?

PRAYER

Father in heaven, as we watch children take their first wobbly steps, may we be reminded that our faith journey is just as courageous and beautiful. Help us to embrace each falter as a moment of growth, trusting in Your grace to lift us higher. Let our hearts glow with hope as we move ever closer to Your Light, knowing that every small victory brings us nearer to Your loving embrace. Amen.

July 27

On this day in the Christian calendar, reflect on the profound lessons of perseverance and reliance on God's strength. Just as a child learns to sit unsupported, we are called to stand firm in faith, trusting that God sustains us even in our most vulnerable moments. Embrace the journey of growth, knowing that His grace is sufficient.

Isaiah 30:15 - "In repentance and rest is your salvation, in quietness and trust is your strength."

DEVOTIONAL

Today, as we reflect on the theme of perseverance and reliance on God's strength, consider the image of a child learning to sit unsupported. There's a sweetness in that struggle—a moment of vulnerability mirrored in our spiritual journeys. Just as a child wobbles and falls, so too do we find ourselves unsteady, but it is in these moments that we discover His unfailing support. Isaiah 30:15 reminds us, "In repentance and rest is your salvation, in quietness and trust is your strength." Here we find an invitation to pause, breathe deeply, and lean into the arms of our Creator. Embrace the gentle assurance that His grace is enough for every fall and every attempt to stand tall. Allow yourself the grace to grow, knowing that each challenge strengthens your faith, and every act of trust deepens your reliance on His unwavering love. Today, let us honor the journey and the lessons it brings, resting confidently in the knowledge that we are never without His comfort and strength.

DAILY REFLECTION

In moments when you feel unsteady in your faith, how can you embrace the vulnerability of your journey and trust that God's strength will lift you to your feet once more?

PRAYER

Dear Father in Heaven, In moments of wobbling and uncertainty, remind us of the sweet strength found in our vulnerability. Help us to lean wholeheartedly into Your embrace, trusting that with each stumble, Your grace lifts us higher. As we navigate our journeys, may we find peace in resting upon Your everlasting support, growing steadfast in faith, and ever reliant on Your unfailing love. Amen.

July 28

Today, as your little one experiences their first hair growth spurt, celebrate the beauty of new beginnings. Just like this precious milestone, God's promises bring growth and transformation in our lives, reminding us that even in the tiniest moments, His love is ever-present and nurturing.

Matthew 6:28-29 - "And why do you worry about clothes? See how the flowers of the field grow. They do not labor or spin. Yet I tell you that not even Solomon in all his splendor was dressed like one of these."

DEVOTIONAL

As you marvel at the sight of your little one's first hair growth spurt, take a moment to celebrate this beautiful sign of new beginnings. Just as each delicate strand emerges, so too do the promises of God bloom in our lives, reminding us that growth often arises from the simplest of moments. In Matthew 6:28-29, we are reminded not to worry about what lies ahead, for even the flowers of the field, with their vibrant beauty, are clothed by God's tender care. Your child's transformation reflects the nurturing love that surrounds them, a divine reminder that every phase of life holds an opportunity for growth. With each small milestone, you can find reassurance that you are not alone; God's presence gently nurtures and guides you both. As you watch your little one flourish, let this moment stir gratitude within you, celebrating not only their growth but your own journey as a parent. Embrace the wonder of these early days, knowing that in every season, His love continues to nourish and sustain us.

DAILY REFLECTION

As you witness your little one's first signs of hair growth, how might you embrace this moment as a tender reminder of God's continuous presence in your own journey of transformation and nurturing love?

PRAYER

Dear Lord, in this tender moment of witnessing my child's first hair growth, I am filled with awe at the beauty of new beginnings. Thank You for Your unchanging love that nurtures us through every phase of life, reminding me that even the smallest signs of growth are within Your divine plan. Help me to embrace these milestones with a heart full of gratitude, trusting in Your guidance as we both flourish in Your care.

As you transition your baby to their own crib, remember that this is a step of faith, just as we trust God's plan for our lives. Allow Him to comfort both you and your little one, knowing that separation can lead to growth and deeper reliance on His love and peace.

Matthew 6:34 - "Therefore do not worry about tomorrow, for tomorrow will worry about itself. Each day has enough trouble of its own."

DEVOTIONAL

As you stand by your baby's crib, preparing to make that significant transition, take a moment to breathe deeply and reflect on the journey ahead. Just as God calls us to trust Him with our dreams and fears, this step into separate spaces is an invitation to lean on His understanding. Remember the tender moments of rocking your little one to sleep, the whispers of love surrounding you both—these memories form a foundation of trust that will carry you through this change. Allow the soothing words of Matthew 6:34 to wash over you: "Therefore do not worry about tomorrow, for tomorrow will worry about itself." Each day brings with it new challenges, but God's presence will envelop both you and your baby through the uncertainty. Embrace this separation as a sacred opportunity for growth, allowing your faith to flourish in the moments you feel their absence. Trust that as you release your little one to sleep safely in their crib, you are entrusting them—and yourself—into the boundless love and peace of God's embrace.

DAILY REFLECTION

How can you find solace in God's unwavering love and guidance as you prepare to let go, knowing that this small act of separation is a profound step towards fostering both your baby's independence and your spiritual growth?

PRAYER

Dear Lord, as I make this tender transition of placing my baby in their own crib, I ask for Your comforting presence to surround us both. Help me to release my fears and embrace this leap of faith, trusting that You are weaving our paths with love and purpose. May Your peace fill my heart and my little one's nursery, reassuring us that even in moments of separation, we are always held in Your embrace. Amen.

In the wake of the resurrection, find joy in the simplicity of faith. As new life blossoms, let it inspire you to refresh your spirit and nurture your soul, reflecting God's love in every moment.

Matthew 28:6-7 - "He is not here, for he has risen, as he said. Come, see the place where he lay. Then go quickly and tell his disciples that he has risen from the dead."

DEVOTIONAL

In the hush of early morning, as the sun spills golden light over the earth, we are invited to witness the wondrous promise fulfilled: "He is not here, for he has risen, as he said." Just as the beauty of spring births new life from the barren soil, let the resurrection awaken within us a refreshing joy—a gentle reminder that faith can bloom even in the simplest moments. In the quiet of a child's nap routine, we find echoes of God's love, nurturing our souls and calling us to pause, breathe, and reflect. Take a moment today to step away from the chaos, to linger in silence, and to savor the grace of new beginnings. As the disciples were instructed to go and share the good news, so too are we called to carry this joy into our daily lives— through laughter, kindness, and love. In this simplicity, we discover that every moment holds the potential to reflect the beauty of His resurrection. Let this truth embrace you today, nurturing your spirit and inspiring you to spread the light of His love as springtime renews the world.

DAILY REFLECTION

In what simple moments today can you allow the joy of the resurrection to fill your heart, nurturing your spirit and reminding you of the profound love God has for you and others?

PRAYER

Dear Lord, in the stillness of this sacred moment, we thank You for the gift of renewal and the joy that springs forth from the truth of the resurrection. As we pause to embrace the simplicity of faith, may we feel Your love nurturing our souls, reminding us that in every pause and every breath, Your grace is at work. Help us to carry this newfound joy into our daily lives, reflecting Your light and love in even the smallest acts of kindness. Amen.

When frustration emerges in our smallest moments, we are reminded of the power of patience and grace. Just as God nurtures us through our tears, let us extend that same compassion to our little ones, teaching them to find comfort in Him amidst their struggles. Embrace the opportunity to model faith and understanding as they navigate their first feelings of frustration.

James 1:19-20 - "My dear brothers and sisters, take note of this: Everyone should be quick to listen, slow to speak and slow to become angry, because human anger does not produce the righteousness that God desires."

DEVOTIONAL

In the soft glow of a late afternoon, you might find your little one clutching a toy, their face scrunching with confusion and frustration. In these tender moments, echoing the wisdom of James 1:19-20, we are gently reminded of our own journey in the art of patience. As their small cries fill the room, we feel the warmth of God's grace enveloping us, urging us to mirror that same compassion back to our children. It's in these fragile instances that we hold the beautiful opportunity to teach them — to listen, to breathe, and to find solace in the Lord even when emotions swirl. Let us kneel beside them, offering understanding rather than a quick fix, guiding them to see that frustration is simply a stepping stone on the path of growth. With every reassuring hug, we can foster their faith, reminding them that their struggles are seen and embraced by both us and God. Together, may we learn to transform these moments into lessons of grace, acceptance, and love, nurturing hearts that trust in His ever-present comfort.

DAILY REFLECTION

In the stillness of your little one's struggle, how can you cultivate a moment of grace that not only comforts them but also deepens your shared understanding of God's unwavering love amidst life's frustrations?

PRAYER

Dear Lord, in these moments of frustration when our little ones' tears fall like gentle rain, help us to embody Your patience and grace. May we kneel beside them, offering a listening ear and a tender heart, reflecting Your love as they navigate their first feelings of struggle. Teach us, Lord, to transform their cries into lessons of comfort and faith, so that they may learn to seek solace in You amid life's little storms. Amen.

August 1

Seek the light of Christ in every moment, for today reminds us that even in awaiting seasons, His presence is our true comfort and guide. Let this be a day of hope and reflection as we prepare our hearts for the journey ahead.

Matthew 5:14-16 - "You are the light of the world. A city set on a hill cannot be hidden. Nor do people light a lamp and put it under a basket, but on a stand, and it gives light to all in the house. In the same way, let your light shine before others, so that they may see your good works and give glory to your Father who is in heaven."

DEVOTIONAL

In this season of waiting, when every moment feels heavy with anticipation, remember that Christ's light shines the brightest in our darkest hours. Just as a child delights in the simple game of peekaboo, revealing joy and laughter in the most unexpected places, so too does the Lord invite us to seek Him in every unseen moment. His presence is like a lamp on a stand, illuminating our path and guiding our hearts through uncertainty. As you reflect today, consider how your own light can shine, illuminating the lives of those around you, even in your waiting. Let your good works, born from faith and love, be a testament to His glory, drawing others closer to the warmth of His embrace. Embrace this day as a precious opportunity to be a beacon of hope, showing the world that even in stillness, God is at work. Lift your head, dear one, and prepare your heart for the journey ahead—His light will not lead you astray.

DAILY REFLECTION

In the quiet moments of waiting, how might you open your heart to witness the unexpected joy of Christ's presence, and in turn, share that light with someone who feels forgotten or lost?

PRAYER

Dear Lord, in this season of waiting, help us to seek Your light in every moment, trusting that it illuminates even our darkest hours. May our hearts burst with hope and joy as we reflect Your love and goodness to those around us, shining like beacons of Your grace. As we prepare for the journey ahead, remind us that Your presence is our true comfort and guide, even in the stillness.

August 2

In this sacred moment of holding your newborn, remember the gift of life reflected in the manger. Just as the Holy Family welcomed Jesus with love and joy, embrace this little one with hope, knowing that God has great plans for their future.

Luke 2:7 - "And she gave birth to her firstborn son and wrapped him in swaddling clothes and laid him in a manger, because there was no place for them in the inn."

DEVOTIONAL

As you cradle your precious newborn in your arms, take a moment to pause and reflect on the miracle of life. In this sacred instance, you are echoing the moments of the Holy Family, who welcomed the Christ child into a world that offered little comfort yet brimmed with divine purpose. Just as Mary wrapped Jesus in swaddling clothes and laid Him in a humble manger, so too are you wrapping your own child in the warmth of your love and hopes for their bright future. Despite the uncertainties that lie ahead—much like the journey undertaken by the Holy Family—remember that every little one comes with the promise of God's great plans. Let's delve deeper into this moment; your embrace is an affirmation that love overcomes all adversity. Let each breath you share together be a testament to the joy and responsibility of parenthood, and let your heart be open to the incredible adventures that await. As you hold this fragile bundle of life, allow the joy of the season to fill your spirit, reminding you that with hope and faith, marvelous things can unfold.

DAILY REFLECTION

In this tender moment of cradling your newborn, how can you cultivate a heart of hope and faith, remembering that just as the Holy Family embraced unknown futures with love, you too are called to nurture the divine potential nestled within this tiny life?

PRAYER

Dear God, in this sacred moment of cradling my newborn, I thank You for the precious gift of life that mirrors the love shown by the Holy Family. As I embrace this little one with hopes for their future, grant me the wisdom to nurture their spirit and the courage to guide them through life's uncertainties, always reminding them of the joy and purpose that dwells within Your plans. Amen.

On this day, reflect on the miracle of nourishment, both physical and spiritual, as we gather to remember Jesus' feeding of the multitude. Just as He multiplied the loaves and fish, trust that God continues to provide for our needs—body and soul—abundantly. Let us share our blessings, knowing that in giving, we receive even more.

John 6:12-13 - "When they had all had enough to eat, he said to his disciples, 'Gather the pieces that are left over. Let nothing be wasted.' So they gathered them and filled twelve baskets with the pieces of the five barley loaves left over by those who had eaten."

DEVOTIONAL

As we pause to reflect on the miraculous feeding of the multitude, let us take a moment to consider the boundless nature of God's provision. In a world where we often feel overwhelmed by our needs—physical and spiritual—Jesus demonstrates that even the smallest offerings can lead to abundant blessings. Just as He took five loaves and two fish and fed thousands, He invites us to bring our own meager resources into His hands. It is in this act of surrender that we discover not only nourishment for ourselves but a call to share our abundance with others. Today, as you think of those around you, remember that the leftovers from our blessings can fill others' empty baskets. Look for opportunities to share—be it a listening ear, a warm meal, or a kind word—because in giving, we are filled to overflowing. Let us trust that God, who gathers the fragments, will also hold our hearts and needs. As you engage with both the physical and spiritual aspects of nourishment, may you experience His abundant grace and the joy of sharing it freely.

DAILY REFLECTION

In what ways can you surrender your modest resources today, trusting God to multiply them into blessings that nourish not only yourself but also those who hunger for hope and connection around you?

PRAYER

Dear Lord, in the softness of this moment, we remember Your miraculous provision, where scarcity transforms into abundance. Help us to surrender our limited offerings into Your capable hands, trusting that in sharing our blessings, we mirror Your love and generosity. May our hearts overflow with gratitude as we seek opportunities to uplift others, reflecting the nourishment we find in You both physically and spiritually. Amen.

In the quiet stillness of the night, as you cradle your newborn, remember that God's love surrounds you both. Even in sleepless moments, His presence brings peace and strength to your weary heart. Trust in His promise that each challenge is a stepping stone to deeper faith and joy.

Psalm 56:3-4 - "When I am afraid, I put my trust in you. In God, whose word I praise—in God I trust and am not afraid. What can mere mortals do to me?"

DEVOTIONAL

In the quiet stillness of the night, as you cradle your newborn close to your heart, the world outside fades away and you are enveloped in a sacred moment. Each gentle sigh and soft coo reminds you that amidst the sleeplessness, you are not alone. God's love wraps around you both, a comforting blanket against the weariness that seeks to overwhelm. When fear creeps in—perhaps worries of parenting or exhaustion—remember Psalm 56:3-4, which assures you that in your moments of anxiety, you can put your trust in the One who calms even the fiercest storms. With every challenge you face, whether large or small, lean on His promise that these are stepping stones to a faith that is richer and deeper than you ever imagined. Embrace this season, knowing that God sees your struggle and is providing peace and strength in ways you may not yet recognize. Let your heart breathe in His presence, and allow that divine embrace to guide you through the night.

DAILY REFLECTION

In this tender moment of nightwatch, what fears or worries can you lay before God, trusting that His love is your refuge as you nurture both your newborn and your faith?

PRAYER

Dear Lord, in the hushed hours of the night, I lay my weary heart before You, cradling this precious gift of life. Amidst the exhaustion and uncertainty, may Your love be the soothing balm that quiets my fears and renews my spirit. Help me to trust in Your presence, knowing that every sleepless moment is a thread woven into the rich tapestry of faith and joy that You are crafting in our lives. Amen.

On this day of reflection, embrace the joy in life's messy moments, recognizing that God's grace is present even in the chaos. Just as a child's first diaper blowout teaches us about vulnerability and love, let us surrender our imperfections and trust in His unwavering compassion.

Isaiah 61:3 - "...to bestow on them a crown of beauty instead of ashes, the oil of joy instead of mourning, and a garment of praise instead of a spirit of despair."

DEVOTIONAL

Today, as we reflect on the joyful chaos of life, let us consider the unforgettable moment of a first diaper blowout—an event that, while messy, reveals the profound beauty of love and vulnerability. In these moments, we are reminded that our imperfections do not define us; rather, they invite us into a deeper understanding of grace. Just as a child teaches us to laugh amidst the chaos, God gently beckons us to surrender our flaws and embrace His compassion. Isaiah 61:3 tells us that God bestows crowns of beauty instead of ashes—beauty born not from perfection, but from the honest acceptance of our human frailty. Each chaos-laden moment can serve as a reminder of our need for His joy, transforming our mourning into celebration. So let us wear our messiness as a badge of honor and trust that in every blowout, every spilled moment, His love remains steadfast. Today, may we revel in the joy of trusting a God who meets us in our mess and turns it into a masterpiece.

DAILY REFLECTION

In the midst of life's unexpected blowouts, how can we shift our perspective to embrace and celebrate the beauty of our own vulnerabilities as a pathway to deeper trust in God's abundant grace?

PRAYER

Dear Lord, in the midst of our life's messy moments, help us to see the beauty within the chaos. Teach us to embrace our vulnerabilities and imperfections, knowing that they lead us to experience Your unfailing love and grace more deeply. May we find joy in each stumble, trusting that You transform our mess into a beautiful reminder of Your compassionate heart. Amen.

Celebrate the gift of baptism, a profound moment of spiritual rebirth. As you welcome this sacred rite, reflect on the cleansing power of God's grace, washing away the past and renewing your spirit in Christ. Rejoice in the promise of new life!

Romans 6:4 - "We were therefore buried with him through baptism into death in order that, just as Christ was raised from the dead through the glory of the Father, we too may live a new life."

DEVOTIONAL

As you prepare for that first sacred bath at home, let your heart soak in the profound significance of this moment. Today, as you celebrate the gift of baptism, you are not merely engaging in a ritual; you are embracing a transformative act of faith that binds you to the death and resurrection of Christ. Reflect on Romans 6:4—just as Jesus was buried and raised, so too are you being buried in the waters of renewal, emerging cleansed and reborn, free from the shackles of your past. Feel the weight of old burdens lift as you submit to this beautiful symbol of God's grace washing over you, providing a fresh start. With every drop of water, allow yourself to rejoice in the promise of new life—a life infused with hope, purpose, and the unyielding love of your Creator. This is your moment to step boldly into the fullness of who you are meant to be, renewed and radiant in Christ. Bask in this sacred gift, for today marks the beginning of a beautiful journey, drenched in the light of His love.

DAILY REFLECTION

As you prepare to step into this sacred bath, how does embracing the cleansing grace of baptism invite you to let go of past burdens and rejoice in the radiant promise of new life in Christ?

PRAYER

Dear Lord, as I prepare for this sacred bath, I stand in awe of Your grace that washes over me like a cleansing stream. In this moment of baptism, I celebrate the profound rebirth that You offer—a chance to leave behind my past and embrace the hope of new life in Christ. Help me to feel the weight of old burdens lift, filling my heart with joy and purpose, as I step into the journey You have planned for me, radiant in Your love. Amen.

In the quiet moments of changing a diaper, feel God's grace in your hands. It's a sacred act of service, where love meets the mundane, reminding you that even in life's most humble tasks, you reflect Christ's care and compassion.

Matthew 25:40 - "Truly, I say to you, as you did it to one of the least of these my brothers, you did it to me."

DEVOTIONAL

In the stillness of changing a diaper, the world fades and your focus narrows to this precious moment. Here, amidst the gentle coos and the soft rustle of fabric, you are invited into a space where God's grace takes on tangible form. Each movement—washing, wiping, securing—transforms an ordinary task into a sacred act of love. As you care for this tiny being, remember that you are reflecting Christ's compassion, echoing His own acts of service toward the least among us. This is holy work, a powerful reminder that even in the humblest tasks, divine love flows through your hands. Each giggle, each little smile is a testament to the beauty of sacrifice and service, affirming that you are part of a greater narrative of grace. Let this moment ground you in the truth that in loving the least of these, you are truly loving Him.

DAILY REFLECTION

In the stillness of this sacred moment, how can you consciously invite God's grace into your hands, transforming each gentle touch into an expression of love that echoes Christ's compassion?

PRAYER

Dear Lord, in this quiet moment of changing a diaper, may I feel Your grace flow through my hands. Help me to see this simple task as a sacred act of love, a reflection of Christ's compassion resting in my heart. Let the giggles and coos remind me that in caring for this little one, I am participating in Your divine story of grace and servitude. Amen.

For a heart yearning for growth and strength in faith, this time mirrors the quiet resilience of those who sought Jesus in the depths of their need. Reflect on how steadfast prayer nurtures our spiritual development, much like a child's tummy time, building strength and courage to rise and reach for the divine.

Colossians 1:10-11 - "So as to walk in a manner worthy of the Lord, fully pleasing to him: bearing fruit in every good work and increasing in the knowledge of God; being strengthened with all power, according to his glorious might, for all endurance and patience with joy."

DEVOTIONAL

As you embark on the first tummy time session with your little one, pause to reflect on the gentle resilience required for growth. Just as a child learns to lift their head and embrace the world, we too are called to rise in our faith, leaning into the strength that God provides. In moments of struggle and discomfort, we find ourselves vulnerable, yet it is in this vulnerability that our spirit begins to strengthen. Colossians 1:10-11 reminds us that our journey is not in vain; each prayer and each yearning for God's presence nourishes our souls, like the persistent lifting of a baby's body with resolve. As you watch your child work to hold their head up, remember that each effort echoes our own pursuit of a heart and life pleasing to the Lord. With every tear, every desperate sigh, we are cultivating endurance and patience, knowing we are never alone in this journey. May you find joy in the growth, trusting that just as your child learns to rise, so too does God equip you with His glorious might to reach for Him in all areas of life.

DAILY REFLECTION

In the tender moments of your child's first tummy time, how might you embrace the discomfort of your own struggles as sacred opportunities to deepen your trust in God's unwavering strength and love?

PRAYER

Dear Lord, as I witness my child's first efforts to lift their head in this tummy time, I am reminded of my own journey of faith. Grant me the strength to embrace my vulnerabilities and the courage to rise in pursuit of Your presence. May every prayer and every moment of struggle cultivate endurance within me, so I may grow closer to You, nurturing a heart that seeks Your glory in all things. Amen.

At your first postpartum checkup, take a moment to reflect on the miracle of new life and God's unwavering presence. Trust in His guidance as you navigate this sacred journey of motherhood, knowing that each step is filled with His grace and love.

Matthew 18:5 - "And whoever welcomes one such child in my name welcomes me."

DEVOTIONAL

As you sit in the softly illuminated room for your first postpartum checkup, take a deep breath and let gratitude wash over you. This moment, though filled with questions and perhaps a touch of anxiety, is also a sacred pause to celebrate the miracle of new life nestled in your heart. In the tender cries of your newborn, you can hear the echo of Matthew 18:5, where Jesus reminds us that welcoming a child is akin to welcoming Him. Each gentle moment you share is a glimpse of the divine, a reminder of God's unwavering presence in the rollercoaster of motherhood. Trust in His guidance as you navigate this sacred journey, knowing that He walks alongside you, holding your hand through sleepless nights and joyful discoveries alike. With every smile and coo, you are surrounded by His grace, echoing in your baby's innocence and wonder. Embrace this adventure, for it is laced with love, a love that mirrors the very heart of God himself.

DAILY REFLECTION

In this moment of quiet reflection during your first postpartum checkup, how can you open your heart to fully embrace the overwhelming love and grace that God is pouring into your journey of motherhood, even amidst the uncertainties?

PRAYER

Dear Lord, in this quiet moment of reflection during my first postpartum checkup, I thank You for the precious gift of new life that fills my heart with wonder. As I navigate the joys and challenges of motherhood, grant me the courage to trust in Your unwavering presence, knowing that each day is enveloped in Your grace. Help me to embrace the sacred love that reflects Your own, as I cherish every cry, coo, and fleeting moment shared with my baby. Amen.

On this special day, as you take your child for their first pediatrician appointment, remember that God's loving care surrounds your little one. Trust in His plan for health and growth, knowing that each step is part of a divine journey filled with purpose and grace.

3 John 1:2 - "Beloved, I pray that you may prosper in all things and be in health, just as your soul prospers."

DEVOTIONAL

As you prepare to take your little one for their first pediatrician appointment, take a moment to breathe deeply and savor this precious milestone. Every heartbeat, giggle, and tiny finger is a reminder of God's intricate design and unfathomable love. In this moment, as you walk into the doctor's office, let the words of 3 John 1:2 resonate in your heart: "Beloved, I pray that you may prosper in all things and be in health, just as your soul prospers." Know that God's watchful eye is upon your child, and His gentle hands are guiding each step of their journey. Trust in His divine plan for health and growth; even the smallest moments carry significant purpose. Embrace the joy and hope that comes with each new experience, for they are all part of a sacred story woven by His grace. As you nurture your child's well-being, remember that you're never alone—God walks alongside you in this beautiful adventure of parenthood.

DAILY REFLECTION

In the tender embrace of this milestone, what fears or hopes do you feel stirred within your heart as you entrust your child's well-being to God's loving care?

PRAYER

Dear Lord, as I stand on the brink of this significant milestone with my little one, I thank You for the precious gift of life and the love that surrounds us. Grant us peace and assurance as we enter this appointment, knowing that Your guiding hand is upon our journey, filling each moment with purpose and hope. May Your love envelop my child, nurturing them as they grow, and may I always remember that in every heartbeat, You are there, holding us close. Amen.

August 11

As we celebrate the joyous reflexive smiles of a newborn, let us remember that God's love is pure and instinctual, mirroring the untainted joy found in His creation. May these precious moments remind us of the innocence and wonder of our faith, reflecting the simple trust we are called to have in Him.

Psalm 118:24 - "This is the day that the Lord has made; let us rejoice and be glad in it."

DEVOTIONAL

As we gather to witness the awe-inspiring reflexive smiles of a newborn, we are reminded of the pure, instinctual love that God has for each of us. Just as these tiny smiles bring warmth and joy, so too does our Father's love fill our hearts with an unshakeable peace. Psalm 118:24 declares, "This is the day that the Lord has made; let us rejoice and be glad in it." In the same way a baby smiles simply because joy is present, we are invited to bask in the wonder of each day He provides. These innocent expressions echo the trust we are called to have, a trust that is unwavering and joyful. As you cherish these moments with your little one, let them be a reminder of the untainted joy found in God's creation and the simplicity of faith. Embrace the beauty of today; it is a gift crafted by the Creator's hands, just as the child you hold is a testament to His endless love.

DAILY REFLECTION

In the gentle curve of a newborn's smile, what tender reminders of God's pure love and the simple faith He invites us to embody can you uncover in your own heart today?

PRAYER

Dear Lord, in these tender moments of joy, as we witness the beautiful smiles of a newborn, we are reminded of the pure love You shower upon us. May these innocent expressions inspire us to embrace our faith with the same childlike trust, allowing Your light to fill our hearts with peace and wonder. Help us to cherish each day as a precious gift, reflecting the endless beauty of Your creation and the unwavering joy found in Your presence. Amen.

August 12

God's gentle whispers in our lives often arrive unexpectedly, much like a baby's first hiccups. Each little moment reminds us to pause and appreciate His tender presence, guiding us through life's joys and challenges.

Isaiah 43:1-2 - "But now, this is what the Lord says—he who created you, Jacob, he who formed you, Israel: 'Do not fear, for I have redeemed you; I have summoned you by name; you are mine. When you pass through the waters, I will be with you; and when you pass through the rivers, they will not sweep over you.'"

DEVOTIONAL

In the stillness of the night, when a tiny heartbeat echoes softly, a baby's first hiccups ripple through the air—unexpected yet joyful reminders of life's delicate beginnings. Just as these little sounds break the silence, God's gentle whispers often surprise us in our own lives, nudging us to pause and attune our hearts to His presence. In Isaiah 43:1-2, He reassures us of our worth, declaring, "You are mine." The hiccups of a newborn parallel the way we sometimes experience God's guiding hand in the midst of our bewildering moments. As we journey through trials and triumphs, His promise remains steadfast: He is with us, unwavering in our struggles and joys. Let each breath, each little hiccup, stir within us a profound awareness of His love, drawing us nearer to the assurance that we are not alone. Embrace these gentle reminders as milestones on your faith-filled path, and allow them to lead you deeper into the heart of God.

DAILY REFLECTION

In what unexpected moments have you felt God's gentle whispers guiding you, much like the sweet, surprising echoes of a baby's first hiccups?

PRAYER

Dear Lord, in the quiet moments filled with the soft echoes of a baby's first hiccups, may we feel Your gentle whispers wash over us, reminding us of Your tender presence in our lives. Help us to pause amid the chaos and recognize the small graces You sprinkle throughout our days, guiding us even in our bewilderment. As we embrace these moments, deepen our awareness of Your unwavering love, assuring us with each heartbeat that we are never alone. Amen.

August 13

On this special day of firsts, may you find joy in each little moment with your baby, reflecting God's love as you step into the world together. Remember, every outing is a chance to marvel at His creation and share the light of His grace.

Genesis 1:31: "God saw all that he had made, and it was very good."

DEVOTIONAL

As you step out into the world with your precious baby today, take a moment to pause and breathe in the beauty surrounding you. Each tiny gasp of wonder from your little one mirrors the awe that swells in your heart, reminding you of the tender creation that is unfolding before your eyes. Genesis 1:31 tells us that God observed all He had created and declared it very good. In this first outing, may you see the fingerprints of the Creator in the sky's vast blue, the vibrant colors of blooming flowers, and the gentle flutter of leaves. Each moment with your baby is a sacred invitation to witness His goodness and embrace the miracle of life. Let laughter fill the air and joy echo as you both discover the world anew, sharing in the light of His grace. Remember, with every step you take, you are not just nurturing your child's curiosity, but also deepening your bond with the love of the Father who marvels at you both.

DAILY REFLECTION

In the tender moments of your baby's first outing, how can you intentionally pause to recognize and celebrate the divine beauty woven into each experience, allowing it to deepen your gratitude for both the journey of motherhood and the Creator's loving handiwork?

PRAYER

Dear Lord, as we embark on this beautiful journey into the world with our little one, fill our hearts with your joy and wonder. Help us to cherish each small moment, allowing the awe and beauty of creation to ignite our spirits and deepen our love for one another. May your grace shine brightly upon us, guiding our steps as we explore the miracles that surround us. Amen.

August 14

On this day, reflect on the transformative power of faith—how even the smallest steps can lead to profound encounters with God. As you walk, consider the journey of the disciples; just as they followed Jesus, may you find purpose and joy in each stride, trusting in His guidance along the path of life.

Luke 17:5-6 - "The apostles said to the Lord, 'Increase our faith!' He replied, 'If you have faith as small as a mustard seed, you can say to this mulberry tree, "Be uprooted and planted in the sea," and it will obey you.'"

DEVOTIONAL

As you take your first stroller walk today, let the rhythm of your steps remind you of the disciples' journey alongside Jesus. Each movement is not just a physical act but a tangible expression of your faith, however small it may feel. In their request, "Increase our faith," the apostles encapsulated a yearning we all share—a desire to deepen our connection with the Divine. Jesus gently assures us that even faith as tiny as a mustard seed has the power to transform our lives and the world around us. As you breathe in the fresh air and observe the beauty of creation, allow your heart to open to the wonders that unfold with each stride. Trust in His guidance, and let the simple act of walking become a sacred conversation with God. In moments of uncertainty, remember that every step, no matter how small, is significant in the grand tapestry of His plan for you. Embrace this journey, for it is in these humble beginnings that profound encounters with God await.

DAILY REFLECTION

As you stroll today, how might you invite God into your heart's deepest yearnings, allowing each step—no matter how small—to serve as a bridge between your faith and His unfathomable grace?

PRAYER

Dear Lord, as I embark on this first stroller walk, may each step I take draw me closer to You. Help me to embrace the small moments, trusting that just as the disciples found purpose in following Jesus, I too can uncover the beauty of Your presence in the everyday rhythm of life. Let my heart be open to Your guidance, and may this journey fill me with joy and a deeper faith, even in the simplest of strides. Amen.

As you cherish your first car ride with your baby, remember that each journey is guided by God's hand. Trust Him to navigate through every twist and turn, showering your family with grace and love along the way.

Psalm 25:4-5 - "Show me your ways, Lord, teach me your paths. Guide me in your truth and teach me, for you are God my Savior, and my hope is in you all day long."

DEVOTIONAL

As you buckle your precious little one into the car seat for this first ride, pause to embrace the tender beauty of this moment. The soft sounds of their breathing fill the air, a reminder of the new life and endless possibilities ahead. With each turn of the wheel, take heart in knowing that just as you are steering the car, God is masterfully steering your family's journey. Psalm 25:4-5 invites us to seek His guidance: "Show me your ways, Lord, teach me your paths." What a comfort to trust that He is with you in the passenger seat, ready to guide you through every twist and turn of parenthood. Let this first ride be a prayerful journey, steeping your heart in hope and surrender. Cherish this time, knowing that God's love envelops your family, lighting the way forward with grace and joy.

DAILY REFLECTION

As you embark on this sacred journey with your little one, how can you open your heart to embrace God's guiding presence in the uncharted roads of parenthood that lie ahead?

PRAYER

Dear Lord, as we embark on this precious journey with our little one, I thank You for the gift of each moment—each mile filled with joy and wonder. May Your gentle hand guide our path, infusing our travels with grace and love, and reminding us that with every turn, we are never alone. Help us to embrace the beauty of this new adventure, trusting in Your plans as we embrace the joys of parenthood. Amen.

As you dress your little one today, reflect on the gift of new beginnings and the promise of growth. Just as God lovingly nurtures each of us, may your care for this tiny life mirror His unconditional love. Each gentle touch is a reminder of the warmth and hope that comes with faith.

Isaiah 61:10 - "I will greatly rejoice in the Lord; my soul shall exult in my God, for he has clothed me with the garments of salvation; he has covered me with the robe of righteousness, as a bridegroom decks himself like a priest with a beautiful headdress, and as a bride adorns herself with her jewels."

DEVOTIONAL

As you gently dress your little one today, pause for a moment and embrace the miracle of this new beginning. Each soft fabric you wrap around their tiny body reminds us of the tender care God extends towards us, nurturing our spirits with His love. In this sacred act of dressing, consider how your touch is not just a practical necessity, but an expression of the unconditional love that mirrors our Creator's affection for us. Just as God adorns us with the garments of salvation, you are providing your little one with layers of warmth and protection, both physically and spiritually. Hear the promise in Isaiah 61:10 as you clothe your child—a promise of growth, joy, and hope that reflects the beauty of faith. With every gentle motion, you participate in their journey, cultivating a heart that will one day rejoice in the Lord. Let this act be a reminder that in every stitch of love, you are weaving a tapestry of grace and hope for your precious child.

DAILY REFLECTION

As you dress your little one today, how can you allow each gentle touch to become a heartfelt prayer, recognizing that in nurturing their first garments, you are also nurturing the seeds of faith and love that God has planted in both of your lives?

PRAYER

Dear Lord, as I gently dress my precious little one today, I thank You for the gift of new beginnings and the promise of growth that each day brings. May my loving touch wrap around them like Your embrace, reminding them of Your unwavering care and boundless love. Help me to cultivate their spirit with the warmth of faith, so that one day they may rejoice in the beauty of Your grace. Amen.

August 17

Capture the miracle of new life this season, reflecting the joy and wonder of God's creation in your little one. As memory blossoms through your baby's first photos, celebrate the beautiful gift of family and the promise of new beginnings.

Genesis 9:12-13 - "And God said, 'This is the sign of the covenant I am making between me and you and every living creature with you, a covenant for all generations to come: I have set my rainbow in the clouds, and it will be the sign of the covenant between me and the earth.'"

DEVOTIONAL

As you gather to capture the tender beauty of your little one's first moments, remember the profound gift reflected in each photo taken. Genesis 9:12-13 speaks of God's covenant with us, symbolized by the rainbow—a reminder of His promises and a reflection of His love that spans generations. Just as the rainbow bridges the heavens and earth after a storm, so too does your child remind us of hope and renewal. In this season of new beginnings, take a moment to marvel at the miracle of life cradled in your arms. With every click of the camera, you're not just capturing images; you're intertwining moments that speak of faith, family, and the beauty of creation. Celebrate the joy that blossoms in your home and the sacred love that threads your hearts together. Each smile, each tiny hand, is a testament to God's artistry—miniature reflections of His love and a promise that life, like the seasons, is rich with potential and wonder.

DAILY REFLECTION

In the quiet moments as you cradle your little miracle, how does the vibrant beauty of your child remind you of God's promises, inviting you to reflect on the legacy of hope and love that will flourish in your family for generations to come?

PRAYER

Father in heaven, as we cradle this precious new life within our arms, we thank You for the miracle of creation that fills our home with joy and wonder. May each photo we take serve as a living testament to Your love and promises, a celebration of our family's journey intertwined with the beauty of Your artistry. Help us to cherish these fleeting moments, recognizing in each smile and tiny hand the hope and renewal that comes from You, and may we always find delight in the sacred blessings of our lives. Amen.

August 18

As you navigate the joyous surprises of parenthood, remember that even in the messiest moments, God's grace shines through. Each diaper change is an opportunity to reflect on the new life entrusted to you, filled with innocence and the promise of God's love. Embrace the laughter and learn to cherish these fleeting days.

Ecclesiastes 3:12-13 - "I know that there is nothing better for people than to be happy and to do good while they live. That each of them may eat and drink, and find satisfaction in all their toil—this is the gift of God."

DEVOTIONAL

As you lay your little one down for a diaper change, the unexpected happens—a joyful sprinkle, a reminder that parenting is as unpredictable as it is delightful. In these small, messy moments, God's grace shines through, inviting you to embrace the laughter rather than despair over the inconvenience. Reflect on Ecclesiastes 3:12-13, where the writer reminds us that true joy is found in the simple gifts of life, including the fleeting challenges of parenthood. Each tiny laugh, each surprise, connects you deeper to the miracle of life bestowed upon you. Remember that in the midst of chaos, God is cultivating not just your child's life, but your own heart as well. Allow yourself to rejoice in these unfiltered moments, for they are precious opportunities to witness the innocence and beauty of creation. Cherish these days, dear parent, with gratitude, for they are indeed a sweet gift from God.

DAILY REFLECTION

In the midst of playful chaos and unexpected surprises during diaper changes, how can you shift your perspective to see each moment as a cherished reminder of God's tender grace and the beauty of the life you've been entrusted with?

PRAYER

Dear Lord, thank You for the precious gift of parenthood, where even the most unexpected moments become treasures in our hearts. As I navigate the joyful surprises of diaper changes, help me to embrace each little sprinkle with laughter and love, remembering that Your grace is intricately woven into the fabric of these days. May I find joy in the chaos and cherish the fleeting nature of this time, knowing that every challenge is a reflection of the miraculous life You have entrusted to me. Amen.

On this day of reflection, remember that God's promises are our steadfast anchor. In moments of uncertainty, trust in His guidance; with faith as our foundation, every challenge can become an opportunity for growth and renewed hope.

Hebrews 6:19 - We have this hope as an anchor for the soul, firm and secure.

DEVOTIONAL

As we pause to reflect on this season, let us embrace the profound truth embedded in Hebrews 6:19—our hope is an anchor for our souls, unshakeable and secure. In the chaotic currents of life, where uncertainty often threatens to drown our spirits, it's crucial to cling to the promises of God that remind us He is ever-present and faithful. Think of the swaddling of a newborn, enveloped in warmth and comfort; in the same way, God wraps us in His love, holding us firmly through life's storms. Each challenge we face is not merely a hurdle but a divine opportunity for growth, where our faith can blossom into resilience. Trust in His guidance is not just a passive act; it is an active decision to believe in the possibilities He lays before us, even when the path seems murky. Let every moment of doubt transform into a stepping stone, leading us closer to renewed hope. May your heart find rest today, knowing that His steadfast love is your anchor, unfailing in every wave of uncertainty.

DAILY REFLECTION

In the quiet moments of uncertainty, how can you deliberately choose to immerse yourself in God's promises, allowing His love to envelop you like a swaddle, fostering trust and hope amidst life's storms?

PRAYER

Dear Lord, in the quiet moments of today, help us to recognize the embrace of Your love—just as a swaddle enfolds a newborn in safety and warmth. May we find comfort in Your steadfast promises, allowing our hearts to rest in the assurance that through every storm, Your guiding hand leads us toward growth and renewed hope. Grant us the courage to transform our uncertainties into stepping stones, anchoring our souls in the unshakeable hope You provide. Amen.

August 20

In this sacred moment of nourishing life, trust in God's provision and grace. Whether you nurse or bottle-feed, remember that every act of love reflects His nurturing spirit, embracing both mother and child in a holy journey of care. Rest in the assurance that you are beautifully fulfilling your divine calling.

1 Thessalonians 3:12-13 - "May the Lord make your love increase and overflow for each other and for everyone else, just as ours does for you. May he strengthen your hearts so that you will be blameless and holy in the presence of our God and Father when our Lord Jesus comes with all his holy ones."

DEVOTIONAL

In the tender act of nourishing your child, whether through the warmth of breastfeeding or the gentle embrace of a bottle, you partake in a sacred rhythm of life and love. This moment is a profound reminder of God's provision—an echo of His nurturing spirit flowing through you. As you cradle your little one, feel the weight of your divine calling; every loving gaze, every gentle touch, reflects a heart overflowing with grace. In the quiet of these shared moments, trust that God strengthens your heart, making you blameless and holy, enveloped in His presence.
Just as Paul encouraged the Thessalonians, may your love increase and overflow, not only for your child but for everyone who walks this journey with you. Embrace the sacredness of this time, recognizing that it is as much about you as it is about them—both in need of grace, both wrapped in love. Rest assured, you are beautifully fulfilling a holy purpose, one tiny life at a time.

DAILY REFLECTION

In this sacred moment of nourishing your child, how can you open your heart to fully embrace both the joy and the challenges of your divine calling, trusting that each act of love is a reflection of God's nurturing grace flowing through you?

PRAYER

Dear Lord, In this sacred moment of nurturing my child, I seek Your comfort and grace. Help me to remember that each act of love, whether I hold my little one against my heart or cradle a bottle in my hands, is a reflection of Your divine provision. Wrap us both in Your embrace and fill my heart with peace, knowing that I am fulfilling my calling with every gentle whisper and loving gaze. Amen.

August 21

Reflect on the miraculous feeding of the multitude, a testament to God's abundant provision. In moments of need, trust that His grace will satisfy and nourish your spirit, just as it did for those gathered long ago.

John 6:14-15 - "When the people saw the sign that he had done, they said, 'This is indeed the Prophet who is to come into the world!' Perceiving then that they were about to come and take him by force to make him king, Jesus withdrew again to the mountain by himself."

DEVOTIONAL

In the quiet moments of gathering, perhaps like those that fateful day by the sea, we find ourselves in desperate need—not only of physical sustenance but also of spiritual nourishment. The miraculous feeding of the multitude reminds us that in the depths of our hunger and uncertainty, God sees us and knows us. Just as He multiplied the loaves and fishes, He longs to multiply our capacity to receive His grace and love. When challenges arise, it can be easy to feel overlooked or abandoned, yet His abundant provision assures us that we are never alone. As the crowd recognized the miracle and sought to elevate Jesus to earthly power, He chose to withdraw, teaching us that true sustenance comes from a relationship with Him rather than the affections of the world. In these moments of need and want, let us remember to look beyond our circumstances to the One who can satisfy the deepest longings of our hearts. Trust in His grace, for just as it nourished those gathered long ago, it will sustain and fill your spirit today.

DAILY REFLECTION

In what ways can you recognize God's abundant grace in your life, transforming your moments of hunger and desperation into opportunities for spiritual nourishment?

PRAYER

Dear Lord, in our moments of hunger and longing, help us to remember the miraculous provision You offered to the multitude. As we gather quietly before You, may we feel Your grace filling our spirits, assuaging our doubts and fears. Teach us to trust in Your abundant love, and remind us that true nourishment comes not from the world, but from the relationship we nurture with You. Amen.

August 22

In the rawness of postpartum emotions, remember that God sees your struggles and holds your heart close. His strength is made perfect in your weakness, and His love is a refuge in this storm. Lean into His grace, for even in tears, you are deeply cherished.

Psalm 56:8-9 - "You keep track of all my sorrows. You have collected all my tears in your bottle. You have recorded each one in your book. My enemies will retreat when I call to you for help. This I know: God is on my side."

DEVOTIONAL

In the midst of overwhelming emotions, as you navigate the challenges of postpartum life, take a moment to breathe and acknowledge the weight of your heart. Psalm 56:8-9 reminds us that God sees every tear you shed, collecting them as sacred reminders of your journey. He knows the depths of your sorrow, the fears that creep in, and the moments when the world feels too heavy to bear. Yet, in this raw vulnerability, His gentle strength envelops you, urging you to lean into His grace. Each tear is not in vain; they are testimonies of love, resilience, and the profound bond you're forging with your child. Allow yourself to feel, to cry, and to rest in the truth that you are deeply cherished. Remember, you are never alone; He walks beside you, ready to soothe your spirit with His unwavering presence.

DAILY REFLECTION

In your most vulnerable moments of postpartum struggle, how can you invite God's tender presence into your heartache, allowing each tear to transform into a testament of His unwavering love and your growing strength?

PRAYER

Dear Lord, in this fragile moment of postpartum overwhelm, I lay my heart before You, my tears a testament to both my struggles and my love. Embrace me in Your unwavering presence, reminding me that even in my weakest moments, I am held tightly in the embrace of Your grace. Help me to find solace in You, knowing that every tear I shed is seen and cherished by You, a reflection of the beautiful bond I am creating amidst the chaos. Amen.

August 23

As you welcome family for the first visit to meet your precious new addition, may the joy of new beginnings remind you of God's blessings. Each moment with your little one is a testament to His love, a fresh start filled with hope and grace. Cherish the laughter and connection as you share this sacred time together.

1 Chronicles 16:34 - "Give thanks to the LORD, for he is good; his love endures forever."

DEVOTIONAL

As family gathers to welcome your little miracle, take a moment to breathe in the beauty of this new beginning. Each heartwarming smile and cooing sound from your baby speaks of God's unending love and the fresh grace He pours into your life. In the laughter shared around the room, you'll find echoes of His faithfulness, reminding you that every precious moment is a gift to be cherished. Reflect on the promise in 1 Chronicles 16:34: "Give thanks to the LORD, for he is good; his love endures forever." This gathering is not just a celebration of your child's arrival, but a beautiful reminder of the love that binds your family together, a love that mirrors God's own. Embrace the joy that fills the air, knowing that with each visit, your hearts grow closer, knit together by shared memories and the blessings of His grace. As you cradle your baby, let gratitude wash over you, for this sacred time is a glimpse of heaven's delight in your life.

DAILY REFLECTION

How can you intentionally cultivate gratitude in your heart and home during this sacred time, recognizing each joyful interaction as a glimpse of God's enduring love that weaves your family closer together?

PRAYER

Dear Lord, as our family gathers to welcome this precious little one, fill our hearts with gratitude for the gift of new life and the love that surrounds us. Let each smile and coo remind us of Your unending grace and faithfulness, and help us to cherish these fleeting moments as sacred treasures. May this time together deepen our bonds and reflect the warmth of Your love, echoing through generations to come. Amen.

August 24

On this special day of celebration, reflect on the unconditional love that mirrors Christ's own. Just as mothers nurture and guide with grace, let us honor those who embody His love in our lives, cherishing the bonds that draw us closer to Him.
1 John 4:11 - "Beloved, if God so loved us, we also ought to love one another."

DEVOTIONAL

On this special day of celebration, we gather to honor the incredible love that mothers and motherly figures bestow upon us, a love that is often a reflection of Christ's own. Just as God demonstrated His boundless affection for us, so too do mothers pour their hearts into nurturing their children, guiding them through trials, and celebrating their victories. Today, let us pause and recognize the profound grace embedded in these relationships—how they mirror the unconditional love spoken of in 1 John 4:11. As we honor those who have nurtured us, let us also commit to embodying that same love in our interactions with one another. In every embrace, in every word of encouragement, we find a chance to live out the love that God has lavished upon us. Cherishing these bonds draws us closer to Him, reminding us that love, in its purest form, is meant to be shared, multiplied, and made manifest in our daily lives. So, as we celebrate today, may we reflect on how we too can be vessels of His love, ever willing to nurture and uplift those around us.

DAILY REFLECTION

How can you express and live out the unconditional love that mirrors Christ's own, as a tribute to those who have nurtured you in your life?

PRAYER

Dear Lord, on this special day of celebration, we pause to thank You for the nurturing hearts that reflect Your own unfailing love. May we honor those who have poured themselves into our lives, remembering their grace in every moment. Help us to embody this love in our own lives, to be vessels of Your compassion, and to uplift others as we draw closer to You in every embrace and every word. Amen.

On this special day, as you navigate your first grocery run with your baby, may you find joy in the simple moments and strength in God's guiding presence. Trust that each small step is a blessing, and let your little one witness the beauty of everyday grace.

1 Thessalonians 3:9-10 - How can we thank God enough for you in return for all the joy we feel before our God because of you? Night and day we pray most earnestly that we may see you again and supply what is lacking in your faith.

DEVOTIONAL

As you embark on your first grocery run with your precious little one, take a moment to breathe in the beauty of this new chapter. Each aisle is not just a place of purchase but a canvas where you paint memories—of laughter, discovery, and grace. In the hustle of selecting fresh produce and navigating shopping carts, remember that your journey is woven with God's loving presence. Just as Paul expressed his gratitude in 1 Thessalonians, let every item you place in your cart serve as a reminder of the blessings you have—your baby, your love, and the community that supports you. May your heart swell with joy as you reflect on how far you've come, and may you find strength in knowing that every small step you take today is a testament to faith. Allow your little one to soak in these moments, learning that life is found in the simple routines and shared experiences. Trust that God is with you in every moment, nurturing both your child and your faith as you embrace the everyday grace that awaits you.

DAILY REFLECTION

In the midst of this new adventure with your baby, how can you transform the routine of grocery shopping into a sacred moment of gratitude and connection with God, celebrating both the small blessings and the profound grace that surrounds your journey?

PRAYER

Dear Lord, as I take this first grocery run with my baby, I invite Your presence into every moment we share. Help me to uncover joy in the simplest tasks and to cherish the laughter and discoveries that unfold in the aisles. May each blessing I gather reflect the love You've bestowed upon us, nurturing both my little one and my spirit in this beautiful journey of parenthood. Amen.

On this day of reflection, rejoice in the miraculous growth of faith, much like the blossoming of a child. Just as a baby transforms with each passing moment, so too do we grow in grace and love, reminding us of God's continual work within us. Celebrate this journey of growth, for each step brings us closer to His purpose.

2 Peter 3:18 - "But grow in the grace and knowledge of our Lord and Savior Jesus Christ. To him be glory both now and forever! Amen."

DEVOTIONAL

On this special day of reflection, pause and marvel at the wondrous growth within you, much like a child who awakens to new capabilities each day. Just as a baby learns to walk, speak, and experience the world, our faith burgeons with every moment we lean into God's grace. Remember, each small step you take on this journey is not insignificant; it is a testament to His transforming love at work within you. As you celebrate the milestones in your spiritual life, whether they be profound revelations or gentle nudges towards His purpose, rejoice in the beauty of growth. In the tender care of our Lord, you are nurtured and equipped for every challenge ahead. Embrace the promise of 2 Peter 3:18, urging us to continually expand in grace and knowledge. To Him be the glory for the journey we share, one precious moment after another!

DAILY REFLECTION

As you witness the beautiful unfolding of your faith, what new capabilities or understandings have you discovered recently that reflect God's transformative love at work in your life?

PRAYER

Dear Lord, as we stand in awe of the growth we witness in our lives and the lives of our loved ones, may we never lose sight of the beauty that unfolds with each passing moment. Help us to embrace the journey of our faith, recognizing that every step, no matter how small, is a testament to Your grace and love at work within us. We celebrate this miraculous transformation and offer our hearts in gratitude for the purpose You fulfill in our lives. Amen.

August 27

In moments of unexpected chaos, like a baby's spit-up, find grace in the humility of parenthood. Just as God embraces our messiness, we're reminded to love unconditionally, cherishing every moment, however messy it may be. Let each spill serve as a testament to the beautiful, sometimes messy journey of nurturing life.

2 Corinthians 4:7-9 - "But we have this treasure in jars of clay, to show that the surpassing power belongs to God and not to us. We are afflicted in every way, but not crushed; perplexed, but not driven to despair; persecuted, but not forsaken; struck down, but not destroyed."

DEVOTIONAL

In the gentle chaos of parenthood, a baby's spit-up on your freshly laundered shirt is more than just a mess; it's a sacred moment of grace. 2 Corinthians 4:7-9 reminds us that we are like jars of clay—fragile yet filled with the remarkable treasure of life and love, entrusted to us by God. Just as the divine embraces our imperfections, so too are we called to embrace the disarray that comes with nurturing a tiny human being. Each spill is an invitation to reflect on the beauty that lies in vulnerability and the unyielding strength found in humility. In moments when frustration might creep in, let us remember that we are not alone; God walks with us through every perplexing challenge and joyous triumph. Instead of despairing, we can choose to cherish these fleeting instances, reveling in the love that transcends the chaos. May each unexpected mess serve as a reminder that in our nurturing, we are becoming more like Him—crafted in grace, molded by love, and fortified through every trial.

DAILY REFLECTION

In the midst of parenting's delightful chaos, how can you embrace the spills and imperfections as sacred moments that deepen your understanding of God's love and grace in your own life?

PRAYER

Dear Lord, in the midst of this beautiful chaos, help me embrace the spills and the messes as sacred reminders of the love we share. Grant me the grace to see each moment as a precious gift, filled with the nurturing lessons that shape my heart. May I find joy and humility in every unexpected challenge, knowing that through these trials, I am drawn closer to You and the true essence of unconditional love. Amen.

August 28

As dawn breaks, embrace the fresh grace of a new day, remembering that each moment is a gift from God. Stretch your spirit as you awaken to His promises, ready to walk in His light and love today.

Lamentations 3:25-26 - "The LORD is good to those who hope is in him, to the one who seeks him; it is good to wait quietly for the salvation of the LORD."

DEVOTIONAL

As the first rays of dawn caress the world, take a moment to stretch not just your body, but your spirit. In that gentle awakening, remember that each new day is a profound gift from God—filled with untold possibilities and fresh grace. Just as the sun rises, illuminating the darkness, so too does His love pour over you, inviting you to step into His promises. Reflect on Lamentations 3:25-26, which reminds us that the Lord is good to those who place their hope in Him. With every breath, as you wake from the night's slumber, inhale the assurance of His presence and exhale your worries and fears. Embrace the peace in waiting quietly for His guidance, knowing that He walks beside you through the moments of today. As you rise, let your heart rejoice and your spirit stretch, ready to embrace the unfolding beauty of His love in every moment ahead.

DAILY REFLECTION

As you stretch into this new day, how will you actively nurture your spirit to fully embrace the promises of God's love and the endless possibilities He has placed before you?

PRAYER

Dear Lord, as the dawn breaks and the world starts to awaken, I thank You for the gift of this new day. Help me to stretch my spirit wide, embracing the fresh grace You offer, and instill in me a deep awareness of Your unwavering love and guidance throughout the hours ahead. May I step boldly into each moment, trusting in Your promises and finding joy in the beautiful possibilities that You have laid before me. Amen.

August 29

On this special day, we celebrate the joy of nourishment, both physical and spiritual. Just as a mother's first successful latch symbolizes connection and sustenance, may we find reassurance in God's embrace, nourishing our souls with His love and grace. Trust in Him to provide for all your needs, as you nurture the next generation.

Matthew 7:9-11 - "Which of you, if your son asks for bread, will give him a stone? Or if he asks for a fish, will give him a snake? If you then, though you are evil, know how to give good gifts to your children, how much more will your Father in heaven give good gifts to those who ask him!"

DEVOTIONAL

Today, we pause to recognize a moment of profound joy—a first successful latch, a symbol of life, connection, and the nourishment that brings comfort and security. Just as a mother cradles her child and offers them her very essence, so too does our Heavenly Father cradle us in His love, ready to nourish our weary souls. In Matthew 7:9-11, we are reminded that if we, as imperfect beings, instinctively provide for our children, how much more shall God, our perfect Father, shower us with His goodness? Each feeding session is a reminder of this divine provision; it teaches us to trust deeply in His promises and to believe that He truly knows our needs. As you nurture the next generation, reflect on the grace that God extends to you daily, offering bread instead of stones, fish instead of snakes. Embrace the beauty of this sacred connection, and know that in these tender moments, God is whispering His love and reassurance over you. May this day be filled with gratitude, as you experience not only the joy of physical nourishment but also the spiritual sustenance that comes from entrusting your cares to Him. As you pour into your child, remember that you are also being filled, supported by a loving Father who delights in giving good gifts to those who seek Him.

DAILY REFLECTION

In this moment of celebration for nourishment's embrace, how can you open your heart to fully trust in God's provision, allowing His love to flow through you as you nurture and cherish the next generation?

PRAYER

Dear Lord, on this precious day of connection and nourishment, I thank You for the gift of life and the joy of nurturing my child. As I experience the sweetness of each feeding session, may I always remember Your unwavering love, which sustains and fills me beyond measure. Help me to nurture with grace, trusting in Your perfect provision and reflecting Your goodness in every moment we share. Amen.

August 30

In moments of chaos and mess, God's grace offers a fresh start. Just as we change clothes after a blowout, He invites us to shed our burdens and step into His renewed life. Trust in His cleansing power to refresh your spirit today.

Isaiah 1:18 - "Come now, let us reason together, says the Lord: though your sins are like scarlet, they shall be as white as snow; though they are red like crimson, they shall become like wool."

DEVOTIONAL

Life can sometimes feel like an unending mess—a literal blowout of overwhelming emotions and burdens that leave us feeling stained and weary. Just as we reach for a fresh change of clothes after a disaster, our Heavenly Father beckons us to step away from the chaos and into the embrace of His grace. Isaiah 1:18 reminds us that no matter how tangled or dirty our lives may appear, He offers us a transformative renewal: "though your sins are like scarlet, they shall be as white as snow." Imagine the relief of shedding those burdens, as if peeling off a soiled shirt and stepping into a clean, soft fabric that wraps you in warmth and comfort. Jesus invites us to reason together—He understands our struggles and our messes, and He longs to cleanse us from them. In these moments of chaos, we can trust in His cleansing power, allowing Him to refresh our spirits and offer us a newfound clarity. Embrace His invitation today; shed the weight of your past and step into the vibrant life He has prepared for you. Hold onto the promise of renewal and step forward with confidence, dressed in His grace!

DAILY REFLECTION

In the whirlwind of life's messiness, how might embracing God's grace as your fresh start help you shed the burdens that weigh you down and walk confidently in the renewed identity He offers?

PRAYER

Dear Lord, in the midst of life's chaos and the messiness that sometimes overwhelms me, I seek your grace. Help me to let go of the burdens that cling to my spirit and to embrace the fresh start you offer. Wrap me in your love, Lord, and let your cleansing power renew my heart, so I may step boldly into the vibrant life you have for me. Amen.

August 31

On this day of deep reflection as we approach the season of Advent, let the cries of your heart be a call to await the coming of Christ, just as a baby's wail signifies the start of life. Embrace the longing for hope and renewal, knowing that God's perfect plan is unfolding.

Romans 8:22-23 - "We know that the whole creation has been groaning as in the pains of childbirth right up to the present time. Not only so, but we ourselves, who have the firstfruits of the Spirit, groan inwardly as we wait eagerly for our adoption to sonship, the redemption of our bodies."

DEVOTIONAL

As we find ourselves on the threshold of Advent, the season that beckons us to anticipate the coming of Christ, let us pause in the sacred space of longing. Much like the cries of a newborn that announce their arrival into this world, our own heart's cries echo a deep yearning for hope, renewal, and the fulfillment of God's promises. In this moment of reflection, Romans 8:22-23 reminds us that the very fabric of creation groans with us, yearning for redemption and the glorious unveiling of our true identities as children of God. As you cradle your little one, consider how their cries tap into a divine rhythm of expectation—your heart mirrors this cry, longing for the fullness of life that only Christ can bring. This Advent, embrace the ache of anticipation; it is in this very longing that God weaves His perfect plan. With each tear, each sigh, allow them to be a prayer, a testament of faith, as we await the joyous dawning of hope in the form of a humble Child. Trust that in the waiting, you are being filled with the Spirit, preparing to witness the miraculous.

DAILY REFLECTION

In this season of Advent, how can you allow the cries of your heart, much like those of your newborn, to guide you deeper into the sacred anticipation of Christ's coming, embracing the raw beauty of longing as a pathway to renewed hope and divine revelation?

PRAYER

Dear Lord, as we stand at the dawn of Advent, may the cries of our hearts resonate with the deep longing for Your presence. Help us to embrace the beauty of anticipation, allowing each sigh, each tear, to draw us closer to the hope that only You can fulfill. In this sacred waiting, fill our spirits with Your peace, reminding us that each moment of longing is a step toward the miraculous arrival of Your Child, our Savior. Amen.

September 1

Trust in God's timing, even in the quiet moments of your day. Just as the Lord rested on the seventh day, find peace in the stillness, knowing His plans unfold in each gentle breath of your little one. Let this nap remind you of the strength found in surrendering to His will.

Ecclesiastes 3:11 - "He has made everything beautiful in its time."

DEVOTIONAL

As you hold your little one close, surrender to the peaceful rhythm of their breath, a beautiful reminder of God's perfect timing. In this quiet moment, allow the world around you to fade away, knowing that just as the Lord rested on the seventh day, He invites you to find solace in stillness. Each gentle sigh from your baby whispers that life does not rush; it unfolds gracefully, one precious moment at a time. Reflect on Ecclesiastes 3:11: "He has made everything beautiful in its time." Trust that this nap is not merely a pause in your day but a sacred opportunity to align your heart with God's plans for you and your family. Embrace this time of rest as a gift of surrender, knowing that in these slivers of stillness, God weaves His handiwork within your life. Together, in the hush of this moment, nurture the faith that all will come together beautifully, just as it was meant to be.

DAILY REFLECTION

In the tender stillness of this moment, how can you open your heart to God's gentle reminders that even in what feels like rest, His divine orchestration is at work, shaping the beautiful tapestry of your life?

PRAYER

Father in heaven, as I hold my little one close, enveloped in the quiet rhythm of their breath, help me to embrace this stillness as a sacred gift from You. Let me find strength in surrender, trusting that Your plans unfold in each gentle sigh and moment of rest. May this nap be a reminder of Your perfect timing, filling my heart with peace as I align my life with Your beautiful design. Amen.

September 2

As the first belly button stump falls away, reflect on the beauty of new beginnings and the promise of growth in faith. Just as this tiny sign of life signifies a journey starting anew, let it remind us of God's continuous work in our lives, nurturing us toward deeper connections with Him and each other.

1 Peter 1:3 - Blessed be the God and Father of our Lord Jesus Christ! According to his great mercy, he has caused us to be born again to a living hope through the resurrection of Jesus Christ from the dead.

DEVOTIONAL

As we witness the delicate belly button stump fall away, we are invited to pause and reflect on the beauty of new beginnings. This small yet profound change marks not just a physical milestone, but a spiritual awakening that echoes the promise of our faith. Just as a newborn baby begins their life's journey, so too are we reminded of the continuous work God does within us, nurturing growth and transformation. In 1 Peter 1:3, we find assurance of our rebirth in Christ—a living hope birthed from His great mercy. Each moment we experience renewal is an invitation to dive deeper into our relationship with Him, to cultivate connections that reflect His love. May we embrace these fresh starts with open hearts, recognizing that as God guides us through each season of life, we are forever destined for remarkable growth. Let the falling away of this tiny symbol serve as a reminder: in every ending, God graciously ushers in a beautiful new beginning.

DAILY REFLECTION

How does the gentle letting go of the belly button stump resonate with your own experiences of surrendering to God's transformative grace, inviting you to embrace the new beginnings that await in your spiritual journey?

PRAYER

Dear Lord, as this tiny belly button stump falls away, may it serve as a gentle reminder of the new beginnings You weave into our lives. Help us to embrace this small yet significant change as a symbol of Your nurturing presence, guiding us toward deeper connections with You and each other. Let our hearts remain open to the beautiful growth You promise in every season, trusting in the living hope that blooms within us through Your mercy. Amen.

September 3

Loving care is found in the smallest acts; as you trim your baby's nails for the first time, remember that just as God lovingly shapes our lives, you have the opportunity to nurture and protect your little one with gentleness and patience. Reflect on the love that guides your hands in this tender moment.

Psalm 91:11-12: "For he will command his angels concerning you to guard you in all your ways; they will lift you up in their hands, so that you will not strike your foot against a stone."

DEVOTIONAL

As you cradle your little one in your arms, preparing to trim those tiny nails for the first time, take a moment to breathe in the beauty of this act. Each snip, though small, echoes a love that is deep and profound—a reminder of how God meticulously shapes our lives with His attentive care. Just as He commands His angels to guard us, you too are called to protect and nurture your child, guiding their fragile journey with tenderness. Psalm 91:11-12 reassures us that we are never alone in our caregiving; heaven stands vigilant, lifting us in loving hands. In this sacred moment, may your heart resonate with the gentle joy of nurturing, reflecting on the countless ways love envelops us all. Approach this task with patience, knowing that even the smallest acts of care can lay a foundation of security and trust. Let this first experience serve as a cherished memory, forever reminding you of the beauty found in loving the little ones entrusted to you.

DAILY REFLECTION

As you gently clip your baby's tiny nails for the first time, how can this simple act of care deepen your understanding of God's unwavering love and protection in your child's life?

PRAYER

Dear Lord, in this tender moment of caring for my little one, I thank You for the gift of parenthood and the privilege to nurture this precious life. As I gently trim these tiny nails, may Your love guide my hands —infusing each little snip with patience and attentiveness. Remind me that in these small acts of care, I reflect Your profound love, and help me to be ever mindful of the sacred trust placed in me. Amen.

September 4

As you sing your first lullaby, remember that every note is a prayer, cradling your child in God's love. Trust in His guidance, for He watches over both you and your little one, filling your hearts with peace and joy. Let this moment be a sacred reflection of His promise to nurture and protect.

Psalm 31:15 - "My times are in your hands; deliver me from the hand of my enemies and from those who pursue me."

DEVOTIONAL

As you cradle your little one in your arms, the quiet room enveloped in warmth, take a moment to pause and breathe in the beauty of this sacred time. With each gentle note of your lullaby, envision that you're weaving a cocoon of love and safety around your child, an offering of your heart as a prayer to God. Psalm 31:15 reminds us, "My times are in your hands," a profound truth that speaks to the assurance we find in surrendering our worries and fears to Him. Every soft hum and tender melody becomes a testament to your trust in God's unwavering guidance over both your lives. In this intimate moment, feel the peace that surrounds you, knowing He watches over you, filling your hearts with joy and reassurance. Let the soothing rhythm of your voice echo the promise that God nurtures and protects, not just your child, but you as well. As you sing, remember—it is not only a lullaby; it is a profound connection to the divine, a reflection of faith that transcends this fragile moment and enters eternity.

DAILY REFLECTION

As you hum your first lullaby, what emotions stir within you as you trust in God's embrace, knowing that each note carries your heartfelt prayers for your child's journey ahead?

PRAYER

Dear Lord, as I hold my precious baby close and sing this lullaby, I pray that each note carries my love and trust in Your divine care. Wrap us both in Your warmth and grace, granting us peace as we embrace this tender moment. May Your guiding presence envelop our hearts, reminding us always that our lives are cradled in Your gentle hands.

September 5

"God's love shines brightly like a guiding star. As you read together, let every word be a reminder of His light leading us through life's journey."

Isaiah 60:1-2 - "Arise, shine, for your light has come, and the glory of the Lord rises upon you. See, darkness covers the earth and thick darkness is over the peoples, but the Lord rises upon you and his glory appears over you."

DEVOTIONAL

As you cradle your little one in your arms, let the warmth of God's love envelop both of you like a cozy blanket under a starlit sky. The act of reading together becomes a sacred moment, where every word transforms into a gentle reminder of that guiding star leading you both through life's journey. Isaiah reminds us that even amidst the darkness, the glory of the Lord shines uniquely upon us, illuminating our path with hope and tenderness. In these quiet moments, when you share stories, remember that God's light is not just a distant glow but a tangible presence, ready to guide both you and your child. Perhaps, as you read, you might wonder—how will your journey unfold? Let every sentence breathe life and joy, and may it spark curiosity about the world and their Maker. As you instill the love of reading, know that this connection nurtures not just a love for books, but a deeper understanding of God's unwavering light. Together, may you rise and shine in His grace, creating cherished memories that reflect His love brightly.

DAILY REFLECTION

As you share this treasured moment of reading with your little one, how does the thought of God's love as a guiding star inspire you to embrace the beauty of your journey together, illuminating the path with hope and wonder?

PRAYER

Dear Lord, as I hold this precious little one close, I thank You for the gift of Your love that surrounds us like a warm embrace beneath the stars. May each story we share illuminate our hearts with Your light, guiding us with hope and wonder as we embark on this journey together. Help us to see Your presence in every page, nurturing a love for reading that deepens our understanding of Your everlasting grace. Amen.

September 6

Even in the season of change, God's love remains steadfast. Trust that each strand of hair lost is part of the divine plan, paving the way for new beginnings and renewed strength as you nurture both your child and yourself.

1 Peter 1:24-25 - "For all flesh is like grass and all its glory like the flower of grass. The grass withers, and the flower falls, but the word of the Lord remains forever."

DEVOTIONAL

As you stand before the mirror, witnessing the loss of strands that once framed your glowing face, remember that every change is steeped in purpose. Just as the grass withers and the flowers fade, God gently reminds us that our lives are marked by seasons, each one unfolding His divine plan. Your postpartum journey is a beautiful example of this cycle—not only nurturing your child but also nurturing yourself through the shifts that motherhood brings. In these moments of transition, where emotions may run deep and uncertain, hold tightly to the promise of 1 Peter 1:24-25. God's love remains unwavering, like a steady hand against the tempests of change. Each hair that falls is not a loss but a preparation for renewal—a symbol of growth that mirrors your own metamorphosis into mother and nurturer. Trust in the Lord's words, for they endure forever, guiding you through every season with grace and strength.

DAILY REFLECTION

In this season of shedding and renewal, how can you embrace the beauty of your transformation while trusting in God's unwavering love as you navigate the bittersweet changes of motherhood?

PRAYER

Dear Lord, in this season of change, I come before You with a heart both tender and heavy. As strands of hair fall away, remind me that Your love is a constant, a steadfast presence through every shift and transformation. Help me to embrace this journey of motherhood, trusting that each moment of loss is a step toward renewal, shaping me into the nurturer I am meant to be. Amen.

In this season of renewal and grace, turning back to ordinary garments signifies a fresh start. Allow God's love to envelop you as you shed the layers of past struggles, stepping into His light with confidence and joy. Trust in His promise that every day is an opportunity for transformation.

Romans 12:2 - "Do not conform to the pattern of this world, but be transformed by the renewing of your mind. Then you will be able to test and approve what God's will is—his good, pleasing and perfect will."

DEVOTIONAL

As you turn away from the constraints of past struggles and don the simple comfort of ordinary clothes, let this act be a symbol of your renewed spirit. Romans 12:2 reminds us to not conform to the expectations that weigh us down but instead to embrace the transformative power of God. In this season of renewal and grace, each stitch of fabric becomes a reminder that His love envelops you—soft, warm, and inviting. Shed the layers of doubt and fear, stepping boldly into the light that illuminates your path and offers a fresh start. Each day is an invitation to experience His grace anew, trusting that you are not defined by past trials but rather shaped for His good and perfect will. Allow yourself the joy of these moments, where every breath is a declaration of hope and every heartbeat resonates with potential. Embrace this season; let the ordinary become extraordinary as you walk confidently in the love He has for you.

DAILY REFLECTION

In this moment of renewal, how can you consciously embrace the simplicity of everyday life as a canvas for God's transformative work within you?

PRAYER

Dear Lord, as I step into the comfort of ordinary clothes today, let each thread remind me of Your embracing love and grace. Help me to shed the burdens of my past and rise boldly into the light of Your promise, confident in the transformation You are orchestrating within me. May I find joy in the simple moments and recognize that every day holds the potential for renewal, as I walk boldly in the profound truth of Your steadfast presence. Amen.

September 8

In the quiet of night, as you cradle your little one, remember that God's strength is made perfect in your weariness. Each moment of sacrifice is a reflection of His unfailing love, and He is with you in every tired whisper and gentle lullaby. Rest in His promises; He replenishes the weary soul.

Psalm 119:28 - "My soul melts away for sorrow; strengthen me according to your word."

DEVOTIONAL

In the stillness of the night, as you cradle your little one in your weary arms, let the weight of your exhaustion wash over you like a blanket of love wrapped around your heart. Each tired sigh is a testament to the depth of your devotion, a reflection of God's unfailing love that mirrors your own. Remember, it's in these quiet moments, beneath the soft glow of a nightlight, that His strength finds you, reviving the soul that feels heavy with sorrow. "My soul melts away for sorrow," you may whisper, but it is here, in your vulnerability, that the Lord promises to strengthen you. As you rock back and forth, let each gentle lullaby be a prayer, a reminder that He is with you in your fatigue, reassuring you of His presence. Allow yourself to find solace in His Word; it's not about perfect rest, but about resting in His promises. Trust that He replenishes the weary, and even in your darkest hours of sacrifice, His love shines the brightest.

DAILY REFLECTION

In these precious, weary hours, how can you surrender your fatigue to God, allowing His unwavering love to transform your exhaustion into a sacred act of devotion for your little one?

PRAYER

Dear Lord, in this sacred hour of quiet, I come before You with a heart heavy from weariness yet filled with love. As I cradle my little one, let me feel Your gentle embrace, reminding me that in my exhaustion, Your strength sustains me. Help me to see these moments as a canvas where my sacrifices reflect Your everlasting grace, and grant me peace in knowing that even in the darkest nights, Your light shines through my every lullaby. Amen.

As you hold your newborn for the first time, remember that just as God knits us together in His image, He invites you to cherish this divine connection. Embrace the sacred gift of life, reflecting the love of the Father in every heartbeat and gentle touch. May this moment be a holy reminder of the bond that shapes your family's journey.

Genesis 33:5 – "When Esau looked up and saw the women and children, he asked, 'Who are these with you?' Jacob answered, 'They are the children God has graciously given your servant.'"

DEVOTIONAL

As you hold your newborn for the first time, allow this sacred moment to wash over you like a gentle tide. In your arms lies a treasure, a fragile life woven with divine intent, a reminder that God, the master Creator, knits each of us together in His image. Just as Jacob spoke of his children as gifts from God, so too does your heart swell with gratitude for this cherished new life. Each heartbeat is a symphony of love and hope, echoing the very heartbeat of the Father who delighted in your creation. Reflect on the holy bond being formed in these quiet, precious moments—one that will shape your family's journey for years to come. May this connection serve as a foundation of joy and faith, a living testament to God's gracious provision. Embrace this beautiful calling, and let every gentle touch be a prayer of thanks for the gift of life you now cradle within your arms.

DAILY REFLECTION

How can you nurture and deepen the divine bond you are creating with your newborn, allowing each moment to reflect the immeasurable love that God has for you and your family?

PRAYER

Dear Lord, as I cradle this precious life in my arms, I am overwhelmed by the sacred bond we've begun to forge. Thank You for this miracle, this gift woven with purpose in Your image; may each heartbeat be a reminder of Your boundless love. Help me to nurture this child with grace and faith, reflecting Your light in our journey together, and treasure these moments as sacred whispers of Your promise. Amen.

On this special day, as we reflect on our reliance on God's grace, consider how introducing a pacifier can symbolize trust and comfort in our faith journey. Just as a newborn finds peace in their pacifier, we too can seek solace in the gentle support of God's presence. May we embrace His love as our ultimate source of comfort.

Psalm 121:1-2 – "I lift up my eyes to the hills. From where does my help come? My help comes from the Lord, who made heaven and earth."

DEVOTIONAL

On this special day, we pause to reflect on the simple yet profound act of introducing a pacifier, a small symbol that brings immense comfort to a newborn. Just as a baby instinctively reaches for that soft, comforting object when the world feels overwhelming, we too are invited to lean into the tender embrace of God's grace when life's trials arise. Psalm 121:1-2 reassures us, "I lift up my eyes to the hills. From where does my help come? My help comes from the Lord, who made heaven and earth." In this scripture, we find a reminder that our true source of solace and strength lies beyond our circumstances. As we navigate our faith journey, let us remember that God stands ready to offer us peace, much like a parent offers a pacifier to soothe a fussy child. In moments of doubt, let us lift our eyes higher, seeking His presence and comfort in every situation. Today, embrace God's love as your ultimate pacifier—steady, assured, and unwavering. Feel His gentle support, knowing that the Creator of all stands as your refuge, ready to calm your restless heart with His grace.

DAILY REFLECTION

In what ways can you consciously lean into God's presence today, allowing His love to be the comforting pacifier for your heart amid life's uncertainties?

PRAYER

Dear Lord, as I introduce this new source of comfort to my little one, may I also be reminded to seek the gentle peace of Your presence in my own life. Like a pacifier soothes a restless heart, may Your grace cradle my worries and doubts, drawing me closer to the solace found in You. Help me to trust in Your unfailing love, knowing that You are my ultimate source of strength and comfort in every season of life. Amen.

September 11

On this day, reflect on the miracle of new life through the lens of faith. Just as a baby's first sneeze signals growth, let us embrace the fresh beginnings God offers us each day, reminding us of His continual presence and grace in our lives.

Matthew 19:13-15 - "Then little children were brought to Him that He might put His hands on them and pray. But the disciples rebuked them. But Jesus said, 'Let the little children come to Me, and do not hinder them, for to such belongs the kingdom of heaven.' And He laid His hands on them and went away."

DEVOTIONAL

In the soft hush of a newborn's first sneeze, there exists a miraculous echo of life's potential—a gentle reminder that new beginnings are nestled in the very fabric of our daily existence. Just as that tiny sound signals growth and readiness to explore the world, so does each new day invite us to recognize God's vibrant grace stirring within us. Jesus' invitation for the little ones to come to Him reflects a profound truth: That in pure innocence and unguarded faith, we encounter the heart of God. Today, let us rejoice in the beauty of fresh starts, be they grand or seemingly small. Embrace the divine touch that accompanies every moment of awakening in our lives, for in them lies the promise of transformation and hope. Remember, just as the little children are welcomed into the kingdom of heaven, so too are we invited to draw near to the Father, with hearts wide open to receive His blessings. In this sacred space of newness, may we find courage to grow, to learn, and to lean into the abundance of God's love.

DAILY REFLECTION

In the gentle whisper of a baby's first sneeze, how is God inviting you to awaken to the fresh beginnings and transformative grace available in your life today?

PRAYER

Dear Lord, as we witness the tender miracle of a baby's first sneeze, we are reminded of the beauty found in new beginnings. Help us to embrace each day with open hearts, recognizing Your presence in the small moments of growth and transformation. May we always surrender our innocence to Your love, allowing us to explore the boundless grace You have for us. Amen.

September 12

On this joyous day, like a newborn gazing in wonder, may our hearts be drawn to the light of Christ. As we witness His love, let us commit to nurturing faith in our lives, trusting that each moment brings us closer to Him.

John 1:5 - "The light shines in the darkness, and the darkness has not overcome it."

DEVOTIONAL

On this joyous day, as a newborn gazes with awe and wonder, we too are invited to turn our eyes toward the radiant light of Christ. Just as that sweet little one tracks movement with curiosity, may our hearts be drawn to the whispers of God's love that surround us. In John 1:5, we are reminded that "the light shines in the darkness, and the darkness has not overcome it." In moments of uncertainty, let this truth wrap around us like a cozy blanket, illuminating our path and offering reassurance. Let us embrace the beauty of nurturing faith within us, much like a parent cherishes every milestone of their child. Each fleeting moment offers us the chance to deepen our relationship with Jesus, trusting that He is always there, steady and unwavering. May we reflect on His light today, allowing it to guide our thoughts and actions as we step forward, not just as witnesses, but as bearers of His love.

DAILY REFLECTION

How can I open my heart like a newborn to truly embrace the light of Christ in my everyday moments, allowing His love to guide my path and nurture my faith?

PRAYER

Dear Lord, as we stand in awe of the precious gift of new life, may our hearts mirror the wonder of a child's gaze fixed upon Your light. Help us to trust in Your unwavering love, nurturing our faith like tender seedlings, so that we may grow ever closer to You. In moments of doubt, remind us that Your light dispels darkness, comforting us as we embrace the journey ahead, filled with hope and grace.

September 13

As the new life begins a journey, reflect on the miracle of creation and the promise of hope. Each yawn, a reminder of God's tender care and the blessings that come with nurturing love. Celebrate this season of renewal with gratitude for the precious gift of life.

1 Peter 1:3-4 - "Blessed be the God and Father of our Lord Jesus Christ! According to his great mercy, he has caused us to be born again to a living hope through the resurrection of Jesus Christ from the dead, to an inheritance that is imperishable, undefiled, and unfading, kept in heaven for you."

DEVOTIONAL

As we witness the miracle of new life, each yawning moment becomes a sweet reminder of God's tender care. Today, let us reflect on the gentle rhythms of creation—the tiny yawns of a newborn, blossoming with potential, echoing the hope we have in Christ. In 1 Peter 1:3-4, we are assured that through God's great mercy, we embark on a journey of rebirth, awakened to a living hope. This season of renewal invites us to embrace the blessings that surround us, recognizing that every flicker of life holds God's promise. Just as a baby's yawn signals a day filled with possibilities, so does our faith awaken us to the incredible inheritance stored for us in heaven. May we nurture this hope with gratitude in our hearts, celebrating the precious gift of life and the nurturing love that embodies our Creator. Let our lives be a testament to the beauty of His handiwork, as we embrace each moment with joy and wonder.

DAILY REFLECTION

In this sacred season of renewal, how can we, like a newborn's gentle yawn, express our gratitude for the tender care and boundless possibilities that God weaves into each moment of our lives?

PRAYER

Dear Lord, as we marvel at the tender moments of new life, we thank You for each precious yawn that whispers of hope and promise. May we be ever mindful of Your nurturing love, embracing the beauty of creation that unfolds before us. Help us to celebrate the gift of life with gratitude, for in every heartbeat and every gentle sigh, we find a reflection of Your divine care and the endless possibilities that lie ahead. Amen.

September 14

In moments of concern over your baby's temperature, turn your anxious thoughts to God, who cares for each little one. Trust that He holds your child in His loving hands, granting you peace and wisdom in this time of worry. Remember, God's comfort is your anchor amid uncertainties.

Matthew 6:25-26 - "Therefore I tell you, do not be anxious about your life, what you will eat or what you will drink, nor about your body, what you will put on. Is not life more than food, and the body more than clothing? Look at the birds of the air: they neither sow nor reap nor gather into barns, and yet your heavenly Father feeds them. Are you not of more value than they?"

DEVOTIONAL

In those quiet, twilight hours, when your heart races at the thought of your baby's temperature rising, take a moment to breathe deeply and draw near to God. The worries of parenting can feel monumental, but remember that you are not alone; your child is cradled in the same hands that formed the universe. Just as Jesus gently reminds us about the birds of the air—carefree, trusting, and beautifully cared for—trust that your little one is cherished, too. God sees your every concern and understands the depth of your love; they are precious in His sight. Let His peace wash over you, calming the storm of anxiety within. In these moments of uncertainty, cling to the promise that you are held, and every fretful thought can be surrendered to His wisdom. God is your anchor amidst the waves of worry, guiding you toward rest and reassurance in His infinite care.

DAILY REFLECTION

In the stillness of your worry, how might embracing God's unwavering love and presence bring you comfort as you navigate the fears surrounding your baby's well-being?

PRAYER

Dear Lord, in this moment of worry, I bring my anxious heart before You. As I seek reassurance for my baby's well-being, let Your peace envelop me like a warm embrace, calming each racing thought. Grant me the wisdom to trust in Your perfect care, knowing that both my child and I are held securely in Your loving hands. Amen.

September 15

Welcoming new generations into our family embodies God's love and legacy. As your grandparent's visit unfolds, may you cherish the moments that intertwine faith and family, nurturing bonds that reflect the joy of Christ's love.

Proverbs 17:6 - "Children's children are a crown to the aged, and parents are the pride of their children."

DEVOTIONAL

As you prepare to welcome your grandparent into your home, take a moment to pause and reflect on the profound gift of family. Proverbs 17:6 beautifully reminds us that "Children's children are a crown to the aged," a celebration of the love that links generations. Each embrace and shared laugh carries the weight of God's legacy—one rich with stories, wisdom, and warmth. In these cherished moments, you invite not just your grandparent but also the spirit of Christ into your family, creating a tapestry woven with faith and joy. Consider the lessons they bring, the faith they exemplify, and how their presence acts as a living testimony to God's love flowing through your lineage. May you seize this time together to nurture relationships that embody grace, laughter, and reverence for the legacy of faith gifted to you. Hold tight to the beautiful truth that each generation is a chapter in the divine story God continues to write in your family.

DAILY REFLECTION

How does the presence of your grandparent enrich your understanding of God's love and legacy within your family, and what cherished moments will you create together that embody the joy and wisdom of Christ?

PRAYER

Dear Lord, as we open our home and hearts to our grandparent's visit, we thank You for the rich tapestry of love that family provides. Help us to embrace each moment, weaving together laughter and faith, and may our time together be a testament to Your unending love across generations. May we cherish the wisdom they share and honoring the legacy of grace that flows through our family line, reflecting the joy and warmth of Christ in every gathering and conversation.

September 16

On this day, we reflect on the joy and unity found in Christ's resurrection. As siblings in faith, let us celebrate our shared journey, fostering love and support as we grow together in His grace.

Philippians 2:1-2 - If you have any encouragement from being united with Christ, if any comfort from his love, if any common sharing in the Spirit, if any tenderness and compassion, then make my joy complete by being like-minded, having the same love, being one in spirit and of one mind.

DEVOTIONAL

On this day, as we gather in the warmth of our shared faith, we are reminded of the profound joy that springs from Christ's resurrection. It is in this sacred moment that we celebrate not only His victory over death but also the unity that binds us as siblings in faith. Just as He willingly sacrificed for us, we are called to nurture our connection with one another, fostering love and support in our daily lives. Philippians 2:1-2 invites us to embrace that divine encouragement, urging us to be like-minded and to embody His love in our interactions. As we reflect on our journey together, let us cultivate tenderness and compassion, drawing strength from the Spirit that unites us. In our shared laughter and tears, we find the heartbeat of community, where each act of kindness fuels our growth in His grace. Today, let us rejoice in our oneness, knowing that through Christ, we are not merely siblings but a powerful testament to His love in action.

DAILY REFLECTION

How can you deepen the love and support you share with your siblings in faith, reflecting the joy of Christ's resurrection in your daily interactions?

PRAYER

Dear Lord, on this special day, we gather as siblings in faith, united in the joy of Your resurrection. May Your love flow through us, nurturing our bonds and inspiring us to lift one another up in kindness and compassion. Help us to walk together in harmony, reflecting Your grace in all we do, as we celebrate not only the victory over death but the beautiful journey we share in Your light. Amen.

September 17

On this day, as the baby's tiny fingers grasp yours, remember that God's love is like that gentle hold—intimate and steadfast. Just as you nurture this new life, let your heart be open to the divine grip of grace surrounding you, guiding each step of faith.

Psalm 145:18 - The Lord is near to all who call on him, to all who call on him in truth.

DEVOTIONAL

Today, as your baby's tiny fingers wrap around yours, take a moment to breathe in the purity of that bond. In this delicate grasp, you experience a profound intimacy that echoes the nature of God's love—gentle yet unwavering, nurturing yet powerful. Just as you instinctively protect and guide this new life, remember that God, too, is ever-present, inviting you into His embrace with each call of your heart. Psalm 145:18 reassures us, "The Lord is near to all who call on him, to all who call on him in truth." Let your own grasp on faith be as open and trusting as the tiny hand entwined with yours. In this season of new beginnings, allow God's grace to envelop you, serving as your anchor as you navigate the sacred journey of parenthood. In every moment of doubt or fear, know that you are held, guided, and cherished—both by your child and by the eternal love of the Father.

DAILY REFLECTION

How can you embrace the divine love that surrounds you as you nurture this new life, allowing your heart to trust in God's gentle guidance just as you do with your baby's tiny grasp?

PRAYER

Dear Lord, as I feel my baby's delicate fingers wrap around mine, I am reminded of Your unwavering love that surrounds us. May this sacred bond inspire me to lean deeper into Your grace, nurturing not just my child, but also my own heart in the trust of Your presence. Help me to cherish each moment of this journey, knowing that just as I hold my little one, You hold us all in the gentle embrace of Your mercy.

September 18

In the quiet hours of night, even the smallest sounds can awaken great love. As Christ brings light into our darkness, may we find peace in the unexpected moments, fully trusting in His grace to guide us through every challenge.

Psalm 127:2 - "In vain you rise early and stay up late, toiling for food to eat— for he grants sleep to those he loves."

DEVOTIONAL

In the hushed embrace of night, when shadows dance and silence reigns, even the softest cries of a child can echo like thunder, stirring the heart in unexpected ways. It is in these tender hours, as you gently awaken to the needs of your little one, that you are reminded of the profound love Christ has for us—how His light pierces our darkness, guiding us with grace through the unforeseen challenges of parenthood. Psalm 127:2 speaks volumes in this season of your life, reassuring us that our toil, our sleepless nights, and the worries that weigh heavily on our hearts are not for naught. For in the tender moments of rocking a baby back to sleep, you are enveloped by the very love that God bestows upon His children. As you navigate these quiet interruptions, let them be reminders of His presence, showing you that even amidst the chaos and fatigue, there is profound beauty. Each coo and sigh draws forth an ocean of love awakening within you a deeper appreciation for the gift of life, both yours and the little one's. Trust that in these delicate moments, God is at work, inviting you to surrender your worries and rest in His promise of peaceful sleep. In embracing these unexpected disturbances, remember that you are cradled in His eternal love, designed to bring light, joy, and purpose to the night.

DAILY REFLECTION

In the stillness of night, when the gentle stirrings of your little one beckon you from your sleep how might you embrace these quiet interruptions as a sacred invitation to experience the unwavering love of Christ, illuminating your darkest hours with hope and grace?

PRAYER

Dear Lord, in these sacred, silent hours when sleep evades me and my little one stirs, remind me of the beauty hidden within these moments. May I embrace each soft cry as a gentle call to love, trusting in Your grace to guide my weary heart. Help me to find joy in the unexpected, knowing that Your light fills the shadows, and Your presence brings peace to my restless soul. Amen.

September 19

As you sort through tiny garments, remember that just as God knows each of your days, every piece of clothing holds a purpose in your child's journey. Trust in His preparation for new beginnings and cherish the joy of nurturing a life that will grow in His love.

Ephesians 6:4 - "Fathers, do not provoke your children to anger, but bring them up in the discipline and instruction of the Lord."

DEVOTIONAL

As you embark on the tender task of organizing tiny garments, let each piece remind you of the unique purpose woven into your child's life. Just as you sort through these clothes by size and theme, God meticulously plans each day of your journey together. Can you feel the anticipation in the air? Each outfit symbolizes not just warmth and comfort, but the love that envelops your family in His grace. Ephesians 6:4 whispers a gentle reminder – your role as a father is one of nurturing, guiding, and instilling wisdom in the little heart that will wear these clothes. Reflection on this verse may inspire not just discipline, but the joy of teaching through love and tenderness. Trust in God's preparations for your family, embracing the beautiful adventure that lies ahead as you nurture your child's growth in His everlasting love.

DAILY REFLECTION

As you carefully fold and arrange each tiny garment, how does recognizing God's intentional design in both your child's life and your role as a nurturing parent deepen your gratitude and fill you with hope for the journey ahead?

PRAYER

Dear Lord, as I sort through these tiny garments, each one reminding me of the precious life growing within, I thank You for the purpose You have woven into our journey. Help me to embrace this moment of preparation with joy and expectation, knowing that each piece reflects the love and guidance I am to provide. May Your grace fill our home as I nurture this little heart, trusting in Your plans for a beautiful adventure ahead. Amen.

September 20

On this quiet night, as your baby rests peacefully for a longer stretch, reflect on the miracle of new beginnings and God's gift of rest. Just as God grants us respite, cherish this moment of grace, knowing His presence brings peace to both you and your little one.

Exodus 33:14 - "My presence will go with you, and I will give you rest."

DEVOTIONAL

On this quiet night, as your baby sleeps longer and deeper than ever before, take a moment to pause and breathe in the stillness that surrounds you. The gentle rise and fall of your child's tiny chest is a beautiful reminder of God's handiwork — the miracle of new beginnings and the precious gift of rest He bestows upon us. Just as the Lord promises in Exodus 33:14, "My presence will go with you, and I will give you rest," let this be a sacred moment where His peace envelops both you and your little one. In these serene hours, allow the weight of daily worries to lift, for God knows your needs and cradles them with love. Embrace the sweetness of tonight, knowing that His presence brings safety and comfort, allowing you to embrace this fleeting season with gratitude. Cherish the stillness, and let it remind you that even in the midst of chaos, He is with you, granting you a sanctuary of calm. Tonight, as your heart swells with love, surrender to the joy of His presence, finding strength in His promise of rest.

DAILY REFLECTION

In this peaceful moment as your baby sleeps soundly, how can you allow God's promise of rest to transform your heart and fill your home with serenity amidst the joyful chaos of new parenthood?

PRAYER

Dear Lord, on this serene night, I thank You for the precious gift of rest that envelops both my little one and me. As I listen to the gentle rhythm of their breathing, I am reminded of Your unwavering presence, comforting us in this sacred moment. Help me to embrace the stillness, releasing my worries into Your loving care, and may our hearts find peace in the miracle of this new beginning. Amen.

Celebrating the joyful milestone of a baby's first roll, reflect on how God's miraculous creation unfolds in our lives. Just as this small act signals growth and change, so too does faith develop, inviting us to marvel at His wonders each day. Rejoice in God's presence as we nurture our little ones on this beautiful journey.

Psalm 145:4-5 - One generation shall commend your works to another, and shall declare your mighty acts. On the glorious splendor of your majesty, and on your wondrous works, I will meditate.

DEVOTIONAL

Today, we witness a beautiful milestone—a baby's first roll. In this simple act, we glimpse the hand of God at work, guiding the tiny body to reach new horizons. Just as we celebrate this small yet profound leap of physical growth, let us also reflect on the spiritual journeys unfolding around us. Just like a baby's first roll signifies adventure and change, our faith, too, evolves day by day, drawing us closer to God's wondrous creation. Psalm 145:4-5 reminds us that each generation passes down stories of His glory, and as parents, we have the incredible privilege of instilling awe for His works in our children. Let us pause and rejoice in His presence, nurturing the seeds of faith in our little ones while marveling at the myriad ways He shows His love and power. Today, as your baby rolls over, may you also find joy in rolling into deeper communion with the Divine, celebrating every precious moment of growth and transformation.

DAILY REFLECTION

In what ways can you nurture the spirit of wonder in your child, embracing each small milestone as a divine reminder of God's continuous work in both their lives and your own journey of faith?

PRAYER

Dear Lord, with grateful hearts, we celebrate this joyful milestone of our little one's first roll—a reminder of Your wondrous creation at work. Just as our baby begins to explore new horizons, may our faith deepen with each small adventure. Help us to nurture a sense of awe for Your glory in their journey, embracing every moment of growth as a beautiful reflection of Your love. Amen.

"On this day of first smiles, reflect on the joy of new beginnings, just as the angels rejoiced at Christ's birth. Let your heart mirror that innocent joy, spreading warmth and love to those around you, just like His unconditional grace."

Luke 15:10 - "In the same way, there is joy in the presence of the angels of God over one sinner who repents."

DEVOTIONAL

On this day of first smiles, let us pause and reflect on the pure joy that springs from new beginnings. Just as the angels rejoiced over the birth of Christ, we are called to embrace an unfiltered delight when we witness the dawning of hope in others. Each smile, especially a baby's, is a testament to unguarded love and innocence—a glimpse into the beauty of God's creation. In Luke 15:10, we are reminded that there is immense joy in the heavenly realms when even one heart turns towards grace. Today, let us mirror that joy; as we receive the warmth of those first smiles, may we also extend our hands and hearts to uplift and encourage others. In doing so, we participate in the divine dance of love that surrounds us all, reflecting God's unconditional grace. Allow your heart, like the angels', to overflow with joy as you share this grace with the world around you.

DAILY REFLECTION

How can you embrace the innocent joy of a first smile today and share that warmth with someone who needs a glimpse of hope and love in their life?

PRAYER

Dear Lord, on this day of first smiles, we bask in the warmth of your love and the joy of new beginnings. May our hearts remain open to the simple delight of innocence, reflecting the unfiltered joy that fills the heavens. Help us to share this blessed grace with those around us, spreading warmth and encouragement, just as the angels rejoiced at Your birth. Amen.

September 23

Celebrate the joy of Christ's resurrection this Easter Sunday, recognizing that laughter springs from the hope and new life He brings. Let your heart overflow with joy, reflecting the light and love of the risen Savior in every moment of your day.

John 16:22 – "So also you have sorrow now, but I will see you again, and your hearts will rejoice, and no one will take your joy from you."

DEVOTIONAL

As the sun rises on this glorious Easter Sunday, we are reminded that the tomb is empty, and life flourishes anew. In John 16:22, Jesus assures us that while sorrow may touch our hearts, joy is the ultimate promise of His resurrection. Imagine the laughter that must have erupted when the disciples first encountered the risen Christ—laughter woven with relief, disbelief, and overwhelming joy. This is the joy we celebrate today, a joy that springs forth from hope and new beginnings, far surpassing mere happiness. Let this laughter bubble up within you, reflecting the light of Christ to a world that desperately needs to see it. Embrace the transformative power of His love that lingers in every moment, and let it empower you to share that joy with those around you. As you go through your day, remember: no one can take away the joy you possess in the risen Savior.

DAILY REFLECTION

In the light of Christ's resurrection, what joy-filled moments are you inviting into your heart today, and how can your laughter radiate His hope and love to others around you?

PRAYER

Dear Lord, on this glorious Easter Sunday, we come before You with hearts full of gratitude for the laughter and joy that spring from the hope of Your resurrection. May the light of Your love fill our souls, transforming our sorrow into celebration as we embrace the new life You offer. Help us to share this divine joy with everyone we encounter, shining as beacons of Your grace in a world yearning for Your warmth. Amen.

September 24

Rest is a divine gift, a reminder of God's design for renewal. Just as God rested on the seventh day, our souls find restoration in Him during peaceful sleep. Trust that each night spent in His presence strengthens you for the journey ahead.

Exodus 34:21 – "Six days you shall work, but on the seventh day you shall rest; even during the plowing season and harvest you must rest."

DEVOTIONAL

As the sun sets and the world quiets, we are often invited into a sacred rhythm of rest, one that mirrors the divine completion of creation. Exodus 34:21 reminds us, "Six days you shall work, but on the seventh day you shall rest." In a culture that prizes relentless productivity, we can forget that rest is not a luxury; it is a divine gift bestowed upon us by our Creator. Each night, as you surrender to sleep, visualize it as a sweet embrace from God, a moment where He invites you to lay down your burdens and rejuvenate your spirit. Just as He stepped back to admire His handiwork on the seventh day, allow yourself the grace to acknowledge your own accomplishments and recharge for the path ahead. Trust that in the peaceful stillness of sleep, your soul finds solace and strength for tomorrow. Remember, sleep is meant to be a reminder of God's design for renewal and restoration—rest easy in His presence tonight.

DAILY REFLECTION

How can you cultivate a deeper trust in God's invitation to rest, allowing each night of peaceful sleep to be a cherished moment of renewal and a reminder of His unwavering presence in your journey?

PRAYER

Dear Lord, as the day draws to a close, I thank You for the gift of rest, a precious reminder of Your perfect design for renewal. Help me to surrender my burdens into Your capable hands each night, trusting in the peaceful embrace of sleep that strengthens my soul for the journey ahead. May I find gratitude in the stillness, knowing that in Your presence, I am renewed and ready to rise with purpose in the morning light. Amen.

September 25

On this day, we celebrate the profound moment of recognition and connection, akin to how Christ reveals Himself to us. Just as a baby instinctively knows their caregiver, may we grow in our understanding of God's presence in our lives, embracing the joy of our relationship with Him.

John 10:14-15 - "I am the good shepherd; I know my sheep and my sheep know me—just as the Father knows me and I know the Father—and I lay down my life for the sheep."

DEVOTIONAL

In the tender moment when a baby first recognizes the familiar face of their caregiver, we witness the beauty of connection—a bond that speaks of love, trust, and safety. This profound recognition mirrors our relationship with Christ, the Good Shepherd, who lovingly reveals Himself to us. As we reflect on John 10:14-15, we are reminded that just as the sheep know their shepherd, we too are called to recognize and embrace the presence of God in our lives.

In the chaos of our daily routines, may we take a moment to pause and acknowledge the divine face that seeks us amidst our busyness. Like the gentle smile of a parent, God's love envelops us, inviting us to draw nearer and deepen our understanding of Him. Today, let us celebrate the joy that comes from knowing we are seen and known by our Creator, who laid down His life for us, revealing the ultimate act of love. As we grow in recognition of His presence, may our hearts overflow with gratitude for this sacred relationship, nurturing our souls like the sweetest lullaby.

DAILY REFLECTION

In the cherished moment when a baby first beams at the face they recognize, how can we open our hearts to truly see and respond to the gentle, constant presence of Christ in our lives, nurturing the bond of trust and love that He desires with us?

PRAYER

Dear Lord, in the quiet moments of our lives, help us to recognize the gentle warmth of Your presence, just as a baby knows the tender embrace of their caregiver. May we cultivate a deep awareness of Your love and trust, allowing it to nurture our hearts and guide our steps. As we celebrate these precious moments of connection, let our souls sing with gratitude for the gift of being seen and known by You, our Good Shepherd. Amen.

September 26

On this day, as we reflect on the journey of faith, remember that growth often requires patience and perseverance. Just as a child learns to push through challenges during tummy time, we too are called to embrace our spiritual struggles as opportunities for deeper reliance on God's strength. Trust in His timing, knowing that each effort brings you closer to Him.

Galatians 6:9 - "And let us not grow weary of doing good, for in due season we will reap, if we do not give up."

DEVOTIONAL

On this day, as you embark on the tender journey of longer tummy time with your little one, consider how this small struggle mirrors our own walks of faith. Just as your child fortifies their muscles and grows stronger with each effort, so too are we invited to embrace our spiritual struggles. Galatians 6:9 reminds us not to grow weary in doing good, for the fruits of our labor may often take time to reveal themselves. Every time your baby pushes through the discomfort, rejoice in the resilience being built—both in them and in you. In these moments of shared perseverance, trust that God is working within you, shaping your spirit for His divine purpose. Remember, growth is not always easy, but it is always worth it. Lean into His timing and embrace the journey, knowing each challenge is an opportunity to draw closer to His strength and love.

DAILY REFLECTION

In what ways can you embrace the small struggles of your faith journey, just as your child learns to persevere through tummy time, and see them as precious opportunities to deepen your trust in God's unwavering strength?

PRAYER

Dear Lord, as I embark on this beautiful journey of tummy time with my little one, I ask for Your patience and guidance. Help me to see the strength blossoming within both of us through these small struggles, reminding me that each effort brings us closer to You. May we embrace this time together, finding joy in our perseverance and trusting in Your perfect timing as we grow in faith and endurance. Amen.

Celebrate the joy of new beginnings, much like a baby discovering the delight of bath time. In this sacred season, reflect on the cleansing grace of God, who delights in refreshing our hearts and souls, inviting us to bask in His love and renewal.

Psalm 51:10-12 - Create in me a clean heart, O God, and renew a right spirit within me. Cast me not away from your presence, and take not your Holy Spirit from me. Restore to me the joy of your salvation, and uphold me with a willing spirit.

DEVOTIONAL

As you watch a little one revel in the joyful splashes of their bath time, take a moment to reflect on how new beginnings can fill our hearts with pure delight. Just as a baby experiences the refreshing warmth of water, we too are invited to bask in the cleansing grace of our loving God. Psalm 51:10-12 echoes our deepest longing for renewal; in the same way that a gentle wash brings a bubbly laugh, God's Spirit invites us to embrace His refreshing love. Imagine the pure joy that fills that tiny heart, discovering the simple pleasures of life—a reminder that we are never too far from joy ourselves. God longs to create in us a clean heart, to wash away our worries, and to restore the vibrant spirit that brings us close to Him. Let this sacred season be a time of renewal where we, too, shed the old and make space for the new. Allow His love to embrace you, and reclaim the joy of His salvation that overflows in a heart refreshed by grace.

DAILY REFLECTION

In this precious season of new beginnings, how can you embrace the joy of God's cleansing grace, allowing it to wash over you like a warm bath, and fill your heart with renewed delight in His love?

PRAYER

Dear Lord, as we witness the pure delight of a little one in their bath, may we be reminded of the joy found in new beginnings. Refresh our hearts and souls with Your cleansing grace, washing away our worries and restoring us in Your love. Help us to embrace the splashes of joy in life and to rejoice in the renewal You offer, celebrating each moment as a precious gift from You. Amen.

September 28

On this day, as we reflect on the joys of new beginnings, remember that just as children eagerly explore new toys, God invites us to approach Him with the same wonder and trust. Let your heart be open to the gifts of grace and love that He has in store for you today.

Psalm 104:27-28 - "These all look to you to give them their food at the proper time. When you give it to them, they gather it up; when you open your hand, they are satisfied with good things."

DEVOTIONAL

Today, as we bask in the beauty of new beginnings, let us take a moment to ponder the joy children find in their first encounter with toys. With wide eyes and hearts brimming with anticipation, they grasp each vibrant toy, marveling at its possibilities. In the same way, God invites us to approach Him with childlike wonder, ready to explore the depths of His love and grace. Psalm 104:27-28 reminds us that "these all look to you to give them their food at the proper time." Just as a child eagerly awaits the opening of a gift, so too does our Heavenly Father open His hand, offering us blessings crafted uniquely for us. May we not shy away from this divine invitation; instead, let our hearts reach out, ready to gather up every good thing He has in store. Let today be a reminder: each moment is an opportunity to discover the delightful gifts of grace that await us, meant to fill our souls with satisfaction and joy. Embrace the adventure of trusting in God's provision, for He delights in giving us what we need, exactly when we need it.

DAILY REFLECTION

In the midst of life's uncertainties, how can you open your heart like a child, eager to unwrap the daily blessings God has prepared for you, trusting that each moment is a new opportunity for joy and discovery?

PRAYER

Dear Lord, as we embark on this journey of new beginnings, help us to approach each day with the same awe and excitement that children feel when they uncover new toys. Ignite within us a heart that eagerly reaches out to discover the gifts of love and grace You have prepared for us. May we find joy in Your provision and courage in Your embrace, trusting that You delight in our every step of exploration. Amen.

On this joyful day of first giggles, remember that laughter is a precious gift from God, reminding us of His delight in our hearts. Just as a child's laughter brings lightness to our spirits, let us rejoice in the simple joys and celebrate the love that fills our lives.

Proverbs 17:22 - "A cheerful heart is good medicine, but a crushed spirit dries up the bones."

DEVOTIONAL

On this joyful day of first giggles, we are reminded of the pure delight that laughter bestows upon our hearts. The sound of a baby's laughter is a sweet melody, echoing God's love and reminding us to cherish the vibrant moments that life offers. Proverbs 17:22 tells us, "A cheerful heart is good medicine," inviting us to embrace the healing power of joy. Just as a child's innocent laughter lights up a room, let us allow the simple pleasures of life to illuminate our spirits. In times of stress or sorrow, may we remember to seek out the laughter that connects us to one another and to our Creator. As we celebrate this precious milestone, let us commit to cultivating joy, sharing laughter, and appreciating the profound love that fills our everyday life. Today, may your heart be light, and may the joy of the Lord resonate within you, healing and uplifting your spirit.

DAILY REFLECTION

In moments of laughter, how can you intentionally capture and cherish the joy that reminds you of God's unwavering love and presence in your life?

PRAYER

Dear Lord, thank You for the gift of laughter that fills our homes with joy and warmth. As we celebrate this precious milestone of a baby's first giggle, may we be reminded to embrace the joyous moments that connect us to one another and to Your love. Help us to cherish the lightness in our hearts and spread that joy, reflecting Your goodness in all we do. Amen.

As you step into the beauty of creation, let the vibrant colors and gentle whispers of nature remind you of God's boundless love and presence. Take a moment to pause and reflect on the joy that comes from being a part of His masterpiece. Each leaf and flower speaks of grace; let your heart open to the wonder around you.

Psalm 104:24-25 - "O LORD, how manifold are Your works! In wisdom You have made them all. The earth is full of Your possessions—This great and wide sea, in which are innumerable teeming things, living things both small and great."

DEVOTIONAL

As you step into the park, let the world around you ignite a spark of wonder deep within your soul. The vibrant colors of flowers and the lush green trees stand like joyful testimonies to the Creator's artistry, each petal and leaf singing praises of unfathomable love. In the gentle rustle of the leaves and the cheerful chirping of birds, hear the quiet invitation from God to pause and be present. Reflect on Psalm 104:24-25, which reminds us that every inch of creation is part of His grand design, teeming with life and purpose. Allow yourself to breathe in the beauty; it speaks of grace we can hardly fathom. With each step, let gratitude fill your heart, recognizing that you are a beloved part of this marvelous tapestry. Embrace the stillness, for it is here among the wonders of nature that you'll find a deeper connection to the heart of God.

DAILY REFLECTION

As you wander through this vibrant tapestry of creation, what sensations and thoughts arise in your heart that remind you of your unique place within God's masterpiece?

PRAYER

Dear Lord, as I step into the beauty of this park, I am in awe of Your creation and the vibrant expressions of Your love surrounding me. Help me to pause, breathe deeply, and fully embrace the wonder around me, allowing each whisper of nature to stir gratitude and joy in my heart. May I feel Your presence in every rustle of leaves and every note of song, knowing that I am a cherished part of this divine masterpiece. Amen.

A Moment of Gratitude

If this devotional has brought moments of peace, strength, or reflection into your life, a short review on Amazon can help others discover it too.

devo.anchoredgraces.com/newmoms

Even a few words about your experience can make a meaningful difference.

Thank you for continuing this journey.

October 1

In the spirit of new beginnings, cherish the joy of connection and friendship as your little ones play together. May this first encounter be a reminder of God's love in community and the beauty of shared moments. Celebrate the gift of relationships as they bloom under His watchful eye.

Ecclesiastes 4:9-10 - "Two are better than one, because they have a good reward for their labor. For if they fall, one will lift up his companion."

DEVOTIONAL

As you witness your little ones embark on their first playdate, take a moment to soak in the sweetness of this new beginning. There's a spark of joy in those tiny exchanges, the laughter bubbling up like a melody that celebrates connection and innocence. In these early moments of friendship, we are reminded of Ecclesiastes 4:9-10, that "two are better than one." Together, they explore, share, and support one another, echoing the essence of community that God delights in. As they tumble and laugh, remember that these shared experiences are seeds being planted for lifelong bonds. Each giggle and cheer is a reflection of His love, reminding us how beautiful it is to walk alongside one another in life's journey. Cherish the blessing of parenthood, where we can teach our children the art of friendship and connection, all under the watchful eye of our loving Creator. May their camaraderie inspire us to nurture our own relationships, embracing the gift of shared moments that God so graciously provides.

DAILY REFLECTION

How can you cultivate the spirit of connection and joy in your own relationships, inspired by the innocence and laughter of your little ones as they forge their first friendships?

PRAYER

Dear Lord, as we gather to witness the laughter and joy of our little ones on their first playdate, we thank You for the gift of connection and the beauty of friendship. May these precious moments blossom under Your watchful gaze, reminding us of the love You have woven into our lives and our relationships. Help us to nurture the seeds of camaraderie they are planting today, guiding us to celebrate the joy of community, just as You delight in our unity. Amen.

October 2

Celebrate the joy of new beginnings as we reflect on the innocence of faith. Just as a baby's first sounds express wonder and trust, may our hearts voice a pure, childlike love for God this season. Embrace the simple truths that nurture our spiritual growth.

Matthew 18:2-3 - He called a little child to him, and placed the child among them. And he said: "Truly I tell you, unless you change and become like little children, you will not enter the kingdom of heaven."

DEVOTIONAL

As we enter this season of new beginnings, let us pause to embrace the pure joy reflected in a baby's first sounds—those delightful "goo" and "ga" that echo with innocence and trust. Just as a child's babbling fills the air with wonder, our hearts too are invited to express a childlike love for God, a love that is simple yet profound. In the embrace of faith, we discover that our spiritual growth often begins in the small, unrefined moments, where we can bask in the simplicity of His grace. Jesus beckons us to become like little children, reminding us that in our vulnerability and wonder, we uncover the doorway to His kingdom. As we celebrate new beginnings, may we find joy in surrendering our complicated thoughts and simply trusting Him. Let our voices join in the sweetest harmony of praise, as we share in the delight of His love, untainted by the concerns of the world. Together, let us nurture this childlike spirit within us, cherishing the truth that faith can indeed be as pure and joyful as the first sounds of a beloved child.

DAILY REFLECTION

In this season of new beginnings, how can we cultivate a heart that joyfully babbles with trust and wonder, reflecting the innocence of faith as we embrace God's simple truths?

PRAYER

Dear Lord, as we marvel at the innocent sounds of a baby, we are reminded of the pure joy and trust that comes with new beginnings. May our hearts, like their delightful babbling, echo with childlike faith, surrendering to Your grace and embracing the simple truths that nourish our spirits. Help us to find wonder in every moment, cherishing the voice of love that calls us closer to You. Amen.

October 3

On this day, reflect on the transformative power of faith—like a seed blooming in soil, your trust in God can yield vibrant growth and abundant blessings. Embrace each moment as an opportunity to cultivate love and purpose in your journey.

Mark 4:30-32 - "And he said, 'With what can we compare the kingdom of God, or what parable shall we use for it? It is like a grain of mustard seed, which, when sown on the ground, is the smallest of all the seeds on earth; yet when it is sown, it grows up and becomes larger than all the garden plants and puts out large branches, so that the birds of the air can make nests in its shade.'"

DEVOTIONAL

As you grasp a new toy for the first time, consider how this small moment is a glimpse into the transformative power of faith. Just like the tiniest mustard seed, our faith—though seemingly small—holds the potential for monumental growth. In Mark 4:30-32, we are reminded that what begins as a mere whisper of trust can blossom into something magnificent, offering shade and shelter not just for ourselves, but for others as well. Each day presents a new opportunity to nurture this seed within us, cultivating love, kindness, and purpose in every encounter. Embrace these fleeting moments; they are the soil where our dreams and hopes can flourish. As you journey on, let every experience be a stepping stone toward a life rich in blessings and grace. Trust in the process, for your faith, just like that small seed, is destined to grow beyond your imagination.

DAILY REFLECTION

How might embracing the simple joys and surprises in your life, much like a child discovering a new toy, inspire you to nurture your faith and witness the incredible growth it can bring?

PRAYER

Dear Lord, as I hold this new toy in my hands, I am reminded of the beauty of small beginnings. Help me to nurture the seeds of faith within me, trusting that from these tiny whispers of belief, great things can grow. May each moment be a chance to embrace love and purpose, allowing your blessings to flourish in my life and those around me. Amen.

October 4

On this day, reflect on the gift of healing and renewal that comes through faith. Just as vaccination fortifies our bodies, Christ strengthens our spirits, inviting us to trust in His restorative love and to share that hope with a world in need. Let us be vessels of His grace, spreading light and assurance to those around us.

1 Peter 2:24 - "He himself bore our sins in his body on the tree, that we might die to sin and live to righteousness. By his wounds you have been healed."

DEVOTIONAL

As we gather today, let us pause to reflect on the profound gift of healing and renewal that flows from our faith. Just as the first vaccination shots strengthen and protect our physical bodies, we remember that Christ, through His sacrifice, fortifies our spirits. In 1 Peter 2:24, we are reminded that "by his wounds, you have been healed," a testament to His love that transcends our pain and weakness. As we receive this grace, may we also embrace our calling to share that hope with a world longing for reassurance and healing. In moments of doubt or fear, let us turn our hearts to Jesus, finding peace in His restorative love and the promise that we are not alone. Today, let us be vessels of His grace, illuminating the darkness around us with compassion and faith. May our actions reflect His light, inviting others to trust in the same healing power that renews our own hearts.

DAILY REFLECTION

In what ways can we embody Christ's healing love today, offering comfort and hope to those who feel broken and weary in our communities?

PRAYER

Dear Lord, in this moment of quiet reflection, we thank You for the precious gift of healing woven into the fabric of our faith. Just as the first vaccination fortifies our bodies, may we lean into Your restorative love, allowing it to strengthen our spirits and dispel our fears. Help us to be beacons of hope and grace, bringing the light of Your compassion to those who are lost in darkness, reminding them that through You, renewal and healing are always within reach. Amen.

October 5

On this day, reflect on God's unwavering love as you navigate the journey of faith. Trust in His guidance, for He walks beside you, illuminating your path amidst uncertainty. Embrace each moment, knowing that His grace sustains you.

Romans 5:8 - "But God shows his love for us in that while we were still sinners, Christ died for us."

DEVOTIONAL

On this day, as you take your first courageous steps into the embrace of faith, pause to reflect on the depth of God's unwavering love. Romans 5:8 reminds us that even in the messiness of our flaws, God's heart beats fiercely for us—His love expressed most profoundly through Christ's sacrifice. Imagine that love wrapped around you, tender and unyielding, a constant companion guiding you through the uncertainties that life often presents. In moments of doubt or fear, remember that you are not alone; His presence walks beside you, illuminating paths that seem shadowed and unclear. Each moment you embrace is filled with His grace, infusing you with strength to face whatever comes your way. Allow that grace to wash over you, reminding you that His love is relentless, a beacon of hope amidst the storms of life. Trust in this journey, for you are held in the hands of a God whose promise is to sustain you, now and always.

DAILY REFLECTION

How can you intentionally cultivate a deeper awareness of God's unwavering love in your life, especially as you face the uncertainties of your faith journey?

PRAYER

Dear Lord, as I embark on this new journey of faith, I invite Your unwavering love to embrace me deeply. In the moments of uncertainty and fear, help me to trust in Your gentle guidance, knowing that Your grace surrounds me like a protective shield. May I feel Your presence beside me, illuminating my path and reminding me that I am cherished beyond measure, even in my imperfect moments. Amen.

October 6

In this season of rapid change and growth, reflect on God's nourishing grace that sustains us through challenges. Just as a baby thrives during a growth spurt, trust in the Lord's provision to nurture your faith, allowing it to expand and deepen. Embrace the transformation as an opportunity to draw closer to Him.

Isaiah 58:11 - "The Lord will guide you always; he will satisfy your needs in a sun-scorched land and will strengthen your frame. You will be like a well-watered garden, like a spring whose waters never fail."

DEVOTIONAL

As you navigate this season of rapid change, remember that just as a baby experiences and thrives during a growth spurt, so too are you being lovingly nurtured by God. Isaiah 58:11 reminds us that the Lord guides us always, even through the most barren and challenging times. Picture yourself as a well-watered garden, flourishing through His care; He promises to satisfy your needs and strengthen your frame. Embrace this transformation with open arms, for it is in these moments of stretching and expanding that your faith deepens and matures. Trust in His provision, knowing that He is intimately aware of your struggles and delights in every step of your journey. Allow each challenge to draw you closer to Him, nurturing a connection that will sustain you through the seasons of life. In this divine embrace, let your spirit blossom—each new growth, a testament to His unending grace.

DAILY REFLECTION

In this season of growth and transformation, how can you more fully trust in God's nurturing embrace to sustain your faith through the challenges ahead, just as a baby instinctively leans into the love and care of their parent?

PRAYER

Dear Lord, in this season of rapid transformation, I thank You for Your nourishing grace that sustains me through the challenges I face. As I navigate these moments of growth, help me to trust in Your provision and embrace the unfolding of my faith, knowing that each struggle draws me closer to You. May I flourish like a well-watered garden, rooted in Your love, and may every stretch and expansion of my spirit be a testament to Your unending grace.

October 7

As we reflect on the journey of growth and new beginnings, let's remember that even the smallest seeds can bloom into beautiful blessings. In this season of hope and renewal, may we cherish the precious moments and embrace the joy of nurturing what God has entrusted to us.

Matthew 13:31-32 - "He told them another parable: 'The kingdom of heaven is like a mustard seed, which a man took and planted in his field. Though it is the smallest of all seeds, yet when it grows, it is the largest of garden plants and becomes a tree, so that the birds come and perch in its branches.'"

DEVOTIONAL

In this tender season of growth, as we gaze upon those tiny baby clothes that no longer fit, we are reminded of the miracle of transformation that unfolds before us. Each little garment, once a perfect match for a precious life, becomes a testament to the love and care poured into nurturing new beginnings. Like the mustard seed described in Matthew 13:31-32, our moments may seem small and fleeting, yet within them lies the potential for enormous beauty. The kingdom of heaven blooms in unexpected ways, encouraging us to embrace the unfolding journey, both in our children and in our faith. Let us cherish the laughter echoing through our homes and the soft touches that fill our hearts with warmth. In this cycle of letting go, we find the joy of new growth—proof that God faithfully trusts us to nurture the seeds He has planted in our lives. May we find hope in the knowledge that every cherished moment, no matter how small, contributes to the larger tapestry of His grace.

DAILY REFLECTION

In what ways can you celebrate the growth and changes in your life while holding onto the cherished memories of where you began, recognizing that every small step is part of God's beautiful design?

PRAYER

Dear Lord, as we hold these tiny garments and reflect on the wondrous transformation they signify, help us to embrace the beauty of growth in our lives and those we cherish. May we find joy in each fleeting moment, nurturing the seeds of love and faith you have planted in our hearts. Remind us that even the smallest blessings can shape a magnificent legacy, and grant us the grace to celebrate the journey of nurturing your gifts. Amen.

October 8

Embrace the wonder of new beginnings; just as a child delights in the stories of faith, may we too find joy in God's everlasting narrative of love and redemption. Let each moment of laughter and learning remind us that we are beloved children of the Creator.

Isaiah 43:20-21 - "The wild animals honor me, the jackals and the owls, because I provide water in the wilderness and streams in the wasteland, to give drink to my people, my chosen, the people I formed for myself that they may proclaim my praise."

DEVOTIONAL

As we gather for storytime, let us pause and embrace the wonder of new beginnings, just as a child delights in the pages before them, full of colorful illustrations and captivating tales. Isaiah reminds us of a God who provides—who quenches thirst in the wilderness and brings streams to the driest of places. Like the joyful laughter of a baby filled with awe, so, too, should our hearts respond to the abundant love and grace that God pours into our lives. In every story we share, we are reminded of our place within His narrative—a story woven with threads of love, hope, and redemption. We are His beloved children, cherished and known, invited to dance in the richness of His creation. As we reflect on the wild animals that honor Him, let us also honor Him with our praises, recognizing the daily miracles that surround us. May each moment spent in wonder and laughter remind us that we are part of something beautiful—together with our little ones, proclaiming the greatness of our Creator.

DAILY REFLECTION

In the gentle embrace of storytime's wonder, how can we cultivate a heart that mirrors a child's awe, finding joy in the divine narrative that reveals our identity as cherished children of God?

PRAYER

Dear God, thank You for the gift of each new beginning, where laughter and learning bloom in the hearts of our little ones. As we gather in joy for storytime, may we fully immerse ourselves in the wonder of Your everlasting love and grace, cherishing the beautiful narratives You weave into our lives. Help us to nurture their innocence and curiosity, so together we may dance in awe of Your creation and proclaim Your greatness as beloved children of the King. Amen.

October 9

As you savor the sweetness of freshly picked raspberries, remember the joy of new beginnings in Christ. Just as each berry bursts forth with flavor, let your faith flourish and bring forth the fruits of the Spirit in your life today. Celebrate the abundance of God's goodness in every tender moment.

John 15:8 - "This is to my Father's glory, that you bear much fruit, showing yourselves to be my disciples."

DEVOTIONAL

As you savor the sweetness of freshly picked raspberries, let each burst of flavor remind you of the fresh starts we experience in Christ. In the rhythm of the harvest, you can almost hear the whisper of God's promise—the invitation to grow, to flourish, and to bear fruit that reflects His glory. Like these tender berries that come forth in their season, your faith has the potential to thrive in every circumstance. Picture each juice-filled morsel as a symbol of joy and abundance, beckoning you to embrace the new beginnings that await. As you cultivate a heart aligned with Him, the fruits of the Spirit will naturally manifest, revealing the beauty of His presence in your life. Celebrate these moments, for they are evidence of God's relentless goodness, echoing the words of John 15:8. Today, allow your faith to blossom and overflow, just like the sweetest raspberries, as you delight in the richness of His blessings.

DAILY REFLECTION

In what ways can you nurture the fresh beginnings in your life, allowing the sweetness of faith to burst forth and overflow into the lives of those around you, just like the joy of savoring a perfectly ripe raspberry?

PRAYER

Dear Lord, as I savor the sweetness of these freshly picked raspberries, let each burst of flavor remind me of your abundant grace and the joy of new beginnings in Christ. May my heart be tuned to Your whispers, encouraging me to grow and flourish in faith, revealing the fruits of the Spirit in every moment. Help me to embrace the tender blessings of this season, celebrating the beauty of Your goodness and the richness of life found in You. Amen.

October 10

On this day, celebrate the joy of new beginnings, reflecting on the innocence and wonder of a child learning to roll from tummy to back. Just as each small victory in life is a step toward greater growth, trust in God's guidance as you navigate the twists and turns of your spiritual journey. Remember, every effort brings you closer to the fullness of His grace.

Isaiah 43:1 - "Fear not, for I have redeemed you; I have called you by name, you are mine."

DEVOTIONAL

Today, as we witness the simple yet profound milestone of a child mastering the art of rolling from tummy to back, let us pause and reflect on the beauty of new beginnings. Each time they attempt this small victory, their innocence shines through, reminding us that growth often involves both struggle and joy. In Isaiah 43:1, we find assurance in God's unwavering love: "Fear not, for I have redeemed you; I have called you by name, you are mine." Just as this child learns to navigate the twists and turns of their world, God invites us to trust Him with our own journey. Every effort we make, however small, draws us closer to His grace and the fullness of life He intends for us. Embrace your own beginnings today, knowing that your steps matter, and with each attempt, you are not just learning but also delighting in the path God has laid out for you. Let the joy of this moment inspire you to leap forward, trusting that you are forever held in His loving embrace.

DAILY REFLECTION

In what small but significant ways can you embrace the joy of new beginnings in your own life, trusting that each effort draws you into a deeper relationship with God and His grace?

PRAYER

Dear Lord, as we marvel at the joyful determination of a child learning to roll from tummy to back, may we embrace our own journeys with the same spirit of wonder and trust. Help us to see each new beginning as a precious gift, reminding us that even in the smallest victories, we are cradled in Your endless grace. Strengthen our hearts to navigate life's twists and turns, knowing we are always held in Your loving embrace. Amen.

October 11

On this day, celebrate the nurturing love of God, reflecting on how His provision sustains us in every season. Just as a newborn thrives through its first bottle feeding, we are reminded to depend on the Lord's nourishment for our spiritual growth and well-being. Trust in His faithfulness, knowing He equips us for every new step.

Psalm 31:19-20 - "Oh, how abundant is your goodness, which you have stored up for those who fear you and worked for those who take refuge in you, in the sight of the children of mankind! In the cover of your presence you hide them from the plots of men; you store them in your shelter from the strife of tongues."

DEVOTIONAL

On this special day, as we celebrate the milestone of a newborn's first successful bottle feeding, let us pause to reflect on the nurturing love of God. Just as a child learns to trust a bottle for nourishment, we too are invited to lean into the tender provision our Father offers us. In Psalm 31:19-20, we are reminded of the abundance of God's goodness, lovingly reserved for those who seek refuge in Him. Picture the warmth of His shelter, safeguarding us from life's uncertainties and the noise of the world. As you witness this precious moment of growth, remember that spiritual development also requires dependence on Him; we thrive not by our own strength, but through His faithful love. Trust in God as He equips you with every necessary grace for this new season. Embrace His abundant goodness, knowing that just as He nourishes the smallest of His creations, He is ever-present to nurture your soul.

DAILY REFLECTION

In this moment of joy as you celebrate a newborn's first successful bottle feeding, how can you open your heart to God's loving provision, allowing Him to nourish your spirit and guide your journey in this new season of growth?

PRAYER

Dear Lord, on this sacred day, we celebrate the precious milestone of a child's first successful bottle feeding, a tender reminder of Your steadfast love and provision. May we learn to lean into Your nourishing embrace, trusting in Your faithfulness to sustain us through every season of life. As we witness this beautiful moment, may our hearts grow ever closer to You, recognizing that just as You provide for our little ones, You lovingly equip us for the journey ahead. Amen.

October 12

Tonight's the night for sweet freedom! As you trust your little ones to a babysitter, remember that just as God watches over us, He's watching over them too. Embrace this moment of rest, knowing that joy and peace await you both.

Psalm 121:3-4 - "He will not let your foot slip—he who watches over you will not slumber; indeed, he who watches over Israel will neither slumber nor sleep."

DEVOTIONAL

Tonight's the night—a rare moment of sweet freedom, as laughter and anticipation fill the air. As you prepare to hand over the care of your little ones to a trusted babysitter, let your heart be lightened by the truth found in Psalm 121:3-4. Just as a loving parent watches over their children, our Heavenly Father is ever vigilant, ensuring that not even the smallest stumble goes unnoticed. Embrace the unfolding joy of this evening, knowing that while you indulge in well-deserved rest, God's watchful eye stays upon your loved ones. So breathe deeply, savor the fleeting moments of peace, and trust that both you and your children are cradled in His tender care. This trust doesn't merely relieve the weight of worry—it invites joy to flourish in every heartbeat of your night out. Take this time to rejuvenate, for in the tranquility of this break, both you and your little ones can experience the delightful essence of love, safety, and rest.

DAILY REFLECTION

As you relish this rare evening of freedom, how can you embrace the trust in God's unwavering presence, allowing His peace to replace your worries and fill your heart with joy for both you and your little ones?

PRAYER

Dear Lord, as I prepare to entrust my little ones to the care of another, I seek your comforting presence. Help me to release my worries, knowing that just as You watch over us, You surround my children with peace and safety. Let this night of sweet freedom be a reminder of the joy that comes from trusting in Your loving embrace. Amen.

October 13

Cherish the gift of renewed connection on your first postpartum date night. Celebrate the miracle of life in your arms while nurturing the love that binds you together as a couple. Let this time remind you of God's faithfulness in your journey as parents and partners.

1 Peter 3:7 - "Husbands, in the same way be considerate as you live with your wives, and treat them with respect as the weaker partner and as heirs with you of the gracious gift of life, so that nothing will hinder your prayers."

DEVOTIONAL

As you embark on your first postpartum date night, let this sacred moment be a gentle reminder of the miracle you've welcomed into your lives. In the soft glow of candlelight, take a deep breath and savor the joy of connection—both with each other and the precious child in your arms. 1 Peter 3:7 calls husbands to honor their wives, and in this season of new beginnings, consider how vital it is to nurture the love that binds you together. Cherish the laughter, the shared stories, and even the quiet moments that might break into the sounds of parenting. Amid the sweet chaos, remember that you are both heirs of God's gracious gifts, deserving of respect and tenderness. In these simple acts of love and consideration, you reflect God's faithfulness in your journey together. Let this night not just be a celebration of love, but a reaffirmation of your commitment to one another, as partners and co-creators of life.

DAILY REFLECTION

In this tender moment after your beautiful chaos of new parenthood, how can you intentionally weave the threads of gratitude and love into the fabric of your relationship, allowing both your partnership and your faith to flourish?

PRAYER

Dear Lord, as we embark on this first postpartum date night, we thank You for the precious gift of our child and the love that has deepened between us. May the moments we share tonight be laced with joy and gratitude, reminding us of Your unwavering faithfulness in our journey together. Help us to honor one another in this new season, cherishing both the chaos and the calm, as we celebrate the beautiful bond that unites us as partners and parents. Amen.

October 14

Through the strength of Christ, step into your newfound strength today. Every movement, every breath, is a testament to His renewal in your life. Trust in His guidance as you rediscover your body and spirit.

Ephesians 6:10 - "Finally, be strong in the Lord and in the strength of his might."

DEVOTIONAL

As you prepare for your first postpartum exercise session, take a moment to breathe deeply and remind yourself that this journey is not yours alone. Ephesians 6:10 calls us to "be strong in the Lord and in the strength of his might," and today, that strength is quietly working within you. Each movement you make is more than just a physical action; it is a commitment to embracing the renewal that God is providing in this new season of your life. Feel the gentle whispers of His love as you rediscover your body, acknowledging the incredible miracle it has achieved in bringing new life into the world. With every heartbeat, you embody resilience, and with every breath, you are reminded of the grace that sustains you. Trust in His guidance, for He is celebrating each step you take, no matter how small. Embrace this moment; it's a beautiful testament to the strength renewed in Christ—your journey is just beginning.

DAILY REFLECTION

How can you invite Christ's strength into your heart and actions today, allowing each movement to reflect the awe of your body's transformation and the grace of your journey as a new mother?

PRAYER

Dear Lord, as I step into this new chapter of my life, I thank You for the strength that flows through me. Help me to embrace each movement and each breath as a reflection of Your renewal, reminding me of the incredible miracle I have brought into the world. Guide me gently as I rediscover my body and spirit, celebrating every small victory, knowing that You are with me, cheering me on in this beautiful journey of resilience and grace. Amen.

October 15

On this joyful journey of faith, just as a baby finds its feet and takes those first wobbly steps into the world, may you too find strength and courage to move forward, trusting in God's guiding hand with every step you take.

Psalm 119:133 - "Direct my footsteps according to your word; let no sin rule over me."

DEVOTIONAL

As a baby takes those first tentative steps, its heart brims with the thrill of newfound freedom and potential. In the same way, your faith journey beckons you to walk boldly into the world, where each step can feel like an adventure shrouded in uncertainty. Remember the words of Psalm 119:133: "Direct my footsteps according to your word; let no sin rule over me." Just as a parent gently guides their child, God's loving presence is there to steady you when you feel unsteady. While you may stumble and falter at times, take heart: these moments are part of the dance of faith, where every misstep is a lesson in grace. Trust in His word; let it illuminate your path and infuse you with courage. Embrace this joyful journey, and know that with each step, you are never alone.

DAILY REFLECTION

As you take your first wobbly steps in faith today, what fears or doubts can you lay at the feet of Jesus, trusting that His guiding hand will lead you toward the adventure ahead?

PRAYER

Dear Lord, as I take my first steps into this beautiful journey of faith, grant me the courage to move forward with joy and trust. Just as a child leans on their parent for guidance, may I always seek Your loving hand to steady me through the wobbles and uncertainties. Let each step be a testament to Your grace, illuminating my path and filling my heart with hope as I embrace the adventure ahead. Amen.

October 16

Joyful beginnings herald the promise of new life in Christ. In this season of hope, may our hearts resonate with the pure delight of His love, embracing the innocence and wonder of faith.

Isaiah 65:17 - "For behold, I create new heavens and a new earth, and the former things shall not be remembered or come into mind."

DEVOTIONAL

As we celebrate this radiant season, let us pause and embrace the truth nestled within Isaiah 65:17: "For behold, I create new heavens and a new earth, and the former things shall not be remembered or come into mind." Just as the first high-pitched squeal of a baby fills a room with awe and delight, so too does the promise of new life in Christ awaken within us a profound sense of joy. Each new day is a gentle reminder of His faithfulness, where old burdens are lifted and glimmers of hope arise, painting our lives with the vibrant colors of His grace. In this season of hope, may our hearts overflow with the pure delight of His love, echoing the innocent wonder of faith. Just like a child marvels at the simplest of joys, let us approach our lives with that same eagerness, finding beauty in the ordinary and the extraordinary alike. Embrace the newness He offers, for in letting go of the past, we open our hearts to the infinite possibilities of His divine plan. Trust in His promise, and allow the joy of new beginnings to reignite your spirit, as we step into the beautiful future He has ordained for us.

DAILY REFLECTION

In this season of new beginnings, how can you embody the joy and wonder of a child, letting go of past burdens to fully embrace the fresh possibilities of life in Christ?

PRAYER

Dear Lord, with hearts full of gratitude, we celebrate the joyful beginnings You offer us each day. Help us to embrace the innocence and wonder of faith, allowing the pure delight of Your love to fill our spirits, just as a baby's first cry fills a room with delight. May we find joy in the present, letting go of the past, and open ourselves to the vibrant possibilities of the future You've designed for us in Christ. Amen.

On this day, as we celebrate the beauty of creation, reflect on the joy that music brings to our hearts—just like a baby's first reaction to a melody. Let your spirit dance in praise, recognizing that even the smallest moments of joy are reminders of God's love and creativity in our lives.

Psalm 150:4-6 - "Praise him with the sound of the trumpet; praise him with the lute and harp! Praise him with the timbrel and dance; praise him with stringed instruments and flutes! Praise him with loud cymbals; praise him with clashing cymbals!"

DEVOTIONAL

On this beautiful day, as we witness the moment a baby first reacts to the magic of music, let our hearts be stirred in wonder and joy. Just as that little one's eyes light up at the sound of a melody, we too are called to rejoice in the symphony of creation around us. Psalm 150 reminds us to praise God with every instrument at our disposal—our voices, our laughter, our very lives—because music has the power to awaken our spirit and draw us closer to His love. In those soft, innocent giggles and curious coos, we see God's handiwork—a reminder that He delights in our joy. Each note we hear whispers of His creativity, urging us to dance and celebrate life's sweetest moments. So let us embrace the sounds that move us, allowing them to become a language of praise, filling our hearts with gratitude for the beauty that surrounds us. Today, may we find joy in the simplest of things, realizing that even fleeting sounds are echoes of God's eternal love.

DAILY REFLECTION

How can we, like a baby enchanted by music, rediscover and celebrate the simple joys of creation in our lives, allowing each moment to unfold as a symphony of God's love?

PRAYER

Dear Lord, as we gather to witness the pure delight of a baby's first reaction to music, may our hearts be as tender and open to the wonders around us. Let us find joy in the simplest melodies, appreciating the whispers of Your creativity that echo in our lives. May each note remind us of Your abiding love, inviting us to dance in gratitude and celebrate the beauty of this world You have crafted. Amen.

On this day, reflect on the simple joy of new beginnings and the wonder found in childhood faith. Just as a baby discovers delight in their first toy, may we rediscover the purity and simplicity of our relationship with God, cherishing the small moments that awaken our spirit.

Psalm 103:17-18 - But the steadfast love of the LORD is from everlasting to everlasting on those who fear him, and his righteousness to children's children, to those who keep his covenant and remember to do his commandments.

DEVOTIONAL

On this day, as we celebrate the simple joy of newfound treasures, let us pause to reflect on the wonder and innocence found in a child's heart. Just as a baby experiences pure delight in their first toy, may we allow ourselves to unearth the same joy in our relationship with God. In Psalm 103:17-18, we are reminded that the steadfast love of the LORD abides across generations, binding us together in a tapestry of faith and grace. Each day brings the opportunity to rediscover what it means to embrace Him with childlike wonder, to cherish the covenant we share, and to be mindful of His commandments. As we hold onto the small moments—those little triumphs of faith and fleeting encounters with His presence—let us remember to celebrate the beauty of new beginnings. May our hearts awaken to the simple yet profound love God extends to us, inspiring us to pass this legacy of faith on to our children. Today, may we all nurture and rediscover the purity of our connection to the divine, just like a child who finds endless joy in a beloved toy.

DAILY REFLECTION

How can you intentionally nurture a childlike sense of wonder in your daily walk with God, allowing the simple joys of faith to awaken your spirit and deepen your connection to His enduring love?

PRAYER

Dear Lord, as we pause to celebrate the joyous discoveries of life, help us to embrace the wonder that resides within a child's heart. May we find delight in our journey with You, cherishing each small moment that ignites our spirit, just as a baby treasures their first beloved toy. Awaken in us a childlike faith that seeks Your love and grace, inspiring us to pass on this treasured legacy to our children and nourish our connection to the divine. Amen.

October 19

Today, reflect on the journey of faith as you take your first long stroll. Just as Jesus walked with His disciples, let every step remind you of His presence guiding and strengthening you along the way.

Luke 24:15-16 - "While they were talking and discussing together, Jesus himself drew near and went with them. But their eyes were kept from recognizing him."

DEVOTIONAL

As you embark on this first long stroll, take a moment to breathe in the world around you. Each step forward is not just a movement but a journey through faith, reminiscent of those quiet moments when Jesus walked alongside His disciples. In Luke 24:15-16, we find that in their shared discussions, Jesus drew near; He was there, even when they did not recognize Him. As you walk, consider how often His presence surrounds you, gently guiding your path, even when life feels uncertain or overwhelming. Let the rhythm of your footsteps remind you that God is with you, illuminating your way like the sun breaking through the clouds after a storm. With each moment of reflection, allow His peace to wash over you, anchoring your heart in the knowledge that you are never alone on this journey. Embrace the beauty of your stroll, and let it become a sacred space for communion with the One who walks beside you always.

DAILY REFLECTION

As you take each step on this first long stroll, how can you open your heart to recognize the quiet ways Jesus walks with you, even in the moments when His presence feels hidden?

PRAYER

Dear Lord, as I take these first steps on my long stroll, help me to feel Your presence beside me, just as You walked beside Your disciples. May each footfall echo with the assurance of Your guidance, reminding me that even in moments of uncertainty, I am never alone. Grant me the grace to embrace this journey of faith, allowing Your peace to envelop my heart and illuminating my path with hope and love. Amen.

October 20

In this season of new beginnings, just as every meal is a chance to nourish our bodies, bringing your little one into the world of shared experiences is a precious opportunity to nourish your spirit. Trust in God's grace to guide your first restaurant adventure, where every moment is a reminder of His abundant blessings and love.

Psalm 145:15-16 - "The eyes of all look to you, and you give them their food at the proper time. You open your hand and satisfy the desires of every living thing."

DEVOTIONAL

As you prepare for this special outing, take a moment to reflect on the beauty of new beginnings. Bringing your baby into the vibrant world of shared meals is not just about tasting new flavors; it's about creating cherished memories that nourish your spirit. Each small smile from your little one, each curious glance at the bustling surroundings, reminds us of the wonders that God unfolds in our lives. Psalm 145:15-16 rings true: "The eyes of all look to you, and you give them their food at the proper time." Just as God provides for our needs, He invites you to trust in His grace during this adventure. Let each bite you share symbolize the abundance of love and blessings surrounding your family. Remember that with every giggle and spill, God's hand is there—guiding, sustaining, and filling your hearts with joy in this beautiful journey of parenthood.

DAILY REFLECTION

As you savor this first meal together, how can you embrace the joy of this moment as a reminder of God's faithfulness and the beautiful journey of growth unfolding in your family's life?

PRAYER

Dear Lord, as we embark on this first dining adventure with our little one, we thank You for the gift of new beginnings. May each shared moment be a reminder of Your abundant grace, filling our hearts with joy as we embrace the wonders of parenthood. Guide us through every giggle and spill, reminding us that in this journey of love and discovery, You are ever present, nourishing our spirits as we create lasting memories together. Amen.

Capture the joy of new life this Christmas season as you celebrate your baby's first holiday. Reflect on the miracle of Christ's birth and the promise of hope and love that comes with each tiny hand and joyful smile. Let this moment be a reminder of the joyous gift God has given us all.

Luke 2:14 - "Glory to God in the highest, and on earth peace among those with whom he is pleased!"

DEVOTIONAL

As you gather this Christmas to capture the joy of your baby's first holiday, let each smile remind you of the miraculous gift of life mirroring the divine moment when Christ was born. In that small, precious face, you can see the embodiment of hope, a promise whispered long ago that continues to unfold today. Just as the angels proclaimed, "Glory to God in the highest," let your heart swell with gratitude for the blessing of new beginnings and the peace that envelops your family during this sacred season. Each coo and giggle resonates with the promise that God is with us, bringing joy and light where there was once darkness. In the simplicity of those tiny hands and wide-eyed wonder, you are reminded that love walks among us, quiet yet powerful, transforming ordinary days into cherished memories. Embrace this moment fully as a reminder that in giving and receiving love, we reflect the heart of God Himself. This Christmas, as you capture these fleeting moments, remember that your little one is a testament to the hope and joy that can only come from Him.

DAILY REFLECTION

How can you embrace the joy and wonder of your baby's first Christmas as a reflection of the love and hope that Christ's birth brings into your life and the world?

PRAYER

Dear Lord, as we gather this Christmas to celebrate our baby's first holiday, fill our hearts with a profound sense of gratitude for the miracle of new life. Let each smile and soft giggle remind us of the hope embodied in Christ's birth, and may we cherish these fleeting moments, recognizing them as precious gifts from Your boundless love. Help us to embrace this season with open hearts, inspired by the joy that our little one brings and the promise of love that envelops our family. Amen.

The joy of a baby recognizing their name mirrors God's profound love for us. Just as a child responds to their name, may we turn our hearts to the Shepherd who knows us intimately, inviting us to respond to His call with trust and wonder.

John 10:27 - "My sheep hear my voice, and I know them, and they follow me."

DEVOTIONAL

In those precious moments when a baby first recognizes their name, there lies an unspoken bond—a spark of connection that resonates deep within the heart. This sweet awareness reflects a profound truth: just as a little one responds with delight to the sound of their name, we too are invited to acknowledge the tender call of our Shepherd. In John 10:27, Jesus assures us, "My sheep hear my voice, and I know them, and they follow me." How humbling it is to realize that we are known so intimately by the Creator of the universe! Imagine the joy in a parent's eyes as their child turns towards them, the warmth of love enveloping that shared moment. In the same way, let us respond to God's voice—filled with affection and purpose. When we turn our hearts toward Him, we step into a relationship rich with trust and wonder. Today, may we take delight in the knowledge that our names are lovingly spoken by Him, inviting us to thrive in His embrace.

DAILY REFLECTION

In the tender recognition of your own name, how might you respond to the gentle call of your Shepherd, knowing He delights in your presence just as a parent rejoices in their child's first acknowledgment?

PRAYER

Dear Lord, in the sweet simplicity of a child's first recognition of their name, we glimpse the depth of Your love for us. Help us to respond to Your gentle call with the same joy and delight, reminding us that You know us intimately and cherish each of our hearts. May we always turn toward You, embracing the warmth of Your presence and the purpose You offer, as we flourish in the beauty of our relationship with You. Amen.

October 23

On this day, reflect on the transformative power of grace in your life. Let the love of Christ renew your spirit, guiding you toward compassion and forgiveness. Embrace the call to serve others, knowing that in giving, we truly receive.

Titus 3:4-5: "But when the goodness and loving kindness of God our Savior appeared, he saved us, not because of works done by us in righteousness, but according to his own mercy, by the washing of regeneration and renewal of the Holy Spirit."

DEVOTIONAL

On this day, as you bring both hands together in prayer, pause to reflect on the transformative power of grace in your life. Recall that moment when God's goodness and loving kindness broke through your darkness, washing over you with the renewal of the Holy Spirit. It's a staggering truth: we were not saved by our own righteousness but by His unfathomable mercy, a gift freely given to each of us. As you embrace this grace, let it fill your spirit and spill over into the lives of those around you. Compassion and forgiveness are not merely aspirations; they are responses to the love you have received. Today, consider how acts of service—small or great—allow you to share that same grace with others. In giving, you discover the profound joy of receiving, reflecting Christ's heart to a world in desperate need of His light. Let this day be a reminder that grace is most deeply understood not as something to hold tightly but as a call to extend open hands to those around you.

DAILY REFLECTION

In what ways can you open your heart and hands today to let the grace you've received flow into the lives of others, transforming both their spirits and your own?

PRAYER

Dear Lord, as I bring my hands together in prayer, I am awed by the grace that has transformed my heart. Fill me with Your love, that I may extend compassion and forgiveness to others, allowing Your light to shine through me. Guide me in serving those around me, reminding me that in every act of giving, I am enriched by the beauty of Your unfailing mercy. Amen.

October 24

On this day, we celebrate the gift of new life, reflecting God's creative power in every tiny handprint and footprint. Just as each print is unique, so is every child a cherished part of His creation, reminding us to nurture and guide them in faith's journey.

Isaiah 44:2 - "This is what the Lord says— he who made you, who formed you in the womb, and who will help you: Do not be afraid, Jacob, my servant; Jeshurun, whom I have chosen."

DEVOTIONAL

On this day, as we celebrate the precious gift of new life, we pause to marvel at the intricate beauty of God's creation in every tiny handprint and footprint. Each mark is a testament to His creative power, a reminder that just as no two prints are alike, neither are any two children. In Isaiah 44:2, we hear the Lord's tender words: "He who made you, who formed you in the womb, and who will help you." How comforting it is to know that our little ones are part of a divine design, crafted with purpose and love. As parents and guardians, we are entrusted with guiding these treasures, nurturing their faith and helping them discover the world with wonder. Let each footprint inspire us to cultivate a path of faith, leading them closer to the heart of God. May we embrace our role with joy, trusting that He walks beside us every step of the way.

DAILY REFLECTION

How can I treasure and nurture the unique gifts of faith within each of my children, reflecting God's love and creativity in their lives as they take their first steps into the world?

PRAYER

Dear God, as we celebrate the miracle of new life and the tender handprints and footprints that reflect Your creative love, we thank You for the unique journey of each child. May we embrace our calling to nurture and guide them in faith, always reminding them of the wonder of Your presence. Help us to walk alongside them, trusting in Your guidance as they take each precious step in this world. Amen.

Dive into the refreshing waters of faith this week, just as you take your first splash in the pool. Embrace the opportunity to grow, trusting that with each stroke, God is guiding you deeper into His love and grace.

Isaiah 12:2 - "Surely God is my salvation; I will trust and not be afraid. The Lord, the Lord himself, is my strength and my defense; he has become my salvation."

DEVOTIONAL

As you prepare for your first swim class, take a moment to reflect on the act of plunging into water—how it invites you to let go of your fears and embrace new experiences. Much like stepping into the pool, your journey of faith invites you to trust in God's unwavering presence. Isaiah 12:2 whispers a truth that calms our anxious hearts: "Surely God is my salvation; I will trust and not be afraid." Imagine each splash representing your prayers, your doubts, and your hopes as you glide through the water of His grace. Embrace this week as an opportunity to grow deeper in your relationship with God, knowing that with each stroke, He is guiding you closer to His love. Just as your body learns to float and swim, allow your spirit to thrive in the knowledge that He is your strength and defense. Dive headfirst into this adventure, trusting that God is with you, ready to catch you when you falter, and eager to help you soar.

DAILY REFLECTION

As you take a deep breath and prepare to immerse yourself in the pool, what fears can you release into God's hands this week, allowing His love to carry you deeper into the waters of faith?

PRAYER

Dear Lord, as I prepare to take my first splash into the pool, I humbly ask for Your guidance and strength. Help me to let go of my fears, embracing this new experience as a reflection of my journey in faith. May each ripple in the water remind me of Your unwavering love, assuring me that with every stroke I take, You are there, catching me in Your grace and leading me deeper into the refreshing waters of Your presence. Amen.

As you hit the road for your first family adventure, let each mile remind you of God's promise to guide and protect your journey. With every coo and giggle from your baby, cherish the joy and blessings of new beginnings, trusting that God is with you in every moment.

Psalm 32:8 - "I will instruct you and teach you in the way you should go; I will counsel you with my eye upon you."

DEVOTIONAL

As you embark on your first road trip with your little one, take a moment to breathe in the excitement of this new adventure. Each mile you travel is not just distance covered, but a testament to God's unwavering promise to guide you. Picture the coos and giggles of your baby filling the car—these joyful sounds are reminders of the blessings that come with new beginnings. In the unpredictable turns of your journey, lean into the assurance of Psalm 32:8, knowing that God is actively instructing you, illuminating the path ahead. Every smile exchanged and every peaceful snooze is a moment infused with His presence. Trust that with every stop, every snack, and even the unexpected detours, He is watching over you with loving care. Embrace the beauty of this shared experience, and let the faith that has brought you this far propel you into the thrill of what lies ahead.

DAILY REFLECTION

As you navigate the winding roads of this new family journey, how can you open your heart to see God's guidance in both the joyful moments and the unexpected challenges that lie ahead?

PRAYER

Dear Lord, as we set off on this journey as a family, fill our hearts with gratitude for this precious time together. May the laughter of our little one echo in our minds, reminding us of Your endless blessings and the joy of new beginnings. Guide us safely down each road, embracing every moment with faith, knowing that Your love surrounds us in every mile. Amen.

October 27

As you step into your family's home, remember that every gathering is an opportunity for grace and connection. Let your heart reflect the love of Christ, fostering unity and joy in the ties that bind you. Embrace this time as a sacred chance to share blessings and build deeper relationships.

Colossians 3:14 - "And over all these virtues put on love, which binds them all together in perfect unity."

DEVOTIONAL

As you step into your family's home, take a moment to breathe deeply and invite God's presence into this sacred space. Each greeting, each shared laugh, is a thread in the tapestry of love that binds you together—woven by grace and intentionality. Remember Colossians 3:14: "And over all these virtues put on love, which binds them all together in perfect unity." Let your heart overflow with the love of Christ, for it is through this love that you can foster true connection and understanding. In gatherings like this, every conversation can become a blessing, every shared memory a chance to deepen bonds. Embrace the joy that comes from being fully present, for these moments are not just moments but divine invitations to reflect God's heart. As you navigate the time with your loved ones, allow the spirit of unity to flow freely between you, letting go of conflicts and embracing the grace that sets you all free. This time together is a precious gift—an opportunity to build a foundation of relationship that endures in love.

DAILY REFLECTION

How can you intentionally weave moments of grace and love into your interactions today, transforming what might feel like just a family gathering into a sacred opportunity for connection and heartfelt understanding?

PRAYER

Dear Lord, as I step into this cherished space filled with family, I invite Your presence to envelop every moment we share. May each laugh and conversation be a thread of Your love woven into our hearts, cultivating unity and joy among us. Help me to be fully present, embracing the grace You offer, and let our time together be a sacred opportunity to reflect Your heart and deepen our bonds. Amen.

October 28

When your little one coughs, remember that even in small challenges, God's presence is with us. Trust in His comfort and guidance, for He cares for every detail of our lives, including our children's health. Lean on prayer and support, knowing that healing comes in His perfect timing.

Psalm 91:1-2 - "He who dwells in the secret place of the Most High shall abide under the shadow of the Almighty. I will say of the Lord, 'He is my refuge and my fortress, my God, in Him I will trust.'"

DEVOTIONAL

In those quiet moments when your little one coughs softly in the night, it's easy for worry to creep in, isn't it? As you sit by their bedside, let the soothing words of Psalm 91 wash over you: "He who dwells in the secret place of the Most High shall abide under the shadow of the Almighty." Remember that with each gentle cough, God invites you to trust in His faithful presence. He cares for every detail of our lives, including your precious child's health, and He is with you in this small challenge. You may feel anxious, but lean into prayer, for it is your lifeline, a way to release your fears into His capable hands. Just as the sun rises, so too will the hope of healing in His perfect timing. Trust that you are not alone; He is your refuge and fortress, ready to wrap you both in His comforting embrace. In these moments, stay close to Him, and let His peace envelop your heart.

DAILY REFLECTION

In those tender, vulnerable moments when your little one coughs softly in the night, how can you open your heart to embrace God's comforting presence and trust Him to cradle both your fears and your child in His loving care?

PRAYER

Dear Lord, as I listen to my little one's soft cough in the stillness of the night, I feel a wave of worry crash over me. Remind me, in these tender moments, of Your unwavering presence and comforting embrace; help me to release my fears into Your hands. Grant us both peace and assurance in Your perfect care, knowing that healing will come in Your time, and fill my heart with the trust that we are never alone. Amen.

In the midst of sleepless nights and tender moments, find comfort in God's unwavering presence. Just as He cares for us through every trial, may you embrace the journey of your little one's growth with hope and love, knowing that each struggle brings forth new joys.

Psalm 34:17-18 - The righteous cry, and the Lord hears, and delivers them out of all their troubles. The Lord is near to those who have a broken heart, and saves such as have a contrite spirit.

DEVOTIONAL

In the tender moments of sleepless nights, you may feel overwhelmed as your little one navigates the challenges of teething. Yet, it is precisely in these struggles where we can find the comforting embrace of God, a reminder that He is always present, even in our weariness. Psalm 34:17-18 reassures us that the righteous cry out, and the Lord hears—He understands your exhaustion and your heart. As your child experiences the discomfort of their first teeth, remember that this journey, while painful, is also filled with the promise of growth and new beginnings. Each tear shed is met with grace, and each cry is a step towards joy, a testament to the miraculous ways God nurtures His children. Embrace these moments of tenderness, knowing that through this trial, you are not alone; you are surrounded by divine love and care. Let hope fill your heart as you witness the beautiful transformation happening before you, trusting that your cries and disappointments are heard by the One who saves.

DAILY REFLECTION

In the quiet chaos of teething nights, how can you actively invite God's comforting presence into your moments of exhaustion, transforming your struggles into a deeper connection with your little one and with Him?

PRAYER

Dear Lord, in these quiet, weary hours of the night, I seek Your tender presence as we navigate the challenges of teething. Wrap my little one in Your comfort, and grant me strength to embrace this journey with love, recognizing that even in moments of struggle, Your grace shines through. Help us to cherish each tear and every cry, knowing that growth and joy are just around the corner, held securely in Your caring hands. Amen.

Taste and see that the Lord is good (Psalm 34:8). Just as a child savors their first solid food, may we savor the richness of God's Word, nurturing our souls and growing in faith with each nourishing experience.

Matthew 5:6 - "Blessed are those who hunger and thirst for righteousness, for they will be filled."

DEVOTIONAL

As you embark on this new culinary adventure with your little one, consider how akin this experience is to our journey with God. Just as your child savors their very first bites of solid food, exploring new textures and flavors, so too are we invited to taste and see the goodness of the Lord. Psalm 34:8 beckons us to engage with the richness of God's Word, allowing it to nourish our souls and expand our understanding of His love. In moments of hunger and thirst, Matthew 5:6 assures us that those who seek righteousness will be filled. Each time you share a meal with your child, reflect on the ways God provides for our every need, not just physically but spiritually as well. Together, as you delight in these precious moments, may your heart echo the wonder of God's abundant grace. Together, let's savor each bite of His truth, for in doing so, we cultivate a lasting appetite for holiness and richness in faith.

DAILY REFLECTION

As you witness your little one's joyful discovery of solid foods, how can you open your heart to explore the depths of God's Word with the same eager delight, allowing each verse to nourish your spirit and deepen your faith?

PRAYER

Dear Lord, as we embark on this precious journey of sharing solid food with our little one, may we also open our hearts to taste and see Your goodness in every moment. Help us to savor not only the new flavors before us but also the nourishment of Your Word, allowing it to fill us with joy and understanding. Remind us, in these small yet profound gatherings, of Your abundant grace, and let our hearts grow in faith as we delight in the gifts You provide each day. Amen.

October 31

On this day, we celebrate the joy of communion—sharing moments with loved ones that can be messy but are full of grace. Just as Jesus transformed ordinary moments into sacred ones, let us find beauty in the messy faces around our family tables, reflecting the warmth of His love and acceptance.

Luke 22:19-20 - "And he took bread, gave thanks and broke it, and gave it to them, saying, 'This is my body given for you; do this in remembrance of me.' In the same way, after the supper he took the cup, saying, 'This cup is the new covenant in my blood, which is poured out for you.'"

DEVOTIONAL

On this day, as we gather around our tables, let us remember the sacredness hidden in the mess. Just as Jesus took the bread and broke it, transforming a simple meal into a profound act of communion, we are invited to do the same with our moments—especially the messy ones. Picture the joyful chaos: splattered pasta sauce, sticky fingers, and laughter bouncing off the walls. These are the rich moments that reflect the essence of love and acceptance that Christ showed us. Each smudge on a child's face is a reminder of the grace that meets us in our imperfections, inviting us to cherish the company of those we hold dear. Let us lift our cups in gratitude, understanding that the new covenant Jesus established is about embracing the beautiful mess of life together. May we find joy in these shared moments, letting them deepen our connection with each other and with Him.

DAILY REFLECTION

In the beautiful chaos of our shared meals, what moments of grace and love can we embrace amidst the messiness, reflecting the sacredness of our communion with Christ and one another?

PRAYER

Dear Lord, as we gather around our tables today, help us to embrace the sweet messiness of our shared moments. May every splatter and sticky finger remind us of Your grace that flows through our imperfections, binding us together in love and laughter. Let us celebrate the sacredness found in these joyful chaos, reflecting the warmth of Your acceptance in our hearts and homes. Amen.

November 1

On this day, reflect on the theme of patience and nurturing love, just as God cares for us in our struggles. Just like tending to a baby's first diaper rash, our faith journey may require gentle attention and compassion. Trust that through discomfort, growth and healing are on the horizon.

1 Peter 4:8 - Above all, keep loving one another earnestly, since love covers a multitude of sins.

DEVOTIONAL

As you navigate the unsettling experience of your baby's first diaper rash, you are reminded of the fragility that comes with new life. Each whimper and cry triggers a wave of instinctual love, compelling you to minister to their discomfort with tender hands and a gentle heart. In these moments, you embody God's grace, pouring out patience and nurturing love just as He does for you in your own struggles. Just as a baby's skin needs careful tending, our souls require the same gentle attention to heal and flourish. Reflect on how your faith journey mirrors this experience—a series of tender moments where God lovingly attends to your pains and growing edges. With each challenge, remember that discomfort often leads to growth, and trust that through every trial, you are being molded into someone stronger and more compassionate. Above all, let your love overflow, embracing the small steps of progress and trusting the promise of healing on the horizon.

DAILY REFLECTION

In the tender moments spent comforting your baby through their first discomfort, how might you recognize God's patient and nurturing presence in your own struggles, and how can you allow that awareness to deepen your faith and compassion?

PRAYER

Father in heaven, thank You for the gift of new life and the opportunity to nurture it with love and care. Amidst the discomfort of my baby's first diaper rash, help me to mirror Your patience and compassion, embracing this journey with grace. May my heart remain open to the lessons within this season, as I trust in Your promise of healing and the beautiful growth that awaits us both. Amen.

November 2

On this day of reflection, recognize the joy in God's creation—laughter is a divine gift! Let your heart resonate with gratitude as you celebrate the abundant grace that fills your life. Seek joy, share love, and let your laughter echo as a testament to His goodness.

Proverbs 15:13 - A glad heart makes a cheerful face, but by sorrow of heart the spirit is crushed.

DEVOTIONAL

Today, let's bask in the radiant beauty of God's creation, where laughter emerges as a divine melody, a testament to His boundless grace. As the sun's rays dance through the trees, let your heart respond with joy and gratitude, savoring the moments that spark your first loud belly laugh. Proverbs 15:13 reminds us that a glad heart brings a cheerful face; let your spirit be unburdened, celebrating the simple joys that weave through your days. Reflect on the laughter shared with loved ones, the whimsical moments that catch you off guard, and the echoes of joy that fill your life. How often do we overlook these gifts, focusing instead on our worries or burdens? Today, take a step back—allow your spirit to be lifted by the laughter that God has woven into the fabric of life. Share that joy with others; let your laughter ripple outward, a contagious reminder of His goodness and the abundant grace that envelops you in every moment.

DAILY REFLECTION

In the midst of life's noise, how can you attune your heart to the laughter that reflects God's joy, allowing it to transform your perspective and draw you closer to His love?

PRAYER

Dear Lord, in the sacred space of this day, I pause to celebrate the laughter that paints my life with joy. Thank You for every hearty laugh shared with loved ones, every unexpected moment that brightens my spirit, and the grace that fills each fleeting second. May my heart overflow with gratitude, and may my laughter serve as a joyful echo of Your goodness in the world. Amen.

November 3

On this date in the Christian calendar, reflect on the theme of perseverance in faith. Just as a child learns to crawl by trying again and again, we are reminded that God's grace supports us through our struggles, urging us to keep moving forward, trusting His plan and timing in every step we take.

Hebrews 12:1-2 - "Therefore, since we are surrounded by such a great cloud of witnesses, let us throw off everything that hinders and the sin that so easily entangles. And let us run with perseverance the race marked out for us, fixing our eyes on Jesus, the pioneer and perfecter of faith."

DEVOTIONAL

As we gather our thoughts on this day, consider the humble beginnings of a child learning to crawl. With each tentative rock forward, there is both an eagerness and a wobbly determination—an embodiment of the perseverance we are called to embody in our faith. In Hebrews 12:1-2, we are reminded that the journey of faith is not merely a sprint, but a race filled with challenges that require us to shed the burdens of sin and distraction. Just as a child falls only to rise again, so too are we encouraged to rise despite the setbacks that may seek to entangle us. The great cloud of witnesses surrounding us—those who have walked before—reminds us that we are never alone in our efforts. With each push against the ground, we must fix our eyes on Jesus, the pioneer and perfecter of our faith, who holds our frailty in His tender hands. Let's step forward, even when the path feels uncertain, trusting in the divine grace that supports our every move. In our striving, may we remember that it is not just the destination that matters, but the journey of becoming, one inspired crawl at a time.

DAILY REFLECTION

As you ponder the tender steps of faith you are taking today, what burdens do you need to lay down in order to embrace the grace that empowers you to keep crawling forward in your spiritual journey?

PRAYER

Dear Lord, as we reflect on the journey of faith today, teach us to embrace the wobbly steps of our own spiritual crawling. May we find strength in Your grace to rise again after every fall and trust that each small attempt draws us closer to You. Help us to fix our eyes on Jesus and persevere through life's challenges, knowing that our struggles shape us into the beings You have designed us to be. Amen.

November 4

On this day, reflect on the steadfast love of Christ that upholds us in times of uncertainty. Trust in His promise that even in our vulnerability, He strengthens us to rise and walk in faith.

Isaiah 54:10 - "Though the mountains be shaken and the hills be removed, yet my unfailing love for you will not be shaken nor my covenant of peace be removed," says the Lord, who has compassion on you.

DEVOTIONAL

On this day, let us take a moment to embrace the steadfast love of Christ, a love that remains unshakable even as the world around us trembles. In times of uncertainty, when the mountains of our lives feel as if they are crumbling and the hills seem to threaten our peace, God whispers to our hearts through Isaiah 54:10. His promise of unfailing love is not just a distant echo but a present reality, holding us close and reminding us that we are never alone in our vulnerability. As we navigate the challenges that arise, let us trust that it is in our weakest moments that His strength is revealed most profoundly. When we feel we cannot rise, it is His grace that lifts us and propels us forward in faith. Remember, dear friend, that each time we falter, we are met with His compassion, an assurance that there is always hope. Let your heart rest in the certainty of His covenant of peace, for His love is the anchor that grounds us amid the storm.

DAILY REFLECTION

In the quiet moments of your uncertainty, how can you open your heart to truly experience the unwavering love of Christ that not only sustains you but empowers you to rise and walk confidently in faith?

PRAYER

Dear Lord, In this moment of uncertainty, I surrender my fears and weaknesses to you, resting in the steadfast love that holds me firm. When the tides of life threaten to sweep me away, let your promise be my anchor, reminding me that even amidst the storms, it is Your grace that empowers me to rise, walk, and trust in Your unwavering faithfulness. Amen.

On this momentous occasion of your baby's first hair growth spurt, reflect on the beauty of new beginnings. Just as God nurtures us through each stage of growth, may this milestone remind you of His faithful hand guiding your child's development and the wonderful journey ahead.

Isaiah 40:30-31 - Even youths grow tired and weary, and young men stumble and fall; but those who hope in the Lord will renew their strength. They will soar on wings like eagles; they will run and not grow weary, they will walk and not be faint.

DEVOTIONAL

As you celebrate this precious milestone of your baby's first hair growth spurt, pause and reflect on the beauty of new beginnings. Just as each strand emerges with its own unique texture and brilliance, so too does God's plan unfold in your child's life—every stage infused with purpose and promise. In Isaiah 40:30-31, we are reminded that even the strongest can grow weary, but those who place their hope in the Lord find renewal, much like the fresh strength that comes as your little one grows. This moment is an invitation to envision the incredible journey ahead, where each curl or wave signifies the love, guidance, and nurturing you provide as a parent. Trust that God's faithful hand is upon your child, just as He cradles your heart during this beautiful yet fleeting season. Embrace this time of growth with joy, knowing that as your baby's hair flourishes, so too will their spirit soar under the love and grace of our Lord. Together, let us celebrate not just the changes in appearance, but the profound journey of faith and love that lies ahead.

DAILY REFLECTION

How can you nurture your child's spirit in this season of growth, while trusting in God's unwavering provision and plan for their unique journey ahead?

PRAYER

Dear Lord, in this tender moment of witnessing my baby's first hair growth spurt, I pause to marvel at Your handiwork and the beauty of new beginnings. As each delicate strand reminds me of Your faithful presence, I pray for Your guiding hand to nurture my child's journey ahead. Help me to embrace these fleeting days with gratitude, knowing that in every curl and wave, Your love and purpose are unfolding in their precious life. Amen.

Trust in God's perfect timing as you transition your little one to their own crib. This moment is a step of faith, reflecting God's love and care for both you and your child. Allow His peace to fill your heart in this new season of independence.

Isaiah 41:13 - For I, the LORD your God, hold your right hand; it is I who say to you, "Fear not, I am the one who helps you."

DEVOTIONAL

As you stand before the crib, a mixture of excitement and anxiety swells in your heart. This moment, filled with both joy and apprehension, marks a significant step in your baby's journey towards independence. Remember, dear parent, that God's timing is perfect, even in the quiet moments spent transitioning your little one to their own space. Reflect on Isaiah 41:13: "For I, the LORD your God, hold your right hand; it is I who say to you, 'Fear not, I am the one who helps you.'" In this new season, trust that just as He holds your hand, He holds your child too, wrapping them in His love and protection. Allow His peace to wash over you, assuring you that He is present in both the gentle coos and the quiet stillness of their new room. Step forward in faith, knowing that releasing your little one to sleep alone is a reflection of your trust in God's unfailing care for both of you. Embrace this transition as an unfolding story of love, courage, and the beautiful journey of growing in faith.

DAILY REFLECTION

In this pivotal moment of laying your precious baby in their crib, how can you consciously release your worries into God's hands, embracing the peace that comes from trusting His perfect plan for both your child and yourself?

PRAYER

Dear Lord, as I place my little one in this crib, I feel a blend of hope and uncertainty. Hold my heart steady in this new chapter, reassuring me of Your perfect timing and unwavering love. Help me to trust in Your presence, knowing that while my child begins a journey of independence, we are both wrapped in Your gentle care and surrounded by Your peace. Amen.

November 7

On this day, remember that rest is a divine gift, reflecting God's own pause after creation. Embrace the stillness of His presence and allow His peace to renew your spirit as you cultivate a purposeful nap routine. Seek strength in the quiet moments, trusting that God revitalizes us for His work.

Genesis 2:2-3 - And on the seventh day God finished his work that he had done, and he rested on the seventh day from all his work that he had done. So God blessed the seventh day and made it holy, because on it God rested from all his work that he had done in creation.

DEVOTIONAL

As we gather today, let us remember that rest is not merely a pause in our busy lives, but a sacred gift from our Creator. In Genesis 2:2-3, we see the God of the universe take a moment to step back, to breathe, and to reflect on the beauty of His creation, blessing the seventh day and making it holy. Embracing a purposeful nap routine can be an invitation into that divine rhythm— a chance to disconnect from the noise and reconnect with the stillness of His presence. Just as the earth finds renewal in the quiet of the night, so too can our weary souls be revitalized in those gentle moments of rest. Allow His peace to envelop you as you lay down your burdens, trusting that in the stillness, God is working in you. Each nap can be a sacred act, reminding you that even in our need for rest, His strength flows abundantly. Today, let us cultivate this rhythm of rest, knowing it prepares us for all the beautiful work He has in store.

DAILY REFLECTION

In the stillness of your next nap, how might you open your heart to experience the profound peace and renewal that only comes from resting in God's presence, allowing Him to prepare you for the beautiful tasks ahead?

PRAYER

Dear Lord, as I pause to embrace the precious gift of rest, I thank You for the gentle reminder of Your own sacred rhythm in creation. Help me to find solace in the stillness, to lay down my burdens, and to open my heart to Your renewing presence. May each moment of rest be a cherished time of reconnection, filling me with the strength and peace I need to carry out the beautiful work You have prepared for me. Amen.

November 8

On this day, as we reflect on the joy of new beginnings, let us also embrace patience in the small frustrations. Just as a baby learns to express needs, we are reminded that God listens to our cries and nurtures our growth in faith and understanding.

Psalm 40:1-3 - "I waited patiently for the Lord; he inclined to me and heard my cry. He drew me up from the pit of destruction, out of the miry bog, and set my feet upon a rock, making my steps secure. He put a new song in my mouth, a song of praise to our God."

DEVOTIONAL

On this day, as we celebrate the beauty of new beginnings, we are invited to notice the small frustrations that arise in our lives—those moments akin to a baby's first tiny tantrum. These little expressions of need remind us of our own journey of growth and understanding. Just as a child learns to voice their desires, so too are we called to bring our cries to the Lord, trusting that He hears us in our moments of desperation. Psalm 40:1-3 beautifully reflects this truth, illustrating how the Lord not only listens but acts, lifting us from our struggles and placing our feet on solid ground. As we encounter our own frustrations today, let us practice patience, knowing that each tear shed is a step toward deeper faith. He transforms our cries into songs of praise, teaching us that even in discomfort, His presence is a source of strength and joy. May we celebrate the process of growth, resting in the assurance that God nurtures our souls along the way.

DAILY REFLECTION

In the midst of life's small frustrations, how can we open our hearts in patience, trusting that just as a child is nurtured through their first expressions of need, God is lovingly guiding us toward a deeper understanding of His faithfulness and grace?

PRAYER

Dear Lord, as we navigate the small frustrations of our day, help us to embrace the lessons they bring. Teach us to express our needs with the same honesty as a child, trusting that You hear our cries and cradle our hearts with love. May our moments of discomfort become catalysts for growth, allowing us to rest in the comfort of Your presence and transform our struggles into songs of hope and praise. Amen.

November 9

On this day, reflect on the profound love of Christ demonstrated through His sacrifices. As we journey through this season, may we find strength in His grace and deepen our commitment to serve others with the same compassion He showed us. Let your heart be a vessel of His light in a world seeking hope.

John 15:13 - "Greater love has no one than this: to lay down one's life for one's friends."

DEVOTIONAL

As we gather today, let us pause and reflect on the extraordinary depth of Christ's love, a love that knows no bounds. In John 15:13, we are reminded, "Greater love has no one than this: to lay down one's life for one's friends." Imagine the ultimate sacrifice made not just for friends, but for each of us—for our flaws, our struggles, and our deepest longings. In this season of reflection, let His grace wash over us, strengthening our hearts and empowering us to extend that same compassion to others. Each day is an opportunity to embody His light, to be a vessel of hope in a world that often feels dark and uncertain. Just as Christ lovingly surrendered for our sake, may we choose to live sacrificially, giving of ourselves in small, meaningful ways. As we commit ourselves to serve and support those around us, let's carry His profound love in our actions, making our lives a testament to His unyielding faithfulness.

DAILY REFLECTION

How might your life reflect the boundless love of Christ today, inviting you to embrace small acts of sacrifice that illuminate hope for those around you?

PRAYER

Dear Lord, as we immerse ourselves in the depth of Your love this day, we are reminded of the ultimate sacrifice You made for us. May Your grace fill our hearts and empower us to pour out that same boundless compassion to those around us. Let our lives shine with the hope of Your light, so that in our small acts of service, we may reflect Your unwavering faithfulness and love in a world aching for Your embrace. Amen.

November 10

On this day, as you cradle new life in your arms, reflect on the miracle of beginnings. Just as God gifted us His Son, cherish this sacred moment of hope and love, reminding us that every child is a divine promise for the world.

Isaiah 9:6 - "For to us a child is born, to us a son is given; and the government shall be upon his shoulder, and his name shall be called Wonderful Counselor, Mighty God, Everlasting Father, Prince of Peace."

DEVOTIONAL

On this day, cradling the weight of new life in your arms, pause to marvel at the extraordinary gift you hold. In this tender moment, you are reminded of the profound blessings wrapped inside the fragile form of a child. Just as the angels heralded the birth of Jesus, the greatest gift of all, cherish this sacred life before you as a divine whisper of hope that echoes through time. Each coo and breath is a testament to God's promise—a reminder that in the heart of every child lies an unspoken potential, waiting to change the world. Consider the names given to Christ: Wonderful Counselor, Mighty God, Everlasting Father, Prince of Peace. Let these attributes envelop you and this little one, inspiring you to nurture their spirit with love and wisdom. As you hold them close, recognize that you too are part of this beautiful tapestry, woven together in faith and grace.

DAILY REFLECTION

In this precious moment of cradling new life, how will you embody the love and wisdom of Christ as you nurture this child's unique journey, ensuring they feel the embrace of hope and promise in a world that longs for light?

PRAYER

Dear Lord, As I cradle this precious new life in my arms, I am filled with awe at the miracle of beginnings. May Your divine love guide me as I nurture this little one, and may their future be brightened by the promise of hope and grace that You embody. Remind me daily of the powerful potential within them, and help me to be a wise and loving steward of their spirit, just as You have modeled for us through Your Son. Amen.

November 11

On this day of the Christian calendar, reflect on the nourishment found in Christ's love, akin to a first feeding experience. Just as a newborn depends on sustenance for growth, may you draw from the wellspring of His grace, discovering how His word fuels your spirit and fosters deeper faith.

John 7:37-38 - "On the last day of the feast, the great day, Jesus stood up and cried out, 'If anyone thirsts, let him come to me and drink. Whoever believes in me, as the Scripture has said, "Out of his heart will flow rivers of living water."'"

DEVOTIONAL

On this significant day in our Christian calendar, we are invited to contemplate the profound nourishment that flows from Christ's love, reminiscent of the sacred moment when a newborn first tastes sustenance. Just as a tiny infant experiences that pure, instinctive reliance on milk for strength and growth, we too are called to come with eagerness to the wellspring of grace that Jesus offers. He beckons us, saying, "If anyone thirsts, let him come to me and drink." Can you hear His voice? In our parched lives, filled with the dryness of this world, His promise quenches our deepest longings, flowing like rivers of living water into the crevices of our weariness. As we draw near to Him, let us recognize that His Word is the lifeblood that nourishes our spirits, infusing us with the strength to grow and thrive in faith. In Christ, each moment spent in His presence is an opportunity for our souls to flourish, burgeoning under the weight of His love. So let us approach with the trust of a newborn, ready to be filled anew, allowing His grace to shape us, and reveal the beautiful person He designed us to be.

DAILY REFLECTION

In what ways can you allow yourself to be vulnerably nourished by Christ's love today, trusting that His grace will cultivate growth and strength within your spirit as you embrace the sweetness of His Word?

PRAYER

Dear Lord, today I come before You with the humble heart of a newborn seeking nourishment. As I reflect on the sweetness of Your love, help me to fully rely on the sustenance that flows from Your grace, quenching my deepest thirst with Your living waters. May I find strength and growth in Your Word, trusting that in every moment spent with You, my spirit is renewed and my faith deepens.

November 12

In the stillness of a sleepless night, remember that even in the darkest moments, God's light shines brightest. Just as He entrusted the world to a humble manger, He walks with you now, guiding your heart in this sacred journey of parenthood. Rest in His promises, for every cry is a song of hope.

Luke 2:12 - "And this will be a sign for you: you will find a baby wrapped in swaddling cloths and lying in a manger."

DEVOTIONAL

In the stillness of a sleepless night, as the world around you slumbers, take a moment to breathe in the profound peace that envelops you and your newborn. These hours may feel long, but they are woven with sacred significance, much like that holy night when Christ came into the world, wrapped in swaddling cloths and lying in a manger. Remember, dear parent, that in this tender yet challenging journey, you are not alone; God walks with you, His light shining brightly even in the shadows of fatigue and uncertainty. Each cry echoes the promise of new beginnings, a song of hope that the world so desperately needs. Every moment spent cradling your child is a precious reminder of God's own love and faithfulness. As you rock them gently, let your hearts be filled with the assurance that He holds the future of this little one in His hands, just as He did on that fateful night in Bethlehem. Trust in His guidance, lean into the stillness, and rest in the beauty of this sacred chapter, knowing that the dawn will come, bringing with it a renewed hope and joy.

DAILY REFLECTION

In this tender hour of quiet restlessness, how can you embrace the whispers of God's presence amidst the cries and coos of your newborn, finding solace in the knowledge that each moment of this journey is a sacred reflection of His eternal love?

PRAYER

Dear Lord, in this stillness of the night, I come before You with a weary heart, cradling my newborn and seeking comfort in Your presence. May Your light shine brightly through my moments of doubt and fatigue, reminding me that each cry is a precious reminder of Your promises and the hope of new beginnings. Wrap us in Your love tonight, Lord, and grant me the strength to embrace this sacred journey of parenthood, trusting that You are guiding us both in this beautiful unfolding. Amen.

In the midst of life's unexpected messes, like a diaper blowout, we find an opportunity for grace and laughter. Just as God cares for our every need, He invites us to trust in His presence through all of life's challenges, reminding us that His love covers every situation.

Psalm 103:13-14 – "As a father shows compassion to his children, so the Lord shows compassion to those who fear him. For he knows our frame; he remembers that we are dust."

DEVOTIONAL

In the whirlwind of parenting, there's nothing quite like facing your baby's first diaper blowout—a messy, chaotic moment that seems to catch you off guard. Amidst the laughter and the frantic dash for wipes, we can find a beautiful reminder of God's grace. Just as we approach our children with compassion and understanding, our Heavenly Father approaches us with unfathomable love and care. Psalm 103:13-14 gently reminds us that while we are imperfect and, at times, messy in our own lives, God knows our weaknesses and loves us fiercely regardless. Perhaps in that moment of chaos, we are invited to pause, breathe, and trust in His presence—after all, He is well-acquainted with our frailty and offers His strength in our shortcomings. Every blowout becomes a chance to experience grace that surprises us, teaching us to find joy even in messy situations. Embrace those moments; they are not just challenges but opportunities for growth, laughter, and an ever-deepening connection with our Creator.

DAILY REFLECTION

In the midst of the chaos of a first diaper blowout, how can you pause and recognize God's unwavering presence, inviting you to embrace both the mess of parenting and the grace that teaches you to trust His love in every moment?

PRAYER

Dear Lord, in the midst of the chaos that comes with parenting, especially those unexpected moments like a diaper blowout, help us to pause and see your grace at work. Remind us of your unwavering love that covers our imperfections and leads us to joy, even in the messiest situations. May we embrace these challenges as invitations to grow closer to you, trusting in your presence as we navigate both the laughter and the tears of this beautiful journey.

As Jesus found solace in familiar places, may we also discover His presence in the simple joys of home. In every corner and moment, recognize that God's love dwells among us, reminding us that true comfort comes from Him.

Matthew 18:20 – "For where two or three gather in my name, there am I with them."

DEVOTIONAL

In the sacred spaces of our homes, where laughter mingles with quiet moments of reflection, we oftentimes discover the essence of true comfort—an echo of the peace that Jesus Himself cherished. Just as He found solace in familiar surroundings, we, too, can encounter His presence in the simplicity of our everyday lives. Imagine the warmth of a shared meal, the gentle rustle of turning pages, or even the silence that wraps around us like a cozy blanket; these are more than mere routines; they are moments where God's love resides. Matthew 18:20 reassures us that when we gather, even in life's intimacies and mundane rhythms, He is with us. In the tender act of gathering around the table, or in the quietude of a shared afternoon, we can feel the divine embrace, reminding us that home is more than a place— it is a posture of the heart. So let us be attentive to the whispers of love that permeate our homes, realizing that it is here, amidst the warmth, we can truly find Him. In the company of loved ones, may we celebrate the extraordinary gift of togetherness, knowing that in every heartbeat shared, we are cradled in His grace.

DAILY REFLECTION

In what ways can you open your heart to recognize God's presence in the everyday moments of warmth and connection within your home?

PRAYER

Dear Lord, in the gentle embrace of our homes, may we always recognize Your presence, weaving through the laughter and quiet moments alike. As we gather with loved ones, help us to cherish these sacred spaces, remembering that true comfort dwells in Your love, cradling us like a familiar melody. Teach us to find You in the ordinary and to celebrate every heartbeat shared, knowing that home is not just a place, but a haven of Your grace. Amen.

November 15

Today, as you change that diaper, remember the humble service of Christ, who washed the feet of His disciples. Each act of care reflects His love—embrace this sacred moment of nurturing with grace and joy.

John 13:14-15 - "If I then, your Lord and Teacher, have washed your feet, you also ought to wash one another's feet. For I have given you an example, that you should do as I have done to you."

DEVOTIONAL

Today, as you find yourself changing that diaper for the first time alone, take a moment to embrace the significance of this humble task. In this act of care, you mirror the heart of Christ, who knelt to wash the feet of His disciples, showing us that true leadership is found in service. Just as He offered His hands to cleanse the dirt, your hands today embody a love that nurtures and protects. This moment, though it may feel ordinary, is infused with grace, a gentle reminder that the smallest acts can reflect the greatest love. Allow yourself to feel the joy and purpose in this nurturing; you are not just changing a diaper, but cultivating a bond that echoes the love Christ has for us all. Let your heart overflow with gratitude as you recognize that in serving, you are walking in His footsteps. Embrace this sacred time, knowing that every act of love, no matter how small, is a reflection of His grace.

DAILY REFLECTION

In this quiet moment of changing a diaper, how can you open your heart to recognize the profound beauty and grace in this simple act, reflecting on how Christ's humble service informs your journey as a caregiver?

PRAYER

Dear Lord, as I change this diaper today, may I remember that in each gentle touch, I am living out the love You have shown us. Help me to embrace these humble moments with joy and gratitude, recognizing that in nurturing, I reflect Your heart. Allow me to find strength and grace in this sacred task, knowing that even the smallest acts of service are a powerful testimony of Your love. Amen.

November 16

As the season of Lent begins, reflect on the call to humility and self-denial. Like a seed that must break open to sprout, let your burdens release to God, allowing His transformative grace to nurture your spirit. Commit to a journey of deeper faith, trusting in His purpose for growth.

Mark 8:34-35 - "And calling the crowd to him with his disciples, he said to them, 'If anyone would come after me, let him deny himself and take up his cross and follow me. For whoever would save his life will lose it, but whoever loses his life for my sake and the gospel's will save it.'"

DEVOTIONAL

As we enter this season of Lent, our hearts are drawn to the profound call of humility that resides within the words of Mark 8:34-35. Jesus invites each of us to reflect on the weight of our burdens and consider what it truly means to deny ourselves. Like a seed that must break open to uncover its potential, we too are called to release our fears, desires, and distractions into the nourishing hands of God. This journey of self-denial is not an act of loss but a beautiful exchange— trading our burdens for His grace, our struggles for His strength. As we embark on this path of deeper faith, let us trust that God has a purpose for our growth, even in the moments when we feel like we're losing ourselves. Embrace this time to dig deep, allowing the transformative grace of Christ to cultivate new life within you. May your spirit blossom as you faithfully follow Him, bearing the fruit of His love and light in this world.

DAILY REFLECTION

In this Lenten season of humility and self-denial, how might surrendering your burdens to God reveal the untapped potential of your spirit, leading you to a deeper understanding of His transformative grace?

PRAYER

Dear Lord, as this Lenten season unfolds, help me to embrace the call of humility and self-denial. I surrender my burdens and distractions into Your loving hands, trusting that in letting go, I may uncover the depths of my true potential. May Your transformative grace nurture my spirit, allowing me to blossom in faith and bear the fruit of Your love in every moment of my journey. Amen.

During your first postpartum checkup, reflect on God's faithfulness as you navigate this new season of motherhood. Remember that just as He knitted your child together, He brings healing and renewal for you too. Trust in His plan as you embrace this journey of care and growth.

Psalm 30:2 - "O Lord my God, I cried to you for help, and you have healed me."

DEVOTIONAL

As you sit in the waiting room for your first postpartum checkup, take a moment to breathe and soak in the miracle of this new life. The journey of motherhood is filled with joy, but it can also bring a whirlwind of emotions and uncertainties. Psalm 30:2 reminds us, "O Lord my God, I cried to you for help, and you have healed me." In these words, you can find solace; the same God who meticulously fashioned your child in the womb is actively knitting healing and renewal into your own life. Amidst sleepless nights and newfound responsibilities, remember that every tear, every prayer has a purpose. Your body has journeyed through profound change, and today you can trust that God is tenderly restoring you. Embrace this guide to health, both physical and spiritual, as an opportunity to reflect on His faithfulness. The road ahead may feel daunting, but with each step, know that He walks beside you, weaving together your story and your child's in a beautiful tapestry of love.

DAILY REFLECTION

In this season of newfound motherhood, how can you actively recognize and embrace God's tender presence as He guides your healing and growth amidst the beautiful chaos of caring for your little one?

PRAYER

Dear Lord, as I sit in the waiting room, I am filled with a mix of joy and uncertainty. Thank You for the precious life You have blessed me with and for the journey of motherhood that lies ahead. Please grant me the grace to trust in Your healing touch and the strength to embrace this beautiful yet challenging season, knowing that You walk beside me every step of the way. Amen.

Trust in God's design as you nurture your little one from the very first appointment. Just as Jesus welcomed children, may you find peace in His guidance and wisdom for each step of this precious journey.

Matthew 18:5-6 - "And whoever welcomes one such child in my name welcomes me. But if anyone causes one of these little ones who believe in me to stumble, it would be better for them to have a large millstone hung around their neck and to be drowned in the depths of the sea."

DEVOTIONAL

As you prepare for your child's first pediatrician appointment, take a moment to breathe and reflect on the sacred gift of parenthood. Trust in God's design; every heartbeat and tiny giggle is part of His grand plan. Just as Jesus lovingly embraced the little ones, recognize that this journey is drenched in divine purpose. The nerves you feel are a testament to the love that envelops your heart, guiding you to protect and nurture this precious life. Let Matthew 18:5-6 remind you that the vulnerability of children is held in the highest regard by our Savior. In each decision you make, from choosing a doctor to following their advice, surrender your worries into His capable hands, finding peace in the guidance He provides. May the wisdom of the Lord envelop you, inviting you to cherish every moment, and empowering you to cultivate an environment where your little one can flourish.

DAILY REFLECTION

How can you embrace the sacred journey of parenthood by surrendering your anxieties to God, trusting in His design to guide you as you nurture your little one from that very first appointment?

PRAYER

Dear Lord, as I prepare for my child's first pediatrician appointment, I lay before You my hopes and worries. Grant me the grace to trust in Your divine design, knowing each heartbeat is a precious part of Your plan. May Your wisdom illuminate my path, helping me nurture this little one with love and purpose, just as You embrace all children. Amen.

In the radiant joy of a baby's first smile, we glimpse the pure and spontaneous love of God. Just as these innocent moments reflect divine grace, may our hearts respond with gratitude, recognizing the simple yet profound gifts of life that point us back to the Creator's joy.

Psalm 35:9-10 - "And my soul shall be joyful in the Lord; It shall rejoice in His salvation. All my bones shall say, 'Lord, who is like You?'"

DEVOTIONAL

In the enchanting moment when a baby first smiles, we witness a glimpse of pure, unfiltered joy—an echo of the divine love that flows from the heart of God. This radiant expression, innocent and spontaneous, becomes a window into the very nature of grace, reminding us of the simplicity and depth of His affection for us. Just as the baby's smile can melt our hearts, so too does God's joy encompass us, inviting us to embrace life in its most uncomplicated beauty. Psalm 35:9-10 reminds us that our souls find true joy in the Lord, an invitation to celebrate the profound gift of His salvation that dances in the life of every cherished moment. Let our hearts, like the contented coos of a baby, respond in gratitude for the simple yet profound blessings that surround us. In the glee of a child's innocent laughter, may we rediscover the Creator's joy, leading us to a deeper appreciation for each day. As we marvel at these small wonders, let us come to know that in every smile given and received, we are touched by the very hands of God.

DAILY REFLECTION

In the sweetness of a baby's first smile, how might we open our hearts to recognize and rejoice in the spontaneous gifts of grace that God places before us each day?

PRAYER

Dear Lord, in the tender magic of a baby's first smile, we are reminded of the depth of Your love and the purity of Your grace. May our hearts be forever grateful for these small yet profound gifts, recognizing that in every innocent laugh, we are invited to experience the joy of Your presence. Help us to embrace each moment with wonder, reflecting the simple beauty of life that points us back to Your divine joy.

As we celebrate the joy of new beginnings, let the laughter of our little ones remind us of God's blessings each day. In every giggle and hiccup, we find His presence, guiding us toward a deeper faith and grateful heart. Embrace the miracle of life, for in each moment, His love is revealed.

Psalm 149:4 - "For the Lord takes delight in his people; he crowns the humble with victory."

DEVOTIONAL

As we celebrate the joy of new beginnings, the sweet sound of a baby's hiccup becomes a gentle reminder of the blessings that fill our lives each day. Each tiny giggle bursts forth like a promise, echoing the delight the Lord finds in us, His beloved children. In moments when our little ones stumble through their hiccups, let us pause and recognize the grace and humor woven into the tapestry of parenthood, where every sigh and soft laugh points us toward a deeper connection with our Creator. Psalm 149:4 reminds us that God takes delight in His people, crowning the humble with victory—victory that often comes in the simplest of joys. How beautiful it is to see His love unfolding in the innocent moments, to know that each hiccup is a celebration of life and divine purpose. Embracing our little ones as they navigate this world anew, we see our faith deepening, our hearts becoming more grateful for the miracle of existence. Let us cherish every fleeting moment, knowing that through laughter and love, God's presence is ever near, guiding us on this wondrous journey of parenthood.

DAILY REFLECTION

In the joyful symphony of your baby's hiccups and laughter, how might you pause to recognize the divine presence of love and purpose in each precious moment, and how can you celebrate these simple yet profound blessings as a reflection of God's delight in you?

PRAYER

Dear Lord, as we watch our little ones giggle and hiccup, may we be reminded of the joy and blessings that fill our lives. Help us to embrace the precious moments of parenthood, even in their simplest forms, and deepen our hearts with gratitude for the miracle of life. May each hiccup serve as a tender reminder of Your love, guiding us on this beautiful journey together. Amen.

As you take your first outing with your baby, cherish the gift of new life and the promise of hope. Today, reflect on the joy of creation and the love that surrounds you, reminding yourself of God's unwavering presence in every moment.

Genesis 1:28 - "God blessed them and said to them, 'Be fruitful and increase in number; fill the earth and subdue it.'"

DEVOTIONAL

As you embark on your first outing with your precious baby, take a moment to breathe in the beauty of new life that surrounds you. With each tiny coo and gentle sigh, you are reminded of the promise woven into creation itself—an assurance of hope and love that stretches far beyond the moment. Genesis 1:28 encourages us to be fruitful, a call that resonates deeply in your heart, knowing that you are now a part of this sacred cycle. Each step you take today holds a significance—your small yet mighty contribution to filling the earth with love and joy. Cherish the sounds of nature, the warmth of the sun, and the kindness of strangers as they catch a glimpse of your bundle of joy; these are expressions of God's unwavering presence in all things. In this shared journey of motherhood, recognize that you are never alone; God walks beside you, guiding your steps with a gentle hand. Embrace the miracle of today and the countless tomorrows to come, trusting that through your baby, you bear witness to the wonder of His creation.

DAILY REFLECTION

How can you intentionally cultivate gratitude for the fleeting moments of joy and connection as you navigate this new adventure with your baby, recognizing each smile and coo as a testament to God's promise of hope in your life?

PRAYER

Dear Lord, as I step into the world with my precious baby, help me to be fully present in each moment, savoring the beauty of this new life and the hope it brings. May your love envelop us, reminding me that every coo and sigh echoes your promise of joy, guiding my heart as I embrace the miracle of motherhood. Please walk beside us, Lord, illuminating our path with your unwavering presence, and fill our days with the wonder of your creation. Amen.

On this day, reflect on the transformative power of God's love that guides our steps. Just as a stroll unfolds new paths, God's presence opens our hearts to grace and purpose. Trust in Him as you journey forward, allowing His light to illuminate every decision you face.

Romans 8:38-39 - "For I am convinced that neither death nor life, neither angels nor demons, neither the present nor the future, nor any powers, neither height nor depth, nor anything else in all creation, will be able to separate us from the love of God that is in Christ Jesus our Lord."

DEVOTIONAL

As you step out for your first stroller walk, take a moment to breathe in the fresh air and feel the gentle rhythm of your surroundings. Just like this stroll opens new paths before you, God's love invites you to explore the journey of life with courage and wonder. Romans 8:38-39 assures us that nothing can sever the bond we have with God—neither the weight of worries, the shadows of doubt, nor the uncertainties of tomorrow. Each step you take is a testament to His faithfulness, illuminating the way forward, even when the path seems unclear. Embrace this moment; let His grace guide your decisions and fill your heart with purpose. As you explore the world around you, remember that you are wrapped in the unconditional love of Christ, a love that transforms every ordinary day into something extraordinary. Trust in His light as your companion, and allow your journey to blossom with hope.

DAILY REFLECTION

As you take each step on this first stroller walk, what fears or doubts might you need to surrender to God's love, allowing His grace to transform your journey into one filled with purpose and hope?

PRAYER

Dear Lord, As I take this first stroller walk, may I feel the warmth of Your love cradling me and my little one, guiding each step with purpose. Help me embrace the beauty of this moment, trusting that Your grace will illuminate the path ahead, even when the road feels uncertain. Let every breath of fresh air remind me of Your ever-present faithfulness, and may my heart overflow with hope as I journey forward in Your light. Amen.

November 23

Celebrate the joy of new beginnings as you take your baby's first car ride. May this journey be filled with tender moments, reminding us that each step in life is guided by God's loving hand. Trust in His safety and grace as you explore the world together.

Psalm 148:1-4 - "Hallelujah! Praise the Lord from the heavens; praise him in the heights. Praise him, all his angels; praise him, all his heavenly hosts. Praise him, sun and moon; praise him, all you shining stars. Praise him, you highest heavens and you waters above the heavens."

DEVOTIONAL

As you buckle in your little one for their very first car ride, take a moment to breathe in the beauty of this new beginning. With every turn of the wheel, you are not only steering the car but also guiding your child's first exploration of the world outside. Psalm 148 calls us to praise the Lord from the heavens, reminding us of the vast beauty that surrounds us, mirrored in the tiny hands that grasp your fingers. Each chirp of the birds and flutter of leaves signifies God's handiwork, a natural soundtrack to this journey you're embarking on together. Trust that His loving hand cradles both of you, showering you with grace as you navigate the open road. In this tender moment, let your heart swell with gratitude, embracing the joy of discovery and the warmth of your baby's presence. May this adventure, filled with laughter and wonder, be a testament to the life unfolding before you, beautifully orchestrated by the Creator.

DAILY REFLECTION

As you embark on this precious journey with your little one, how can you intentionally celebrate each moment of discovery, trusting that God's love and guidance will illuminate your path together?

PRAYER

Dear Lord, as we embark on this beautiful journey with our little one, fill our hearts with wonder and gratitude for the gift of new beginnings. May each mile we travel be a reminder of Your loving guidance, wrapping us in Your grace and illuminating the world outside with splendor. Help us to cherish these precious moments, celebrating the joy of discovery together, trusting that Your hand leads us every step of the way. Amen.

November 24

As you dress your little one today, remember that just as you lovingly wrap them in warmth and care, God envelops us in His grace and love. Each button and fold can be a reminder of the new life and hope found in Christ during this season of preparation. Celebrate each moment as a blessing and a promise of His faithfulness.

Ephesians 4:32 - "Be kind and compassionate to one another, forgiving each other, just as in Christ God forgave you."

DEVOTIONAL

As you gently dress your little one today, take a moment to pause and reflect on the love that envelops them. Just like the softness of the fabric you tie around their tiny limbs, God wraps us in His boundless grace and unwavering love. Each button you fasten, each fold you make, serves as a reminder of the new life and hope we find in Christ, especially during this season of preparation. Allow your heart to be filled with gratitude as you cherish this precious moment, for within these simple acts lies a profound opportunity to demonstrate kindness—both to your child and to those around you. Ephesians 4:32 calls us to embody compassion, mirroring the forgiveness we receive from Christ. Let's celebrate this beautiful journey of parenthood, where every touch becomes an expression of love and every outfit an opportunity to reflect His faithfulness. In dressing your baby, you are not just preparing them for the day but also nurturing a spirit of grace that will carry them throughout their life.

DAILY REFLECTION

As you thoughtfully dress your little one today, how can you embrace the tender moments of this simple task as sacred opportunities to express the love and grace you wish to nurture in their heart, reflecting the divine warmth of God's unchanging love?

PRAYER

Dear Lord, as I dress my little one today, help me to see the beauty in each gentle touch and every careful fold. May these moments of wrapping them in warmth remind me of Your infinite love that envelops us all. Grant me the grace to nurture not just their physical being, but their spirit, fostering kindness and compassion that echoes the gifts You have so generously given us. Amen.

Capture the miracle of new life this season, reflecting on the beauty of creation and the love that surrounds your little one. Just as Christ brought light into the world, let your baby's first moments shine brightly in your heart.

John 1:9 - The true light that gives light to everyone was coming into the world.

DEVOTIONAL

In this sacred season of new beginnings, as you cradle your newborn and prepare for that first precious photoshoot, take a moment to bask in the wonder of creation. With each click of the camera, remember that just as Christ came into the world as the true light, your little one brings their own unique brilliance, illuminating your life in ways you never imagined. These are fleeting moments, so let each captured smile and gentle coo resonate in your heart, echoing the beauty of God's perfect design. As you lay your baby down in soft blankets, surrounded by tender reminders of love, reflect on the miracle of life that has entered your home. The warmth of their little body, the peaceful rhythm of their breaths, all point to the intentional, loving artistry of our Creator. Embrace this time, where every giggle and sigh is a testament to the love that swells around them—a love that mirrors the light that has come into the world. Cherish these early days, for they are not just photographs but sacred reminders of the hope and joy that surround you, a glimpse of the divine nestled in your arms.

DAILY REFLECTION

In this tender season of your baby's first moments, how can you consciously marvel at the divine love cradled in your arms, allowing each fleeting smile and soft sigh to deepen your gratitude for the miracle of life entrusted to you?

PRAYER

Dear Lord, as we prepare to capture the fleeting beauty of our newborn's first moments, fill our hearts with gratitude for this miracle of new life. Help us to see in each smile and coo the reflection of Your love and light, reminding us that our little one is a precious gift and a shining testament to Your perfect creation. Guide us to cherish these early days, holding them close as sacred memories, and may our hearts always echo the joy and hope that surround us in this holy season. Amen.

November 26

In the joyful chaos of parenthood, celebrate the miracle of new life! Each unexpected moment, like a first diaper change, reminds us of God's blessings and the wonder of creation. Trust in His guidance as you navigate this beautiful journey of nurturing.

Luke 18:15-17 - "People were also bringing babies to Jesus to have him touch them. When the disciples saw this, they rebuked them. But Jesus called the children to him and said, 'Let the little children come to me, and do not hinder them, for the kingdom of God belongs to such as these. Truly I tell you, anyone who will not receive the kingdom of God like a little child will never enter it.'"

DEVOTIONAL

In the whirlwind of parenthood, each unexpected moment – like the joyful surprise of a first diaper change – is a gentle reminder of the beauty intricately woven into the fabric of life. As you navigate this new territory, remember that these seemingly chaotic instances are blessings wrapped in grace, echoing God's promise of new beginnings. Just as the children in Luke 18 were brought to Jesus, marking their innocence and desire for connection, we are invited to approach our journey of nurturing with that same childlike faith and trust. Embrace the giggles, the messes, and even the little pees, for they are milestones in a miraculous adventure. In these moments, God's love shines brightly, illuminating the path of your parenting journey, filled with both challenges and joys. Let each smile, each coo, and each messy moment draw you closer to Him, reinforcing the truth that the hearts of these little ones belong to the kingdom of God. Trust in His guidance as you celebrate the wonder of new life and the extraordinary love that unfolds with each passing day.

DAILY REFLECTION

In the delightful chaos of your baby's first experiences, how can you find God's presence in the seemingly small moments that remind you of the miracle of life and the joy of nurturing this new soul?

PRAYER

Dear Lord, in the midst of this joyful chaos, I thank You for the precious gift of new life and the laughter that fills our home. Help me to embrace each unexpected moment as a beautiful reminder of Your love and the journey we share. May I always find grace in the messes and trust in Your guiding hand, celebrating the miracle of parenting with a heart full of joy. Amen.

Embrace the peace of Christ this Advent season, finding hope in the promise of new beginnings and the light that shines in the darkness. Let every moment of preparation draw you closer to the heart of God as you anticipate His coming.

Luke 1:78-79 -: "Because of the tender mercy of our God, whereby the sunrise shall visit us from on high to give light to those who sit in darkness and in the shadow of death, to guide our feet into the way of peace."

DEVOTIONAL

As we journey through this Advent season, let us pause to embrace the profound peace that comes from Christ's tender love. In the stillness of our preparations, may we open our hearts to the promise of new beginnings, just as the dawn breaks into the darkest hours of night. Luke 1:78-79 beckons us to consider the gentle mercy of our God, who sends His light to guide our feet when we feel lost in shadows. Each flicker of hope that we nurture invites us closer to His heart—not merely lighting our path, but illuminating the depths of our being. Let us surrender our anxieties, knowing that in Christ, every chaotic moment can transform into a tranquil step toward peace. This Advent, as we anticipate His coming, may we find solace in the love that wraps around us like a warm swaddle, embracing us in our vulnerabilities. Let His light shine brightly in our lives, igniting our spirits with hope as we wait expectantly for the Christ child.

DAILY REFLECTION

In this Advent season of anticipation, how can you intentionally create space in your heart to nurture the peace of Christ, allowing His light to softly dispel the shadows of your worries and illuminate your journey toward hope and new beginnings?

PRAYER

Dear Lord, as we enter this sacred season of Advent, fill our hearts with the tranquil peace of Your presence. Help us to release our burdens and anxieties, allowing Your light to illuminate our path and nurture hope within us. May we wrap ourselves in Your abiding love, finding strength in our vulnerabilities as we await the joyful arrival of the Christ child. Amen.

November 28

On this day, find strength in the simple act of nurturing. Just as Jesus fed the multitude, your care sustains life. May you feel God's presence, blessing every moment you share with your child in love and grace.

Matthew 14:13-14 - "When Jesus heard what had happened, he withdrew by boat privately to a solitary place. Hearing of this, the crowds followed him on foot from the towns. When Jesus landed and saw a large crowd, he had compassion on them and healed their sick."

DEVOTIONAL

On this day, as you embrace the simple yet profound act of nurturing your child, remember that you are echoing the heart of Jesus. In Matthew 14:13-14, we see Him respond not with reluctance but with deep compassion, healing and feeding those who sought Him. Like Jesus, you too are a source of sustenance—physically and emotionally—offering nourishment that carries the essence of love and grace. In every moment spent breastfeeding or bottle-feeding, reflect on the sacredness of your role as a caregiver, understanding that the act is not merely a necessity but a holy gift. When you feel the weight of the world judging your choice to nurture in public, let the Holy Spirit wrap you in warmth, reminding you that your efforts are seen and cherished. Each glance you share with your child is a tender reminder of God's overwhelming love for us, filled with assurance that you are not alone in this journey. Allow yourself to feel God's presence blessing each moment, reinforcing the truth that your care is an embodiment of His grace, sustaining life in its most beautiful form.

DAILY REFLECTION

As you nurture your child today, how can you embrace the truth that each act of love, no matter where it takes place, reflects God's grace and the sacred bond you share?

PRAYER

Dear Lord, in this sacred moment of nurturing, I turn to You for strength and reassurance. May I find comfort in knowing that my love echoes the compassion of Your Son, as I nourish my child in both body and spirit. Grant me the courage to embrace each shared glance as a gentle reminder of Your presence, wrapping us in grace and filling our time together with the beauty of Your eternal love. Amen.

In this sacred moment, reflect on Jesus as the Bread of Life, nourishing our souls with His presence. Just as the early disciples shared in the feeding of the multitudes, let us open our hearts to both give and receive grace, sharing in the abundance of God's love.

John 6:51 - "I am the living bread that came down from heaven. If anyone eats of this bread, he will live forever."

DEVOTIONAL

In this sacred moment, pause and envision Jesus standing before you, the Bread of Life, extending His arms of love and grace. Just as the early disciples witnessed the miraculous feeding of the multitudes, we too are invited to partake in His endless provision. **John 6:51** reminds us, "I am the living bread that came down from heaven. If anyone eats of this bread, he will live forever." These words echo with a promise that transcends our deepest hunger, both physical and spiritual. As we gather in His presence, let us open our hearts wide, ready to receive His nourishing love and to share it with others. Reflect on the abundance around you—the laughter of loved ones, the beauty of creation, and the grace that flows through everyday moments. In sharing our own stories of grace, we become vessels of His mercy, feeding those who may feel empty or lost. May this sharing draw us closer to the heart of God, where we find not just sustenance, but a vibrant life forever anchored in His goodness.

DAILY REFLECTION

In what ways can you open your heart today to both receive the nourishing love of Jesus, the Bread of Life, and to extend that grace generously to those around you who may be in need of His abundance?

PRAYER

Dear Lord, in this sacred moment, we come before you with hearts both hungry and grateful. As we reflect on Your promise as the Bread of Life, may we embrace the grace You offer, allowing it to fill our spirits and overflow to those around us. Help us to recognize the beauty in our shared journey, nourishing one another with kindness and love, so that we may all be strengthened in Your abundance. Amen.

Amidst the overwhelming waves of emotion following the arrival of your little one, remember that Jesus wept, too. In your vulnerability, find strength in His comforting presence, knowing He understands your struggles and walks with you in this journey of motherhood. Seek solace in prayer, for His mercies are new every morning.

John 11:35 - "Jesus wept."

DEVOTIONAL

Amidst the overwhelming waves of emotion that engulf you after the arrival of your little one, take heart in the simple truth that Jesus wept, too. In that moment, we see the depth of His compassion, the grace in His shared humanity, and the profound understanding of our struggles, especially the uncharted waters of motherhood. Your tears are not a sign of weakness; rather, they are a testament to the love you feel for your child and the daunting challenges you now face. In your vulnerability, find strength wrapped in His comforting presence, as He gently walks beside you through each sleepless night and tearful moment. Allow yourself to be present in these feelings—acknowledge them, cry if you must, and then let them wash over you like the tide. Bring your heart to Him in prayer, laying bare the fears and anxieties that hold you captive, for His mercies are new every morning, like a sunrise after a stormy night. Remember that you are never alone in this journey; the One who knows your heart intimately meets you here, ready to guide you with love and grace.

DAILY REFLECTION

In this season of sleepless nights and overwhelming emotion, how can you invite Jesus into your vulnerabilities, trusting that He not only understands your tears but also offers you unwavering strength and comfort amidst the chaos of new motherhood?

PRAYER

Dear Lord, in this whirlwind of emotions and sleepless nights, I come to you with a heart heavy and tender. Remind me, in my tears, that I am cradled in your understanding embrace, just as you walked alongside those who mourned. Help me to see my vulnerability as a testament to the fierce love I hold for my baby and guide me through this uncharted territory of motherhood with your unwavering grace. Amen.

December 1

As you welcome your baby's first visit from family, remember that just as Christ brought joy to those around Him, your little one embodies new life and hope. Celebrate the gift of family and the love that deepens through shared moments. May each smile and coo echo the light of God's love in your home.

Luke 2:30-32 - "For my eyes have seen your salvation, which you have prepared in the sight of all nations: a light for revelation to the Gentiles, and the glory of your people Israel."

DEVOTIONAL

As you gather to welcome family and share in the joy of your baby's first visit, take a moment to pause and reflect on the profound gift before you. Just as Simeon declared in Luke 2:30-32, your little one is a light of revelation, embodying hope for all who meet them. Each smile, each gentle coo, radiates the love that God has so freely given, deepening the bonds of family in ways that words often fall short of expressing. With every embrace and tender glance, remember that this precious life is woven into the tapestry of God's promises — a reminder that joy can flourish even in the quietest of moments. Celebrate not only the arrival of your baby but also the legacy of love being built within your home. Let laughter echo as divine light fills the space around you, nurturing connections that will last a lifetime. In this sacred gathering, may you find grace in each shared moment, reflecting the fullness of God's love revealed through your child.

DAILY REFLECTION

In the warmth of your baby's first family visit, how can you open your heart to recognize the sacred joy and divine connections being woven into the tapestry of your new life together?

PRAYER

Dear Lord, in this sacred moment of gathering with family, I lift my heart in gratitude for the gift of our little one, a radiant symbol of hope and joy. May every smile and coo remind us of Your everlasting love, weaving us closer together in bonds that reflect Your divine grace. As we share in laughter and embrace, let us cherish these fleeting moments, allowing the light of our child to illuminate our home and deepen our connections for generations to come. Amen.

December 2

Celebrate the love and sacrifice of mothers reflecting God's unconditional love this Mother's Day. Honor the nurturing spirit that mirrors Christ's care for us, rejoicing in the gift of family and the blessings they bring.

Proverbs 31:25-28 - "Strength and dignity are her clothing, and she laughs at the time to come. She opens her mouth with wisdom, and the teaching of kindness is on her tongue. She looks well to the ways of her household and does not eat the bread of idleness. Her children rise up and call her blessed; her husband also, and he praises her."

DEVOTIONAL

As we gather to celebrate Mother's Day, let us take a moment to reflect on the profound love and sacrifice found in the heart of every mother. The words of Proverbs 31:25-28 resonate now more than ever, illuminating the strength, dignity, and wisdom that mothers embody. Like Christ, who tenderly cares for us, mothers nurture their families with an unwavering spirit, pouring out love that mirrors God's own unconditional grace. They laugh in the face of tomorrow's uncertainties, rooted in faith and bold confidence. In the everyday moments— preparing meals, offering guidance, and supporting dreams—they teach us the beauty of kindness. Let us honor them, acknowledging the blessings they bring into our lives, and celebrating their roles as gifts from God. May we rise up today and call them blessed, reflecting on the deep legacy of love they impart.

DAILY REFLECTION

In what ways can you express gratitude today for the unique sacrifices and unwavering love your mother has given, mirroring the boundless grace that God extends to us?

PRAYER

Dear Lord, today we celebrate the incredible gift of mothers—their unwavering love, sacrifice, and nurturing spirit that reflect Your own unconditional grace. As we honor their strength and wisdom, may we recognize the blessings they bring into our lives, and may our gratitude overflow, echoing the love You pour into our hearts. Help us to cherish these precious moments with our families, embracing the legacy of love that mothers impart, and let us always rise up to call them blessed. Amen.

December 3

As you navigate your first grocery run with your little one, remember that even in the hustle, God's presence guides each step. Trust in His provision for every need and find joy in these cherished moments of newfound responsibility.

Psalm 37:25 - "I was young, and now I am old, yet I have never seen the righteous forsaken or their children begging for bread."

DEVOTIONAL

As you embark on your first grocery run with your little one, breathe in the whirlwind of this new adventure. Each cart push and aisle turn reflects a sacred rhythm—a dance of love and responsibility that you never anticipated. Remember, even amidst the busyness, God is intricately woven into each moment. Psalm 37:25 reassures us, "I was young, and now I am old, yet I have never seen the righteous forsaken or their children begging for bread." This journey may feel overwhelming, but trust that God's provision covers all your needs, both for you and for your little blessing. Embrace the beautiful chaos; it's a reminder that you are never alone. Let joy seep into the corners of your heart, for these days, though fleeting, are filled with His grace. Cherish these moments, for in them lies the heartbeat of family and faith.

DAILY REFLECTION

In the midst of your grocery run, how can you open your heart to see God's grace in the everyday moments, transforming the chaos of this new journey into a celebration of His unwavering provision and love?

PRAYER

Dear Lord, as I navigate this first grocery run with my little one, I seek Your guidance in the hustle of this beautiful chaos. Grant me patience and joy as I embrace each moment, trusting in Your provision for our needs. May I feel Your presence in the rhythm of our day, reminding me that I am never alone on this journey of love and responsibility. Amen.

December 4

On this day, reflect on the sacred growth of Christ, who began as a vulnerable infant and blossomed into our Savior. As we witness the milestones of our own lives, may we cherish each moment and recognize the divine hand guiding us, transforming our hearts as He did from the manger to the cross.

Luke 2:40 - "And the child grew and became strong, filled with wisdom. And the favor of God was upon him."

DEVOTIONAL

As we pause on this sacred journey, we are reminded of that wondrous moment when a fragile infant cradled in swaddling cloth embodied the infinite potential of God's love. In the stillness of the night when angels sang, the world was introduced to a child destined to illuminate our hearts and transform our lives. "And the child grew and became strong, filled with wisdom. And the favor of God was upon him" (Luke 2:40). In reflecting on Christ's growth, we are invited to consider our own. Each milestone, each tender moment of development, beckons us to see the divine hand at work in our lives. Just as the Savior emerged from the manger, we too are called to blossom, to allow our faith and strength to flourish under His watchful gaze. Let us cherish every footstep of our journey, recognizing how the God who nurtured His Son also nurtures us, guiding us from the innocence of infancy to a deeper understanding of His purpose for our lives.

DAILY REFLECTION

As you reflect on the sacred growth of Christ from a vulnerable infant to our Savior, what milestones in your own life can you cherish today, recognizing the gentle and transformative hand of God guiding you toward your unique purpose?

PRAYER

Dear Lord, in this sacred moment, we stand in awe of the growth we witness in our lives and in our loved ones, especially as we reflect on the journey of Your Son. Help us to embrace each milestone with gratitude, recognizing Your nurturing hand guiding us from moments of vulnerability to strength and wisdom. May we cherish the beauty of transformation within us, just as You transformed an infant in a manger into our eternal Savior. Amen.

December 5

On this day, let us find grace in the unexpected moments of parenthood. Just as our Heavenly Father provides for us amidst our messiness, may we learn to embrace every spit-up and smile as a reminder of His abundant love and the joy in nurturing His creation.

Hebrews 12:11 - "No discipline seems pleasant at the time, but painful. Later on, however, it produces a harvest of righteousness and peace for those who have been trained by it."

DEVOTIONAL

In the early days of parenthood, the moments of joy are often accompanied by unexpected surprises—like the first time your little one spits up on you. In that instant, it's easy to feel overwhelmed or frustrated, but today, let us pause and find grace amid the chaos. Just as our Heavenly Father lovingly embraces us in our messiness, this fleeting moment serves as a reminder of His abundant love. The discomfort we experience, akin to the discipline mentioned in Hebrews 12:11, can lead us to deeper wisdom and greater joy. As we nurture this tiny life, each spit-up becomes a symbol of growth—both for our child and ourselves. Embrace the laughter that follows, for these are the moments that weave the tapestry of parenthood, rich with love and learning. May we find peace, even in the unexpected, knowing that each experience nurtures our hearts and souls in extraordinary ways.

DAILY REFLECTION

In the midst of the joyful chaos of parenthood, how can you shift your perspective to see each unexpected moment—like a gentle spit-up—as a sacred opportunity to experience and share the profound grace of God's love?

PRAYER

Father in heaven, in the tender chaos of parenthood, help us to see beyond the messiness of spit-up and sleepless nights. Grant us the grace to embrace each unexpected moment as a beautiful reminder of Your love and provision, and allow laughter to fill our hearts as we nurture the fragile beauty of this gift. May we find joy in the journey, trusting that You are with us in every season of growth and embracing our imperfect paths with Your perfect love. Amen.

December 6

Awaken to the grace of new beginnings today, just as the dawn breaks anew each morning. Let your heart stretch toward God's love, and be reminded that His mercies are fresh with every sunrise. Trust in His faithfulness to guide your steps as you move into this day.

Psalm 148:1-2 - "Praise the Lord! Praise the Lord from the heavens; praise Him in the heights! Praise Him, all His angels; praise Him, all His hosts!"

DEVOTIONAL

As you gently rise from slumber, take a moment to stretch your body and heart, embracing the promise of a new day. The dawn's first light is a reminder of God's unwavering grace that greets us each morning—much like the tender embrace of a parent welcoming their child into the day. Psalm 148 calls all creations, from the heavens to the deepest corners of the earth, to lift their voices in praise, and so too are we invited to join this heavenly chorus. As you breathe in the freshness of the day, allow your spirit to awaken to the boundless love that surrounds you, nurturing your hopes and guiding your steps. Know that each moment holds the potential for renewal, echoing the promise that His mercies are ever new. Trust in His faithfulness to illuminate your path, leading you with gentle whispers of encouragement as you stretch into the fullness of today. Embrace this fresh start, feeling God's love wrap around you like the warmth of the sun, invigorating your soul for the journey ahead.

DAILY REFLECTION

As you stretch into this new day, how can you open your heart to embrace the fresh grace that God offers, allowing His love to guide your steps amidst the unfolding beauty around you?

PRAYER

Dear Lord, as the dawn breaks and I rise to greet this new day, help me to stretch my heart towards Your love and embrace the grace that surrounds me. May I find comfort in the warmth of Your mercies, reminding me that every moment offers a chance for renewal. Guide my steps today, Lord, as I trust in Your faithfulness and allow Your light to illuminate my path. Amen.

December 7

On this day of nurturing, celebrate the sacred bond of motherhood as you embrace the gift of life through breastfeeding. Just as Christ nourishes our souls, may each successful latch and feeding session be a reminder of His abundance, sustaining both mother and child in love.

Psalm 84:11 - "For the Lord God is a sun and shield; the Lord bestows favor and honor. No good thing does he withhold from those whose walk is blameless."

DEVOTIONAL

On this day of nurturing, as you cradle your child close to your heart, reflect on the sacred bond that breastfeeding embodies. Each successful latch is a testament to the unique connection you share—one that mirrors the love Christ has for us, a love that nourishes and sustains. Just as He is our sun and shield, bestowing favor and honor, so too does He fill your moments of motherhood with grace, reminding you that no good thing is withheld from you. In each feeding session, celebrate the miracle of life, the rhythm of breath, and the soft murmurs of contentment as your little one draws sustenance from your love. Embrace the beauty of this nurturing role, recognizing that your dedication is a reflection of His abundant care. Let the warmth of this experience fill your heart, affirming that your journey is blessed, and every effort is cherished by the One who knows your needs. May you find joy in this holy task, knowing that you are held in His light, just as your child is held in your arms.

DAILY REFLECTION

How does each moment of nurturing through breastfeeding deepen your understanding of God's unconditional love and provision in your life?

PRAYER

Dear Lord, as I embrace this precious moment of nurturing with my child, I thank You for the sacred gift of motherhood. May each successful latch remind me of Your unwavering love and abundance, filling my heart with joy and gratitude. Grant me strength and peace in this journey, knowing that, just as You nourish my soul, I am honored to nourish this little life held so closely in my arms. Amen.

December 8

As you change garments after a challenging moment, remember that God's grace offers a fresh start. Just like new clothes represent renewal, so too does His mercy transform our hearts, allowing us to rise above past struggles. Trust in the promise of restoration today.

Colossians 3:9-10: "Do not lie to one another, seeing that you have put off the old self with its practices and have put on the new self, which is being renewed in knowledge after the image of its creator."

DEVOTIONAL

On this day of renewal, as you slip into fresh garments after a challenging blowout, let each piece of clothing remind you of God's transformative grace. Just as you discard the soiled attire, think of the old burdens and struggles you're shedding, trusting that they no longer define you. Colossians 3:9-10 calls us to put off the old self, not merely through our actions, but in the very core of our identity. With each new garment, picture the mercy of God wrapping around you, inviting you into a space of restoration and hope. Trust in His promise; your past does not dictate your future. You are being renewed, each day offering a fresh start filled with possibility. Embrace this truth as you dress for the life God has planned for you, one of resilience, grace, and new beginnings.

DAILY REFLECTION

As you embrace the joy of changing into fresh clothes after a messy moment, how can you allow God's grace to envelop not only your outward appearance but also your heart, enabling you to let go of past struggles and step confidently into the new life He has designed for you?

PRAYER

Dear Lord, as I stand here, changing my clothes after a challenging moment, help me to embrace the renewal that comes from You. Like this fresh garment, may Your grace wrap around my heart, reminding me that my past struggles do not define me but instead prepare me for a brighter future. Grant me the courage to shed the burdens I've carried and to trust in Your promise of restoration, knowing that each day is a new beginning filled with Your mercy and hope. Amen.

December 9

As the dawn of resurrection approaches, may the cries of our hearts reflect the depths of our longing for Christ, who transforms tears into joy. In this sacred waiting, let faith arise, trusting that even in our darkest moments, the light of His promise shines brightly.

John 16:20-22 - "Very truly I tell you, you will weep and mourn while the world rejoices. You will grieve, but your grief will turn to joy. A woman giving birth to a child has pain because her time has come; but when her baby is born she forgets the anguish because of her joy that a child is born into the world."

DEVOTIONAL

As the dawn of resurrection approaches, our hearts may feel like restless echoes, each cry a testament to our deep longing for Christ. In this sacred waiting, we embrace the tension between grief and joy, knowing that our tears are not in vain. Like a mother in labor, we face moments of anguish, yet we hold fast to the promise that joy is coming. With every cry of our spirits, we declare our trust in the One who transforms sorrow into celebration. When we turn to Him, even in our darkest nights, the light of His resurrection promises to pierce through, reminding us that these trials are but the birth pangs of something beautiful. So let us weep, let us mourn, and let us trust that what lies ahead is worth every tear we have shed. For in the embrace of His love, we find our deepest yearnings fulfilled, and our hearts, once heavy, will finally dance in joy.

DAILY REFLECTION

In this sacred season of waiting, what cry of your heart is longing to be heard by Christ, and how might you embrace that ache as a pathway to discovering the joy that lies just beyond the dawn of resurrection?

PRAYER

Dear Lord, in this sacred space of yearning and waiting, we lift our hearts to You, acknowledging every tear that falls as a testament to our longing for Your presence. As we navigate the depths of our sorrow, may Your light pierce through our darkest nights, reassuring us that joy is on the horizon. Help us to embrace this journey, trusting that with each cry of our spirits, we are drawing closer to the transformative hope of Your resurrection. Amen.

December 10

In this quiet moment of rest, let gratitude bloom in your heart. Just as God cradles us in His love, find solace in His embrace while your little one sleeps. Trust that in the stillness, His peace will refresh your spirit for the day ahead.

Psalm 62:1-2 - "For God alone my soul waits in silence; from Him comes my salvation. He alone is my rock and my salvation, my fortress; I shall not be greatly shaken."

DEVOTIONAL

In the gentle hush of this moment, as your little one nestles in your arms, take a deep breath and allow gratitude to swell within you. Just as a mother cradles her child, so too does God envelop us in His tender care. Psalm 62 reminds us that in silence, we can find our deepest strength; it is here, in these fleeting minutes of serenity, that He whispers promises of salvation and support. Let the weight of the world slip from your shoulders as you embrace the stillness; this is where His peace washes over you. Remember, your heart, like a fortress, can withstand the trials of the day ahead, anchored in His love. Allow this calm to refresh your spirit, nurturing your soul for the challenges that may come. Trust that in His embrace, you are never alone—each quiet moment is a reminder of His unwavering faithfulness.

DAILY REFLECTION

In this precious pause, how can you more fully embrace God's love and let it transform your weary moments into a sanctuary of peace and gratitude?

PRAYER

Dear Lord, in this sacred pause while my little one sleeps, may my heart overflow with gratitude for Your unwavering love and gentle care. As I cradle this precious life, remind me of the solace I find in Your embrace, that in these quiet moments, I can lay my burdens down and be replenished by Your peace. Strengthen my spirit for the journey ahead, knowing that I am never alone, and let my heart rest in the promise of Your faithfulness.

December 11

As the belly button stump falls away, it symbolizes new beginnings and the shedding of the old. This moment reminds us of the transformative power of God's grace, inviting us to rejoice in the new life and opportunities He offers us every day.

Romans 8:1-2 - "Therefore, there is now no condemnation for those who are in Christ Jesus, because through Christ Jesus the law of the Spirit who gives life has set you free from the law of sin and death."

DEVOTIONAL

As you witness the gentle detachment of the belly button stump, take a moment to rejoice in this tangible symbol of new beginnings. Just as this small remnant from infancy falls away, so too does God invite us to shed the remnants of our past—those burdens of guilt and shame which, like the stump, no longer serve our journey. In Romans 8:1-2, we are reminded that in Christ Jesus, we are free; there is no condemnation that can hold us down. Picture this moment in your child's life as a reflection of your own spiritual transformation—each day stands as a fresh opportunity to embrace the grace that God so generously offers. As you celebrate this milestone, let it stir in you a deep gratitude for the multitude of new beginnings that await us. The old has passed away; rejoice in the freedom and joy that fills the space it leaves behind. In Christ, every end is but a herald of new life, so hold tightly to the promise that God continually renews your spirit and leads you on.

DAILY REFLECTION

As the belly button stump detaches, what remnants of the past is God gently urging you to let go of in order to embrace the abundant new beginnings He is offering you today?

PRAYER

Dear Lord, as my child's belly button stump falls away, I am reminded of Your grace that clears the old to make way for the new. Help us to embrace this moment as a sacred reminder of our own transformations, shedding the burdens that weigh us down and rejoicing in the new life You offer. Fill our hearts with gratitude for each new beginning, and guide us to fully experience the freedom and joy that comes from trusting in Your enduring promise of renewal. Amen.

December 12

Trust in God through the small tasks; even trimming a baby's nails is a reminder of His care in the delicate moments of life. Just as He tends to our needs, let us approach new challenges with faith and patience, knowing He guides our hands.

Proverbs 16:3 - "Commit your work to the Lord, and your plans will be established."

DEVOTIONAL

As you prepare to trim your baby's tiny nails, take a moment to reflect on the trust required in this delicate task. In these small moments, we discover profound truths about God's care for us. Just as He intricately crafted your little one, He meticulously attends to the intricate details of our lives—never overlooking even the smallest of our needs. Proverbs 16:3 reminds us, "Commit your work to the Lord, and your plans will be established." In this act of trimming, you are not merely cutting nails; you are committing a tender moment into God's hands. Let this simple task serve as a gentle reminder that He guides our every movement, infusing even mundane activities with purpose and grace. Approach this new challenge with faith, knowing that with each careful clip, you are nurturing not only your child but also a deeper trust in God's faithful provision.

DAILY REFLECTION

How can you embrace the small, seemingly routine tasks of your day as sacred moments to entrust to God, allowing His gentle guidance to transform your worries into deeper faith and connection?

PRAYER

Dear Lord, as I delicately trim my baby's tiny nails, help me to embrace this moment with trust and gratitude. May each careful clip remind me of Your unwavering care and attention to even the smallest details of our lives. Grant me patience and faith as I navigate this new challenge, knowing that Your guiding hands nurture both my child and my heart in every tender task. Amen.

December 13

On this precious night, as you cradle your sweet child, let your lullaby be a gentle echo of God's love—a reminder that His presence is always near. With each note, you instill peace, weaving faith into the fabric of their dreams, showing them the warmth of your heart and the grace of the Divine.

1 John 4:16-19 - So we have come to know and to believe the love that God has for us. God is love, and whoever abides in love abides in God, and God abides in them. In this way, love is made complete among us, so that we will have confidence on the day of judgment; for in this world we are just like Him. There is no fear in love. But perfect love drives out fear, because fear has to do with punishment. The one who fears is not made perfect in love. We love because He first loved us.

DEVOTIONAL

On this precious night, as you cradle your sweet child, let your lullaby be a gentle echo of God's love—a reminder that His presence is always near. Each tender note sways like the whispers of the Holy Spirit, wrapping your little one in a cocoon of warmth and security. As you sing, imagine how the melody threads your faith into their very dreams, introducing them to the grace that envelops our lives, even in the quietest moments. Reflecting on 1 John 4:16-19, you are reminded that love is not just an emotion; it is the essence of both God and parenthood. With every soothing phrase, you convey the perfect love that drives out fear, giving your child a glimpse of the divine love that will always protect and uplift them. Know that as you hold them close tonight, you're imbuing their hearts with confidence and hope for the journey ahead. In this sacred act, you are not just singing a lullaby; you are planting seeds of faith that will bloom for a lifetime.

DAILY REFLECTION

As you sing your lullaby tonight, how can you be more intentional in weaving the profound love of God into your child's heart, illuminating their dreams with faith and comfort?

PRAYER

Dear Lord, on this tender night, as I cradle my precious child and sing this lullaby, I invite Your holy presence to envelop us both. May my voice carry whispers of Your unending love and create a safe harbor of peace in their dreams. Help me nurture their heart with faith and hope, so they may always know the warmth of Your embrace, guiding them through every season of life.

December 14

In this moment of gentle wonder, as you share the joy of reading with your little one, remember the wisdom in Proverbs 22:6: "Start children off on the way they should go." Each page turned opens a world of faith and love, guiding them towards a future filled with God's light and grace.

Psalm 111:10 - "The fear of the Lord is the beginning of wisdom; all who follow his precepts have good understanding."

DEVOTIONAL

In this moment of gentle wonder, as you cradle your little one and embark on the beautiful journey of reading, your heart swells with anticipation. Each page turned not only nurtures their imagination but serves as a crucial stepping stone in their spiritual growth. Proverbs 22:6 reminds us to "Start children off on the way they should go," and in this simple act of sharing stories, you are instilling a foundation of faith and love. Your voice carries whispers of God's grace, planting seeds of wisdom that will flourish in their hearts. As Psalm 111:10 assures us, the fear of the Lord is the beginning of wisdom, and this early exposure to His word gives them a treasure trove of understanding to draw from later in life. Embrace these precious moments; they are not merely about the stories you read, but about the love and faith they inspire. Together, you are weaving a tapestry of hope and light that will guide your child well beyond the pages you share today.

DAILY REFLECTION

In these quiet moments with your baby, how can you intentionally weave God's love and wisdom into the stories you share, nurturing a heart that will seek Him throughout life's journey?

PRAYER

Dear Lord, as I hold my little one close, I thank You for this precious gift of time shared together. May these moments of reading nurture their heart and mind, planting seeds of Your love and wisdom deep within their soul. Guide our journey with Your light, allowing the stories we share to flourish into faith that will carry them through life's many chapters. Amen.

In this season of renewal, remember that God sees your journey through postpartum changes, including hair loss. Trust in His promise to restore and strengthen you as you care for your growing family. Your worth is not defined by outward appearances, but by the love and grace that fills your heart.

Matthew 10:30-31 - "And even the very hairs of your head are all numbered. So don't be afraid; you are worth more than many sparrows."

DEVOTIONAL

As you stand before the mirror, perhaps feeling a twinge of sorrow over your postpartum hair loss, take a moment to breathe deeply and center yourself in the truth of God's love. In this season of renewal, remember that every strand of hair that has fallen is known by the Creator of the universe; He sees you in your vulnerability and understands your fears. Matthew 10:30-31 reminds us that not only are the hairs on your head numbered, but your worth transcends all outward appearances. In caring for your growing family, you may feel as though you are losing pieces of yourself, but know that each moment spent nurturing your loved ones adds to the beauty of who you are becoming. Your identity is not defined by how full your hair is, but by the love, grace, and strength you embody as a mother. Allow yourself to be wrapped in His embrace, trusting in His promise to restore you, both inside and out. Take heart; you are cherished far beyond measure.

DAILY REFLECTION

In this season of renewal, how might you embrace the journey of transformation and find your identity rooted not in physical change, but in the unwavering love and grace that God has for you as a beloved mother?

PRAYER

Dear Lord, as I stand before the mirror, feeling the weight of change upon me, I ask for Your gentle reassurance. Help me to embrace this season of renewal, knowing that in my vulnerability, You see my strength and my worth. May Your love wash over me, reminding me that my beauty radiates from within, and in caring for my family, I am dancing in Your grace. Amen.

December 16

On this day of renewal and restoration, find joy in stepping back into the ordinary, just as Christ brought the extraordinary into the everyday. Celebrate the beauty of God's grace that clothes you anew, bringing hope and purpose to every moment.

2 Corinthians 3:17-18 - "Now the Lord is the Spirit, and where the Spirit of the Lord is, there is freedom. And we all, who with unveiled faces contemplate the Lord's glory, are being transformed into his image with ever-increasing glory, which comes from the Lord, who is the Spirit."

DEVOTIONAL

On this day of renewal and restoration, pause to consider the beauty of stepping back into the ordinary. As you wear your normal clothes again, let this moment symbolize the extraordinary grace of Christ that transforms our everyday lives. Reflect on 2 Corinthians 3:17-18, where we are reminded of the freedom found in the Spirit—the very essence of true renewal. Just as we are cloaked in the fabric of our daily routines, we are also draped in the glory of His transformative love, reflecting His image day by day. Each moment carries with it the potential for hope, purpose, and joy, as God's grace springs forth in the simplest of tasks. Embrace this gift; relish the comfort of normalcy knowing you wear it anew, illuminated by the Spirit's work within you. Today, find delight in the ordinary and celebrate the extraordinary freedom that comes from being made whole in Him.

DAILY REFLECTION

In what ordinary moment today can you recognize and celebrate the extraordinary grace of Christ that renews your spirit and fulfills your daily purpose?

PRAYER

Dear Lord, as I step back into the comfort of the ordinary today, help me to recognize the extraordinary grace that envelops me. May each article I wear remind me of the renewal You offer—the freedom to embrace hope and purpose in every moment. Fill my heart with joy as I celebrate this newfound normalcy, and let Your Spirit illuminate my path, transforming the mundane into moments of divine beauty. Amen.

Near the End of Our Journey

You have spent many days reflecting through these devotionals.

If this book has supported your spiritual journey, sharing a short review on Amazon helps more women discover these pages of encouragement.

devo.anchoredgraces.com/newmoms

Your story may be the reason another woman finds hope.

December 17

In the quiet of the night, as you cradle your little one, remember that even in exhaustion, God's presence surrounds you. He hears your whispered prayers and sees your sacrifices, filling these moments with purpose and grace. Each feeding is a reminder of His sustaining love, nurturing both you and your child.

1 Peter 4:11 - "If anyone speaks, they should do so as one who speaks the very words of God. If anyone serves, they should do so with the strength God provides, so that in all things God may be praised through Jesus Christ."

DEVOTIONAL

In the stillness of the night, as you rock your little one in your weary arms, take a moment to breathe deeply and embrace the silence. This sacred hour, albeit exhausting, is where God's presence envelops you, whispering reassurances that you are not alone. Each soft coo and gentle sigh from your baby echoes the tender love that cradles you both, reminding you that even in fatigue, there is profound purpose. As you offer this nurturing care, remember that God sees your every sacrifice and hears your muted prayers—each one a fragrant offering to Him. In these fragile moments, you are both speaking and serving, embodying the very heart of Christ's love. Lean into the strength He promises, allowing His grace to surge through you, igniting the mundane with divine significance. May you find joy and peace in this rhythm of feeding, knowing that in all things, God is glorified through your faithful witness.

DAILY REFLECTION

As you rock your little one in the quiet of the night, how can you let God's abiding love transform this moment of exhaustion into a sacred act of worship and connection?

PRAYER

Dear Lord, in these quiet hours of midnight, I seek Your presence amidst the weariness. Fill my heart with Your strength as I cradle my little one, reminding me that every moment of sacrifice is steeped in Your love. May I embrace this sacred time, finding joy in the gentle rhythm of nurturing, knowing that even in my exhaustion, You are weaving a tapestry of grace and purpose through our sleepless nights. Amen.

December 18

"Lord, as we share this sacred moment, may our hearts and souls unite in Your love, fostering a bond that mirrors the Holy Spirit's connection. Bless this time together, enriching our family with grace and strength."

1 John 4:12 - "No one has ever seen God; if we love one another, God abides in us and His love is perfected in us."

DEVOTIONAL

As we cradle our little one close, our hearts beat in rhythm, echoing the sacred dance of love that transcends time. In this tender embrace, we are reminded of the profound truth in 1 John 4:12: "No one has ever seen God; if we love one another, God abides in us and His love is perfected in us." In the sweet simplicity of this moment, let us invite the Holy Spirit to weave our souls together creating a tapestry of love that will warm and protect our family through all seasons. Each touch, each sigh, is a testament to our commitment not just as parents, but as vessels of divine grace. As we lean into this bond, may our fears fade and our hearts expand with the strength of God's unwavering presence. We bless this time, dear Lord, asking that our unity be a reflection of Your love—a seed planted deep within, nurturing our family with faith and resilience. Amen.

DAILY REFLECTION

In this sacred moment of closeness, how can we open our hearts even wider to let the love of Christ flow through us, nurturing not just our child, but the very essence of our family?

PRAYER

Dear Lord, as we embark on this sacred journey of skin-to-skin connection, may Your divine love envelop us, fostering a bond that echoes the sacred unity of the Holy Spirit. Bless this precious moment, Lord; let our hearts intertwine in grace and strength, nurturing our family with the warmth of Your embrace. Amen.

December 19

On this date, reflect on the simplicity of trust, just as a child finds comfort in a pacifier. Embrace the assurance of God's presence in our lives, inviting us to surrender our worries and find peace in His everlasting love.

Matthew 10:14 - "And if anyone will not welcome you or listen to your words, shake the dust off your feet when you leave that home or town."

DEVOTIONAL

In the early moments of parenthood, when the world feels both exhilarating and overwhelming, introducing a pacifier to your little one can be a beautiful reminder of how simple comfort can be. Just as a child instinctively knows to seek solace in a gentle object, we are invited by God to find peace in trusting Him completely, surrendering our worries into His capable hands. Matthew 10:14 teaches us about the importance of walking away from unwelcoming spaces, reminding us that not every heart will receive our truth. Yet, we do not carry the burden of rejection alone; God whispers that we can shake the dust off our feet and still find security in His constant presence. Like the soft embrace of a pacifier, God offers us His everlasting love, a soothing balm for our anxious hearts. When we allow ourselves to let go and embrace His gentle guidance, we discover that true peace lies not in our circumstances, but in our willingness to trust. Today, let us find comfort in the presence of the One who welcomes us with open arms, inviting us to rest and relinquish our fears as we journey forward.

DAILY REFLECTION

In moments of uncertainty, how can you cultivate a heart that, like a child reaching for a pacifier, instinctively seeks the comforting embrace of God's unwavering love and presence?

PRAYER

Dear Lord, as I introduce this small comfort to my child, remind me of the profound simplicity in trust. Help me to surrender my worries, allowing Your gentle presence to cradle my heart, just as a pacifier brings peace to my little one. May I find solace in Your everlasting love, embracing Your assurance as I navigate this beautiful yet unpredictable journey of parenthood. Amen.

December 20

On this day of reflection and renewal, let the first whispers of spring remind us of God's promise of new life. Just as a baby's first sneeze signals awakening, may we embrace the fresh beginnings He offers in our hearts.

2 Corinthians 4:16-17 - "Therefore we do not lose heart. Though outwardly we are wasting away, yet inwardly we are being renewed day by day. For our light and momentary troubles are achieving for us an eternal glory that far outweighs them all."

DEVOTIONAL

On this day of reflection and renewal, we pause to notice the whispers of spring stirring around us—like the gentle tickle that precedes a baby's first sneeze. Each sneeze is a reminder of new beginnings, a soft herald of life awakening from its slumber. Just as a child's innocent reaction to the world is both comical and precious, so too are the moments God brings to us when we least expect them. In our lives, we may feel every burden and ache; we may see the cracks that age and trials have brought. Yet, as Paul reassures us in 2 Corinthians 4:16-17, it is precisely in these moments of vulnerability that we can experience God's renewing touch deep within our souls. As spring unfolds, let us embrace the promise of renewal, recognizing that our struggles—light as they may seem in the light of eternity—are shaping us for something far more glorious. Let each new day be an invitation to shed our weariness and breathe in the hope of transformation, just as nature comes alive again.

DAILY REFLECTION

How can you open your heart today to the gentle stirrings of new beginnings, allowing the promise of God's renewal to breathe life into the weary places within you?

PRAYER

Dear Lord, as the gentle whispers of spring awaken the world around us, may we too feel the stirring of new life within our hearts. Help us to embrace each moment of renewal with gratitude, shedding our weariness and welcoming the fresh beginnings You offer. Just as a baby's innocent sneeze brings smiles and laughter, let the joys of Your creation remind us of the hope and transformation that lie ahead in our journey with You. Amen.

On this special day, reflect on the wonder of new life, where every gaze of a baby reveals curiosity and innocence. Just as the eyes of a child seek our faces, may we also seek the face of God, trusting in His guiding love as we navigate our own journey. Today, let's celebrate the beauty of beginnings and the divine purpose woven into each new life.

Psalm 34:11-14 - "Come, my children, listen to me; I will teach you the fear of the Lord. Who among you loves life and desires to see many good days? Keep your tongue from evil and your lips from telling lies. Turn from evil and do good; seek peace and pursue it."

DEVOTIONAL

On this day, as we bask in the delight of a baby's first explorations, let us reflect on the pure innocence displayed in their wide, curious eyes. Each gaze, filled with wonder, invites us to remember the beauty of beginnings—the sacred potential held within every new life. In Psalm 34:11-14, we hear God beckoning us to listen closely, to absorb the wisdom meant for our growth and joy. Just as a baby seeks the warmth of a familiar face, may we seek the light of God's presence, drawing strength and security from His love. Every moment, every blink, is a reminder to engage in life with childlike trust and openness. Today, let us commit to turning away from negativity and embracing the goodness that God desires for us. In nurturing the innocence of new life, may we also strive to cultivate a heart that seeks peace and pursues righteousness, reflecting the divine purpose woven into our own journeys.

DAILY REFLECTION

In the gentle gaze of a baby, what hidden invitation is God offering you today to rediscover the wonder of His love and the simplicity of trusting in His perfect plan for your life?

PRAYER

Dear Lord, as we marvel at the wonder of a baby's gaze, filled with curiosity and innocence, may our hearts be stirred to seek Your face with the same fervor. Help us to embrace the beauty of new beginnings and the sacred purpose You have placed within each life. Inspire us to nurture not only the precious lives around us but also our own spirits, fostering trust and openness as we journey forward in Your guiding love. Amen.

On this special day of new beginnings, let us marvel at the gift of life and the joy that comes with each tender moment. Just as a baby's first yawn reminds us of God's fresh mercies, in the quiet simplicity, may we recognize His presence in our daily rhythms and celebrate the grace woven into our lives.

Ephesians 2:8-9 - For by grace you have been saved through faith, and that not of yourselves; it is the gift of God, not of works, lest anyone should boast.

DEVOTIONAL

On this special day of new beginnings, we pause to celebrate the miracle of life captured in the simple wonder of a baby's first yawn. In that gentle release, we are reminded of the fresh mercies that God pours into our lives each day, inviting us to see beauty in the mundane and joy in our daily rhythms. Just as a newborn stirs from slumber, may our hearts awaken to the grace that envelops us, reminding us that we are cherished beyond measure. Ephesians 2:8-9 softly assures us that our salvation is not earned but freely bestowed—a precious gift from our Creator. Let us embrace the truth that every moment holds the potential for transformation, as we reflect on the countless ways God weaves His grace through our experiences. In the quiet simplicity of life's tender moments, may we recognize His presence, find gratitude in our hearts, and celebrate His unending love. Today, let us breathe in deeply and hold close the beautiful truth that our lives are a tapestry of God's grace, unfolding with each new beginning.

DAILY REFLECTION

In the stillness of today's new beginnings, how can we open our hearts to cherish the small miracles around us, recognizing that each moment—like a baby's first yawn—invites us to embrace the profound grace of God woven into our daily lives?

PRAYER

Dear Lord, on this beautiful day of new beginnings, we stand in awe of the simple yet profound miracle of life that unfolds before us. As we witness the gentle yawn of a newborn, may our hearts awaken to Your fresh mercies each day, reminding us of the beauty woven into our ordinary moments. Help us to cherish the grace that surrounds us, filling our lives with gratitude and joy, as we recognize Your loving presence in every tender experience. Amen.

December 23

In moments of worry for your baby's temperature, find peace in the reassurance of God's watchful care. Trust that just as He knows every hair on your child's head, He faithfully holds each moment of concern in His loving hands. Lean into His comfort and wisdom as you navigate this new journey.

Luke 12:6-7 - "Are not five sparrows sold for two pennies? And not one of them is forgotten by God. Indeed, the very hairs of your head are all numbered. Don't be afraid; you are worth more than many sparrows."

DEVOTIONAL

In the quiet moments of worry, as you gently check your baby's temperature, remember that you are not alone in your anxiety. God, who created the heavens and the earth, is intimately aware of your little one, just as He knows every detail about you. Luke reminds us that not one sparrow falls to the ground without His notice, and in this, we find comforting assurance: your precious child is cradled in His loving hands. Each rise and fall of your baby's breath echoes with divine attention; every concern is met with His steadfast love. When doubts creep in, lean on the truth that you are worth so much more than many sparrows. You have been entrusted with this beautiful life, and His grace will guide you through even the hardest nights. Trust in His watchful care, for God's heart beats with love for you and your child, reminding you that peace is always within reach.

DAILY REFLECTION

In this moment of worry over your baby's temperature, how can you actively surrender your fears to God, embracing the full depth of His unwavering love and promise to care for both you and your little one?

PRAYER

Dear Lord, in these tender moments of worry as I check my baby's temperature, I seek Your peace that surpasses all understanding. Wrap Your loving arms around both of us, reminding me that just as You know every detail of Your creation, You hold my child close and guard their well-being. Grant me the strength to trust in Your divine care, allowing my anxious heart to find solace in Your unwavering presence.

December 24

On this day of joy and connection, celebrate the gift of family as you welcome your grandchild into a new chapter of life. Just as God cherishes each generation, let this visit be a time for sharing stories of faith, love, and the joy of shared blessings. May the bond you create today echo through the years, nurturing hearts in His grace.

Psalm 100:5 - "For the Lord is good; His steadfast love endures forever, and His faithfulness to all generations."

DEVOTIONAL

On this joyful day, as you embrace your grandchild for the first time, take a moment to reflect on the beautiful tapestry of family woven by God's hands. Each hug and shared laughter is a thread connecting generations, a reminder that His steadfast love endures forever. In the innocence of your grandchild's smile, see the promise of new beginnings, where faith can blossom in ways you may never have imagined. Share stories that cradle the wisdom of your own journey and the love that has sustained you, nurturing their spirit with the legacy of grace you have received. Let this visit be more than just a moment in time; let it be a sacred occasion where memories are painted with joy and laughter. Trust that the bonds forged today will echo across the years, a harmonious melody of love in His faithfulness. For within this cherished connection lies the beauty of God's plan, uniting us in His unwavering goodness.

DAILY REFLECTION

In the tender embrace of your grandchild, what stories of faith and love can you share that not only honor your own journey but also plant seeds of grace and hope for generations to come?

PRAYER

Dear Lord, as I welcome my grandchild into my arms today, I am filled with gratitude for this moment of connection and love. Help me to weave the stories of my faith and the legacy of our family into their heart, nurturing a bond that will flourish through the years. May our time together be a sacred reminder of Your steadfast love, echoing in joyful laughter and shared blessings, guiding us all in Your grace.

December 25

Reflect on the unity and love demonstrated in the early Christian community, as we gather with brothers and sisters in faith. Celebrate the shared bonds of fellowship, encouraging one another to walk in grace and truth, just as the early disciples did. Let this meeting be a reminder of our call to support each other in our journeys of faith.

Acts 2:44-47 - "All the believers were together and had everything in common. They sold property and possessions to give to anyone who had need. Every day they continued to meet together in the temple courts. They broke bread in their homes and ate together with glad and sincere hearts, praising God and enjoying the favor of all the people. And the Lord added to their number daily those who were being saved."

DEVOTIONAL

As we come together in this sacred space, let us embrace the beautiful tapestry of our shared faith, woven with threads of love and unity, much like the early Christian community in Acts. Picture the early believers, gathered with glad and sincere hearts, embodying a spirit of generosity and connection that transcended mere fellowship. Here, in our own gathering, we reflect the same grace, supporting one another as we share both our joys and burdens—each meeting an echo of their commitment to one another. In the simplicity of breaking bread together, we find depth in our relationships, a reminder that every act of kindness we extend becomes a sacred thread binding us closer. Just as they witnessed growth and favor in their community through their shared faith, may our time together not only reinforce our bonds but inspire us to reach out to those in need around us. Let us encourage one another to walk boldly in grace and truth, cherishing this call to lift each other up as we journey together in faith. May this meeting ignite within us the same fervor for unity, compassion, and hope, so that our lives together reflect the love Christ has bestowed upon us.

DAILY REFLECTION

How can we, like the early disciples, actively foster an atmosphere of love and support in our gathering that transforms not only our own faith journeys but also those of others around us?

PRAYER

Dear Lord, as we gather in this sacred moment, may Your unifying love envelop us, knitting our hearts together in a tapestry of fellowship. Just as the early Christians shared their lives with gladness and sincerity, help us to embody that same spirit, encouraging one another to navigate our journeys with grace and truth. Let our time together be a reflection of Your love, igniting in us a fervent desire to support each other and reach out to those in need, so that we may shine brightly in our communities as a testament to Your goodness. Amen.

December 26

As your baby's tiny hand wraps around your finger, remember the profound truth that we are all held firmly in the loving grip of God. Just as your child looks to you for guidance, trust that our Heavenly Father is always close, supporting us through every moment of our journey. Cherish this bond, knowing it reflects the unconditional love He offers us all.

John 1:12-13 - "But to all who did receive him, who believed in his name, he gave the right to become children of God, who were born, not of blood nor of the will of the flesh nor of the will of man, but of God."

DEVOTIONAL

As you feel your baby's tiny hand wrap around your finger, take a moment to pause and reflect on the profound truth woven into this simple gesture. In that delicate grip lies the promise of unconditional love and trust, a reminder that we are all held tightly in the loving embrace of our Heavenly Father. Just as your child instinctively looks to you for comfort and guidance, God invites us to lean into His arms, knowing He is always near, ready to support us on our unique journey. This intimate connection mirrors the relationship He desires with each of us, one defined by acceptance and grace. In John 1:12-13, we are reminded of our identity as children of God—not born of earthly expectations, but by His divine will. Take heart in this truth: as you cherish this bond with your little one, let it serve as a reflection of the boundless love that God offers to all who receive Him. Embrace each moment, for within these tender interactions lies a sacred invitation to trust and to love deeply, just as we are loved.

DAILY REFLECTION

In the gentle grasp of your baby's tiny hand, how can you more deeply embrace the truth that, just as they rely on your love and guidance, you too are called to trust in the unwavering embrace of God's care and presence in your life?

PRAYER

Dear Lord, as my baby's tiny fingers wrap around mine, I am reminded of the profound love and trust that exists between us. May I always cherish this bond, knowing it reflects Your unwavering presence in our lives. Help me to lean into Your embrace as my child looks to me for comfort, trusting that just as I hold my little one, You hold us all securely in Your loving grip. Amen.

December 27

On this date, reflect on the profound joy that springs from knowing God's grace. Let today's moments be infused with gratitude, as we embrace the laughter and light that faith brings, reminding us that in Christ, we find our true delight.

Nehemiah 8:10 - "Do not grieve, for the joy of the Lord is your strength."

DEVOTIONAL

As we reflect on the beauty of God's grace today, let us pause to celebrate the laughter that bubbles up from our souls, a sign of the joy that our Creator has woven into the fabric of our lives. In moments of doubt, we often overlook the vibrant light that faith can illuminate. Nehemiah reminds us, "Do not grieve, for the joy of the Lord is your strength." This truth becomes our anchor, inviting us to release our burdens and embrace a lighter spirit. When we allow God's grace to wash over us, we find not only strength but also the profound delight in simply being His beloved children. Let each smile today serve as a beacon of gratitude, echoing the joyful laughter of those assured in His promises. In Christ, we are reminded that joy is not merely a fleeting emotion but a deep-seated assurance that uplifts our hearts and enhances every moment. Cherish the grace that ignites your joy, and may that joy, in turn, bless those around you with the infectious laughter of faith.

DAILY REFLECTION

How can you invite God's grace to transform your daily experiences into moments of laughter and gratitude, reminding you of the profound joy found in simply being loved by Him?

PRAYER

Dear Lord, today, we come before You with hearts overflowing, grateful for the joy that Your grace bestows upon us. May our laughter be a reflection of the light You bring into our lives, reminding us that in the embrace of Your love, we find our true delight. Help us to release our burdens, welcoming Your strength, and let every smile we share echo the profound joy rooted in our faith, showering those around us with the goodness of Your promises. Amen.

December 28

Rest in the assurance that God renews our strength as we surrender our worries at His feet. As you enjoy this newfound peace of sleep, remember Psalm 127:2, "He grants sleep to those He loves." Trust in His provision, knowing that each moment of rest is a gift from Him.

Hebrews 4:9-11 - "There remains, then, a Sabbath-rest for the people of God; for anyone who enters God's rest also rests from their works, just as God did from his."

DEVOTIONAL

As you drift into the comfort of your newfound slumber, let the warmth of God's embrace wrap around you like a cozy blanket. Each hour of rest is not just a reprieve but a divine gift—a testament to His unwavering love, as reflected in Psalm 127:2: "He grants sleep to those He loves." In surrendering your worries at His feet, you exchange your anxieties for His peace, allowing Him to cradle your burdens while you rejuvenate in His presence. Remember, Hebrews 4:9-11 invites you into a Sabbath-rest, a sacred pause where you can cease striving and simply be. Just as God rested after creation, you, too, are called to lay down your burdens and trust in His perfect provision. Embrace this time of renewal, knowing that in each dream and quiet moment, He whispers assurance that you are cherished and cared for. As you open your eyes to a new day, recognize that His strength has been at work, preparing you to step boldly into His plans, refreshed and ready to shine His light.

DAILY REFLECTION

How does the peace of restful sleep remind you of God's loving provision in your life, and in what ways can you surrender your worries to Him today?

PRAYER

Dear Lord, as I settle into the comforting embrace of sleep, I surrender my worries into Your gentle hands, trusting in Your promise that You grant rest to those You love. May each moment of slumber be a reminder of Your unwavering care and provision, renewing my spirit and strength for the day ahead. Help me to cherish this time of peace, knowing that in my quiet moments, You are working all things for my good, filling me with the assurance that I am beloved and held close to Your heart.

On this day, celebrate the incredible moment when your baby recognizes your face—much like how God knows each of us intimately. Just as your child finds comfort in your presence, remember that God's love surrounds us, inviting us to draw closer to Him with every new revelation.

Jeremiah 31:3 - "I have loved you with an everlasting love; I have drawn you with unfailing kindness."

DEVOTIONAL

Today, as you revel in the sweet joy of your baby recognizing your face for the first time, take a moment to reflect on the depth of that connection. It's a profound moment—a silent understanding that speaks of safety and love. Just as your little one finds comfort in your warm smile, consider how God knows you intimately, loving you with an everlasting love, as Jeremiah 31:3 reminds us. His kindness is unfailing, wrapping around you like a gentle embrace during the most ordinary or chaotic moments of your day. This recognition is a glimpse of the divine; it invites you to draw closer to Him, much like your child reaches for you with trust and anticipation. In those fleeting moments, remember that you are known, cherished, and held by a love that is steadfast and true. Celebrate this miracle of recognition, both in your child and in your own heart, for God delights in every moment of growth and understanding we experience.

DAILY REFLECTION

In this precious moment of your baby's first recognition, how can you embrace the truth that just as they see you as their safe haven, you too are invited to fully see and respond to God's unwavering love in your life?

PRAYER

Dear Lord, in this precious moment when my baby looks into my eyes and recognizes me for the first time, I am reminded of Your intimate knowledge of my heart. Help me to embrace this profound love, celebrating the simple yet profound way You cradle each one of us in Your embrace. May I, like my child, turn to You with trust and anticipation, ever aware that I am cherished and known by You. Amen.

Tummy time signifies growth and resilience, as little ones learn to lift their heads and engage with the world, we too are called to rise with faith, strengthening our spirits even in the face of challenges. Each small effort in faith nurtures a deeper relationship with God, just as every tummy time session fosters a child's development

Ephesians 3:16-17 - "I pray that out of his glorious riches he may strengthen you with power through his Spirit in your inner being, so that Christ may dwell in your hearts through faith."

DEVOTIONAL

As you settle onto the floor beside your little one, ready for another tummy time session, pause for a moment to reflect on the beauty of this simple act. Just as your child struggles to lift their head, discovering their strength amidst gentle discomfort, we too are invited to rise in our faith, navigating the challenges that life brings. Ephesians 3:16-17 reminds us of God's glorious riches, where His Spirit empowers us from within, fortifying our hearts just as your presence strengthens your child's spirit. Each moment of effort during tummy time is a tender reminder that growth often comes through perseverance. Like the little ones striving to engage with the world, every small step we take in faith draws us closer to Christ, nurturing a deeper relationship with the One who calls us beloved. So, as you encourage your baby to push through, let it also serve as an encouragement for your own journey – that in every effort, no matter how small, you are building resilience and fortitude. Lift your head, embrace the struggle, and let your heart dwell in the promise of His strength.

DAILY REFLECTION

How can you embrace the small challenges in your own life as opportunities for deeper faith and connection with God, just as your little one learns to rise with each tummy time session?

PRAYER

Dear Lord, as I watch my little one struggle and grow during tummy time, I'm reminded of the divine strength you provide in our own journeys of faith. Help us to embrace the challenges with courage, just as our children learn to lift their heads and engage with the world around them. May every push towards resilience be a testament to your love, drawing us closer to you with each small step we take. Amen.

As the waters gently envelop the little one, may we remember our own baptism—an invitation into God's boundless love and grace. Just as this baby finds joy and freedom in the cleansing waters, let us rejoice in the renewal of our spirits through Christ.

John 3:5 - *"Jesus answered, 'Very truly I tell you, no one can enter the kingdom of God unless they are born of water and the Spirit.'"*

DEVOTIONAL

As we witness a baby's first bath, the joyful splashes remind us of the profound beauty found in our own baptism. The gentle waters wrap around the little one, whispering the love and grace of God that is ever-present. In this moment, we are invited to reflect on our own journey—how we were embraced not just by water, but by the Spirit that breathes life into our souls. Each droplet serves as a reminder of our rebirth, the moment when we were immersed in God's unconditional love. Just as the baby delights in this new sensation, so too should we find joy in our spiritual renewal. Let us celebrate the freedom that comes with being washed clean, knowing that this sacred act opens the door to the kingdom of God. May our hearts, like that baby, dance in the waters of grace today and always.

DAILY REFLECTION

In the tender embrace of those gentle waters, how can we invite the same childlike joy and trust into our hearts as we celebrate the profound gift of our own baptism and the boundless grace it offers?

PRAYER

Dear Lord, as we watch this little one delight in the gentle embrace of water, may we be reminded of the joy and renewal found in our own baptism. Let the splashes and laughter echo your love, awakening in us a spirit of gratitude for the grace that washes over us daily. May we, too, celebrate the freedom and new life you offer, and may our hearts overflow with the same joy as this child, dancing in the waters of your endless affection. Amen.

More Devotionals from Anchored Grace

If this devotional encouraged your heart, you may also enjoy these devotionals from Anchored Grace.

- 365 Day Devotional for Women
- 90 Day Devotional for Women Seeking Peace
- 90 Day Devotional for Women Facing Anxiety and Stress
- 90 Day Devotional for Women 50+
- Guided Prayer Journal for Women

Search **"Anchored Grace Devotional"** on Amazon to discover more devotionals designed to support your journey of faith.

Thank You
for Walking This Journey

Thank you for spending this devotional journey with Anchored Grace.

If this devotional encouraged your heart, strengthened your faith, or brought peace to your daily routine, would you consider leaving a short review on Amazon?

devo.anchoredgraces.com/newmoms

Reviews help other women discover devotionals that may support them through their own seasons of life.

Even a single sentence about your experience can make a difference.

We are grateful you chose Anchored Grace.

www.ingramcontent.com/pod-product-compliance
Lightning Source LLC
Chambersburg PA
CBHW071729120626
46550CB00002B/440

9 7 8 1 9 6 6 2 3 2 2 3 0